ENGINEERING PSYCHOLOGY AND COGNITIVE ERGONOMICS
VOLUME TWO

Engineering Psychology and Cognitive Ergonomics
Volume Two

Job Design and Product Design

Edited by
DON HARRIS

Ashgate

Aldershot • Brookfield USA • Singapore • Sydney

© Don Harris 1997

Published by
Ashgate Publishing Ltd
Gower House
Croft Road
Aldershot
Hants GU11 3HR
England

Ashgate Publishing Company
Old Post Road
Brookfield
Vermont 05036
USA

British Library Cataloguing in Publication Data

Engineering psychology and cognitive ergonomics
   Vol. 2: Job design and product design
   1. Human engineering
   I. Harris, Don
   620.8'2

Library of Congress Cataloging-in-Publication Data

International Conference on Engineering Psychology and Cognitive
   Ergonomics (1st : 1996 : Stratford-upon-Avon, England)
     Engineering psychology and cognitive ergonomics / edited by Don
Harris.
       p. cm.
   "Presentations made at the First International Conference on
Engineering Psychology and Cognitive Ergonomics, held in Stratford
-upon-Avon, between 23 and 25 October 1996".--Pref.
   Contents: v. 1. Transportation systems -- v. 2. Job design and
product design.
   ISBN 0-291-39836-7 (v. 1). -- ISBN 0-291-39847-2 (v. 2)
   1. Human engineering--Congresses. 2. Engineering design-
-Psychological aspects--Congresses. 3. Aeronautics--Human factors-
-Congresses. 4. Aeronautics--Psychology--Congresses.
5. Transportation--Equipment and supplies--Design and construction-
-Congresses. I. Harris, Don, 1961- . II. Title.
TA166.I547 1996
620.8'2--dc21
                                   97-17263
                                    CIP

ISBN 0 291 39847 2

Printed in Great Britain by Galliard (Printers) Ltd, Great Yarmouth

Contents

Acknowledgements   xi
Preface   xiii

Part One: Job Design and Analysis   1

1   Inventing the future: collaborative design of socio-technical systems   3
    Ken Eason

2   CAFE OF EVE: action research in the control room   11
    Neville Stanton, Melanie Ashleigh and Tony Gale

3   Applied cognitive task analysis (ACTA): a practitioner's window into   17
    skilled decision making
    Robert J.B. Hutton and Laura G. Militello

4   Job design in integrated mail processing   25
    Anne Bruseberg and Andrew Shepherd

5   A systems analysis of teamworking in control rooms: methodology   33
    considered
    Melanie Ashleigh and Neville Stanton

6   Models of decision making in emergency management   39
    Mats Danielsson and Kjell Ohlsson

7   Emergency decision making on offshore installations   47
    Jan Skriver and Rhona Flin

8   Cognitive processing and risky behaviour in industrial radiography   55
     Wendy J. Reece and Leroy J. Matthews

9   Modelling of human errors in cognitive processes observed in dynamic   63
     environments
     Ken-ichi Takano and James Reason

10   Mental models of industrial jobs   71
     David Chiasson

Part Two: Learning and Training   79

11   Effects of type of learning on control performance   81
     Rainer H. Kluwe

12   Learning to control a coal-fired power plant: empirical results and a   89
     model
     Dieter Wallach

13   Cognitive technology for knowledge and skill acquisition in   97
     engineering disciplines
     Hitendra K. Pillay

14   Dynamic modelling of a learning system to aid system re-engineering   105
     Nassereddin Eftekhar, Douglas R. Strong and Ostap Hawaleshka

15   Learning statistics: a high level cognitive skill   115
     Tay Wilson

16   Perceptual learning in inspection tasks   121
     Penny Roling, Paul Sowden, Ian Davies, Emre Özgen
     and Margaret Lawler

17   The operator's analysis of the structure of a multi-dimensional video   129
     image of a mosaic subject area given the effects of
     hidden regularities
     Anna Molotova, Igor Schukin and Tatiana Ekonomova

18   Target recognition performance following whole-views, part-views,   135
     and both-views training
     Sehchang Hah, Deborah A. Reisweber, Jose A. Picart
     and Harry Zwick

Part Three: Medical Ergonomics   143

19   Depth perception and indirect viewing: reflections on keyhole surgery   145
     Anthony H. Reinhardt-Rutland, Judith M. Annett and Mervyn Gifford

20   Construction and validation of a model for decision making in   153
     anaesthesia
     Philip M.A. de Graaf

21   Anaesthesiology and aviation: using the analogy   161
     Carole D.B. Deighton and Wendy Morgan

22   Medical cognition and computer support in the intensive care unit: a   167
     cognitive engineering approach
     Robert Logie, Jim Hunter, Neil McIntosh, Ken Gilhooly,
     Eugenio Alberdi and Jan Reiss

23   The patient-monitor system in intensive care: eliciting nurses'   175
     mental models
     Amanda Gilbert

Part Four: Applied Cognitive Psychology   183

24   Audiovisual links in attention: implications for interface design   185
     Charles Spence and Jon Driver

25   A parallel distributed processing model of redundant information   193
     integration
     Matthew Jackson and Steven J. Selcon

26   The magical name Miller, plus or minus the umlaut   201
     Derek J. Smith

27   A partial theory and engineering model of human information-seeking   209
     tasks
     James R. Buck and Steven M. Zellers

28   Model-computer interaction: implementing the action perception loop   215
     for cognitive models
     Gordon D. Baxter and Frank E. Ritter

29   Predicting transaction time for dual-tasks using critical path   223
     Chris Baber and Brian Mellor

30   Engineering psychology: the hidden psychologist - a case study   231
      on the evaluation of the Safer Cities programme using a
      geographical information system
      Ho Law

31   Rewritable routines in human interaction with public technology   239
      Chris Baber and Neville Stanton

32   The function and effectiveness of dynamic task allocation   247
      Andrew J. Tattersall and Catherine A. Morgan

33   Implicit memory: new procedures for cognitive load investigations   257
      in work situations
      Patrice Terrier, Michel Neboit and Jean-Marie Collier

34   Duration estimates: a potentially useful tool for cognitive ergonomists 267
      Alex R. Carmichael

35   Research on auditory comfort by EEG measurement   275
      Min Cheol Whang, Ji Eun Kim and Chul Jung Kim

36   Head orientation and binaural depth perception   285
      Peter J. Simpson and Keith J. Nation

37   The perception of spatial layout in telepresence systems   293
      Andy Parton, Mark F. Bradshaw, Bart DeBruyn, Alison Wheeler,
      John Pretlove, Jörg Huber and Ian R.L. Davies

38   Validation: the best kept secret in Ergonomics!   301
      Neville Stanton and Mark Young

39   Performance anxiety and coping strategies for musicians
      Sture Brändström and Anna-Karin Gullberg   309

40   Fatigue risk assessment for safety critical staff   315
      Deborah Lucas, Colin Mackay, Nicola Cowell and
      Andrew Livingstone

Part Five: Product Design and Evaluation   321

41   Integrating requirements acquisition and user modelling: things users   323
      want, and things users do
      Gordon Rugg and Ann Blandford

viii

42   Knowledge needs analysis for complex systems   331
      Philip J.A. Scown and Janice E. Whatley

43   Generating user requirements from discount usability evaluations   339
      Hilary Johnson

44   'Satisficing' in engineering design: psychological determinants and   347
      implications for design support
      Linden J. Ball, Thomas C. Ormerod and Louise Maskill

45   Modelling design processes of groups in industry: an empirical   355
      investigation of cooperative design work
      Petra Badke-Schaub and Eckart Frankenberger

46   Styles of problem solving and their importance in mechanical   363
      engineering design
      Renate Eisentraut

47   Psychology of pointing: factors affecting the use of mice and   371
      trackballs on graphical user interfaces
      Chris Baber

48   Communicating human-computer interaction design intent: 379
      requirements for recycling throwaway prototypes
      Carl Myhill and Peter Brooks

49   Metaphors in software engineering   387
      Briony J. Oates and Helen Gavin

50   Hypertext, navigation and cognitive maps: the effects of a map and   395
      a contents list on navigation performance as a function of prior
      knowledge
      Sharon McDonald and Rosemary J. Stevenson

51   Personal identification code composed of pictures or numbers?   403
      Karl W. Sandberg and Yan Pan

52   Implementing user interface design standards for 'mission critical' IT 411
      systems in telecommunications
      Robert Pedlow

53   Script-based spatial user interface: an approach to supporting   421
      operators of process control systems
      Ivan Burmistrov

54   Theories and interface design: designing interfaces with ecological   429
      and cognitive task analysis
      Marcia Crosland and Eric Sparre

55   A cognitive psychological framework for the description and   437
      evaluation of interfaces
      Torsten Heinbokel, Eric Leimann, Heinz Willumeit and
      Rainer H. Kluwe

56   The effectiveness of using combined mimic/emergent features and   445
      mimic/multilevel flow modelling displays in a pilot process control
      environment
      Mark Gill and Enda F. Fallon

57   Using conversation to model interaction in the MATHS workstation   453
      Carol Linehan and John McCarthy

58   Proposal for the development of an IT-infrastructure for the disabled   461
      person
      Karl W. Sandberg

59   Application of human performance theory to virtual environment   467
      development
      Richard Eastgate, Sarah Nichols and Mirabelle D'Cruz

Acknowledgements

I must express my thanks to the various people who contributed, either directly or indirectly, to this venture. Firstly I must thank the members of staff in the Department of Applied Psychology, at the College of Aeronautics, Cranfield University, who worked so hard to make the First International Conference on Engineering Psychology and Cognitive Ergonomics such a success. The contributions in this volume were derived directly from the papers presented at the conference. My thanks go out to Ann Cobbett, Carole Deighton, Sarah Duggan, Tricia Forrest-Holden, Karen Lane, Joel Morley, Siobhan O'Malley, Emma Parry and our Head of Department, Prof. Helen Muir, who was the one who had the faith to support the undertaking. I should also thank all the members of staff in the Department who were not directly involved in the conference for being so tolerant of the staff who were (especially in the few weeks immediately preceding the event)! I would also like to thank all the contributors to this volume for their efforts. Without them neither the conference nor the books would have been possible. Additionally, a word of gratitude is due to John Hindley of Avebury, who has helped immensely in the publication and production of these proceedings. Finally, I should also mention Fiona, who had to put up with me while I edited these volumes (no easy task at the best of times, I'm told). My apologies if I have omitted anyone from this list who deserves my thanks, however, they can be content in the knowledge that their efforts were most appreciated.

Don Harris
Cranfield University
February 1997

Acknowledgements

Preface

The papers in this book are all derived from presentations made at the First International Conference on Engineering Psychology and Cognitive Ergonomics, held in Stratford-upon-Avon, between 23 and 25 October 1996. More than 110 papers were presented at the conference, which attracted delegates from 18 countries.

This is the second of two volumes of papers from the conference. In this volume the papers are generally concerned with human factors in job design and product design. The first volume in the series is concerned with the human factors in transportation. As mentioned in the preface to the first volume, deciding upon which papers should be contained in which of the volumes was no small task. Perhaps the arrangement of the material into these two volumes reflects the professional interests of an editor which are contained solely within the field of transportation. As such, the composition of the sections in this book and the editing of the papers posed a far greater challenge that the material in the first volume. I can only hope that I have done justice to the work presented.

I feel that it is also worth re-iterating a point that I made in the preface to the first volume. Producing a book composed of the work of authors from many countries places its editor in a moral quandary. The standard of English from the authors from non-English speaking countries is to be applauded, however there are occasional instances where perhaps a word or the phraseology used would not be the first choice of a native speaker. The quandary that results is this: what right does a mere editor have to alter the words of a fellow scientist and author? In general, if the meaning was clear I chose to leave an author's words as they were written. If the meaning (in my opinion) was not clear, I have attempted to clarify and modify the English as best I can. Where this has been done, this editor takes full responsibility if the meaning conveyed was not that intended by the author.

The opening chapter of this volume by Ken Eason, was taken from his keynote address to the conference. This paper opens the first section this second volume, which is concerned with job design. It seemed logical (at the time of editing) to follow the section on the design of jobs with a section on learning and training. Both of these sections are essentially concerned with the people doing their job of work. Medical ergonomics is one of the most rapidly growing areas of ergonomics and as such I felt that it was justified in commanding its own section in this book to acknowledge its increasing importance.

This is followed by a section entitled 'applied cognitive psychology'. The focus here is biassed towards basic human capabilities rather than user interfaces or operator training. A sound understanding of the manners in which human beings operate are the building blocks upon which sound human engineering decisions are based.

The first sections were concerned with the human operator in an applied setting. In the final section of this book, 'product design and evaluation', the emphasis is placed firmly on the equipment rather than the human being.

The distinctions between the content of each of the sections may reside solely in the mind of this Editor. However, what I am sure of is that for any system to be safe, effective and efficient, you must ensure that not only is the job fitted to the person, the person must also be fitted to the job. This is not an 'either/or' principle. I hope that the organisation of this volume does not give that impression.

Finally, may I express my thanks once again to all the contributors. Without them these books would not have been possible.

Part One
JOB DESIGN AND ANALYSIS

1 Inventing the future: collaborative design of socio-technical systems

Ken Eason
HUSAT Research Institute
Loughborough University, UK

Abstract

Information technology is transforming work and has many implications for organisations and people at work. It is increasingly common for people at work to be given the opportunity to contribute to the development of future work systems by making early evaluations of socio-technical systems options. This paper discusses the difficulties that people have in making effective contributions to future planning and identifies some of the cognitive processes involved. It presents a range of ways that have been found in practice to help people make an effective contribution. These include the creation of realistic and concrete socio-technical systems scenarios, the engagement of people in role play exercises in the scenarios and the systematic review of implications from stakeholder perspectives.

The challenge of change

One of the greatest challenges facing engineering psychologists and ergonomists is the pace of change in the world of work. A particular force for change is the impact of information technology and the creation of the information society. We are moving rapidly towards a world in which work is characterised by networking, teleworking, virtual teams, automation, outsourcing, globalisation etc. These changes transform the tasks that people undertake and the way they undertake them. For the optimists the world of work will be one of empowerment; when we have the knowledge of the world at our fingertips, enormous processing power and the opportunity to communicate with anyone, anywhere. For the pessimists it will mean a world of separation from the real work materials (because we are dealing with a virtual world), isolation from our fellows, a lack of privacy and a lack of personal control of our lives.

Whatever our views of these great trends they do constitute enormous forces for change. For many organisations and the people who work in them these forces are opportunities and threats - opportunities for new forms of business, threats that they will be left behind by their competitors, opportunities for new careers for staff, fears they may not be able to cope etc. But the information revolution is not deterministic; there are many ways of applying the technology and changing the world of work. This means that organisations and their staff have many choices and could select outcomes in their best interests. Many people are now being given opportunities to help choose future work systems. This is a wonderful opportunity to shape the future for human effectiveness and human well being. But how are they to undertake this task and can we help? Detailed analysis of current work practices may help but the future will be significantly different. How to we help invent the future?

In the HUSAT Research Institute we have assisted many organisations to develop future work systems. Most of these engagements have been within an organisational frame of reference - developing future socio-technical systems - and most have involved a social process in which human actors have evaluated future options. To be effective in this process we have to manage the cognitive processes of the human factors. The aim of this paper is to describe the process by which future systems are being developed and then to identify the cognitive issues which we need to address.

The process of scenario development and evaluation

The majority of change processes consist of technical innovations in order to achieve business objectives. There is usually very little analysis of the human or organisational implications and, as a result, implementation is often followed by the realisation of significant implications which may limit the effectiveness of the change. Figure 1 provides a description of a process by which an organisation might examine the opportunities for change and assess the human and organisational implications very early in the process (Eason, 1988; Eason and Olphert, 1996) in order to select the most effective route forward. In this approach the application of new technology to an existing work system is used to construct a number of different scenarios for the future. Each of these scenarios is evaluated by the stakeholders who would be affected by the implementation of the scenario.

The aim in this process is to use the knowledge and insights of the stakeholders to predict the implications of each scenario. Since different stockholders will adopt different attitudes to the strengths and weaknesses of each scenario as it affects their own interests, a rounded picture of the likely human and organisational implications can be developed.

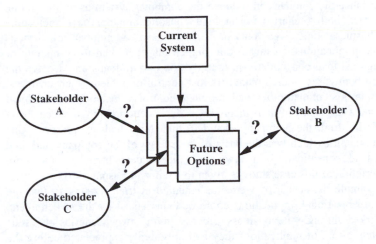

Figure 1   Stakeholder implications of future systems

This approach is part of a general movement to adopt scenario-based design as a means of achieving human-centred design. In most examples of this approach (see Carroll, 1995) the scenario is a technical prototype and the evaluation is an assessment of usability or   individual task performance.   In this instance the scenario is a broader vision, encompassing not only the future technical system but also the network of human roles that uses it within a business process.

An example of a socio-technical systems scenario evaluation

A case study will illustrate the need for a process of evaluating socio-technical scenarios.   We recently assisted a national freight forwarding company in the implementation of a major computer system.   The company had a network of branches across the country each exporting and importing goods on behalf of local clients.   The aim of the computer system was to provide an electronic means of capturing the details of the freight to be transported which could then be used to create the multitude of documents to serve shipping, trucking, insurance, customer, customs and excise and accounting needs.   The company were interested in two scenarios for the application of this system.   In the first scenario each branch would be independent and would use the system to undertake its business quite separately from other branches.   In the second scenario the data base of planned freight movements could be shared between branches in the same region and they could seek load consolidation - sending loads for different clients going to the same destination together to reduce trucking and shipping costs.

In this instance the company introduced the computer system as a pilot in one region and tried both scenarios. The load consolidation approach met some important business objectives but proved to have a number of serious organisational implications. It meant that branch managers had to co-operate or rely on a regional load consolidator to identify appropriate loads and arrange the transport. In both cases Branch managers lost control of some of their business. Traditionally in this company they had complete control to make deals with local companies and a large part of their income was dependent upon their success. At the end of the trial the company decided that they had to preserve this entrepreneurial spirit which was the basis of the energy of the company and they abandoned load consolidation in favour of independent branches. (A more detailed description of this case study is given in Klein and Eason, 1991).

In this example the scenarios were implemented in trial systems so that the human and organisational implications could be experienced by the stakeholders. As they worked through the business process in the two scenarios the staff became acutely aware of implications they had only dimly appreciated before the trial began and they were very clear about the route forward when the trials ended. This approach is effective but it has several drawbacks; it is expensive to mount such trials, they may be disruptive to business and it is difficult to test all the relevant scenarios. To implement a trial it is necessary to have a fully developed technical system which usually means that the trials are undertaken late in the development process and it may be difficult to make major changes in the technical system after the trial. Ideally we require a relatively cheap way of developing and evaluating socio-technical scenarios early in the development process which are sufficiently realistic to give stakeholders the opportunity to evaluate the implications of each scenario with confidence.

Scenario evaluation as a social process

In most system development processes there is now a place for would-be users to play a role. In a number of techniques a social process is created in which stakeholders can consider future opportunities. In the USA, for example, JAD (Joint Application Design, August 1991), provides users and designers with opportunities to meet together in workshops to generate and evaluate future technical systems. In the UK in the ETHICS methodology (Mumford, 1983) users take responsibility for the identification and development of future socio-technical systems. The Search Conference approach developed in Australia (Weisbord, 1990) creates a process for stakeholders to analyse future requirements, search for solutions and seek consensus and commitment to a particular route forward. In Scandinavia (Greenbaum and Kyng, 1991) participative design has been developed with a specific aim of helping shopfloor and craft based users play significant roles in the development of systems which can enhance and develop their skills rather than replace them.

Although there are variations between these approaches they share a common basic structure and have a common purpose. They are participative processes which invite all significant stakeholders in the change process to help create future scenarios. They provide opportunities for stakeholders to evaluate scenarios from their own perspectives and thereby to articulate their requirements from future systems. Underlying these approaches is a belief that, despite different sectional interests, it is possible to find 'win/win outcomes' (Boehm, Bose, Horowitz and Lee, 1994), i.e. scenarios which would be acceptable to all stakeholders. Whilst this may be over-ambitious it is certainly true that the evaluation of a range of scenarios can identify a solution that meets a wider range of requirements than a single solution which is only evaluated against cost and technical criteria.

It is now commonplace for users to participate in systems development processes although it is often less systematic than in the methods described above.

However, there are also regular reports of users struggling when given this opportunity to participate (for example, Hornby and Clegg, 1992) and these difficulties threaten the perceived efficacy of user-centred approaches. We need to understand the difficulties users experience in order to find ways in which they can be helped to make an effective contribution. The difficulties can be listed as:-

(i) Understanding the technology and specifically the way it might be applied in the user's work setting. When an application is presented in technical terms it may be difficult to relate to the work domain. It is often unclear to potential users what the benefits of the technology might be and what problems it might cause.

(ii) Imagining alternative forms of work made possible by the technology. Although there are many different ways of applying information technology it is not easy for people to envisage alternative ways of working that are outside of their experience. What, for example, would it really be like to be a tele-worker?

(iii) Determining realistic requirements for future systems. Because of their lack of knowledge, users tend to have unrealistic expectations of technology; wildly optimistic of what can be achieved or deeply pessimistic of its impact on everything important. Users need to develop realistic hopes and fears before they can make an effective contribution.

(iv) Agreeing system requirements with other stakeholders. Inevitably some choices are more beneficial to some stakeholders than others and some will have more overt power and influence than others. They need a way of examining the options to discover where there is the greatest possibility of consensus and support.

7

Scenario evaluation as a cognitive process

As a result of the increasing use of scenario based design a number of practices are emerging to help stakeholders play their role in this process. They constitute largely untested ways of dealing with the problems listed above. These practices, summarised in figure 2, also involve the users in specific kinds of cognitive tasks and underpinning them are a set of beliefs about how users can best tackle these tasks.

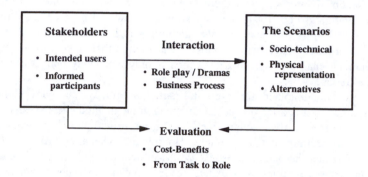

Figure 2 **Towards the effective management of the evaluation of future systems**

The first set of beliefs concern the nature of the scenarios that have to be created to help the stakeholders. They need to be socio-technical representations; if they are just technical representations the stakeholders have difficulty working out how they affect the work people do. The scenarios therefore have to be expressed in terms of the set of human work roles needed to accomplish the business process and the manner in which the technology will support each work role. The enterprise modelling approach included in the ORDIT methodology (Olphert and Harker, 1994; Eason, 1996; Eason, Harker and Olphert, 1996) provides a means of creating such scenarios by relating work roles and information services through responsibility analysis. The scenario also needs to be instantiated in a physical representation to make it as near as possible to the everyday experience of the stakeholders. This is the equivalent of the traditional ergonomic practice of building prototype workstations out of cardboard boxes or of the modern practice in software design of creating a prototype interface for users to evaluate. Another requirement is to be able to represent more than one future socio-technical system. People need to be able to perceive there are alternatives before they can be creative in generating their own alternatives.

The second requirement is to construct a process by which stakeholders can engage in the scenario in order to appreciate its implications. The stakeholders and users themselves need to be involved in order that they can use their knowledge of tasks, culture etc to judge the scenario from the perspective of their aims and concerns. The prevailing view is that stakeholders need to engage in a two stage process. First they have to have an active engagement with the scenario in order to develop their understanding of it and, as a result, they cannot evaluate the broader implications. The active engagement is often undertaken as the simulated performance of a cooperative task with the stakeholder playing their normal role in the performance of the task. This provides the most immediate evidence of the direct effects of the scenario.

The final part of the process is to structure the evaluation of the scenario by the stakeholder. As a result of working through the scenario people usually see primary implications, eg. a lack of technical support for specific task needs, but they need help to identify secondary and tertiary implications. We have adopted a checklist approach which asks stakeholders to assess direct implications for tasks and then work through their work role to relations with other roles to help them explore possible organisational and cultural implications. Working outwards in this way helps to identify alternative possibilities of the 'if we implemented the system so that ...' kind. In this process we also ask users to rate each change from their perspective. The outcome is a systematic review of the requirements from the stakeholder perspective's and a view of the directions they would like systems development to take. Putting the different stakeholder perspectives together begins the process of identifying whether there is a solution space that would represent a 'win-win' outcome for the development.

Conclusions

Bringing stakeholders into development processes which define their future working systems is a significant opportunity to work on human factors issues. It is now quite a well established procedure as a social process within many systems development methodologies but it represents a difficult opportunity for stakeholders to exploit because of the unfamiliar issues which they have to address. The processes described above of formulating scenarios, helping stakeholders experience them and then evaluating them seem to help stakeholders make the most of the opportunity to shape future systems. However, these are conclusions borne of practice which have received little systematic attention to understand the cognitive tasks stakeholders undertake in these processes and how best to support them. A major attempt to understand how people can best invent their own futures is needed if we are to exploit the opportunities of information technology for the good of people at work.

Ken Eason

References

August, J.H. (1991) *'Joint Application Design; The Group Session Approach to Systems Design'*. Yourdon Press: Englewood Cliffs, N.J.

Boehm, B., Bose, P., Horowitz, E. and Lee, M.J. (1994) 'Software requirements as negotiated win conditions', in *Proceedings of the International Conference on Requirements Engineering,* IEEE Computer Society Press: Los Alamitos.

Carroll, J.M. (ed.) (1995) *'Scenario-Based Design; Envisioning Work and Technology in System Development'* . Wiley: New York.

Eason K.D. (1988) *'Information Technology and Organisational Change'* Taylor and Francis: London.

Eason, K.D. and Olphert, C.W. (1996) 'Early Evaluation of the Organisational Implications of CSCW Systems'. in P. Thomas (ed.), *'CSCW Requirements and Evaluation'.* Springer-Verlag: London.

Eason, K.D. (1996) 'Division of labour and the design of systems for computer support for co-operative work'. *Journal of Information Technology,* to be published.

Eason, K.D., Harker, S.D.P. & Olphert, C.W. (1996) 'Representing Socio-Technical Systems Options in the Development of New Forms of Work Organization'. *European Journal of Work and Organizational Psychology* , Vol. 5, pp. 399-420.

Greenbaum, J. & Kyng, M. (eds.) (1991) *'Design at Work: Co-operative Design of Computer Systems'.* Erlbaum: Hillside, NJ.

Hornby, P. & Clegg, C. (1992) 'User Participation in Context: A Case Study in a UK Bank'. *Behaviour and Information Technology, Vol.* 11, pp. 293-307.

Klein, L. & Eason, K.D. (1991) *'Putting Social Science to Work'.* Cambridge University Press: Cambridge.

Mumford, E. (1983) *'Designing Human Systems'.* Manchester Business School Publications: Manchester.

Olphert, C.W. & Harker, S.D.P. (1994) 'The ORDIT method for organisational requirements definition', in G.E. Bradley & H.W. Hendrick (eds.) *'Human Factors in Organizational Design and Management'*, Vol.4. Elsevier: Amsterdam.

Weisbord, M.R. (1990) *'Productive Workplaces; Organising and Managing for Dignity, Meaning and Community'.* Jossey-Bass: Oxford.

2   CAFE OF EVE: action research in the control room

Neville Stanton, Melanie Ashleigh and Tony Gale*
University of Southampton, UK
*University of Portsmouth, UK

Abstract

This chapter considers the viability of the CAFE OF EVE concept as a research approach as well as conducting longitudinal investigations into human supervisory control. Neither of these approaches have been undertaken to the extent proposed here and certainly neither have been combined in this way before. Thus, this approach aims to advance our understanding of both issues simultaneously. Firstly, it offers an investigation of a research methodology. Secondly, it aims to determine fundamental aspects of human supervisory control through longitudinal study.

Changes in control room operation

There is a tradition of research being conducted into control room operation, to enhance our understanding of the role of the human operator and learn about new ways of supporting those activities (Edwards & Lees, 1974). According to Kragt (1994) technological developments in process control have led to dramatic changes in the nature of work practices and behaviours. This development has gone through four generations of control system: local manual control, local automatic control, centralised panel displays and SCADA (system control and data acquisition) systems. The first revolution was to automate parts of the process so that workers were able to supervise larger areas of plant. The second revolution was to centralise the controls and displays into a single control room, again enabling workers to supervise larger areas of plant. The third revolution was to put all the information at the workers fingertips via information technology, further reducing the personnel requirements. A review of research into human supervisory control reveals three distinct phases over the past three decades. Research in the 1970s may be characterised by interest in cognitive control (Lees & Edwards, 1974). Interest in the

11

individual shifted to interest in team structure and performance in the 1980s (e.g. Stammers & Hallam). More recently, i.e. the 1990s, researchers have been focussing on human behaviour in context, e.g. Hollnagel's COntext and COntrol Model (CONCOM: Hollnagel, 1993). Zwaga & Hoonhout (1994) argue that all of the technological developments in supervisory control have been based upon the conception of the control room engineers task of 'operation-by-exception': control room engineers only intervening in the process when called to do so by the alarm system (Dallimonti, 1972). However, Zwaga & Hoonhout (1994) argue that this conception is fundamentally flawed. Rather, they propose, control room engineers behaviour is better characterised by a 'management-through-awareness' strategy: control room engineers are actively extracting information from their environment rather than passively reacting to alarms. The dichotomy of 'active extraction' and 'passive reception' were noted by Stanton & Baber (1995) in an analysis of alarm handling activities.

In a review of the impact of control room technology on the behaviour of the operators it was apparent that three research approaches were dominant: the use of surveys and questionnaires, small scale observational studies and simulation of control room environments (Stanton, 1996). Many of the questionnaire studies involved selected samples of employees, often at a time of introducing new technology. This meant that they were being surveyed under conditions of task restructuring, when they were ill-trained for the technology in question, fearful of redundancy and motivated to a particular set of response biases. Observational studies, which appear on the face of it to offer ecological validity, are often of a very short duration that they are likely to suffer from the Hawthorne effect. Social psychologists have drawn a distinction, in the context of observation, between acts and actions, the former relating to behaviours observed by an outsider, the latter to the layers of meaning which surround an act, from the viewpoint of the actual participant or indigenous person. Unless the outsider is au fait with the group's history, purposes, beliefs and values, acts remain as acts. Laboratory studies, which offered more control, often involved relatively brief samples of behaviour generated by unrepresentative samples of volunteer participants with little sense of continuity of employment or of the personal significance of the tasks they were required to perform. We know that workers, after extensive operations in a working context, develop subtle adaptations in their interaction with work interfaces, establishing idiosyncratic patterns and habits which simply cannot be captured in brief simulations. In the search for an alternative approach which yield veridical data, ecological validity and experimental control seem to be at odds with each other; yet without appropriate controls it is hard to plot true causal paths (Stanton & Gale, 1996). This proposal offers to test a compromise research approach which seeks to combine ecological validity with control in a dynamic and developmental way.

Relative benefits and pitfalls of existing approaches

Gale (1984) was quick to realise that the benefits of traditional approaches should be preserved, whilst the disadvantages should be overcome if at all possible. The recognised benefits of laboratory studies include: control over independent variables, limitation on the number of independent variables, control over environmental variables, control over participants' behaviour, event sampling at choice, construction of complete experimental designs, choice of representative or random samples, systematic manipulation of variables, systematic development of a series of studies eliminating specified sources of variability, simplification of data to a level manageable by existing theoretical power, partitioning of subject effects, systematisation of error, capacity for repeated longitudinal measurement over time, planning in advance and replication. However, there are several shortcomings: failure of a differential partitioning of in vivo influences, the generation of statistically significant effects rather than practically significant recommendations, an interest in effects greater than chance rather than effects which apply to large populations, a focus on contemporary theoretical ideas to the exclusion of potential or actual factors impacting on a working environment, theory-driven rather than problem-driven orientation, the use of inexperienced participants (often from an inappropriate background) and sampling which is far too brief to enable participants to develop their own coping strategies. Field studies, whilst being more realistic, typically suffer from: multivariate influences on participants, uncontrolled environmental contexts, uncontrolled and unpredictable disruptive events, restrictions on access for the duration of the study, restrictions on experimental power and status, the use of incomplete designs with incomplete cells, low co-operation and high suspicion by participants, biassed samples, incomplete designs which restrain inference and an inability to replicate.

The CAFE OF EVE methodology

In 1984, Gale presented an internal report to the Human Factors Technology Centre at ITT Europe, in which he proposed a new research strategy for assessing the impact of new technology and for guiding design. In 1987, Gale and Christie set out a detailed blueprint for the approach. The project was called the CAFE OF EVE - a controlled adaptive and flexible experimental office of the future in an ecologically valid environment. Whilst originally conceived as an approach for investigation of human behaviour with office technology, the CAFE OF EVE approach may be equally successfully applied to investigations in control rooms. This requires the researcher to reconceptualise the research paradigm, by applying an action research approach to the investigation of human activity.

The aim of the CAFE OF EVE project is to combine the advantages of both laboratory and field studies, whilst minimising the disadvantages. The proposal involves taking over a control room within a company in a way which allows for the day-to-day operational function, combined with a parallel set of research studies. Staff operating within the selected control room would be included in the research function. The researchers would share some of the control room functions with the aim of understanding the meaning of events and activities for participants. At the same time, through daily exchanges with the permanent employees, the barriers between participant and experimenter would break down. Thus the researchers would take on the role of participant observer as developed in anthropology (Vetere and Gale, 1987) living and working within the human system in question but also recording daily events. Researchers and participants share a social world. As the boundaries between researcher and participant become more permeable, participants feel more free to express their opinions and reactions about their working environment. In daily debriefing sessions, participants interact with researchers, with the goal of identifying problems from the participants' perspectives. Thus, the research questions which are generated are not dictated by existing theories but by the actual perceived experience of control room engineers.

So far as possible, video observation and analysis, diary keeping, interactive recording of subjective responses would be carried out in the control room and integrated with everyday task functions. The aim of the CAFE OF EVE approach is to use a longitudinal and developmental technique to capture real experience and to shape new technological developments (Stanton & Gale, 1996). The research questions are not imposed by prior conceptions but emerge from the working context and the views and analyses of participants. Thus it involves a partnership in exploration in which researcher and participant have equal status. It is argued that objectivity is retained because the researcher is still apart, but ecological validity is ensured by drawing on the participants' day to day experiences (Stanton & Gale, 1996).

The key features of the approach are as follows.
(i)   Ecological validity is approximated.
(ii)   All psychologically significant variables are likely to be identified.
(iii)   Participants and researchers develop a partnership of exploration.
(iv)   Sampling is flexible and by mutual consent.
(v)   Participants reveal and are able to reflect upon coping strategies developed over time.
(vi)   Research studies emerge naturally.
(vii)   Participants themselves will suggest studies or identify salient variables.
(viii) Participant loss will be minimal thereby allowing longitudinal studies.
(ix)   Co-operation will affect broader organisational structures, such as new ways of working.

The CAFE OF EVE methodology offers an action research approach. There is obviously an element of risk associated with investing in such a long term project. The researcher is likely to encounter unpredicted events and difficulties, but this is likely to be outweighed by the quality of the data and the insights gained through research of this nature.

Conclusions

Thus, the CAFE OF EVE approach seeks to draw together a normal working context and a controlled laboratory to create a special human factors environment, capitalising on the benefits of ecological validity and experimental control, while seeking to avoid the disadvantages of the two contrasting approaches. In so doing, the research benefits should surpass the benefits typically yielded by either approach taken separately or sequentially. What we are proposing and its emergent properties could constitute a minor revolution in human factors research.

References

Costall, A. (1995) 'Socializing Affordances'. *Theory & Psychology*, Vol. 5, pp. 467-481.

Dallimonti, R. (1972) 'Future operator consoles for improved decision making and safety'. *Instrumentation Technology*, Vol. 19, pp. 23-8.

Edwards, E. & Lees, F. P. (1974) *The Human Operator in Process Control*. Taylor & Francis: London.

Gale, A. (1984). *Prelude to the Cafe of Eve. Report to the Human Factors Technology Centre,* ITT Europe (ESC Research Centre). ITT Industries Ltd: Harlow.

Gale, A. and Christie, B. (1987). 'Psychophysiology and the electronic workplace: the future', in, A. Gale and B. Christie (eds.) *Psychophysiology and the Electronic Workplace*. John Wiley and Sons: Chichester.

Hollnagel, E. (1993) *Human Reliability Analysis: Context and Control*. Academic Press: London.

Kragt, H. (1994) *Enhancing Industrial Performance*. Taylor & Francis: London.

Stammers, R. B & Hallam, J. (1985) 'Task allocation and the balance of load in the multiman-machine system: some case studies'. *Applied Ergonomics*, Vol. 16, pp. 251-257.

Stanton, N.A. (1996) *Human Factors in Nuclear Safety*. Taylor & Francis: London.

Stanton, N. A. & Baber, C. (1995) 'Alarm initiated activities: an analysis of alarm handling by operators using text-based alarm systems in supervisory control systems'. *Ergonomics*, Vol. 38, pp. 2414-2431.

Stanton, N. A. & Gale, A. (1996) 'CAFE OF EVE: A method for designing and evaluating interfaces'. In, M. Cook & J. Noyes (eds.) *Interfaces - the leading edge*. IEE Digest No. 96/126. IEE: London.

Neville Stanton et al.

Vetere, A. and Gale, A. (1987). *Ecological Studies of Family Life*. John Wiley and Sons: Chichester.

Zwaga, H. J. G. & Hoonhout, H. C. M. (1994) 'Supervisory control behaviour and the implementation of alarms in process control', in N. A. Stanton (ed.) *Human Factors in Alarm Design*. Taylor & Francis: London.

3 Applied cognitive task analysis (ACTA): a practitioner's window into skilled decision making

Robert J.B. Hutton and Laura G. Militello
Klein Associates Inc., USA

Abstract

Cognitive task analysis (CTA) is a method of identifying cognitive skills, or mental demands, needed to perform a task proficiently. CTA is used to complement traditional 'behavioural' task analysis. The product of the task analysis can be used to inform the design of interface and training systems. However, CTA is resource intensive and has previously been of limited use to design practitioners. A streamlined method of CTA, applied cognitive task analysis (ACTA), is presented in this paper. ACTA consists of three interview methods which help the practitioner extract information about the cognitive demands and skills required for a task. ACTA also allows the practitioner to represent this information in a format that will translate more directly into applied products, such as improved training scenarios or interface recommendations. The paper will describe the three methods, an evaluation study conducted to assess the usability and usefulness of the methods, and some potential applications of the representations and output from ACTA.

Introduction

Designers of training and man-machine systems have traditionally relied on task analysis to provide the tasks, information, and procedures that must be supported by their interventions. Cognitive task analysis (CTA) provides additional information about how operators conceptualize tasks, how they recognize the critical information and patterns of cues, and the strategies that they use to assess situations, solve problems, and make judgments and decisions (Cooke, 1994; Gordon, Schmierer, & Gill, 1993; Hall, Gott, & Pokorny, 1995). CTA techniques have previously been restricted to the domain of researchers rather than that of instructional systems design (ISD) professionals or systems and interface designers who implement interventions.

17

This paper describes applied cognitive task analysis (ACTA), streamlined CTA methods for practitioners to elicit and represent cognitive components of skilled task performance, and the means to transform that data into design interventions.

Task analysis has traditionally attempted to describe procedures and behaviours required to accomplish a task by decomposing it into its component operations. The methods are general, flexible, and provide a logical approach to providing input into training and human-computer interface design. However, these methods have emphasized primarily observable behaviours and procedures rather than the thinking skills, decisions, and judgments which are very often critical components of skilled performance.

The goal of cognitive task analysis (CTA) is to identify the cognitive skills, or mental demands, that are needed to perform a task. These include: the critical cues and patterns of cues; assessment, problem solving and decision making strategies; why these are difficult for novices; and, common novice errors. The goal of ACTA is to provide a means for practitioners to elicit this kind of information and incorporate it into their design interventions.

Applied cognitive task analysis

The impetus for this project came from a need to incorporate thinking and decision making skills training into US Navy training programs. Navy instructional designers have no formal methods for analysing a task in terms of the cognitive demands of a task or the cognitive skills required to perform proficiently. The Navy Personnel Research and Development Center (NPRDC), San Diego, sponsored two efforts to try to address this problem.

We conducted a six month Phase I effort to assess the feasibility of the project and suggest potential solutions for streamlining cognitive task analysis. In the two year Phase II effort we took those potential analysis tools, refined them, conducted an evaluation study, refined the tools again, and we are now currently involved in producing a computer-based training tool for ACTA.

The ACTA methods were developed from techniques that Klein Associates Inc. has been using and improving for over fifteen years in domains as diverse as nursing, firefighting, consumer products design, air crew decision making, driver decision making, and army air defense planners to name but a few. The ACTA methods are adaptations of several core techniques: concept mapping (McNeese et al., 1990); knowledge audit (aspects of expertise); and, the critical decision method. The techniques are primarily interviewing techniques for knowledge elicitation.

Task diagram

The first tool is the task diagram which helps the interviewer get a broad overview of the task of interest by having a subject matter expert (SME) break the task down

18

into three to six steps or sub-tasks. The interviewer then identifies which of these is the most cognitively challenging. The task diagram provides a road-map and focus for the remaining interviews.

Knowledge audit

The knowledge audit relies on an understanding of expert/novice performance differences and aspects of expertise as identified from a broad literature base on expert performance and expert decision making. The SME is asked to provide specific examples of expertise as explained by the interviewer. The SME is asked to provide detail about the cues and strategies relied on in the example, and to provide an insight into why the situation would have been difficult for a novice to handle.

Simulation interview

This interview is based on the critical decision method (Klein, Calderwood, & McGregor, 1989). A specific incident is presented to the SME in the form of a scenario or simulation. The SME is required to participate in the simulation or describe the scenario as if they were there. The incident is broken down into key events or decision points. Each decision point is probed about the individual's assessment of the situation at that point in time, the specific cues or pieces of information that led to that assessment, what actions were taken and why, and what common novice errors might occur at that point in time. The intent of this interview is to follow the decision making process from a specific incident, as opposed to getting the less concrete information that may be obtained in the other interviews.

The three interview techniques are intended to complement each other and provide the practitioner with an understanding of the cognitive demands and how experts deal with them. Furthermore, Klein Associates has addressed means of analysing the data and translating the findings into training and interface design implications. This is achieved by providing the means to consolidate the information from multiple interviews into a common place in order to identify common themes and any conflicting SME accounts. The cognitive demands table (CDT) provides a framework for this. From the CDT, specific design interventions can be identified either in terms of cognitive training objectives, improved training scenarios or simulations, or text revisions.

As yet, specific interface design interventions have not been incorporated into ACTA, but our work on decision-centered design will provide the perspective that will be addressed by ACTA at a later date.

Evaluation study

An evaluation of the ACTA techniques was conducted to evaluate its usefulness and usability. The concept of CTA and its training implications was introduced to two groups of 12 psychology graduate students. One group of students was provided with instructions to conduct unstructured interviews with SMEs, while the other group was provided with a three hour workshop on the ACTA techniques. Each group interviewed SMEs from either the firefighting domain or US Navy Electronic Warfare Operators. Each student participated in two interviews with SMEs, followed by a session to collate the data and develop training materials. They were required to consolidate the data from the interviews in the Cognitive Demands Table format, prepare cognitive learning objectives for a course, and revise or add to existing training manuals. Subjective ratings from interviewers and SMEs were also collected.

Several sets of data were collected for the evaluation. We collected questionnaire data from both the participants in the study and the SMEs that were interviewed. These included ratings on an ACTA usability questionnaire, an interviewer questionnaire which addressed the experiences of the participants with interviewing and creating the training materials, and an interviewee questionnaire which the SMEs filled out expressing their experience in the interview and what kinds of information they had been able to discuss. We also collected the participants' interview data, and notes. We collected the participants' completed cognitive demands tables, the cognitive learning objectives, and the training manual additions/revisions from the training material development session. Finally, we recruited SMEs to evaluate the materials for content accuracy, importance, and relevance to training. We also conducted SME evaluations of the cognitive nature of the information contained in the CDTs and training materials.

Key findings

Few significant differences were found between the unstructured interview group and the ACTA trained group. The reasons for this are discussed later. However, the key findings are summarized below.

Questionnaires

The ACTA usability questionnaires indicated that ACTA was easy to use, flexible, and provided clear output. The interviewer questionnaires indicated that both the ACTA and unstructured groups were able to conduct interviews that provided information that the interviewers considered useful and relevant to the training interventions. The ACTA group was more confident in their ability to conduct the interviews. The SME questionnaires indicated that the interviews allowed them to articulate their experience and expertise at the task.

SME evaluations

Independent EW and firefighter SMEs were brought in to evaluate the content of the learning objectives and manual revisions. They rated the manual revisions for both groups as both accurate and important for training. They rated the learning objectives as containing information that was both accurate and important for training purposes. Over eighty percent of the content was also judged to be very or somewhat helpful for the training of the task of interest.

To answer the question whether ACTA actually elicited cognitive information beyond that which is already captured in current courses and textbooks, SMEs assessed whether a new person on the job would be likely to know the information in the table. In spite of large individual differences in content, the Cognitive demand tables were judged to contain experience-based knowledge rather than text-book procedural information. The information in the tables was also judged to be relevant to the task of interest.

Group differences

Only very small differences were found between the ACTA group and the unstructured interview group. This was at first surprising. On further qualitative analyses of the data, however, we discovered large individual differences in interviewing skill resulting in large intra-group variance, making group differences difficult to interpret. Also, on reflection, we realized that we had helped both groups by providing an introduction to cognition, expertise, and CTA, and by providing the means to analyse the data for cognitive training interventions. We believe that the introductory workshop was influential in the favorable outcomes from both groups. The implications for ACTA are twofold. We must provide practitioners with an introduction to cognition, expertise and the purposes of CTA so that they are aware of the types of information that they are looking for during the interviews, and can learn to adapt and be flexible with the ACTA methods that we provide.

We also learned that providing practitioners with a way to consolidate and analyse the data from the perspective of providing training interventions was also useful in that it provided a means for practitioners to be aware of the types of information elicited by ACTA that would benefit a training programme.

These lessons-learned from our evaluation study have been put to good use in refining the ACTA methods and the way that they are packaged for practitioners in a computer-based training tool that we are currently developing for ACTA (ACTA has previously been presented in workshop format).

Applications of ACTA

The products of the ACTA interviews are geared towards interventions for training and for systems design. Currently the Navy is looking at ACTA for use by instructional designers for implementing training interventions to improve the rapid acquisition of cognitive decision making and judgment skills in Navy domains. Based on existing CTA methods, training interventions have been created for urban fireground incident commanders, wildland firefighters, nursing patient assessment, training of air traffic controllers' display scanning for improved situation awareness, training of decision making by Tactical Action Officers in ships' Combat Information Centers, training surgical skills, and in many other domains.

We also believe that the data from ACTA can support cognitive engineering and decision-centered design approaches to designing interventions for systems and user interfaces. Examples of such interventions using existing CTA methods have included: the successful modification of the AWACS Weapons-Director workstation, the creation of an electronic patient recording chart that helps nurses recognize the early onset of subtle problems in neonatal intensive care units, a tool to help weaponeers choose effective munitions for precision bombing missions and to assess the munitions effectiveness (bomb damage assessment), and a set of implications for air traffic control system design, to name but a few.

Future issues

Klein Associates currently conducts workshops to teach ACTA, but we are also working on a computer-based training application for the US Navy instructional designers that runs on CD-ROM. This application includes an introduction to cognitive task analysis, cognition and expertise, the three ACTA methods, how to consolidate the data into a cognitive demands table, and how to use that information to produce training interventions (including cognitive learning objectives, improved training simulations, and instructor guides for making more effective use of old training simulations).

The key areas of future research for ACTA include:
- *Team CTA methods*: additional methods for the acquisition of expert knowledge and skills as it relates to team decision making.
- *ACTA+ISD*: means to improve the incorporation of ACTA into more traditional ISD approaches to task analysis.
- *Representations*: additional means to represent the data in such a way that it allows the practitioner to translate the data into effective training and design products.
- *Cognitive skills training*: how training needs to change to encourage the more rapid acquisition of judgment and decision making skills to take advantage of the data gathered with ACTA.

- *Systems & interface design*: how to provide designers with the tools to incorporate a decision-centered design approach into their systems and interface designs.

References

Cooke, N. J. (1994). 'Varieties of knowledge elicitation techniques'. *International Journal of Human-Computer Studies,* Vol. 41, pp. 801-849.

Gordon, S. E., Schmierer, K. A., & Gill, R. T. (1993). 'Conceptual graph analysis: Knowledge acquisition for instructional systems design'. *Human Factors,* Vol. 35, pp. 459-481.

Hall, E. M., Gott, S. P., & Pokorny, R. A. (1995). *A procedural guide to cognitive task analysis: The PARI methodology.* AL/HR-TR-1995-0108. Manpower and Personnel Division: Armstrong Laboratory, Brooks AFB, TX.

Klein, G. A., Calderwood, R., & McGregor, D. (1989). 'Critical Decision method for eliciting knowledge. Special issue: Perspectives in knowledge engineering'. *IEEE Transactions on Systems, Man, and Cybernetics*, Vol 19, pp. 462-472.

McNeese, M. D., Zaff, B. S., Peio, K. J., Snyder, D. E., Duncan, J. C., & McFarren, M. R. (1990). *An advanced knowledge and design acquisition methodology: Application for the Pilot's Associate.* AAMRL-TR-90-060. Human Systems Division Armstrong: Aerospace Medical Research Laboratory, Wright-Patterson AFB, OH.

Acknowledgements

Funding was provided by the Naval Personnel Research and Development Center, San Diego, under contract # N66001-94-C-7034. Many thanks for the efforts and support of Dr. Josephine Randel, of NPRDC, and to the team at Klein Associates Inc.

4   Job design in integrated mail processing

Anne Bruseberg and Andrew Shepherd
Loughborough University, UK

Abstract

A common motivation in automating manufacturing is to create continuous processes, using production staff to undertake system supervision rather than manual activity. This issue is emerging in Royal Mail, with the introduction of new mail sorting technologies. We have used hierarchical task analysis (HTA) to understand these new tasks and to inform issues concerned with the design of jobs and other human factors. Much of the analysis of this novel context was made possible by recognising the similarities with existing process control plants. Results of analysis show a mix of manual and cognitive tasks. Manual skills required are similar to present arrangements in sorting offices, but supervisory monitoring, problem solving and planning skills are not. Despite similarities between the operating philosophy of Royal Mail and process control, several cognitive skills in Royal Mail appear unique to sorting office supervision. The need to understand more fully how these systems should be supervised has prompted the development of task simulation in order that supervisory skills might be studied further.

Introduction

Royal Mail is currently involved in intensive organisational change driven by the introduction of an integrated mail processing system (IMP) - an advanced machinery for letter sorting. A major issue when introducing new technology is the design of jobs. New technology offers flexibility to configure jobs in novel ways and requires job-holders to take on new responsibilities. Royal Mail has experienced several generations of radically different technology but has accommodated these changes within broadly consistent work organization. A challenge currently facing Royal

Mail is whether the changes implied by IMP constitute another small step or are more revolutionary, warranting a new approach to system operation.

Changes within several generations of sorting technology

Mail processing entails several stages. After posting, letters are transported to a sorting office, to be: (i) *segregated* into different types of mail; (ii) *pre-sorted* into larger areas, then (iii) *final sorted* for dispatch. Originally, these processes were entirely manual. However, to handle mail more efficiently, a number of machines have been introduced over the years. Mail *segregation* is automated through using large drums to enable separation of letters from packages, and through reading bars on stamps to discriminate 1st from 2nd class mail. Mail *sorting* was facilitated by the introduction of post-codes which are translated into phosphor-dots by 'coding-desk' operators. Later technologies used optical character recognition (OCR). Even with these advances, mail processing was a 'batch-process' with manual work entailed in transferring batches of letters from one machine to the next.

Integrated mail processing - IMP

In the IMP system each stage is automated using state-of-the-art technology with individual items of mail transferred between units in a continuous, rather than batch, flow. The technology thus eliminates the need for pre-sorting and intermediate transport and storage. The computer technology used in OCR is now sufficiently powerful to offer customers additional services based on an analysis of the addresses of mail items, such as overprinting selective advertisements. This commercial development adds a commercial dimension to the system control strategy. High volumes of letters will be processed at high speed with very little delay between input and output. Decisions to change processing parameters will need to be made much faster. Control decisions will need to incorporate information from all intermediate processing steps. Technical failures or even minor stoppages will be much more wasteful.

The similarity between IMP and more traditional 'process control' is marked; thus, staffing strategies in IMP could reflect those that have been proven in other process industries. Royal Mail supervisors have traditionally overseen a number of postal workers carrying out the separate tasks around the sorting office. Supervisors have not been directly engaged with the system other than in monitoring and scheduling general performance. In view of the integrated nature of IMP, there now seems to be a role for system supervision, which monitors the system as an integrated whole, diagnosing and planning strategies which may affect the whole process.

Task analysis of supervising IMP

Job design should be based on a functional analysis of the task. Hierarchical task analysis (HTA; Duncan, 1974), which has been used extensively in process control environments is a rational approach to identifying task information in terms of functions and the skills and knowledge necessary to carry these functions out. HTA redescribes a task into sub-tasks and specifies the 'plan' stating the conditions under which sub-tasks must be carried out. Analysing a task that has not yet been developed is a common problem but one that can be overcome by reference to existing work organization. Indeed, it has been possible to understand the new IMP system by analysing the tasks involved in previous generations of postal-sorting. In previous generations of sorting office the functions are organised according to the major processing stages. Figure 1 represents the top levels of the HTA for the current automated mail sorting systems. It reflects the general pattern of activity of current and previous generations of sorting office, though further detail will vary according to the technology employed.

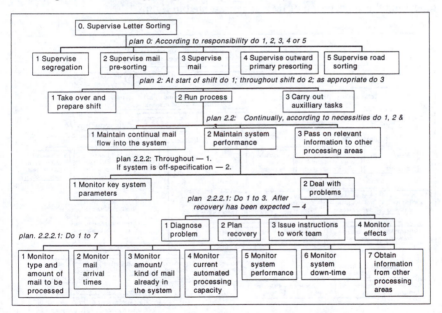

Figure 1   HTA of current and previous mail processing

Office supervision in existing and earlier generations of sorting office requires watching the mail inflow, ensuring high sorting performance, detecting problems and

27

allocating staff to duties. It also entails communicating with staff in the other sorting areas to determine respective system capacities and work-load. Current sorting offices entail substantial manual activity, even though individual units are served by advanced technology. Batches of mail are held in 'buffer storage' which makes work-scheduling easier, but at the cost of inefficiency. IMP is designed, in part, to reduce opportunities for intermediate buffer storage of mail, though mail which cannot be processed is removed for separate manual treatment. The system is totally integrated across hitherto separate sections. It is soon becomes clear that the traditional organization of work is inappropriate. Manual activity is still needed to provide back-up for processing non-machinable items and to deal with blockages, but these activities are required less as equipment becomes more reliable. The key task that is emerging with IMP is that of *system supervision*, including monitoring system performance to ensure that quality of service is maintained, and that all components are working and in harmony. When problems arise, there is a need to deal with them swiftly, both to rectify the problem and devise strategies to optimise performance until the problem is solved. These are common characteristics observed in system supervisory tasks in the process industries and embody the principles for modelling the supervision of IMP as represented in figure 2.

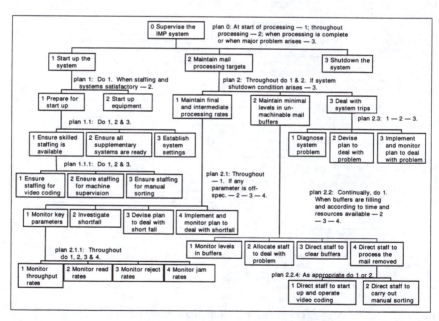

Figure 2   Top levels of the analysis of the task of supervising IMP

Figure 2 shows the main tasks entailed in monitoring and maintaining the performance of IMP. It does not specify the tasks of individuals, but describes the functional responsibility of the overall team. The main duties specified in the redescription of the top goal are typical system supervisory task descriptions. Development of the analysis for system start-up {goal 1.2} reflects the stages identified in the earlier generations of mail sorting, as described in figure 1. A great deal of activity is concerned with maintaining and monitoring key parameters {2}. Where parameters are outside acceptable tolerance, remedial action is prompted (e.g. {2.1.2}, {2.1.3}, {2.3.2}). When remedial plans have been made, they must be implemented (e.g. {2.1.4}, {2.2.2}, {2.3.3}). To ensure that any of this work gets done requires appropriate duties be allocated to team members. When this is done, the issues of interface design and training can be addressed.

Job design for cognitive, process control related tasks

Activities described in figure 2 are varied. 'Cognitive' work entails making judgements concerning system status and planning remedial action (e.g. {2.1.1}, {2.1.2}, {2.1.3}); there is also manual intervention into the system (e.g. {2.2.3}). Because much of the monitoring, diagnosis and planning requires analysis of the interaction between information drawn from all parts of the system, it is necessary to carry it out in one place and represent it on an appropriate interface. Moreover, the information gained through the execution of task elements such as monitoring, is likely to influence the effectiveness with which subsequent diagnosis or planning is carried out. So, these tasks are best carried out by the same person. Despite the importance of cognitive skills, manual work, carried out in specific places, remains crucial, and this manual work must be informed by decisions about the system, i.e. *what* to do in specific circumstances and *when* to do it. Moreover, this crucial manual work cannot be done at the expense of maintaining system supervision. It follows that running the IMP system must be done by team members with different skills, but working in close collaboration.

The effective distribution of task functions between members of a team entails consideration of:

- the information network within the task - how information must flow between individual operations and between operatives and equipment;
- time and order constraints - when things must be done and which things must be done in temporal proximity to each other;
- layout and space restrictions - where physical location for executing task elements is constrained;
- operational importance - where error or delay can and cannot be tolerated;
- cognitive demands/loading - where workload is unacceptable at any point in time or across the profile of the shift;

- common information - where working knowledge is common to more than one task element;
- shared skill base - where different task elements exercise the same or similar skills.

The design of jobs and the design of the tasks that job-holders must carry out are complementary activities. For the design of jobs containing high amounts of cognitive activity it is especially crucial to specify the information requirements. Effectiveness of control is decreased by factors such as lack of, or unsuitability of information, information delay or information overload. The problem of information fragmentation (Shepherd, 1993) needs special consideration. This occurs if data required in a certain context is divided between different people or between locations with different access to them. So decisions based on the sum of the information are impeded. These factors cause even lower performance if combined with problems such as lack of skill or time pressure. Many of these issues are discussed by Bainbridge (1987). Organisational structure must enable effective information flow with no barriers to prevent information being available where it is needed.

The novel job structures that must be applied to IMP will require Royal Mail personnel carrying out tasks of a kind with which they are unfamiliar. Manual and procedural tasks in IMP will not be completely familiar, but their purposes will be easy to discern from the physical affordances of the system. Hence, procedures will be easy to design, and activities will contain many of the features familiar in current generations of sorting office - information necessary to support work design, job design, training and support in manual tasks will be easily forthcoming from existing task analysis (e.g. figure 1). Understanding the system supervision skills of monitoring, diagnosis and planning is far from straightforward, because operating behaviour does not map simply onto the structures of plant and equipment. Skills are covert and skilled personnel in these domains extract practical working knowledge from their experience with the task. Understanding how experienced people operate in such domains helps us devise measures to help novices through training etc. (e.g. Marshall et al., 1981).

In more familiar domains, such as process control in petrochemical or power plant, task analysis often shows how new tasks may be rendered into elements where operating principles are familiar, for example, the filling and emptying of vessels, or the control of cooling systems. In a *new* domain, we reach a point in task analysis where there are no promising models for how to proceed. Figure 2 shows how we have used HTA to configure the main activities likely to govern the operation of IMP. This was done by drawing the analogy between the operating philosophy of IMP and the operating philosophies of automated process with which we are familiar, e.g. power generation and petrochemical plant. Thus, it has been possible to model the main activities entailed in supervising IMP. However, when we encounter cognitive tasks in this novel domain, there are no templates for comparison

30

to suggest how the system should be controlled. There are no real 'experts' from whom to distil expert wisdom. Understanding how people can operate IMP is a problem which must be solved before information requirements, cognitive loading and training can be understood.

The examination of cognitive skills

By analogy with more familiar process control tasks, HTA models a framework which situates the cognitive tasks of concern in controlling IMP. This shows how task elements relate to one another, hence, how information will or will not be available as the task is carried out; it indicates which tasks need to be carried out concurrently; and it indicates the task elements which are performed later and which the current task element must serve or inform. Thus, while examination of cognition is necessary, the task is placed in the context defined by the HTA (Shepherd, 1995).

Our method for understanding these cognitive strategies has been to develop a task simulator to enable the development of expertise. This is not a full mission simulator, because the work environment has not yet been designed, and because the tasks and team structures are not yet resolved. The simulator is currently being used in a series of experiments where, first, the system and the performance targets are explained to the subject, and then subjects are required to explore and resolve likely operational problems. As expertise emerges so ideas will be tested to establish whether this operating knowledge is useful to the next 'expert' being developed. In this way, we aim to establish a useful knowledge-base of operating practice in this domain on which to base formal experiments on training and task loading.

The simulation (Mini-IMP) comprises a mathematical model of the IMP process, which drives a prototype interface. The model was produced using the spreadsheet Microsoft EXCEL[a], which provides convenient calculation and macro programming capabilities, with good graphics facilities to represent a dynamic interface. The process of producing the Mini-IMP in EXCEL was, itself, very useful because it helped significantly in learning about system interactions and understanding the emergent properties of IMP. This is helpful both in making suggestions to initial experimental subjects and in understanding their resultant behaviour. Fuller detail about Mini-IMP, its application and its findings will be described elsewhere.

Concluding remarks

The paper describes a strategy for understanding the tasks of supervising a new automated mail-sorting system (IMP) with a view to prescribing how operating teams should be configured and how team members should be supported. Hierarchical analysis of the tasks of operating the existing 'manual' system proved informative in understanding the various system elements. Analysis of operating the *new* system was achieved by recognising the analogy between the manufacturing philosophy of IMP and more familiar process control domains. Thus, the new task analysis used task structures familiar from process control. This strategy revealed a number of important cognitive tasks which complement the more obvious physical tasks of sorting offices, pointing to a need for a supervisor to monitor system parameters across the whole office and direct the activities of 'manual' operatives in dealing with, for example, equipment jams. However, because this level of automation in sorting offices is so new and different to process plant, the actual strategies and the information needed to support these strategies, must be discerned empirically. This is necessary to establish the information to be presented, the informational interdependencies between job elements and the training that people will require. However, the novelty of the domain precludes there being experts from whom to distil operating knowledge. To this end, a simulator has been developed on which to develop and study this expertise with a view to informing subsequent human factors decisions.

References

Bainbridge, L. (1987), 'Ironies of automation', in J. Rasmussen, K.D. Duncan & J. Leplat (eds.), *New technology and human error*. John Wiley & Sons: Chichester.

Duncan, K.D. (1974), 'Analytical techniques in training design', in E. Edwards and F.P. Lees (eds.), *The human operator in process control*. Taylor and Francis: London.

Marshall, E.C., Scanlon K.E., Duncan, K.D. & Shepherd, A. (1981), 'Panel diagnosis training for major-hazard continuous process installations', *Chemical Engineer*, Vol. 365, pp. 66-69.

Shepherd, A. (1993), 'An approach to information requirements specification for process control tasks', *Ergonomics*, Vol. 36, pp 805-817.

Shepherd, A. (1995), 'Task Analysis in HCI tasks', in A.F. Monk & M. Gilbert (eds.) *Perspectives in HCI*. Academic Press: London.

5   A systems analysis of teamworking in control rooms: methodology considered

Melanie Ashleigh and Neville Stanton
University of Southampton, UK

Abstract

This   paper considers some of the research problems that are incurred when evaluating team effectiveness and offers an approach to the problem. It focuses on the development of a practical methodology which is based on a theoretical framework of the socio-technical paradigm. A taxonomy of methods is offered which is both practical for the researcher and culminates into a holistic approach towards analysing teams in control rooms.

Introduction

As teams are an integral part of organisational structure, evaluating their effectiveness has become an important part of enhancing development per se, as well as furthering academic research. With the introduction of highly integrated technical systems, teamworking in control room environments has enabled fewer people to cope with increased workload as well as facilitating personal growth and development; allowing employees to become more adaptable with higher skill levels. This has also promoted dependency on others in terms of job sharing, cross training, culminating ideas and collaborative decision making. However, developing methods of evaluating team 'synergy' can be problematic for researchers.

Problems with analysing teams

Teams are social units operating in larger social systems, bounded together by a multitude of interdependent factors, and as such are hard to define and even more difficult to measure. Teams can present many problems to the researcher, especially

33

when carrying out natural studies. Evaluation problems may occur from the fact that there is no way of generalising how and when teams should be trained or managed (Guzzo, Salas and Associates, 1995). This is a contextual issue and often dependent upon the way a team is structured as well as the organisational culture it is working in.

Another dilemma in evaluating teams is the one of unit analysis, mainly because typically, approaches tailored for individual-differences are being used to carry out team research. Guzzo et al (1995), argue that when studying team behaviour, one is trying to study behaviour of the 'aggregate' of team members and make inferences on the population of teams and not on the individual members themselves. This presents problems, as generally the population of teams are relatively small in size, few in number across an organisation and therefore the large samples which are the usual requirement for normal statistical methods, are difficult to come by.

Approaches and methods

In attempting to develop appropriate methods of evaluating team performance, various models have been used to identify and categorise the many determinants of teamwork. Recent research has been based on the socio-technical paradigm, using a systems analysis (Hettenhaus, 1992). This model identifies two sub-systems, the technical, which denotes the hardware and software (e.g. the SCADA system), whereas the social system is made up of the control room engineers, support staff, management etc. This approach realises a more holistic view and incorporates both objective and subjective data collection. Similarly, Foushee & Helmreich (1988) when considering control-room teams, used three classification elements as:
- Inputs - those determinants which are brought into the team situation; the characteristics of the individual members of the team, the characteristics of the team and of the environment.
- Process - the elements which make the actual functionality of the team.
- Outcomes - the performance of the team, both for task and team processes.

Development of methodology

Initial framework

For the purposes of the current project a team can be likened to an open system, defined as 'a set of interrelated elements, each of which is related directly or indirectly to every other element' (Ackoff & Emery, 1972). In order to capture the many different elements of teamworking, a systems framework was used based on the 'general systems theory' (von Bertalanffy, 1950). The model was adapted from Foushee and Helmreich (1988), which provided a comprehensive, yet standardised way of measuring different teams. Initially, during the design phase of the study, measurement of a multiplicity of variables was envisaged, which in hindsight was a little over optimistic. The final measures were contingent upon the contextual environment, the aims, in trying to measure the interdependency of human activity, attitudes and performance from a psychological focus, based upon Stanton (1996).

Inputs

It is important to differentiate between the three factors under this heading of inputs; 'individual', 'team' and 'context', and their relationship with the team processes and outputs. The measures taken and methodology used for these elements are described as follows.

Individual inputs Accumulated individual behavioural competency scores, were a useful measure of baseline scores in order to make across team comparisons. However, care must be taken to preserve strict anonymity, together with consideration of ethical issues, as such data is extremely sensitive. The purpose of using these measures was to try and eliminate differences, rather than find them. Other biographical data e.g. age, length of tenure in control room can also provide useful co-variates or matching variables.

Team inputs As indicated by past research, optimal task separation is contingent upon the structure of a team. Stammers & Hallam, (1985) identified two main methods of team organisation; vertical and horizontal. Different permutations of these two basic structures can be extended, depending on the operational environments and the size of the team leading to more complex and hybrid combinations. This implies that possible differences may be found in major structural factors such as work roles and responsibilities, tasks, lines of communication and how they are assigned to each other. These differences, specifically in task structure, roles and responsibilities may be identified by undertaking a hierarchical task analysis, (Annett et. al, 1971).

Contextual inputs In order to assess the intrinsic characteristics of work in the control rooms we used the 'core job characteristics model developed by Hackman & Oldham, (1980). A self-reporting questionnaire, which is divided into seven sections, identifies five principle characteristics of work that predict job performance and satisfaction. These are:
- Skill variety - the degree to which the job challenges a person to use a range of skills and abilities.
- Task identity - the degree to which the job results in an identifiable and visible outcome.
- Task significance - the degree to which the job has a perceivable impact upon others.

35

- Autonomy - the degree to which the job provides the individual with freedom and discretion in scheduling work and how it will be undertaken.
- Feedback - the degree to which the individual is provided with information about the effectiveness of their efforts.

A human factors review comprising ten factors relating to the SCADA system, provided a measurement of the technical context of the control room. These included: visual clarity, consistency, compatibility, informative feedback, explicitness, appropriate functionality, flexibility and control, error prevention, user guidance and usability problems. An in-depth usability study was undertaken with a sample of control room operators in each area, using a structured evaluation checklist (Ravden & Johnson, 1989). This was done on a one to one interview basis, whilst sitting at a terminal. This allowed users to relate their views directly to the tasks they were performing, whilst providing the researcher with examples which facilitated context and understanding.

Processes

In an attempt to measure the processes, both attitudinal and direct behavioural observations were taken.

Traffic analysis The method of link analysis (Drury, 1995) was adapted and was a useful tool in tracking the physical movements of people in and out of the control room as well as monitoring demand of resources and equipment (e.g. fax/printer machines). It was considered that this data would provide a necessary insight into spatial layout of the control room, as well as information regarding social interactions and communication behaviours. The data was gathered over a comparable eight hour shift period in each control room, where all movements were monitored, using two independent researchers; this was in order to gain some measure of inter-reliability.

Direct observation In order to successfully evaluate any system, it is preferable to observe it in its naturally occurring state. Other researchers have found that direct observation procedures provide a high degree of face validity as one is recording actual events as they happen (Drury, 1995). Unfortunately experimental control is usually low in such situations as one cannot manipulate any of the many interacting variables. A 'shadowing' technique was used to gather both quantitative and qualitative data by monitoring frequency and duration of various activities within the control room. From the researchers perspective this one to one monitoring is beneficial as participants can provide contextual information through verbal protocol. In order to limit observer error and test reliability, a simultaneous video recording was taken, which was coded and analysed in real time in the laboratory using a powerful software package. Although these methods allow both technical and social interaction processes to be recorded in detail, it is acknowledged that any direct observation technique is invasive for the participant and is likely to have some effect on behaviour.

Teamworking questionnaire   In order to gain the team members perceptions of their own synergy, it was necessary to obtain qualitative data.   A self reporting questionnaire was developed based on performance shaping factors (Glendon et al 1994) and a review of team performance undertaken by Stanton (1996). The principle behind this was that 'teamwork', as distinct from 'taskwork' (Guzzo et al, 1995) incorporate factors which 'include activities that serve to strengthen the quality of functional interactions, relationships, co-operation, communication and co-ordination of team members' (p. 15; 1995). The questionnaire was produced from seven 'teamwork' dimensions, namely: consensus, co-ordination, control, communication, co-operation, coaching and culture.

Outputs

Two methods of output measures were considered to be relevant. One from an individual perspective in terms of life and job satisfaction. This was undertaken by using a questionnaire taken from the work of Warr, Cook & Wall (1979). It was considered that these variables were significant measures in the context of the project as the company had recently undergone a restructuring programme. This had implications on peoples' life style in terms of relocation; living away from home for long periods, and/or commuting over long distances. The team outputs were measured using the critical success factors (CSFs) that were pertinent to the company. From the company's own operating philosophy, seven factors were identified that directly related to their own vision statements. These were developed into a questionnaire that are to be targeted at their customers. Both these measures are important and constitute feedback into the system, which in turn can determine changes in input and/or process.

Conclusions

This revised systems approach illustrates the relevant measures that were appropriate for evaluating teamworking in control rooms.   This approach identifies a comprehensive and practical methodology, using standardised measures across control rooms; this was confirmed by a recent pilot study. By using this approach it is hoped   that comparisons between control rooms can be made and predictions made on possible outcomes on the basis of the inputs and processes. By combining data and using multivariate analysis techniques, we will hopefully be able to establish what factors if any, affect the outputs. Similarly by treating the inputs and processes as alternate independent variables, using a quasi-experimental model, we will determine whether specific input factors determine team processes and outputs as well as if particular processes determine CSFs. Although there are an infinite amount of variables that could have been taken, the systems framework provides a practical methodology which gives a broad spectrum of measures feasible for the resource limitations of the study. We anticipate that this methodology, once tested, may be used to evaluate teams in other domains.

References

Ackoff, R.L. & Emery, F.E. (1972) *On Purposeful Systems*. Tavistock: London.

Annett, J. Duncan, K.D., Stammers R.B. & Gray, M.J. (1971*) Task Analysis*. H.M.S.O: London.

Bertalanffy, L. von (1950) 'The theory of open systems in physics and biology'. *Science*, Vol 13, pp. 23-29.

Drury, C.G. (1995) 'Methods for direct observation of performance'. in J.R. Wilson & E.N. Corlett (eds.), *Evaluation of Human Work; A practical ergonomics methodology* (2nd Edition) Taylor & Francis: London.

Foushee, H.C. & Helmreich, R.L. (1988) 'Group interaction and flight crew performance' in, E.L. Weiner & D.C. Nagel (eds.) *Human Factors in Aviation*. Academic Press: New York.

Glendon, A.I., Stanton, N.A. & Harrison, D. (1994) 'Factor analysing a performance shaping concepts questionnaire', in S. Robertson (ed.), *Contemporary Ergonomics.*. Taylor & Francis: London.

Guzzo, R.A., Salas, E., and Associates, (1995*) Team Effectiveness and Decision Making in Organisations* . Josey Bass: San Francisco.

Hackman, J.R. & Oldham, G. (1980) *Work Redesign.* Addison-Wesley: USA.

Hettenhaus, J.R. (1992) 'Changing the way people work: a sociotechnical approach to computer-integrated manufacturing in a process industry', in H. Kragt, (ed.), *Enhancing Industrial Performance.*. Taylor and Francis: London.

Ravden, S. I. & Johnson, G. I. (1989) *Evaluating Usability of Human-Computer Interfaces: A practical method.* Ellis Horwood: Chichester.

Stammers, R.B. & Hallam, J. (1985) 'Task allocation and the balance of load in the multiman-machine system: some case studies'. *Applied Ergonomics*, Vol. 16, pp. 251-257.

Stanton, N.A. (1996) 'Team Performance: communication, co-ordination, co-operation and control'. In , N. Stanton, (ed.) *Human Factors in Nuclear Safety*. Taylor & Francis: London.

Warr, P., Cook, J. & Wall, T. (1979) 'Scales for the measurement of some work attitudes and aspects of psychological well-being'. *Journal of Occupational Psychology*, Vol 52, pp.129-148.

6 Models of decision making in emergency management

Mats Danielsson and Kjell Ohlsson
Luleå University of Technology, Sweden

Abstract

The Emergency Director's (ED) decision making is decisive for the outcome of an emergency operation. Particularly in large scale operations, the cognitive demands on the ED are severe. Ninety fire chiefs were interviewed about their own accounts of factors affecting difficulty level of decisions. Types of decisions described as especially hard to make concerned prioritizing in life-saving operations, evacuations and whether to adopt an offensive or a defensive fire fighting strategy. Perceived stressors related to lack of information in the initial phase of an operation. Emergency management, being a control task, can be analysed within the framework of distributed dynamic decision making (DDM). Interview data confirmed some findings of previous DDM laboratory research. Information needs differ according to the decision maker's position in the distributed system. A model for evaluation of information transmitted to the emergency management system is proposed.

Decision making in emergency management

The Emergency Director (ED) has the ultimate responsibility for managing emergency operations in the event of forest fires, floods, hazardous material spills or other major incidents. The ED's task may be analysed from different perspectives. In this article, we will discuss the emergency management task in terms of decision making. The ED's decision making authority during an emergency response is crucial for establishment of effective command and control and successful outcome. From a psychological point of view, three criteria are necessary for classification as a decision task. First, there must be a matter of choice between two or more alternatives. Second, the probability of choosing the correct alternative is less than one, either due to a probabilistic relation between the outcome and the information provided, or because of limitations in the decision maker's information processing capacity. Third, there must be some amount of time available for making the decision, at least one second, in order to distinguish decision making from choice reaction tasks (Wickens, 1992).

Traditionally, research on decision making has pitted decision makers' actual performance against normative models, i.e. models outlining behaviour that would be optimal when considering probabilistic relations identified. In emergency management, there is no normative model to rely upon (Brehmer, 1987). An emergency is by definition a unique and unpredictable event and it is seldom possible, even in retrospect, to assess what the outcome of an emergency response had been if alternative measures had been followed. The only kind of normative models available for the rescue service are tactical doctrines codified in manuals and guidelines.

The absence of normative models for emergency management has important consequences for research approaches to an ED's decision making, especially the relationship of the subjective and the objective aspects of his/her decisions. Decision research has thoroughly investigated how a decisions maker's confidence in his/her judgments is related to their actual accuracy. In general, people tend to be overconfident in their decisions, i.e. more confident than warranted by their actual accuracy (Cohen, 1993)

Obviously, the lack of normative models makes the distinction between subjective-objective accuracy difficult to maintain. This is also the case when addressing the difficulty level of various decision tasks. Thus, it is far from apparent whether tasks described as especially difficult by ED's are actually imposing high demands on information processing capacity, or if they reflect other kinds of annoyance.

This discussion, however, from the profession's point of view, might be regarded as specious arguments, since an ED's primary responsibility is not to make decisions, but to control fire fighting or rescue operations. Thus, even if it is not possible to identify optimal decisions, it is apparent that some ED's are better than others in establishing effective command and control in emergency responses.

Emergency management, being a control task, involves *dynamic decision making*. A series of interdependent decisions about continuously changing environments, both spontaneously and as an effect of the decisions made, is required. Time is critical because accurate decisions must be made, not only in a correct order, but also at specific points in time. These are characteristics of tasks that are stressful by their very nature (Brehmer, 1987). Emergency management is a difficult dynamic decision task as compared to other control tasks. Difficulty is mainly due to complexity, - a myriad number of variables have to be controlled and the decision domain is ill-defined.

Furthermore, large scale emergency operations imply *distributed decision making* in that decisions are distributed among many actors of which no single individual has complete knowledge of the current situation. The distribution is structured in a hierarchy determined by the time scales within which the decision makers have to work.

In the following paragraphs we will discuss ED's tasks from the perspective of data obtained in a study that assesses need for decision support systems in Swedish emergency service systems. The results presented are confined to those pertaining to the theoretical issues hinted at above.

Background and aim

On behalf of the Swedish National Rescue Service Agency an interview study was carried out (Danielsson, Mattsson, Ohlsson & Wiberg, 1994). The aim of the study was to survey needs and necessary conditions for implementation of decision support systems in the rescue service organization. The study focussed on conditions in large scale emergency operations and to identify practical strategies for changes that would enhance emergency operation performance.

Method

Seventy-five local fire chiefs were interviewed through telephone contact. The respondents were selected as being representative of various municipal districts in Sweden: rural and urban, low-risk and high-risk environment. The interviews were semi-structured and lasted between thirty and seventy minutes. Responses were tape recorded, copied out in text and content was subsequently analysed and categorized.

Fifteen additional respondents were selected from the very small population of fire chiefs who have ample experiences of major emergency responses, i.e. operations involving a number of fire brigades, rescue squads and other emergency professionals. The repertory grid technique was used in the interviews with these experts.

Results

Response categories for some key items in the interview checklist are presented below.

What is the most difficult aspect of the ED's work in major emergency responses?

Seventy-five percent of the responses were evenly distributed to three categories of difficulty: *lack of routine and practice, communicational shortcomings* and *feelings of isolation.*

Lack of routine and practice refers to the infrequency of major accidents making

41

it difficult to get experiences of the command and control proper. The person acting as ED in major emergencies is usually a fire engineer by training. In most regions, emergencies requiring such competence are to occur on the average of once or twice a year. Fire engineers do not always take part in fire brigade routine operations and are thus unlikely to benefit from experiential training opportunities provided by management of minor emergencies.

Communication shortcomings involve information overload, technical equipment inadequacy and lack of skills in handling communication equipment. Information overload is salient during the initial phase of an emergency response and is seen as especially severe if there are no staff members available to which the communication task may be allocated.

The feeling of isolation is related both to the accumulation of work under time stress without any assurance of timely relief and to a lack of peers with whom to discuss common problems.

Which types of decision tasks are especially difficult?

The most frequent responses referred to *setting priorities in life-saving operations, evacuations* and *'smoke diving'.*

The question of priority in life-saving arises during major operations when many people are injured and resources are scarce. Decisions must be made on order of precedence for first aid treatment. The question also arises in situations where the resources are strained and human lives are at stake and the ED must give priority to at least one populated sector.

Evacuations may be at issue in case of gas leakage and rapidly spreading fires. Difficulty lies in the anticipating unfolding events and ensuing assessment of scope of evacuation necessary for protection of citizens.
'Smoke diving' pertains to the decision to got to a defensive or an offensive tactical approach when fighting a fire.

What are the main stressors related to the command and control tasks?

More than 50 per cent of the responses could be attributed to one factor, *lack of knowledge during the initial phase of an emergency response*. This concerns the period immediately after launching of an emergency response, when there are uncertainties about scale and exact characteristics of damage. Feedback delays from units first arriving on scene are particularly annoying. Respondents reported feelings of distress due to lack of control when confronting such situations.

What are the most important sources of information in major emergencies?

The importance of a specific source of information varies according to type of accident. However, more than half of the respondents mentioned the *SOS alarm operator* as a particularly important informant, especially during the initial stages. Existing computer systems for accessing data bases on hazardous materials were regarded as relevant but too cumbersome to handle, especially under time pressure.

What aspects of the build-up of the staff have to be considered?

The main problem identified by respondents is the scaling-up of an emergency response. There are critical points in time when the ED must size up, not only the nature of an incident and material resources required, but also the scope of the management task per se and to estimate staffing need. Almost all respondents reported that build-up of staff tends to be delayed when accidents escalate. Build-up of staff is more problematic in rural than in urban areas. Typical difficulties are related to information overload, stress and dis-coordination of personal resources.

Discussion

The interview data confirms some core findings of prior decision making research in laboratory settings. The respondents' own accounts of difficulties in command and control correspond to factors identified in research on dynamic decision making in simulated micro-worlds.

First, delay of feedback has detrimental effects on the decision maker's performance in control tasks. However, delays may have different causes with psychological effects that differ accordingly. Types of delays that are especially difficult to handle are those which cannot be visualized while delays related to movements in the system are less severe (Brehmer, 1987; Brehmer & Allard, 1991). In emergency management there are recurrent feedback delays of the former kind due to, for instance, the time it takes to transform the tactical commands from the ED to technical commands from the Fire Ground Commander to fire fighters. As noted above, feedback delay was identified as an important stressor.

Second, delegation of decision making is an efficient strategy for coping with increasing complexity, time pressure and feedback delay. However, this strategy is seldom used spontaneously and under stress a decision maker becomes even more reluctant to delegate responsibility. This bias of over control is consistent with the fact that the build-up of the emergency staff regularly tends to be delayed.

Major emergency responses involve distributed dynamic decision making (DDM). Although the final decision, legally, is the responsibility of only one person, the ED, the global task involves tasks which have to be shared between various operators. The need for distributed decision making arises because of complexity of tasks facing decision makers. As complexity increases, it becomes impossible for a single individual with limited information processing capacity to gain control. DDM means that the decisions are distributed among many actors of which no single person has a complete knowledge of the evolving situation. In emergency management, this distribution is hierarchical and this hierarchy is determined by the time scales within which the decision makers have to work. The ED's long term commands and decisions concerning priorities and coordination of several units represent the uppermost level, implying restrictions for decisions taken by the Fire Ground Commander which, in turn, set restrictions for the Sector Chiefs' concrete minute-operative decisions in the damage area.

Information needs differ according to the decision maker's position in the distributed system. This must be considered when assessing information quality or evaluating computerized decision support system for the emergency service organization. Here we propose a simple model that accounts for quality of

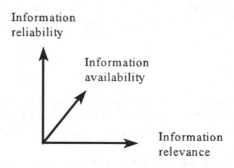

information provided to the emergency system.

The quality of a specific piece of information varies in three dimensions: *reliability*, *availability* and *relevance*.

Figure 1   Quality dimensions of information

Reliability is a basic quality required. Obviously, there is a wide range concerning quality of information provided to the emergency system, from unreliable eye-witness reports of an accident to highly reliable information about hazardous materials in data bases. Availability may differ due to technical capacities of the system conveying the information, the user-friendliness of the information system used and the decision maker's specific knowledge. Typically, an experienced ED develops site specific knowledge about potential hazards and local expertise.

The vertical dimension, relevance, is the most interesting from a DDM perspective, since relevance of information is determined by type of accident and phase of an emergency response but also by the position of the decision maker in the distributed emergency system.

For the ED, information about damage characteristics and extent is most relevant since this constitute the basis for sizing up of a situation and the ensuing overall decisions about pertinent tactical approaches. Thus, information provided by the alarm operator during the initial stage of an emergency response often possess high relevance for this kind of decision. On the other hand, for those decision makers issuing short term commands, like for instance the Fire Ground Commander, information about the damage area provided by maps, flow charts of industrial processes and the like, are more relevant.

Some sources of information in our study could easily be evaluated in terms of these dimensions. For example, information provided by alarm operators generally scores high on each dimension, while on the other hand the Rescue Agency's data base for hazardous materials while having high reliability, relevance varies according to type of accident and low data availability, mainly due to interface deficits.

References

Brehmer, B. (1987). 'Development of mental models for decision in technological systems'. In, J. Rasmussen, K. Duncan & J. Leplat (eds.) *New Technology and Human Error*. John Wiley: New York.

Brehmer, B. & Allard, R. (1991). 'Dynamic decision making: the effects of task complexity'. In, J. Rasmussen, B. Brehmer & J. Leplat (eds.) *Distributed Decision Making: Cognitive Models for Cooperative Work*. John Wiley:New York.

Cohen, M.S. (1993). 'Three paradigms for viewing decision biases'. In, G. Klein, J. Orasanu, R. Calderwood & C. Zsambok (eds.) *Decision Making in Action: Models and Methods* . Ablex Publishing: New Jersey.

Danielsson, M., Mattsson, C., Ohlsson, K. & Wiberg, E. (1994). Beslutsstöd för räddningsledare vid större olyckor: En intervjustudie *(Decision Support for Emergency Management: A survey study*. In Swedish) Research Report TULEA 1994:28.

Wickens, C.D. (1992). *Engineering Psychology and Human Performance (2nd edition)*. Harper Collins: New York.

Acknowledgement

The authors acknowledge the support of the initiator of the project, Jan Ahlberg at the National Rescue Service Agency in Karlstad, Sweden.

7 Emergency decision making on offshore installations

Jan Skriver and Rhona Flin
The Robert Gordon University, Aberdeen, UK

Abstract

Offshore installations are high hazard environments where emergency situations can have devastating effects as seen in the *Piper Alpha* disaster in 1988, which resulted in 167 deaths. In charge of and responsible for handling any incident encountered is the offshore installation manager (OIM). The outcome of an emergency is consequently dependent on the OIM's judgement and decision making. This research sets out to describe the decision making process of experienced OIMs and to link the decisions to a cognitive framework. Fourteen OIMs and five deputy OIMs from two operating companies participated in this study. Each OIM was presented with three paper-based emergency scenarios and asked to identify the first three critical decisions and related situational cues, objectives, expectations, and courses of action. Results indicate that experienced OIMs have emergency response schemata they can utilise to assess the situation and make decisions based on recognition and rules.

Introduction

Command and control skills have been a pre-requisite for senior personnel in the military and the emergency services for as long as those domains have existed. Recently, however, it has been acknowledged that a similar set of skills is essential for senior managers in modern industries where the potential for disaster exists in the shape of large scale loss of life or significant environmental damage. Managers in fields as diverse as sports, entertainment, and the nuclear power industries fall into this category. While the range of possible emergency scenarios which crisis managers from these diverse backgrounds can and have faced is extremely wide, they share a number of broad defining situational characteristics. These are limited time, high risk, multiple players, ill structured problems, and rapidly changing, confusing environments (Orasanu and Connolly, 1993).

One domain where such situations are possible is the offshore oil industry; an environment where the potential dangers posed by the presence of volatile hydrocarbon products are exacerbated by the isolated, often hostile, environments in which exploration and production take place. This study focuses on the emergency decision making skills of the managers of offshore installations. The potential for disaster and the necessity for efficient, self sufficient crisis management in the offshore environment are illustrated by the catastrophic loss of the *Piper Alpha* platform off the coast of Scotland in 1988, which resulted in 167 deaths (Cullen, 1990).

In response to the *Piper Alpha* disaster, the UK government introduced legislation to reduce risks to the health and safety of the offshore workforce, known as the safety case regulations (HSE, 1992). The key feature of the safety case is the requirement that operators must prepare a formal risk assessment for each of their installations and submit the case to the Health and Safety Executive for acceptance. This includes the identification of all major hazards relating to the installation and their consequences, as well as details of emergency response procedures. The outcome, amongst others, is an awareness of what can go wrong in an emergency. This allows the operator to pre-plan responses and provide standard operating procedures for handling the identified hazards from the safety case.

Responsibility for handling an offshore emergency rests with the OIM. The OIM is required to take appropriate action to deal with any emergency such as a fire or an explosion, however, unlike the manager of e.g. a nuclear plant, he or she cannot call upon the emergency services for immediate assistance. In the short term, an emergency must be dealt with by the installation's own personnel. The safety case ensures that the OIM possesses sufficient knowledge of the installation and its emergency procedures not to be surprised in any event. This knowledge is key to effective emergency decision making.

Decision making

Recent developments in decision making research has seen an increasing awareness of the importance of ecological validity. Studies of experienced decision makers working within their domain have emerged from a number of fields. Emphasis is on describing how experienced decision makers actually make decisions, not in prescribing how decisions should be made according to a normative or rational standard. This research has provided alternative, descriptive models of decision making, often containing a recognition based element and a metacognition element (e.g. Cohen, Freeman & Wolf, 1996). However, descriptive models of decision making do not enhance knowledge from a training perspective, as they fail to address the influence and constraints of cognitive processing. That is, to understand how decisions are made, one must take a step further and distinguish between the cognitive processes involved.

Cognitive processing

Cognitive frameworks, such as production system models (Anderson, 1983; Anderson, 1993; Newell, 1990), are useful structures for decomposing and categorising decisions into working memory (WM) or long term memory (LTM) based. WM consists of an immediate memory system containing active information, and LTM of a long term system that contains episodic memory for prior experiences, procedural information about how to react to situations, and semantic memory about how the world is organised. The differentiation between WM and LTM is important in order to address training needs and to focus on particular aspects of learning. For example, training emphasis may be on learning to build a mental model or alternatively to strengthen proceduralised rules of thumb. From a superficial perspective, programmes addressing these needs usually do not differ, but as the building of mental models is strongly associated with WM and proceduralised rules with LTM, the approach should in principle vary.

WM can generally be described as the focus of attention (see Baddeley, 1992 for more details) and is where conscious processing such as thinking, problem solving, reasoning, and imagery take place. It is based on abstract meaning of the current situation. For example, to solve a problem the decision maker has to develop a mental construction of the logical situation at each step in reasoning, and then react to the features of that mental construction. The complexity of the mental models constructed are determined by the capacities of WM. Thus, WM is often the limiting feature in complex decision making and also the processing function most affected by stress (Wickens, 1996).

Through rehearsal, measured in terms of meaningfulness and time, information and knowledge are transferred from WM to LTM (Craik & Lockhart, 1972). There are at present numerous explanations concerning how information is organised and stored as object or relational concepts or combinations of these in LTM (see Van Mechelen, Hampton, Michalski, & Theuns, 1993 for a recent review). One suggestion is the notion of schema. Marshall (1995) suggested that a schema is a vehicle of memory, allowing organisation of an individual's analogous experiences, that include identification, elaboration, planning, and execution knowledge. Schemata in LTM are accessed through a process of pattern or feature matching with external stimuli (Watt, 1988). The accessed schema can then be brought to WM to help establish a mental model of the situation. Alternatively, the schema may provide a proceduralised response without needing to engage WM. Properly applied schemata transfer the information-processing burden from WM, where the decision maker is weak, to LTM, where the decision maker is strong.

Another aspect of importance is attention. The ability to select and reject relevant information has been linked to domain experience and expertise. Dawes (1982) suggested that experts are good at selecting important predictor variables and coding these in some meaningful way. Johnson (1988) similarly reported that experts make better predictions than novices because they focus on important cues. The capacity to focus on important cues is based on pattern recognition. Experts possess more complex domain specific schemata and are, thus, able to perceive large meaningful patterns in their domains. This competence is what permits them to select and reject information at input level.

Acknowledging the complexities of offshore installation emergencies, the positive contribution of descriptive decision making models and the importance of cognition to decision making, this research sets out to describe the decision making process of experienced offshore managers and to link the decisions to a cognitive framework.

Method

The research was based on a grounded approach using semi-structured interviews. In preparation it was necessary for the researcher to acquire considerable domain specific knowledge in order to understand the language and jargon used in the industry as well as gain insight into the emergency response process.

The subjects who participated in this experiment were from three distinctive categories: (i) nine experienced OIMs from one European based operating company; (ii) five deputy OIMs from the same European company; and (iii) five OIMs from an American based operating company. The size of the production platforms they manage varied from POBs (personnel on board) of 30 to more than 250. In some cases nearby flotels provided accommodation for up to 300 additional workers.

Three hypothetical paper-based offshore emergency scenarios were used containing information similar to that which an OIM would receive on arrival at the emergency command centre. Each scenario consisted of a brief description of a crisis incident together with additional information about time of day, wind speed and direction, sea conditions, and the proximity of helicopters. The three scenarios were derived from company training documents and selected to represent various levels of complexity, danger to the platform and danger to the personnel on board and were consistent with the dangers identified through the risk assessment conducted as part of the safety case regulations (HSE, 1992).

The three scenarios were presented to the OIMs in a random sequence. For each scenario, the OIMs were requested to identify the first three critical decisions to be made and to verbalise their thoughts with regard to the scenario, what the problem was, how it could escalate and what had to be done to manage the incident. The focus on the initial phase of the emergencies was selected in accordance with other research (e.g. Orasanu, 1995) stressing the importance of initial situation awareness to decision making and because it was possible at this stage to control the number of variables involved. Probe questions were then asked with regard to issues of importance to the decision making process.

The data were coded into categories of decision points, situation assessment, defined as situational factors and their implications, and options available including the chosen course of action. Furthermore, the data was broken into reasoning and rules in order to illustrate the links to WM and LTM.

Results and discussion

The multifaceted complexity of the environment was reflected in the data collected. Although the research looked at three different groups, the decision making process was found to be similar for all. Any differences could be accounted for by organisational factors and affected sequence of action, not actual decisions. It was, thus, possible to dissect the decisions and to place them into a cognitive framework based on a simple production system model. The model presented corresponds with research on a wide range of memory experts which showed that experts were able to utilise pre-existing, domain specific knowledge stored in LTM in the context of predetermined retrieval plans (Chase & Ericsson, 1982). The experts could then, when recall was required, activate the corresponding retrieval plan, that led to rapid retrieval of the required information. Figure 1 describes the findings.

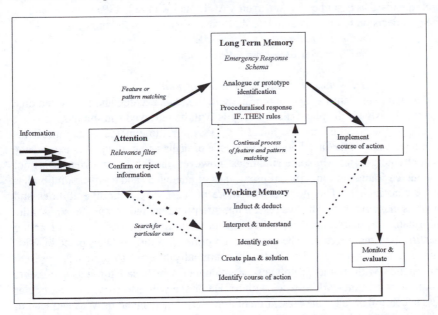

Figure 1   A simple production system model of OIM decision making

51

Initial situation assessment is derived from information received from both internal and external sources e.g. people working in the area, the control room and the standby vessel. The quality of information can vary from specific and correct, to vague and incorrect, depending on the nature of the incident and the people involved. The OIM utilises his or her knowledge of the geography of the installation to visualise where the incident takes place and what is happening. That is, to build a mental model.

Information received is filtered through attention extracting what is of relevance to the ongoing incident. This filter process is based on pattern or feature recognition. Sternberg (1985) called this selective-encoding and described the process as one in which a person realises the relevance of some information at the same time as he or she screens out irrelevant other information. The accepted information is matched to emergency response schemata stored in LTM. Recognition is based on either an explicit experience i.e. a prototype, or an analogue i.e. an incident of similar nature. The retrieved schema helps to identify the incident, provide meaning and also contains information about action plans and means to execute them. Analogies can be derived from own experience, war stories or training manuals and may involve generating a solution to a problem or understanding a solution (Anderson & Thompson, 1989). Decisions are based on simple *IF..THEN* rules that have been proceduralised as described by Anderson's ACT* and R (1983, 1993). For example, the first decision to make is to muster but where depends on the incident:

> *IF the normal muster point is safe*
> *THEN muster at normal muster point.*
> *IF it is not safe*
> *THEN muster at alternative muster point.*

The action plan identified as appropriate will then be executed and monitored on a continual basis. If the plan fails, a new plan will be retrieved and implemented.

This is the common process found for OIMs in routine incidents and it reflects their knowledge of the installation, experience of drills and training, and experience of real emergencies. In some situations, however, the OIMs' experience has not provided a framework in terms of prototypes or analogues and a novel solution has to be constructed. This demands far more of the OIM's cognitive abilities and involves inductive and deductive reasoning, interpretation and comprehension of the information available, goal identification, problem solving, and course of action identification and selection. The construction of novel solutions takes place in WM. Throughout this process the OIM will continually attempt to match the present information with stored prototypes or analogues which can provide a possible solution or a framework to work within. He or she will also search for particular cues to confirm or reject the present mental model. The demand on WM can lead to cognitive overload where the OIM becomes inflexible and may suffer from tunnel vision.

This study found limited evidence for WM based problem solving, a reflection of the routine nature of the incidents used. However, there was plenty of anecdotal evidence suggesting that this process existed. According to the OIMs, in non-routine incidents it involved solving a specific problem rather than dealing with the overall strategy. In such situations, the OIM's focus would move from the 'big picture' to zoom in on the specific problem. For example, if a flange is leaking gas the overall strategy of the OIM would be how to deal with a gas leak. However, the focus of attention would be on stopping the leak.

Conclusion

The general conclusion drawn from this work is that when OIMs are facing familiar emergencies, actual or simulated, they rely largely on previously memorised solution schemata. OIM decision making can be described as a process of pattern matching accessing rules of thumb stored in LTM. Once the appropriate rules are defined, the OIMs know just how to proceed, in a forward-driven manner, rather than by reasoning backward from solution to initial state.

The value of the OIMs' emergency response schemata is that these can be applied as general strategies to the safety case identified emergencies. Reliance on LTM rules of thumb reduces the need for intensive problem solving, thereby releasing WM processing to focus on specific problems. This also ameliorates the obstacle known as tunnel vision caused by stress.

References

Anderson, J.R. (1983) *The Architecture of Cognition*. Harvard University Press: Cambridge, MA.

Anderson, J.R. (1993) *Rules of the Mind*. LEA: Hillsdale, NJ.

Anderson, J.R. & Thompson, R. (1989) 'Use of analogy in a production system architecture', in S. Vosniadou & A. Ortony (eds.), *Similarity and Analogical Reasoning*. Cambridge University Press: Cambridge.

Baddeley, A. (1992), 'Working memory: The interface between memory and cognition'. *Journal of Cognitive Neuroscience*, Vol. 4, pp. 281-288.

Chase, W.G. & Ericsson, K.A. (1982), 'Skill and working memory', in G.H. Bower (ed.), *The Psychology of Learning and Motivation*. Academic Press: New York.

Cohen, M.S., Freeman, J.T. & Wolf, S. (1996), 'Metarecognition in time-stressed decision making: recognizing, critiquing, and correcting'. *Human Factors*, Vol. 38, pp. 206-219.

Craik, F.I.M. & Lockhart R.S. (1972), 'Levels of processing: A framework for memory research'. *Journal of Verbal Learning and Verbal Behavior*, Vol. 11, pp. 671-684.

Cullen, The Hon. Lord (1990), *'The Public Inquiry into the Piper Alpha Disaster'*, Vol. I & II. HMSO: London.

Dawes, R.M. (1982), 'The robust beauty of improper linear models in decision making' in D. Kahneman, P. Slovic & A Tversky (eds.), *Judgment under Uncertainty: Heuristics and Biases.* Cambridge University Press: New York.

Health and Safety Executive (1992) *A Guide to the Offshore Installations (Safety Case) Regulations.* HMSO: London.

Johnson, S.C. (1988) 'Expertise and decision under uncertainty: Performance and process' in M.T.H. Chi, R. Glaser & M.J. Farr (eds.), *The Nature of Expertise.* Erlbaum: Hillsdale, NJ.

Marshall, S.P. (1995) *Schemas in Problem Solving.* Cambridge University Press: New York, NY.

Newell, A. (1990) *Unified Theories of Cognition.* Harvard University Press: Cambridge, MA.

Orasanu, J.M. (1995) 'Situation awareness: Its role in flight crew decision making' in *Proceedings of the Eight International Symposium on Aviation Psychology,* April 24-28, Columbus, Ohio.

Orasanu, J. & Connolly, T. (1993), 'The reinvention of decision making', in G.A. Klein, J. Orasanu, R. Calderwood & C.E. Zsambok (eds.), *Decision Making in Action: Models and Methods.* Ablex Publishing Corp.: Norwood, NJ.

Sternberg R.J. (1985) *Beyond IQ: A Triarchic Theory of Human Intelligence.* Viking: New York.

Van Mechelen, I., Hampton, J.A., Michalski, R.S., & Theuns, P. (1993) *Concepts and Categories.* Academic Press: London.

Watt, R.J. (1988) *Visual Processing: Computational, Psychophysical, and Cognitive Research.* LEA: Hove, UK.

Wickens, C.D. (1996), 'Designing for stress', in J.E. Driskell & E. Salas (eds.), *Stress and Human Performance.* LEA: Mahwah, NJ.

Acknowledgements

We wish to thank the OIMs who participated in this research and the two companies for granting us access.

8 Cognitive processing and risky behaviour in industrial radiography

Wendy J. Reece and Leroy J. Matthews*
Idaho National Engineering Laboratory
*Idaho State University

Abstract

A study was conducted to analyse performance of industrial radiography in incidents where worker errors resulted in radiation exposure to personnel. Results indicated that the most common errors involve diagnosis of system status, development of work strategies, and the proper execution of procedures. An information processing model was applied to characterize the errors. In further examination of the field radiography task, a theoretical framework for cognitive processing is proposed to explain risky behaviour, and to indicate how training could be designed to reduce errors. The premise for this approach is based on the notion that the manner in which information is obtained and stored in memory has a direct influence on how the information will be used.

Introduction

Industrial field radiography uses a sealed gamma radiation source to expose x-ray images of welds and other structural elements. This process provides a nondestructive means of testing the integrity of components in aeroplanes, pipelines, processing facilities and other structures where visual examination does not provide sufficient data. A portable crank-out camera device is used to perform field radiography. The camera body is internally shielded to safely store the radiation source when not in use. A drive cable, with a connection to the source, is attached at one side of the camera. A guide tube is attached to the other side of the camera. The radiographer positions the end of the guide tube at the location to be x-rayed and places films appropriately. A cranking device, located at the other end of the drive cable, is then used to extend the source out of the camera, through the guide tube to the end of the tube where the radiograph is to be taken. After each shot is completed, the radiographer must: i) crank the source back into the camera; ii) secure it inside the camera and lock the source in the shielded position; and iii) perform necessary radiation surveys to ensure that the source has been secured. A hand-held survey meter is used throughout the work process to check for radiation in the area. When ready to move the camera to another location, the radiographer completes all of the previous steps and then removes the cable and guide tube before transporting the equipment to the next site. If the source is left unshielded, the radiographer and other people in the surrounding area may be exposed to levels of radiation that exceed regulatory limits and cause physical injury (McGuire & Peabody, 1982).

Although the field radiography task involves a fairly simple set of manual actions, it provides an interesting scenario for ergonomic and cognitive analysis of human performance. The nature of routine manual tasks, work schedules, and lack of cues to the operator are contributors to the risk of radiation exposure to personnel due to radiographer errors. Another critical element of the task is the lack of immediate contingencies for risky behaviours in handling the radiography equipment; radiation cannot be sensed, and the results of exposure are typically not evident until several hours to many days later.

Performance modelling

In order to identify risky behaviour in radiography, worker overexposure incident reports were reviewed. Of 41 incidents where radiographers were accidentally exposed to the radiation source, sufficient detail was available for a final set of 18 events. In order to best capture and analyse the information available, each of the events was examined using several modelling approaches, including human reliability analysis event trees, operation sequence tables, error influences and effects diagrams, and an information processing failures model. From a cognitive analysis perspective, the latter model provided useful characterization of errors which led to radiographer overexposures.

Information processing

The information processing failures (IPF) model (O'Hare, Wiggins, Batt and Morrison, 1994; Rasmussen, 1982) was used to characterize the types of errors which contributed to the overexposure incidents. The IPF model uses the basic framework of information input, decision-making, and action execution to describe the sub-processes that people use in understanding and acting upon information provided in a specific environment or scenario. The model highlights six error types.

Information error (error in perception of cues) Information errors occur when available cues about system status are not clearly received by the operator. Information errors involve human sensory capabilities (e.g. eyesight, hearing), and existing environmental conditions (e.g. adequate lighting, noise level, relative heat or cold).

Diagnostic error (error in diagnosis of system status)   Diagnostic errors involve difficulties in accurately diagnosing system status. Diagnosis relies on an understanding of the system, equipment, and the information provided.

Goal error (failure to select an appropriate operational goal)   Goal errors involve the selection of unreasonable or inappropriate goals given operational circumstances.

Strategy error (circumvention of procedures or other inefficient strategy for accomplishing the chosen goal)   Strategy errors involve the use of an ineffective plan or strategy for accomplishing the goal. Strategy errors are linked to problem solving or planning skills when operators come to wrong conclusions or develop incorrect plans for handling a situation.

Procedure error (failure to follow proper procedures)   Procedure errors occur when proper procedures are not followed. With the development of a routine or habit in performance of the task, proper procedures can be complied with, even without re-reading written procedures during completion of each task.   Failure to follow procedures may be accidental or intentional. If the procedure error is intentional, the procedure may be difficult to enforce.

Action error (failure to execute steps in the work process)   Action errors concern the failure to properly execute the intended work procedure. This involves the worker's physical motions that are necessary to complete the steps in a work process.

Summary of error characterization

Applying the IPF model, failures for each of the 18 incidents were put into the six IPF error categories to characterize the overexposure incidents. An incident could have multiple information processing failures if there were multiple errors. Table 1 shows the error types involved in each of the incidents. Note that none of the incidents involved goal errors; that is, in all cases the correct goal of retrieving the radiation source to the shielded position was chosen. Strategy errors and procedure errors occurred in most of the incidents. Only two incidents included information difficulties.

Results of this modelling indicate that *procedure errors* occur in the use of survey meters, and in locking the camera after each exposure and retraction of the source to the shielded position. *Strategy errors* are made in equipment set-up and in retrieval of disconnected sources. *Action errors* are also involved with equipment set-up. *Diagnostic errors* occur during inspection of camera equipment and survey meters for proper functioning.

Table 1
Radiography incidents and error types

Incident	Error Types					
	Information	Diagnostic	Goal	Strategy	Procedure	Action
1				X		X
2		X		X	X	
3				X		
4		X		X	X	
5				X	X	X
6				X		
7				X	X	
8	X					X
9		X			X	X
10		X		X	X	
11				X	X	X
12					X	
13	X			X	X	
14						X
15					X	
16					X	
17		X			X	
18				X	X	X

X = Error characterization within each incident.

Cognitive processing framework

To address the radiographer errors and the associated potential for radiation overexposures, a cognitive processing framework was applied. The framework asserts that the way experiences are stored in memory will impact future performance, particularly with respect to how these experiences affect strategy errors. We propose that the manner in which information is gained and stored in memory has a direct influence on how the information will be used.

An underlying premise of this model is that more accurate processing of information occurs when people recognize causal connections between events, particularly when these connections have been formed from their own experiences. Previous research supports the assumption that causal relatedness of information facilitates its utilization. Kahneman, Slovic and Tversky (1982) and Matthews and Sanders (1984) have shown that people tend to integrate information much better if it is causally related.

In further examination of errors committed in performance of the radiography task, our model incorporates Endel Tulving's (1985, 1986) representation of memory, which maintains that information is stored in essentially three different memory systems: semantic memory (words, facts or principles); episodic memory (experiences and events); and procedural memory (how to physically perform tasks, and connections between stimuli and responses). We propose that learning semantic rules about the effects of radiation and storing that information in semantic memory will have a lower probability of being translated into action than rules learned experientially. When rule knowledge is formed from experience and stored in episodic memory, effective causal connections between radiation and its effects are properly achieved. Procedural memory is also enhanced by connections formed through experience, providing stable direction to proper action. We maintain that causal connections formed in episodic memory will lead to more accurate perceptions of risk and hence, improved procedural memory of specific safe task behaviours.

Radiation issues

The radiography task is interesting to analyse because of the issues raised by the nature of radiation. First of all, people do not possess a sensory system capable of detecting radiation, and therefore lack a natural response to the presence of a radiation source. Additionally, the effects of exposure to the radiation source may not be evident until many hours, days, or several years after the exposure. The long temporal delay between unsafe behaviours and consequences to personal health prevents the development of proper causal connections. With no sensory cues to exposure, and no immediate contingencies for risky behaviour, causal connections are never directly experienced. Further, most radiographers will not be involved in an overexposure incident during the course of their careers. Many radiographers have never witnessed an unsafe action that resulted in exposure to a coworker, but have only heard anecdotes of the effects of risky behaviour. Because of the nature of the job and the type of training used, rules about task performance and radiation exposure are stored in semantic memory only.

Discussion

Many of the errors observed in the study of radiographer overexposures were committed by experienced workers. This suggests that they did not have an adequate conception of radiation and its consequences stored in functional or usable memory. Most traditional radiography training builds upon semantic learning of procedures. Operators are indirectly made aware of the causal relationships between risky or unsafe behaviours and consequences through verbal or written information. Because of the infrequency of accidental encounters with an exposed radiation source, opportunities are not presented for developing meaningful experience-based connections between actions and consequences. Cognitive research indicates that experiential learning is more effective in influencing future behaviours. This kind of learning rarely occurs in practice of radiography in the field.

We propose that perceptions of causality may be enhanced by specific experiences during training. Training should be comprised of a representation of the work environment which allows the worker to experience the effects of improper performance and risky behaviours through a simulated overexposure. A representation of radiation could be introduced to simulate worker exposure through visual, auditory, or tactile feedback. Burgeoning virtual reality technologies may provide the perfect avenue for simulating not only the radiography task with high fidelity, but also provide the necessary feedback to promote experience-based learning. With immediate and consistently applied feedback, effective learning is facilitated (Walker, 1995). These experiences, coupled with rules about overexposure and task performance, would support storage of appropriate causal connections between behaviour and consequences for proper action. Additionally, training would be enhanced by exposing workers to varied simulated job conditions. This process would provide workers with elaborated training, an essential component to more firmly embed specific actions in procedural memory (Matlin, 1994).

Table 2
Impact of elaborated training on radiography errors

Error Type	Example	Reduced w/ Training?
Information	Unable to hear alarm due to high noise	
Diagnostic	Fail to recognize equipment problems	x
Procedure	Fail to use survey meter	X
Strategy	Use hand to retrieve disconnected source	X
Action	Improperly connect source assembly	x

X = Direct impact. x = Indirect impact.

Table 2 identifies the types of errors which may be reduced through elaborated training. The major effect of training to enhance workers' conception of the contingencies of risky behaviour is expected to reduce strategy and procedure errors. As the table indicates, this type of training may also reduce diagnostic errors, in addition to providing supplemental action practice and improved overall task performance.

Conclusion

Although the exact role of memory in tasks such as that of industrial radiography remains uncertain, Tulving's three-component representation provides a very useful heuristic for addressing performance errors. Using this representation in analysis of the industrial radiography task, we assert that causal connections between risky actions and the consequential radiation exposure have not been adequately achieved with traditional training. Elaborated training is suggested to improve learning by combining semantic instruction of radiation and performance rules with simulated experiences (stored in episodic memory). This could be accomplished with a representation of the work environment that allows the radiographer to experience direct feedback from improper performance. Using augmented or virtual environment technologies to provide visual, auditory, and tactile indications of worker proximity to the radiation source will help strengthen episodic memory for specific actions, and direct action in procedural memory. The use of such elaborated training methods will provide additional channels of information to help workers gain a more complete scenario of the overall radiography task and associated risks. Improved learning of the relationships between actions and consequences is expected to impact performance of industrial radiography by reducing risky behaviours and consequential overexposures.

References

Kahneman, D., Slovic, P. and Tversky, A. (eds.) (1982), *Judgment under uncertainty: Heuristics and biases*. Cambridge Press: New York.

Matlin, M. W. (1994), *Cognition (Third Edition)*. New York: Harcourt Brace.

Matthews, L. and Sanders, W. (1984), 'Effects of causal and non-causal sequences of information on subjective prediction'. *Psychological Reports*, Vol. 54, pp. 211-215.

McGuire, S.A. and Peabody, C.A. (1982), *Working Safely in Gamma Radiography*. (NUREG/BR-0024). U.S. Nuclear Regulatory Commission: Washington D.C.

O'Hare, D., Wiggins, M., Batt, R. and Morrison, D. (1994), 'Cognitive failure analysis for aircraft accident investigation'. *Ergonomics*, Vol. 37, pp. 1855-1869.

Rasmussen, J. (1982), 'Human errors: a taxonomy for describing human malfunction in industrial installations', *Journal of Occupational Accidents*, Vol. 4, pp. 311-333.

Tulving, E. (1985), 'How many memory systems are there?'. *American Psychologist*, Vol. 40, pp. 385-398.

Tulving, E. (1986), 'What kind of hypothesis is the distinction between episodic and semantic memory?'. *Journal of Experimental Psychology: Learning, Memory, and Cognition*, Vol. 12, pp. 307-311.

Walker, T. (1995), *The Psychology of Learning.* Prentice Hall: New Jersey.

9 Modelling of human errors in cognitive processes observed in dynamic environments

Ken-ichi Takano and James Reason*
CRIEPI, Japan
*University of Manchester, UK

Abstract

In order to identify error types observed in the dynamic operational environment, the following material was analysed: (i) 13 human factors analyses of US nuclear power events, and (ii) 40 cases of errors made in the simplified plant simulator. In the resulting analysis, the most frequently identified cognitive process associated with error production was situation assessment, and following varieties were knowledge based (KB) processes and response planning. This suggested that the more significant human errors originated in the conscious thought processes. The error mechanisms were judged to fall into three categories: psychological bias, arousal and KB problems. In conclusion, several of the most frequent error patterns identified in each cognitive process were modelled with regard to their relationship between performance shaping factors, biases and error types.

Introduction

Human performance has been considered to play a major role in incidents occurring in a dynamic environment, such as a nuclear power plant (INPO, 1985) . Especially, crew performance in coping with non-normal situations played a crucial contribution to previous severe accidents (Roth, 1994; Woods, 1987; Reason, 1990). However, the possibility has not yet been extensively investigated of the possible paths which escalate the situation into a severe accident arising by the combinations of both mechanical failure and human error. Thus, finding these paths can contribute to countermeasures in advance to avoid this possibility. CRIEPI has been developing the team behaviour simulation model, *SYBORG: Simulation system for behaviour of an operating group* (Takano, 1995) , for which the fundamental simulation model has already been completed, however, this model did not possess any error mechanisms. This paper presents the modelling of typical error occurrence patterns, which can be observed in an operator's cognitive processes, to be integrated into *SYBORG*. In order to identify these patterns, US event reports and results of simulator experiments were analysed. Main items studied here are summarized as follows.

(i) Fundamental understanding of error occurrence patterns.
(ii) The variety of possible cognitive errors (errors occurred in cognitive processes).
(iii) Identification of cognitive errors associated with these mechanisms and PSFs derived from US event reports and simulator experiments.
(iv) Modelling of occurrence patterns of typical cognitive errors with relation between PSFs, biases and error types.

Method

As a method to derive the typical cognitive error patterns, the following premises were adopted in the analyses of the event reports.

(i) The development of a basic human error occurrence model.
(ii) The definition of cognitive processes divided into 11 categories.
(iii) The identification of possible error types occurred in each cognitive process.

Human error occurrence model

It is necessary to take a wider view to understand the overall structure of the concepts relating to human error mechanisms. Based on several previous considerations of human error classification (Rasmussen, 1980; Reason, 1987, 1990; Wreathall, 1995), the human error occurrence model was developed (see figure 1). In this model, error occurrence patterns including the relationships between PSFs, error mechanisms and error types were identified. As in the figure, obtained information via HMI and HHI is often associated with inaccuracies such as time delays or improper salience. On occasions, there are disturbances in cognitive processes due to external PSFs such as heavy work requests. Some of the external PSFs would activate any internal PSFs: arousal level, workload or attention allocation. On the other hand, psychological biases often take an important role in the context of human cognitive processes (Wason, 1966; Reason, 1990).

[EXTERNAL]

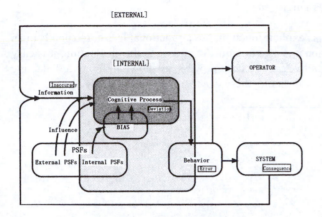

Figure 1   An envisaged human error occurrence model for this study

Operator's cognitive processes

The operator's cognitive processes were divided into 11 parts according to the operator behaviour simulation model developed by the authors (Takano, 1995). Figure 2 shows the schematic diagram of an individual operator model. The *thought MM* was divided into two areas based on behaviour levels: one is the *skill-based response* and the other is *knowledge-based processing*. The knowledge-based one was further divided into four stages: (i) situation assessment; (ii) response planning; (iii) response implementation; (iv) effect monitoring.

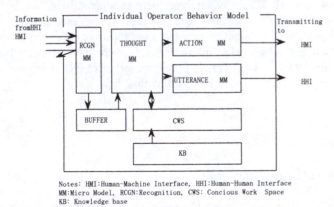

Notes: HMI:Human-Machine Interface, HHI:Human-Human Interface
MM:Micro Model, RCGN:Recognition, CWS: Concious Work Space
KB: Knowledge base

Figure 2   A schematic diagram of an individual operator model

Possible cognitive errors envisaged

Each cognitive process has explicit functions, so a functional loss corresponds to an omission and a malfunction is a commission. According to this distinction, it is easy to list every possible cognitive error in each process, as shown in figure 3. Selecting the principal cognitive errors among these is a main aim in this study.

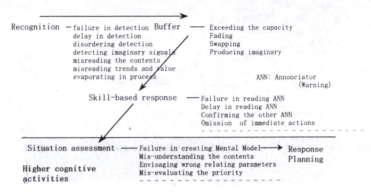

Figure 3   Possible cognitive errors envisaged for each cognitive process

Analysis procedure

The incident reports analysed were those prepared by US-NRC (US NRC, 1994). A total of 13 reports were analysed, however, that was not enough to extract the typical principal error examples. Simulator experiment data, using a simplified BWR plant simulator, were also used to complement the incident reports. The number of cases involving human errors was 40. Basically, analyses were conducted based on the model shown in figure 1 using the systematic analysis procedure (Takano, 1993). There were three aspects studied: (i) cognitive error types and location; (ii) PSFs; (iii) error mechanisms including biases. The following biases were also considered: (i) salience bias; (ii) cognitive trap; (iii) improper persistence; (iv) frequency bias;(v) recency bias; (vi) brief bias; (vii) confirmation bias; (viii) similarity matching.

Results and discussion

Cognitive error types and location identified

In 13 US incident cases, there were a total 28 cognitive errors extracted, and 40 errors in the simulator experiments. In those 25 error types were identified. The error types observed will be discussed later. A histogram of the locations of cognitive errors is shown in figure 4. Roughly speaking, regarding to the locations where cognitive errors occurred: (i) situation assessment was the most frequent process; (ii) the next most common varieties were KB processes and response planning. These locations identified belong to the higher cognitive activities.

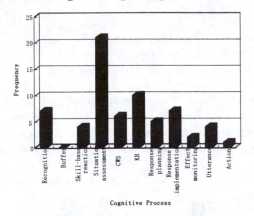

Figure 4   Distribution of cognitive errors' location in cognitive processes

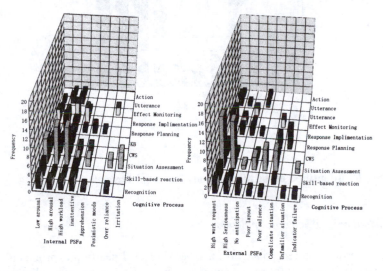

Figure 5   Identified external and internal PSFs

PSFs

Observed external PSFs were classified into eight categories as shown in figure 5. Internal PSFs were also classified into eight categories. Among external PSFs, high levels of *work request* and *seriousness* became major factors influencing cognitive processes. As for internal PSFs, low/high *arousal*, high *workload* and *inattentive* were the major contributors.

Error mechanism

For each cognitive error observed in this analysis, it was attempted to identify the principal factor that determined the cognitive error type. Those mechanisms identified could be classified into four groups: (i) psychological bias properties, 40%; (ii) resource properties (overload and inattention), 30%; (iii) knowledge properties (KB defects and inert knowledge; Woods, 1994), 20%. A summary of the error mechanisms evaluated is shown in figure 6. The most dominant bias was the frequency bias, especially in situation assessment. Resource properties, like overload and inattention, were common mechanisms underlying errors in many cognitive processes.

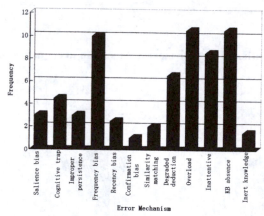

Figure 6   Identified error mechanisms for cognitive errors

Principal error occurrence patterns

Typical error occurrence patterns have been selected nearly proportionally to the occurrence frequency for each cognitive process. Each patterns involve the inter-relationship between PSFs, error mechanisms and cognitive error types as shown, for example, in figure 7. A total of 20 patterns were chosen as representatives.

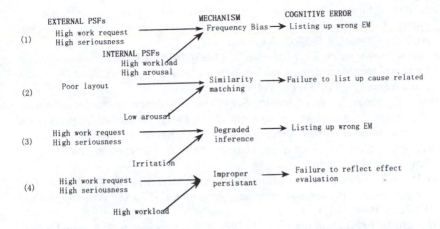

Figure 7   Principal error occurrence patterns in situation assessment

Conclusions

The purpose of the present paper is to identify crucial cognitive errors associated with error mechanisms and PSFs as seen in dynamic operational environments from a review of US incident reports and simulator experiments. The cognitive errors identified are to be integrated into *SYBORG*, in order to find paths resulting in severe accidents due to the combination of both machinery mal-functions and human error. The results obtained would also be useful to improve the operational procedures and operator support in dynamic situations.

References

Institute of Nuclear Power Operations (INPO). (1985) *An analysis of root causes in 1983 and 1984 significant event reports*, INPO 85-027.

NUREG/CR-6093 (1994) *An analysis of operational experience during low power and shutdown and a plan for addressing human reliability assessment issues.* NRC, Washington DC.,USA.

Rasmussen, J. (1980) 'What can be learned from human error reports?' In, K.D. Duncan et al. (eds.) John Wiley & Sons: London.

Reason, J. (1987) 'Part I: Definition and Taxonomies of human error'. In: J. Rasmussen, et al (eds.), *New Technology and Human Error*. John Wiley & Sons: London.

Reason, J. (1990) *Human error*. Cambridge University Press: Cambridge.

Roth, EM., Mumaw, RJ., & Lewis,PM. (1994) *An empirical investigation of operator performance in cognitively demanding simulated emergencies.* NUREG/CR-6208,US-NRC: Washington DC.

Takano, K., Sawayanagi, K., & Kabetani, T. (1993) 'Analysis and evaluation system for human related incidents in nuclear power plants'. *Journal of Nuclear Science and Technology,* Vol. 31, pp. 894-913.

Takano, K., Sasou, K., & Yoshimura, S. (1995) 'Simulation system for behaviour of an operating group'. *In, Proceedings of XIV European Annual Conference on Human Decision Making.* Netherlands: Delft University of Technology.

Wason, P.C. (1966) 'Reasoning'. In, Foss, B. (ed.), *New horizons in psychology, I.* Penguin Books: London.

Woods, D.D., Johannesen, L.J., Cook, R.I., & Sarter,N.B. (1994) *Behind human error: Cognitive systems, computers and hindsight.* CSERIAC: Wright-Patterson Air Force Base, OH, USA.

Wreathall, J. (1995) *Draft version of NUREG/CR report section 3,* Personal letter.

10 Mental models of industrial jobs

David Chiasson
Dalhousie University, Canada

Abstract

In making use of recent computer technology, a study was conducted to examine the mental models of industrial jobs. Cognitive differences in the mental models of engineers, healthcare professionals, and trades persons pertaining to industrial job tasks were examined. Elements consisting of video presentations of task examples and the sorting manipulation of the examples were combined for a clear and consistent interface that allowed ease of use with minimum practice. Subjects used the system to categorize and sort twenty-five different video clips of industrial job tasks into file folder icons. A cluster analysis was used to examine differences in the categorization and sorting patterns of subjects. Results established differences in the mental models of engineers, healthcare professionals, and trades persons pertaining to industrial job tasks. The results are discussed in terms of their theoretical and methodological significance; their practical significance as a means of educating individuals involved with maintaining industrial and ergonomic factors; and further uses of this computer program in research.

Introduction

The mental models theory of knowledge representation began appearing in the literature as long as fifty years ago and remains a popular topic of discussion in cognitive psychology and human factors. Even before the introduction of digital computers to the world, Craik (1943) put forth the idea that 'small scale models' of external reality existed within our heads. By combining models of external reality with models of our possible actions, we can prepare ourselves to predict future situations before they arise and react to them by utilizing knowledge of past events in dealing with the present and the future. It is this ever-evolving ability to process

71

and utilize information that plays a key role in the results of our day-to-day interaction with objects in our environment and, ultimately, in our survival.

Mental models can be referred to as the models people have of themselves, others, the environment, and the things with which they interact. As described by Sanford (1987), 'a mental model is that set of representations which is used in drawing a conclusion about something, in going beyond the evidence given.' People form mental models through experience, training, and instruction. These models are essential in helping us understand our experiences, predict the outcomes of our actions, and handle unexpected occurrences.

Though varied, inconsistent, and confusing at times, previous research into the origins and applications of mental models has resulted in several points that have been agreed upon in the literature. Payne (1991), recognized four conclusions that could be drawn from the research in psychology and human factors that mental models promote.

(i)   Our beliefs predict our behaviour.
(ii)   Inferences can be made from mental simulations, particularly when reasoning about devices or just the physical world in general.
(iii)   Mental representations can be analogical.
(iv)   Mental models are based on physical experience with the content domain.

Benefits of studying individual's mental models

Loss of time due to work related injuries or illnesses have been a fact of life for all major industries and businesses and remains a key ingredient in determining a company's stability and growth. Ergonomic principles continue to be introduced into the design of jobs as a treatment for and prevention of work related injuries. Brehmer (1987) notes that work is becoming mental and abstract, rather than physical and concrete. As a result, it would seem that greater amounts of lost time on the job are being attributed to emotional and psychological factors that manifest themselves in the workplace. In addressing this issue, worker rehabilitation programs are beginning to shift their focus more towards improving the mental well being of affected individuals and less on their physical state. From the perspective of injury prevention, perhaps there is a need to study the mental aspect of work from the viewpoint of individuals who are familiar with different areas of work-specifically, their mental models of industrial jobs.

This investigation was unique in that it attempted to examine the cognitive differences in the mental models of three groups of individuals (engineers, healthcare professionals and tradespeople), each group being experts in a particular domain. This investigation provides a unique window into gaining a clearer understanding of the bases for expert differences in knowledge representation and organization regarding industrial jobs.

Methods

Subject selection

The experiment consisted of thirty subjects, ten from each of the following professions: engineering (two architects; four civil; four structural; two mechanical), health-care professions (seven physiotherapists; two occupational therapists; one kinesiologist), and manual trades (three plumbers; two electricians; two carpenters; two technicians; one trades helper). All subjects had a minimum of four years professional experience in their field of expertise and were currently employed in the indicated profession.

Apparatus for experiment one and experiment two

(i) Twenty-five video taped segments of various industrial jobs were chosen from a variety of occupational health and safety videos obtained from the Nova Scotia Department of Labour, Department of National Defense Health and Safety Division, and the Department of Kinesiology at Dalhousie University. The descriptive statistics of the videos were: mean length, 6.04 seconds; standard deviation, 1.37 seconds; standard error, 0.27 seconds; variance, 1.87 seconds; coefficient of variation, 0.227; minimum length, 3.00 seconds; maximum length, 8.00 seconds; and range, 5.00 seconds.
(ii) A VHS video cassette recorder was used to download the video segments onto the hard drive of a Power Macintosh 6100/60av computer.
(iii) Software programs Fushionrecorder and Adobe Premier were used to record and edit the video segments on the computer's hard drive.
(iv) The program 'Mental Model Manager' was written using the software development program FaceSpan 2.0.1.
(v) A tape recorder and cassette tapes were used to record the subjects' verbal descriptions of their sorting procedures.
(vi) Subjects' raw data was recorded in AppleScript and was transferred into Microsoft Excel 5 in spreadsheet form for further statistical processing.
(vii) The sorting procedures were analysed using a cluster analysis option available in the 'S Plus' statistical analysis software package.

Procedure

Three groups of ten subjects from the indicated professions participated on an individual basis. Using the 'Mental Model Manager' software program, (figures 1 and 2), each subject was allowed to view each video entirely and then categorize according to this information. After completing the sorting task they were asked individually to explain the methodology behind their actions.

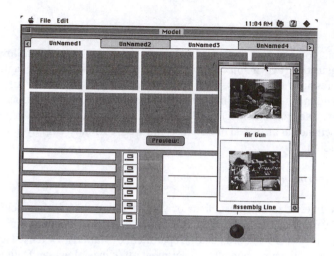

Figure 1   'Mental Model Manager' computer interface

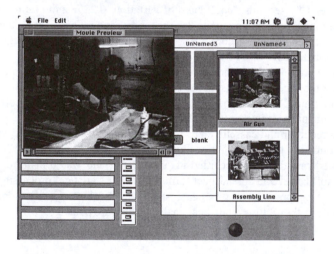

Figure 2   'Mental Model Manager' computer interface with the movie preview window for movie 'Air Gun' open after double clicking on the movie image in the scrolling pallet

Results

Engineers

In demonstrating a great amount of diversity in their sorting strategies, four engineers, subjects five, six, eight and nine, confirmed a knowledge of physical and human factors involved with the design of industrial jobs similar to the group of healthcare professionals. Two engineers, subjects three and seven, demonstrated sorting strategies that were similar to the tradespeople in that they appeared to use sorting strategies that focussed on the superficial variables in the videos without providing any introspection. Two engineers, subjects four and ten, appeared to employ a sorting strategy that could be described as viewing all the videos as being contributing parts of some larger manufacturing process or skill hierarchy and then breaking this larger process down into its component parts based on the information they were focussing on in the videos. The two remaining engineers, subjects one and two, used folder names and descriptions of their sorting strategies that were similar to the tradespeople in content but differed in that these subjects provided more introspection during the interviews into what was happening in the videos.

Two of the engineers (subjects eight and nine) indicated during the post-experiment interview that they were familiar with the principles of ergonomic design and that they attempted to relate their sorting strategies to designing the job to fit the worker by focussing on the physical factors, limitations, and safety issues that were apparent to them in the videos. Their professional focus as engineers had been on redesigning machines to be more efficient and physically less stressful to operate. Subject five explained during the post-experiment interview that educational background and experience in space planning influenced this subject's sorting strategies. This individual based the sorting strategies on the degree of physical movement that was associated with performing each job as portrayed in the videos. These observations lend strength to the theory that people form mental models through experience, training and instruction and it is possible to predict the behaviour of individuals based in relation to these variables.

Healthcare professionals

The healthcare professionals consistently based their sorting strategies on the physical movement components associated with the jobs represented in the videos and related these movements to make predictions of future injuries to those workers performing the jobs. They did not appear to demonstrate any sorting strategies that overlapped with the engineers, as the engineers did with the healthcare professionals and the tradespeople, or the tradespeople. This finding suggests that it would be in the best interest of these individuals to broaden their knowledge through learning about the contributions of these other professional groups with which they will inevitably interact.

In order to be an effective occupational therapist, physiotherapist, kinesiologist, occupational health and safety nurse or any health professional that deals with the care and prevention of work-related injuries it becomes essential to be able to see the 'big picture' in the workplace through successful interactions with a variety of different professional groups operating in the workplace that bring their own particular biases and perspectives to the workplace. This can only be accomplished by recognizing one's own professional shortcomings with regard to knowledge of the contributions of other professionals in the workplace.

Tradespeople

Tradespeople consistently based their sorting strategies around the superficial variables apparent in the videos. They neglected to provide a great degree of introspection into what they were seeing in the videos in the form of industrial processes and did not attempt to make any predictions about the potential for injuries to employees because of the current job design. As was previously suggested with the healthcare professionals, the tradespeople could improve their interactions with other contributing members of the workplace, engineers and healthcare professionals, by learning about the roles and contributions of these groups to workplace.

Discussion and conclusions

Cognitive differences were detected in the mental models of engineers, health-care professionals, and tradespeople pertaining to industrial tasks. Tradespeople tended to base their categorization on the superficial details of the tasks as they were depicted and did not attempt to go into any detail when asked to explain their method of categorization. Healthcare professionals consistently focussed on the physical movements that were required of the workers to perform their tasks as illustrated in the videos. When appropriate, they determined if there was a concern for injury with the related work and in several instances gave suggestions to reduce the chance of injury occurring. Engineers showed some clustering behaviours that were similar, although more in depth, to the tradespeople and some clustering behaviours that related to physical movement and injury potential in decidedly similar fashion to the health professionals while also exhibiting some unique clustering behaviours of their own.

In considering the definition of mental models offered by Sanford (1987), 'a mental model is that set of representations that is used in drawing a conclusion about something, in going beyond the evidence given', one concrete conclusion can be drawn from the results of this investigation. The engineers and healthcare professional who participated in this study demonstrated mental models of industrial jobs that were more developed than the mental models of the tradespeople. The engineers and healthcare professionals demonstrated the ability to draw conclusions from the information shown to them in the videos by applying introspection to the work they were viewing which required evidence which was not always apparent in the videos.

Previous studies by Parker (1989), Mitchell (1991), and Parks (1992) demonstrated that the type of knowledge about a particular domain, as demonstrated by an individual, appeared to be related to the role of the participant within that particular domain. This finding is somewhat consistent with the work of Gillan, Breedin, and Cooke (1992) in which role (human factor expert, software development expert) also appeared to influence the cognitive components of individual's knowledge within the domain of human-computer interaction. The results of this investigation are consistent with the findings of these studies in that individuals who have very different roles in the workplace (engineer, healthcare professional, and trades person) appeared to represent and organize their knowledge of industrial jobs differently.

This investigation examined the experimental methods of previous sorting task studies that examined human information processing in the domains of physics (Chi, Feltovich and Glaser, 1981), sports (Allard and Burnett, 1985; Parker, 1987; Mitchell, 1990, and Parks, 1992), and human factors (Gillan et al, 1992) and attempted to improve on these methods by creating a computer program, the 'Mental Model Manager', that provided subjects with the ability to simultaneously view and sort videos. Due to the apparently successful use of this new technology in this investigation in cognitive ergonomics, it is recommended that the 'Mental Model Manager' could be used as a testing protocol for related studies on expertise in sport and other physical strategies.

The results of this investigation demonstrated fundamental differences among engineers, healthcare professionals, and tradespeople in their representation and organization of knowledge regarding industrial jobs. Based on these results, it is hypothesized that these differences may adversely affect interactions among these individuals in the workplace. Continuing examinations related to how different groups of individuals think about work behaviours and how this might affect their communicative interactions in the workplace are necessary.

References

Brehmer, B. (1987). 'Development of mental models for decision in technological systems'. In, J. Rasmussen, K. Duncan, & J. Leplat (eds.), *New Technology and Human Error*. John Wiley and Sons: Chichester.

Craik, K. J. W. (1943). *The Nature of Explanation*. Cambridge University Press: Cambridge.

Johnson-Laird, P. N. (1983). *Mental Models*. Cambridge University Press: Cambridge.

David Chiasson

Mitchell, D., (1990). *An analysis of cognitive and perceptual abilities of coaches and players in basketball*. Unpublished Master's thesis, Dalhousie University.

Parker, S. G. (1989). *Organization of knowledge in ice hockey experts*. Unpublished Master's thesis, University of New Brunswick.

Parks, S. L. (1992). *Perceptual and cognitive differences in sport expertise*. Unpublished Master's thesis, Dalhousie University.

Payne, S. J. (1991). 'A descriptive study of mental models'. *Behaviour and Information Technology*, Vol. 10, pp. 3-21.

Sanford, A. (1987). *The Mind of Man: Models of human understanding*. Harvester Press Limited: Sussex.

Part Two
LEARNING AND TRAINING

11 Effects of type of learning on control performance

Rainer H. Kluwe
Universität der Bw, Hamburg, Germany

Abstract

Two types of learning were compared when training operators to operate a simulated system: learning by being told plus practicing provided rules, versus learning by being told plus exploratory search. On a general level of analysis both groups do not differ with regard to control performance. More finegrained analyses reveal important differences: learning by being told plus practicing rules goes together with a temporary drop of control performance when control demands change and become more difficult. Shifting to a modified control strategy is connected with a decrease of performance and requires time.

Introduction

Appropriate operator training is of central importance for efficient and reliable man-machine-interaction. The benefits of different methods to provide knowledge for process control are not very well proven. It is rather unclear which attributes of individual process control are influenced by different training methods. Few results are available from empirical studies with respect to the content of knowledge to be provided for control. However, they do not support specific interventions. Perhaps the most comprehensive study with respect to the problem of providing knowledge in the domain of system control has been performed by Morris & Rouse (1985). Providing operators with different types of knowledge resulted in knowledge differences between operator groups as assessed by a questionnaire, but did not engender performance differences.

The following experiment is designed to examine the effects of specific conditions when training individuals to operate a dynamic system. Rather than studying the 'what' of knowledge, the experimental conditions refer instead to the 'how' of learning, i.e. the modes of learning. It is assumed here that different learning modes contribute to differences in control performance, control activity, and knowledge. The plan was to examine the effects of a more active mode of learning compared to the effects of learning by being told. With regard to a classification proposed by Michalski (1993) based on the type of input and output knowledge, the acquisition of a new skill on the basis of provided declarative knowledge can be viewed as an example of declarative-to-procedural learning. Knowledge acquisition by means of exploratory search and learning by doing can be conceived of as procedural-to-procedural learning. It is usually assumed, though less demonstrated that a more active mode of learning and of self guided knowledge acquisition is advantageous. For example, the results of Kamouri et al. (1986) suggest that an exploratory mode of knowledge acquisition may provide for a more abstract representation of the system. Carroll et al. (1985) discuss learning by doing as a useful method to acquire knowledge about text processing systems. It can be shown that this type of learning provides a powerful method for acquiring knowledge especially in complex domains (Kluwe et al., 1990).

The goal of this experiment is to compare two learning conditions when preparing operators for process control: (i) learning by being told how to operate a dynamic system versus, (ii) learning by providing opportunities for exploratory search. It is expected that control performance of subjects given the opportunity for exploratory serach during training will be superior to the performance of those subjects who are learning by being told how to operate the system.

Method

The control task of the subjects in this experiment was to operate system 'MIX' which is a simulation of an asphalt mixing plant. An operator of system MIX is provided with a formula for the production of a specific asphalt mixture. It specifies the attributes of the desired outcome of the productionprocess. Process control requires starting processes, like mixing of different minerals, heating of minerals, adding of bitumen, monitoring processes, etc. Formulas can be varied with regard to their difficulty.

The experimental factor 'learning mode' has two levels: (i) condition TOLD: learning by being told, practice and application of provided rules; (ii) condition EXPL: learning by being told and exploratory problem solving. In condition TOLD subjects are provided with knowledge in terms of facts about the system, and about the interface as well as with knowledge in terms of rules for operating the system via the interface. This is followed by applying rules. In condition EXPL subjects acquire knowledge about the system and its control in the same way like in the TOLD group. However, an essential part of the training is reserved for exploratary search. This refers to the acquisition of knowledge about the system by solving provided problems in a self regulated, exploratory manner. The training followed two steps: first, all subjects were provided with the same knowledge on the basis of the manual developed for the system MIX. The manual was always available for the subject. Introduction to the manual and to the system was guided by the experimenter. Second, the different learning arrangements were implemented. Since this cannot be done for the entire instruction about the system it was decided to focus on one system component. The dry drum of the plant has been selected for this purpose since this is the most central system component with the highest control demands. Under condition TOLD the subjects are provided with a set of rules for this system component. In addition they apply these rules. In condition EXPL subjects were provided with a set of selected problems that have to be worked on. Knowledge about the control of the dry drum has to be acquired in the course of exploratory search. A subject was encouraged to find a solution by himself through goal directed interaction with the system and in a self guided manner. It was ensured that te subjects found a solution.

Forty-two male subjects aged 22-24 yrs were studied. Their occupational background was mainly electrical engineering and mechanical engineering. All subjects were studied individually in the presence of one experimenter. They participated on a voluntary basis and were paid. The training procedure lasted for three days, ending with the first assessment of knowledge. It was followed by six days with process control, where all subjects had to accomplish 24 production tasks. On the 10th day the second assessment of knowledge was performed. Control actions were registered on line, refering to the type and time for control inputs; control performance was assessed by a set of production variables derived directly from the description of the plant and of the production lines. Subjects were informed to keep the consumption of time, energy and materials as low as possible.

Results

Control performance

In general, the results showed no significant differences between the experimental groups with respect to the quality of production (P) as well as with regard to the costs of production (C). P is an indicator for satisfying the goal criteria: low values correspond to major deviations from the goal criteria. Variable C indicates the efficiency of the production process as implemented by the operator: high values correspond to high consumption of energy, fuel, bitumen, raw materials, and of time.

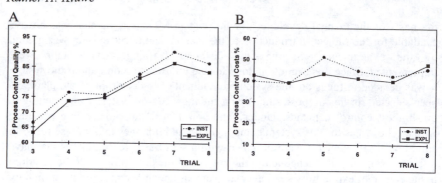

Figure 1   Control performance

Control activity

Though members of the EXPL-group perform a significantly higher amount of control inputs, the two groups do not differ with respect to the average decision time per control input.

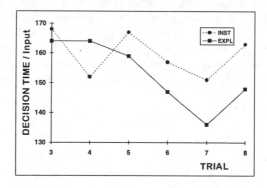

Figure 2   Decision times

Knowledge

Comparisons of both groups with regard to knowledge variables as assessed by questionnaires were performed taking into account different types of knowledge: knowledge about the components of the interface, about inputs to be performed on the interface, furthermore knowledge about the structure of the technical system and about its internal causal relationships (Kluwe, in press). There were no significant differences between the groups EXPL and TOLD with respect to these types of knowledge. Also, both groups do not differ when analysing the changes of knowledge scores in the course of control practice from assessment I to II.

As a general conclusion derived from these results one could assume that the different learning arrangements as implemented in this study do not affect control performance and knowledge acquisition when trained to operate a complex device. However, a more detailed analysis of operator performance on a more finegrained level reveals differences between the groups that may be important in real control environments.

'Repair'- strategy of control

For a specific set of control actions there result significantly higher frequencies for the EXPL group compared to the TOLD group. These actions refer mainly to the drydrum of the plant; the pattern of increased activities indicates that the EXPL group seems to accept that there are differences between the set values for masses and the actually resulting amounts at the end of the production process. The observed pattern of actions can be understood as supplementary intervention which becomes necessary because of imprecise actions in initial stages of the production. This results holds also for the control of temperatures. Altogether, the control procedure of operators who were given the opportunity for exploratory search can be characterized as a 'repair'-strategy, in order to adjust masses and temperatures.

Impact of changing control demands

When accomplishing production tasks, trial five seems to be crucial. Members of the TOLD group show increases of specific losses (losses of minerals, filler, binder), and increased deviations of masses (binder, filler). Due to these changes the costs C of the production process in trial five are significantly higher for group TOLD compared to group EXPL.

The performance differences are presumably caused by modified control demands in tiral five; there are only difficult formulas provided (formulas with high amounts of masses, high temperatures). Compared to the EXPL group the TOLD group responds to these requirements with a clear drop of control performance. It is assumed that subjects in the TOLD group tend to develop rather soon in the course of practicing control a standard repertory of rules which is applied quickly. This is also indicated by the changes of the average decision times for inputs: EXPL does not decrease its decision time from trial three to four (t=0.12; p=0.91), while the TOLD group decreases decision times considerably (t=2.18; p=0.04). When confronted with the difficult formulas in trial five the EXPL group again does not change the decision times (t=0.09; p=0.93), the TOLD group however, significantly *increases* the decision times per input (t=2.66; p=0.016).

It can be assumed that changing control requirements, as in trial five with less familiar and more difficult formulas, require the TOLD group to abandon the developed control routines. This may cause a temporary drop of control performance. The EXPL group on the other hand, may develop less quickly routines for control. Instead this group keeps some flexibility and thus, does not react with performance decreases to the changing requirements in trial five. It takes the TOLD group some time in the subsequent trials six to eight until it reaches again a similar performance level like the EXPL group.

Adopting a modified strategy

Connected with this point there is another important difference between EXPL and TOLD group indicated by the differences for mixdrum overflow MOF. While the overflow values increase significantly for the TOLD group in trial five, there are no significant changes for the EXPL group. The MOF values for the EXPL group remain on a low level. The difference between both groups is highly significant (Chi-square=6.46; df=1; p=0.01). Clearly the EXPL group operates the system more efficiently with regard to this component. The changes of MOF values indicate the application of a modified, more advanced strategy for accomplishing the difficult formulas. The strategy, when applied for the first time is initially connected with higher mental load. This causes temporary decreases of production performance.

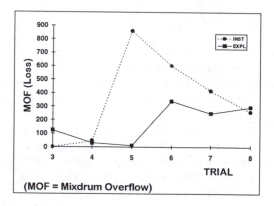

(MOF = Mixdrum Overflow)

Figure 3   Mixdrum overflow

Subjects in the TOLD group adopt the advanced strategy earlier than those in the EXPL group (trial five versus six). But this is done less successfully, and it results in a remarkable overflow. This indicates that subjects in the TOLD group may be more distracted when having to abandon a control strategy (basic strategy of partitioning recipes), and when trying to adopt a modified advanced strategy (releasing additional mixing cycle). Subjects in the EXPL group on the contrary adopt that strategy without those performance deficits   (the proportion of subjects adopting the advanced strategy is nearly the same in both groups: 52% in the TOLD group, 50% in the EXPL group).

Conclusion

The goal of this experiment was to examine the effects of two modes of learning on control performance when training operators to control a dynamic system. For one group of operators the training procedure was mainly based on declarative input, that is on learning by being told how to operate the system and on practicing provided rules for control. The training for the other group of operators provided for self guided knowledge acquisition, by including as a central part exploratory search in order to acquire knowledge about the control of a central component of the system. On a global level of analysis there are no performance differences between the two operator groups.

A more detailed analysis taking into account specific control requirements reveals however differences in control performance between these groups that may be of importance in real control environments. Differences emerge where control demands change and become more difficult.

Operators who were given the opportunity for exploratory problem solving with the system are less affected by changing and increasing control demands. On the contrary, the group of operators instructed by being provided with knowledge and by applying knowledge shows a severe drop of performance when confronted with less familiar, more difficult control demands after initial practice of control. Also, this group is inferior when trying to modify its control procedure, in order to apply a more efficient strategy.

It is suggested that operator training mainly based on learning by being told how to operate the system may foster the development of routine procedures after initial practice. This raises however difficulties when being confronted with new demands: it is necessary to abandon the developed routines and to configurate a modified control strategy. On the contrary, operators who were given the opportunity for exploratory problem solving during training may keep some flexibility with regard to their control actions.

The cognitive causes of these differences have still to be analysed. The results of this study suggest that different types of learning when training operators may engender rather different performance potentials. Rather than claiming the superiority of one or the other mode of learning it becomes evident that the training of operators has to take into account the range of possible control demands. Training procedures based on different types of learning presumably differ with regard to the type and range of control tasks which they prepare for.

References

Carroll, J.M., Mack, R.L, Lewis, C.H., Grischkowsky, N.L. & Robertson, S.R. (1985), 'Exploring exploring a word processor'. *Human Computer Interaction* Vol. 1, pp. 283-307.

Kamouri, A.L., Kamouri, J. & Smith, K.H. (1986), 'Training by exploration: facilitating the transfer of procedural knowledge through analogical reasoning'. *International Journal of Man-Machine-Studies,* Vol. 24, pp. 171-192.

Kluwe, R.H. (in press), 'Acquisition of knowledge in the control of a simulated technical system'. *Le travail Humain.*

Kluwe, R.H., Misiak, C. & Haider, H. (1990), 'Learning by doing in the control of a complex system'. In, H. Mandl, N. Bennet, E. de Corte & H.F. Friedrich (eds.), *Learning and instruction.* Pergamon Press: Oxford.

Michalski, R.S. (1993), 'Toward a unified theory of learning', in, G. Buchanan & D.C. Wilkins (eds.), *Knowledge acquisition and learning.* Kaufman: San Mateo.

Morris, N.M. & Rouse, W.B. (1985), 'The effects of type of knowledge upon human problem solving in a process control task'. *IEEE Transactions on Systems, Man, Cybernetics*, Vol. SMC 15(6), pp. 698-707.

Acknowledgement

This work was supported by a grant from Volkswagen-Foundation, Hannover (Germany).

12 Learning to control a coal-fired power plant: empirical results and a model

Dieter Wallach
Saarland University, Germany

Abstract

In 1986 Donald A. Norman coined the term *cognitive engineering*, which denotes a cognitive science approach within the engineering sciences. The research outlined in this paper follows this tradition and exemplifies a cognitive science methodology for the investigation of knowledge acquisition processes in a semantically rich task domain. To tackle this, an experimental design is combined with the construction of a simulation model that is based on a single case study. It is suggested to adopt a complementary view of both approaches towards the understanding of human learning processes. Whereas experimental results may demonstrate certain effects of different learning modes, a cognitive modelling approach offers a framework for their explanation.

Introduction

Although problem-solving research in psychology formerly concentrated on knowledge-lean tasks such as the *Tower of Hanoi*, attention during the eighties shifted to questions of knowledge acquisition, its organization and application in knowledge-rich task domains. A new paradigm, labelled *complex problem solving* (CPS), deepened cognitive psychology by investigating the effects of complexity and uncertainty in dealing with computer-simulated dynamic systems. Usually subjects in CPS-settings have to deal with a set of interrelated variables that are to be controlled to reach specified goal states. Generally speaking, there are two different approaches in CPS: the first type being task environments that bear superficial resemblance to real-life situations. For this type, unfortunately, the postulated realism often amounts to hardly more than the use of a more or less elaborated semantic cover story by labelling system components with commonplace vocabulary. In addition, these so-called *naturalistic* environments frequently lack a sound mathematical basis, which would allow the derivation of evaluation scales for the subject's performance in system control. This leads to the second type of environments that are based on well-defined equation systems which offer the benefits of precise analyzability and known problem structure. In order to control for subjects' background knowledge these environments are typically presented as abstract problems, abandoning a meaningful semantic cover story. This, as a result, weakens the *ecologically validity* of the experiments - a claim that has often been associated with the use of naturalistic scenarios.

The POWERPLANT environment

When comparing the advantages of both approaches to CPS, an integration is obviously required. With this goal in mind, POWERPLANT, a systems-theoretically well-defined model of an existing coal-fired power plant was constructed. Figure 1 shows the main screen of the user interface.

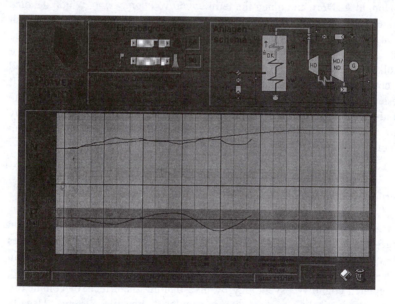

Figure 1   POWERPLANT main screen

Formally, POWERPLANT is based on a set of differential and algebraic equations. A task analysis was carried out in which central systems-theoretical attributes such as *stability, controllability* and *observability* of POWERPLANT have been mathematically proven (Wallach, in press). To operate POWERPLANT subjects have to fix two input variables, namely the *fuel mass flow*, (supply of coal in kg/s) and the *position of the turbine valve* (indicated in percent). As output-variables, the *power* generated (N; indicated in megawatts) and the *steam pressure* in the steam generator (P; indicated in bar) are considered. The control problem the subjects are faced with involves following given time-dependent power curves by appropriate settings of the control elements for the fuel mass flow and the valve position. In addition to this goal, the subjects are supposed to ensure that the steam pressure does not leave a specified tolerance range (shown as the grey bar in figure 1). This second goal makes the control task especially difficult: in many situations, interventions to attain the desired power may interfere with the achievement of the pressure goal and vice versa. As a performance index for the quality of control, an additive measure, based on the integral squared error of approximating the power curve and the maintenance of the pressure range is calculated.

Effects of participatory modes on system control

While subjects in CPS settings generally are supposed to actively control a computer-simulated environment, operators of real technical systems primarily become monitors of the system. By definition, the central task of monitors is process observation with active involvement primarily in cases of system and/or automation failures. Although literature on the consequences of different participatory modes (e.g. active control vs. system monitoring) exists, basic research has primarily concentrated on the effects on *manual* or *motor* control as opposed to *cognitive* control investigated in CPS. Usually, these studies report a superiority of active engagement in system control that is attributed to additional proprioceptive information in contrast to system monitoring where only visual cues are available. In CPS, Funke & Müller (1988) conducted an experiment to explore the role of different participatory modes. They found that active control in an initial learning phase led to better control performance in a subsequent test phase. Unexpectedly, the application of a knowledge assessment technique revealed that subjects who only monitored the system in the initial phase seemed to have acquired more verbalizable knowledge on involved system variables and their interrelations.

In general, as Kluwe (this volume) notes, the assumption that an active mode of learning to control a dynamic system is superior has been more widely claimed than empirically substantiated through CPS experiments. To investigate the effects of different participatory modes on control performance and system knowledge an experiment was conducted using the POWERPLANT environment.

Dieter Wallach

Procedure and design

Two variables, (i) the participatory mode and (ii) the demand to think aloud while controlling POWERPLANT, were experimentally manipulated as orthogonal factors, with two conditions each.

With respect to the first factor two experimental phases were introduced, namely, a *knowledge acquisition* phase and a phase of *knowledge application*. To separate effects of the active system control from those of pure system observation, a yoked control design was used:

- A *system control* group (SC) was allowed in the knowledge acquisition phase to actively explore POWERPLANT, e.g. to freely make interventions, gather data, test hypotheses by introducing signals and analysing their effects, and so on.
- In contrast, subjects in a *system monitoring* group (SM) were restricted to the observation of a yoked operator from the SC group controlling POWERPLANT in the knowledge acquisition phase. That is, each SM subject observed exactly the system course that the yoked subject from the SC-group generated. This method of *experimental twins* ensures that the respective twins are provided with identical data about POWERPLANT's dynamic behaviour while having to cope with the situation either actively or passively.

During the subsequent knowledge application phase, all subjects had to control POWERPLANT by following given power curves. The introduction of the second factor 'think aloud', was motivated by methodological and theoretical considerations. Methodologically, this on-line method of knowledge assessment is frequently accused of being reactive. That is, the request to think aloud may change the investigated primary process. Although there is a considerable body of evidence against this objection when committing to certain methodological standards (see Wallach, in press), experience with this method in CPS research is still rare. On theoretical grounds, think aloud protocols offer an extraordinarily rich data source for the knowledge and the cognitive activity underlying subjects' control behaviour. To further diagnose the acquired knowledge, additional off-line assessment techniques (e.g. questionnaires, a sorting-task, teach-back) were applied after the acquisition and application phase. The position taken here favours the application of multiple methods of knowledge elicitation, to take into account their differential adequacy in diagnosing certain aspects of system knowledge.

Subjects

Forty subjects participated in this experiment. To control background knowledge only third-year students from an electrical engineering department were chosen.

Subjects were paid according to their control performance in the knowledge application phase.

Main results

Close inspection of the data gathered by the knowledge assessment techniques revealed that the vast majority of all the subjects did not take into account extensive structural knowledge on the causal and topological relationships of POWERPLANT's components when operating the system. Instead, rather shallow knowledge in the form of idealized, heuristic input-output rules was used to attain the control goal. Following a distinction made by Kieras and Bovair (1984), subjects relied primarily on simple *'how to work it'* knowledge as opposed to comprehensive *'how it works'* knowledge. Obviously, successful goal attainment did not require subjects to acquire deep knowledge about POWERPLANT's causal structure. Therefore, knowledge acquisition was directed in a goal-adaptive manner towards the development of efficient control heuristics. This result supports a position, exemplified by Kluwe (1995), that successful system control does not necessarily require a comprehensive and complete internal model of the system, but that the learning process is essentially oriented on the respective operating goals.

Although there was no significant influence of the think aloud condition on process control or acquired system knowledge, clear differences concerning the *content* of verbalizations in the SC and the SM group were found. Subjects from the SC group essentially described their actions and paraphrased the resulting system states whereas verbalizations in the SM group mainly contained *self-explanations* (Chi et al., 1989). That is, SM subjects tend to explain to themselves the dynamic relationships between system variables, review the adequacy of earlier predictions about the effects of observed interventions, refer to exemplary system states to justify or revise assumptions, etc. The difference in verbalization content between the SC and the SM group reached statistical significance at the $p<0.001$ level (Kruskall-Wallis test). In sum, this result can be taken as substantiation of a more elaborate processing of observed system states by SM subjects.

Contradicting the prevailing assumption in CPS *no* performance differences between the SC and SM group with respect to process control in the knowledge application phase were found. Instead, a significant superiority ($p<0.001$, Kruskall-Wallis test) referring to the acquired system knowledge of the SM group was demonstrated. System knowledge was assessed using two questionnaires in which the prediction of system states after given system interventions was requested.

Interestingly, the two participatory modes led to different patterns of relationships between system knowledge and control performance. While there

93

was a strong association between system knowledge and control performance in the SC group (Spearman's r=0.76; p<0.001), *no* significant correlation was found in the SM group. Thus, although subjects from the SM group seem to have acquired better verbalizable system knowledge, this superiority was not reflected by a correspondingly better performance in system control.

Modelling approach and single case study

As a framework for the interpretation of the results obtained, the cognitive architecture ACT-R (Anderson, 1993) is used. A cornerstone of this framework is the distinction between two types of knowledge: *declarative* vs. *procedural*. Declarative knowledge comprises so-called *chunks* that encode facts that can be recalled and explicitly reported. Procedural knowledge on the other hand is represented by *productions*, condition-action pairs that encode knowledge about how to carry out actions, but that are inaccessible to verbalization. Although declarative knowledge is acquired from direct encodings of the environment, procedural knowledge must be compiled from declarative knowledge through practice. According to this framework, skills in the form of productions are acquired by *analogy* to declarative representations of examples.

From the perspective of ACT-R, the pairs of *intervention* and *resulting system state* SC subjects monitored in the knowledge acquisition phase can be represented as declaratively encoded examples for (more or less) successful system control. Because active control was not required, subjects from the SM group benefited from this reduced workload in the knowledge acquisition phase and generated self-explanations of the observed control examples. In contrast to pure paraphrasing, these elaborations led to an enriched declarative base of verbalizable knowledge which was helpful in working on the questionnaires. Thus, SM subjects were restricted to the acquisition of declarative knowledge in the learning phase, however, subjects from the SC group were given the opportunity to practice system control and thereby to acquire procedural knowledge on how to achieve target system states by appropriate interventions.

According to this interpretation, the superiority of the SM group with respect to declarative system knowledge is due to a more elaborated processing of monitored control examples. To explain the observed dissociation of knowledge and performance in this group, two interpretations can be suggested: (i) the successful attainment of the control task did not require the exploitation of better system knowledge, thus, SM subjects were not able to take advantage of such; (ii) the dissociation is a consequence of the separation of the opportunity to learn declarative knowledge and the opportunity to practice it for the acquisition of procedural knowledge. In Wallach, (in press) the empirical and theoretical support for both interpretations is discussed in detail.

Kluwe (1995) notes that it may be inadequate to reduce the manifold processes involved when controlling a dynamic system and to summarize the stream of activity in one performance score. The results obtained from the knowledge assessment techniques support this position in providing evidence for a broad heterogeneity of the mental representations and strategies subjects acquired when controlling POWERPLANT. To analyse the acquired knowledge on a finer grain level, a single-case study using the best thinking-aloud subject from the SM group was conducted. Based on the results of this study an ACT-R model was implemented. To prevent confounding model construction and its empirical evaluation, only data (i.e. verbalizations, observed pairs of interventions and resulting states) from the knowledge acquisition phase of the subject was used for implementing the model, whereas it was tested in predicting the knowledge application phase. Intentionally, no productions for fixing interventions in the knowledge application phase were coded. Instead, the goal was to explore the generality of the ACT-R analogy mechanism to learn such productions. Although a closer description of the model is beyond the scope of this paper, a comparison of the interventions in the knowledge acquisition phase of ACT-R and the modelled subject (see figure 2) indicate a close fit of their respective control behaviour.

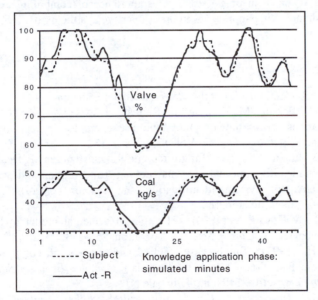

Figure 2   Control behaviour single case subject vs. ACT-R

The ACT-R model learns heuristics for operating POWERPLANT by recalling and elaborating observed examples of system control and compiling these into productions. In my opinion, modelling approaches on the basis of a cognitive architecture such as ACT-R offer a fruitful framework at the interface of engineering psychology and cognitive science. The exploitation and extension of this framework seems to me a promising way to arrive at an integrative theory of complex problem solving, comprising assumptions about the human cognitive architecture as well as the knowledge necessary for successful process control.

Discussion

The goal of this study was to investigate the effects of different participatory modes on system control and system knowledge. Although there was no difference in control performance, a significant superiority of the monitoring mode with respect to system knowledge was found. In sharp contrast to the prevailing view in CPS, this result at least questions assumptions about the benefits of an active learning mode. Further research is necessary to clarify the implications of different participatory modes on the training of human operators. Using data from a single-case study, a cognitive simulation model based on ACT-R was implemented and empirically evaluated. The insights gained from this model (see Wallach, in press) stress the importance of combining experimental designs with modelling approaches in order to arrive at a theory of CPS.

References

Anderson, J.R. (1993), *Rules of the Mind.* Hillsdale: Erlbaum.

Chi, M.T.H., Bassok, M., Lewis, M., Reiman, P. & Glaser, R. (1989), 'Self-explanations: how students study and use examples in learning to solve problems'. *Cognitive Science,* Vol. 13, pp. 145-182.

Funke, J. & Müller, H. (1988), 'Eingreifen und Prognostizieren als Determinanten der Systemidentifikation und Systemsteuerung' [Intervention and prediction as determinants for system identification and system control]. *Sprache & Kognition,* Vol. 7, pp. 176-186.

Kieras, D.E. & Bovair, S. (1984), 'The role of a mental model in learning to operate a device'. *Cognitive Science,* Vol. 8, pp. 255-273.

Kluwe, R.H. (1995), 'Single case studies and models of complex problem solving', in P.A. Frensch & J. Funke (eds.), *Complex Problem Solving: The European Perspective.* Erlbaum: Hillsdale NJ.

Wallach, D. (in press), *Kognitionswissenschaftliche Analyse komplexer Problemlšseprozesse* [A cognitive science approach to complex problem solving]. Westdeutscher Verlag: Wiesbaden.

13 Cognitive technology for knowledge and skill acquisition in engineering disciplines

Hitendra K. Pillay
Queensland University of Technology, Australia

Abstract

Recent research in cognitive science and information processing has identified and analysed many cognitive activities which provide insight into the mental manoeuvres that learners engage in when trying to increase efficiency and effectiveness of knowledge acquisition processes. These cognitive activities constitute the elements of a cognitive technology for the design of tasks information. Many of these findings suggest that enhanced knowledge acquisition and skill development can be obtained by effective management of cognitive resources. This paper provides an overview of the theoretical rationale for some of the elements of the cognitive technology together with discussion of selected empirical studies.

Human cognition and knowledge acquisition

The memory system has three major components namely, long term memory (LTM), the short term memory (STM) and sensory receptors. LTM is the storage house of the memory system and has infinite capacity. Every type of knowledge that learners acquire is categorised into knowledge types, structured and networked into prior knowledge and then stored in LTM. The STM is where we actively process information and construct knowledge before it can be stored in LTM. The sensory receptor acts as the input device for all information that passes through the STM and LTM memory. When individuals interact with new tasks they encode essential information, retrieve related information form the LTM and synthesise the two sets of information to construct meaningful understanding. The amount of information that can be processed at any one time is limited and

97

depends upon the individual's cognitive resources (Bower, 1975; Anderson, 1990). The limitation is mainly, due to the inability of our STM system to attend concurrently both to a vast amount of information and to the various cognitive activities associated with processing information (Kyllonan & Christal, 1990; Bower, 1970). This limitation has serious implications for knowledge acquisition and skill development. Recent research in cognition and instruction has attempted to find ways to circumvent this limitation and enhance knowledge acquisition.

One of the factors that influences the ability to process information and engage in knowledge acquisition is the design of task information as presented to our sensory receptors. Kotovsky and Fallside (1989) found that by manipulating the format of given information we can increase processing difficulty by as much as 16 times. They argue that the difficulty is caused by the increased demands made on the limited cognitive resource. Halford (1993) describes cognitive resources as the individual's cognitive ability to deal with a task, and cognitive load as the demand made by the task on the individual's mental effort for successful completion of that task. Cognitive load may be imposed either by the inherent complexity of the task or by the manner in which the information is presented as is the case in split attention. Split attention is an element of cognitive technology which requires individuals to direct their attention to multiple sources of information and synthesise them before proceeding any further. Often it may not be possible to reduce the inherent complexity of the task but the task format can be manipulated. The effect of the cognitive load of tasks on knowledge acquisition first became apparent in studies concerned with relationships between learning and problems solving. It is argued by Sweller (1989) and Halford (1993) that cognitive load imposed by poor task format often directs cognitive resources to extraneous activities associated with problem solving rather than to activities that facilitate knowledge acquisition. If the extraneous cognitive activities and the cognitive activities that facilitate knowledge acquisition draw from the same pool of cognitive resources then insufficient resources may be available for knowledge acquisition. As a result, they found that sometimes, individuals can solve a problem but learn little about its structures or heuristics to solve (Sweller, 1989). Knowledge acquisition is seen as a process of acquiring knowledge about the problem structure and categorising information in problem types in order to facilitate accessing at a later stage for applying in other similar tasks.

Cognitive technology is concerned with identifying extraneous cognitive activities in task information formats and developing ways of reducing or eliminating the associated cognitive load. Recent research in cognitive technology indicates that task information formats can be manipulated to reduce their difficulty and enhance knowledge acquisition and skill development (Sweller, Chandler, Tierney and Cooper, 1990; Sweller, 1989;). Some of the elements of cognitive technology attributed to knowledge and skill acquisition are: split attention instructional formats (Sweller, 1989), poor task formats requiring search heuristics (Ward and Sweller, 1990), having to reorganise information to bring it into congruence with existing mental models (Carballis, Zbrodoff & Roldan, 1978), constructing hidden details not given in the task information (Carpenter and Just, 1986) and internalising extraneous information and performing transformation (Kosslyn and Pomerantz, 1977). These elements have been found to impose a large cognitive load which may not be essential for many knowledge acquisition tasks.

An example of an element of cognitive technology hindering knowledge acquisition can be seen when trainees attempt to comprehend drawings drawn from an odd perspective. They tend to move their eyes and head until they recognise a 'neutral position' which fits their existing knowledge base before they proceed to learning the drawing. The search for a neutral position and the relating of the problem elements to the neutral position is not necessary for learning the drawing. It only becomes necessary because of the manner in which the given information is presented. A similar situation can be seen in the learning of engineering mechanics. Problems presented in text form require trainees to encode and construct the relationship between the various elements in the problem. In most cases the trainees use tools such as space diagrams or equations to identify and comprehend the relationships of the elements. Without the space diagrams and/or equations it is difficult to recognise the elemental relationships and consequently a large amount of memory resource is wastefully utilised in searching, constructing and transforming the elemental relationship in an attempt to comprehend the problem. This can be easily overcome by integrating diagrams and schematics with text (Ward and Sweller, 1990).

These types of discordance among the elements of cognitive technology occur in learning many engineering-related tasks. The remaining part of this paper will discuss how we interact with task information formats in engineering graphics, computer numerical control programming and learning assembly procedures. Conventional task information formats are compared with those developed according to the guidelines of cognitive technology.

Empirical studies to find means to resolve the discordance in cognitive activities and knowledge acquisition

Knowledge acquisition in engineering graphics problems

Engineering graphics is considered a difficult subject by many students. Pillay (1994) investigated the cognitive activities associated with comprehending such information and provided insights into why students found it a difficult subject. Consider the manner in which three dimensional objects are represented as two dimensional drawings in engineering graphics. Three orthogonal views are drawn directly from the top, front and the left. To comprehend the rotational transformation and the object, trainees are required to encode information from the three views and construct a three dimensional (3D) mental representation of the object which is subsequently rotated so that it presents a sight line perpendicular to each of the three faces to be drawn. When the objects are simple and physically available the rotation may be physical, but in the absence of a physical model, which occurs frequently, trainees engage in mental rotation of the constructed 3D mental representation (Metzler and Shepard 1982; Cooper, 1988). As we rotate 3D mental representations we construct intermediate stages in the rotation trajectory. While the construction of the 3D mental representation of intermediate stages may be essential to solving the problem, paradoxically, it is not essential to learning how to construct the orthogonal images.

In order to construct intermediate images, a person may engage in a trial and error process involving a search for the correct set of elemental relations between the various entities, such as corners, sides, edges, faces, angles and dimensions of the rotated object as it moves through the rotation trajectory. These activities are an essential precursor to learning the relations because it allows students to trace the movements of the above elements as the 3D image is transformed into a 2D image. However, to monitor the elements as they move along the trajectory we need to construct the 3D mental representations of the intermediate stages. If the 3D representation of the intermediate stages is given then students can focus their attention on the elements and how they transform in the trajectory, rather then focusing on constructing the 3D representations of intermediate stages which exhausts their cognitive resources and prevents learning the structure of the total transformation. Searching for and constructing appropriate intermediate images requires different mental processes to learning but draws on the same pool of memory resources, hence the search process may impose a heavy memory load that interferes with learning. Through a series of experiments Pillay (1994) found that when rotation transformation is simulated by a series of intermediate stages from the rotation trajectory, it eliminated the high demands imposed on the memory resources by the need to search and construct intermediate images. There were sufficient cognitive resources to learn the transformation, which was evident in subsequent test tasks. On the other hand, trainees who received instructional material without the simulation had to search and construct the rotated intermediate images thus increasing the cognitive load. As a result they performed poorly on test tasks.

It is suggested that when designing instruction for tasks which require the construction and manipulation of intermediate mental representations in order to comprehend the problem, it is more beneficial to the learner if the complex mental representations and manipulations are provided in some form such as simulated video instruction, computer simulation or even a pictorial simulation.

Knowledge acquisition in computer numerical control programming (CNC)

In 1992, Chandler and Sweller studied the effect of task information format on teaching CNC programming. Conventional instructional method for CNC programming instruction has textual information describing the various function keys and how they actuate specific responses on the CNC machine together with information describing how to use 'G' codes to programme a specific tool movement. In order to present this information, frequent reference to diagrams is made to illustrate points better communicated through graphical display. Trainees are required to integrate information from the text and diagram, and at the same time learn the relation between the elements (key functions, programming codes, tool path movement, coordinates defining the path) described in the instruction. Consider learning the function G01 X-20, Y10. Trainees need to learn and maintain that G01 is a cut command, X-20 is a position 20 units to the left of the origin, Y10 is 10 unit above the origin and GO1 X-20, Y10 is cut from G00 to a point which is the intersection of X-20 and Y10. If trainees have to process all the above information and maintain it in their memory and, at the same time attend to integrating information from other sources such as the drawing of the object and the tool path movement this imposes a large cognitive load. As a result they do not learn much of the programming commands. Considering the elements of cognitive technology such as information overload and split attention an alternative instructional format was developed. Through a series of experimental studies Chandler and Sweller (1992) compared conventional instruction with integrated instruction. The findings demonstrated that learning is enhanced when instructional material is modified by integrating the text into the diagrams. The instruction normally presented in text form is decomposed into little steps, coded for sequence, and placed at relevant positions on the diagrams to simulate the thought process necessary to understand the programming commands. This brings the information within the attentional focus of the trainee thereby eliminating split attention and also the need to internalise all the information prior to learning the relationships. The instructional format acts as an external memory aid bringing all the information together as a meaningful unit thus reducing extraneous memory load. The key functions, coded programs and the corresponding tool movements (contextual and procedural information) are all put together in one instructional frame. The presentation format may appear crowded and, intuitively it might be supposed that it would interfere with learning. But field trials in CNC programming suggest the opposite (Chandler and Sweller 1992). Trainees presented with integrated instructional material performed better in subsequent CNC programming tasks. Once again, this illustrates the benefits of cognitive technology for knowledge acquisition.

Hitendra K. Pillay

Knowledge acquisition when learning assembly procedures

In a recent study Pillay (1995) investigated how students interacted with different instructional formats when learning assembly procedures. The manner in which assembly procedures are taught varies, for example in trade apprenticeship, trainees are allowed to study physical objects whereas in design subjects drawings are used to instruct the sequence, orientation and position of components in an assembly task. Among the graphical styles, orthographic drawing has three, two dimensional views as described earlier in the paper. To understand such drawings subjects need to encode information from all three views, synthesise, construct hidden details, construct 3D representation of individual components and while maintaining the components in the memory, learn the sequence, size, orientations etc of the whole assembly (Cooper, 1988). The other graphical style commonly used has exploded isometric drawings which have pictorial representation of the components aligned for assembly. By contrast to the orthographic format in this style the construction of 3D representation of individual components is not necessary. However, there are parts of the object that are obscured, which the observer is expected to construct mentally in order to comprehend fully the nature of the object. When studying from physical models students could physically manipulate the object and view it from different perspectives. They did not have to construct 3D mental representations because the image was available in 3D form. They also did not have to construct hidden information which could be viewed by manipulating the model. The orthographic drawing, isometric and a physical model instructional formats were compared to establish the most efficient format for knowledge acquisition. The finding indicated that the group presented with a physical model performed better on similar tasks presented at a later stage, than the other groups. The findings of the study suggest that working from a physical model seemed to be most beneficial (Pillay, in preparation). This was largely due to the reduced cognitive demand made by the given information. It is argued that students did not have to engage in encoding and synthesising information from multiple sources, constructing hidden lines, hold information in memory as they perform transformation all of which, according to Carpenter and Just (1986) is a cognitively very demanding exercise. Presenting task information in the form of physical models may eliminate many of the extraneous cognitive activities and thereby facilitate knowledge acquisition. It may not be possible to use a physical model for all tasks. Computer simulation with 360 degrees rotational capabilities and virtual reality images may be a solution when a physical model is not a possibility. In the case of orthographic drawing it is argued that it may be a convenient way to present detailed information about a object but this type of drawing is very difficult to comprehend.

Conclusion

Cognitive technology has provided trainers with a powerful tool for facilitating knowledge and skill acquisition. Whereas in the past difficulties in these areas have been attributed to such uncontrollable factors as inherent task complexity and /or lack of mental capacity it is increasingly recognised that the design of task format is crucial in the process of knowledge and skill acquisition.

Understanding the elements of cognitive technology has promoted the design of efficient instructional formats for engineering tasks. Use of split attention, information overload, redundant information and misdirected attention techniques has thrown new light on why certain information and skills has always been considered difficult to acquire. The perceived difficulties in many engineering-related tasks may not be intrinsic to the task but lie in the manner in which task information is presented. An understanding of how we learn from these instructional materials will generate greater understanding and empathy towards students who exhibit apparent inability to learn certain concepts.

References

Anderson, J.R. (1990) *The adaptive character of thought*. Lawrence Erlbaum Associates: Hillsdale, NJ.

Bower, B.H.(1975), Cognitive Psychology: an introduction. In W. K. Estes (ed.) *Handbook of learning and cognitive processes: Vol 1. Introduction to Concepts and Issues*. Erlbaum: Hillsdale NJ.

Carpenter, P.A & Just, M.A (1986), Spatial ability: An information processing approach to psychometrics. In R. Sternberg (ed) *Advances in the Psychology of Human Intelligence*. Erlbaum: Hillsdale NJ.

Chandler, P. & Sweller, J. (1992), 'The split attention effect as a factor in the design of instruction', *British Journal of Educational Psychology*, Vol. 62, pp. 223-246.

Cooper, L.A. (1988) The role of spatial representations in complex problem solving, in S. Schiffer and S. Steele (eds.) Cognition and Representation. Westview Press, Boulder, Colorado.

Corballis, M.C, Zbrodoff, N.J. & Butler, P.B. (1978) 'Decisions about identity and orientation of rotated letters and digits'. *Memory and Cognition*, Vol 6, pp.98-107.

Hafford, G. S. (1993) *Children's Understanding: The Development of Mental Models*. Erlbaum: Hillsdale NJ.

Kotovsky,K. & Fallside, D. (1989), Representation and Transfer in Problem Solving, in, D. Klahr and K.Kotovsky (eds.) *Complex information processing: the impact of Herbert Simon*, Erlbaum: Hillsdale NJ.

Kossyln, S.M & Pomerantz, J.R (1977) 'Imagery, proposition and form of the internal representation', *Cognitive Psychology*, Vol. 9, pp. 52-76.

Kyllonen, P.C & Christal, R. (1990) 'Reasoning ability is (little more than) working memory capacity', *Intelligence*, Vol. 14, pp. 389-433.

Metzler, J. & Shepard, R. N. (1982) Transformational studies of the internal representation of three-dimensional objects, in R. N. Shepard & L. A. Cooper (eds.) *Mental Images and their Transformation*. MIT Press: London.

Pillay, H K 1994, 'Cognitive load and mental rotation: structuring orthographic projection to enhance learning and problem solving', *Instructional Science*, Vol. 22, pp. 91-113.

Pillay, H.K (1995) Cognitive Processes and Instructional Format: Structuring Instruction for Learning Assembly Procedures. *2nd International Symposium on Cognition and Education: A Multi-disciplinary Perspective*. December 14-18, India.

Sweller, J. (1989) 'Cognitive technology: some procedures for facilitating learning and problem solving in mathematics and science', *Journal of Educational Psychology*, Vol. 81, pp. 457-466.

Sweller, J, Chandler, P, Tierney, P & Cooper, M (1990), 'Cognitive load as a factor in structuring of technical material, *'Journal of Experimental Psychology; General*, Vol. 119, pp. 176-192.

Ward, M. & Sweller, J. (1990), 'Structuring effective worked examples', *Cognition and Instruction*, Vol. 7, pp. 1-39.

14 Dynamic modelling of a learning system to aid system re-engineering

Nassereddin Eftekhar, Douglas R. Strong
and Ostap Hawaleshka
University of Manitoba, Canada

Abstract

This work is an ambitious undertaking that implements a unique effort combining education metrics and engineering simulation modelling. It is a package of a simple control engineering concept, a model of a learning process, and a computer simulation. This work ultimately develops a model by which one can gain a better insight into the possible dynamic behaviour of a learning system. The methodology used by this study is known as 'system dynamics.' It generally includes a qualitative and a quantitative phase. The qualitative phase is based on mapping the resource flows and interrelations of the learning system and converting the map to a simulation model. The quantitative phase is a quantitative computer simulation modelling using a purpose-built software. This phase is based on investigating the dynamic behaviour of the system to obtain a better understanding of how a learning system works, and applying some proposed changes to the model to improve the performance of the system. This paper describes the first stage of the study.

Introduction

This study attempts to apply industrial engineering simulation modelling techniques to the analysis of a learning system. The intent is to give some information about cause and effect relationships that would allow educators and education administrators to make necessary changes to the system, with greater knowledge of the ramifications than is presently available. This is an essentially uncharted area, and will use information that is not as reliable as that usually used by engineers. However, it seems that research into simulation modelling of learning systems is a worthwhile direction. It is likely that this will be useful in helping define the direction of change for learning systems that are about to go through a massive change, driven by the continuing decrease of funds and the continuing improvement of technology.

The methodology

This work uses system dynamics as a suitable methodology to analyse the process of student learning. System dynamics is a specific system analysis approach that is being increasingly used in research in very diverse areas. The unique characteristic of this approach is its ability to represent the real world. Figure 1 illustrates the system dynamics process for a learning system (Forrester, 1994). The investigation starts at step one, 'description (mapping) of the learning system'. It is the most important and the least straightforward of the stages in system analysis. In step one, a model of a real learning system is defined. It requires taking various bits of information about learning systems in the real world and turning them into a unified theory. Step two begins the formulation and construction of a simulation model. The system description is translated and converted into the level and rate equations of a system dynamics model by providing the requisite parameters. As with every step, active recycling occurs back to prior steps. In step two, writing equations reveals gaps and inconsistencies that must be remedied in the prior description. Step three, simulation of the model, will start after the equations of step two pass the logical criteria of an operable model, such as all variables being defined, and consistent units of measures. Step four identifies policy alternatives for testing. Simulation tests determine which policies show the greatest promise. Step five works toward a consensus for implementation. In this step proposed policy changes will be tried to the model to maintain or obtain sustainable improvement in performance while considering the feasibility of implementing these changes in its real world. Questions will arise that require repeated recycling through steps one to five. Finally, step six implements the changes in policies and structure of the system. If the model is relevant and persuasive, then step six can progress smoothly. Evaluation of the policy changes comes after implementation.

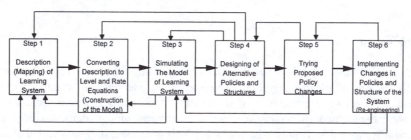

Figure 1   System dynamics process for a learning system, adopted and modified from Forrester (1994)

106

The tool

The model of a learning system is constructed using the STELLA modelling language (Paterson and Richmond, 1994). This computer program is a continuous simulation package with an appropriate multi-level, hierarchical environment for constructing and interacting with complex models. The language is built around a progression of structures that is particularly compatible with the nature of a learning system. At its lowest level are stocks and flows, the primary building blocks of structure. Stocks represent 'accumulations' while flows are the 'actions'. Infrastructures are the next step in the progression. They are built up from various combinations of stocks and flows. The final step is the. feedback loops. They are the relationships that link stocks to flows in various ways. and enable infrastructures to exhibit interesting dynamic behaviours.

The parameters

Many parameters and situations are considered in this study. Some main examples are: types of learning (memorizing, close-problem solving and open-problem solving), types of teaching system, types of subject matter, types of student (surface learners and deep learners), and the learning and teaching environmental factors (Feldman and Paulsen, 1994).

Development of the theory

Globally, any model of a learning process can be conceptualized in a simple control engineering approach as shown in figure 2.

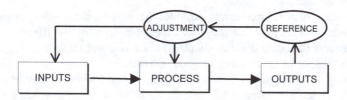

Figure 2   The structure of a simple control process

The above control process structure is easily applicable to each student's unique learning behaviour. Inputs are the resources. They drive the learning process and through the process create the outputs. Outputs are the different outcomes of the learning process. A feedback loop represents feedback information that exists in the learning system. The feedback loops persistently seek adjustments in the inputs and process of the learning system. For instance, through a feed-back signal, an output, say the amount of knowledge acquired by the student, is assessed against a reference policy, say the student's target knowledge, and subsequently a corrective measure, say his or her higher or lower effort for study hours, is taken accordingly (cause-effect). The resulting behaviour of the system for each student may overlap with those of other students, or may not. However, to facilitate this approach, we have to identify what components each part of the system possesses.

The result of the literature search on aspects related to learning system indicates that there seems to be a consensus on the following general items.

- The process of learning includes cognitive, behavioral, and experimental dimensions or components.
- Learning and teaching are dual and complementary processes. But in any attempt to model an educational system, the heavier part should go to the 'learning side' rather than to the 'teaching side'.
- Learning is mainly a function of students interacting with the instruction method and subject matter variables.
- Some student learning results from instruction and some from other forms of organized experience. Similarly, the main conditions under which the learning situation occurs were identified as follows.
- The individual differences of the students themselves; i.e., their academic ability, their previous preparation at the secondary level, and the various motives that bring them to the university classroom.
- The nature of the learning materials, tasks, equipment, and facilities that will be involved in the academic course work including the structure and content of the academic programs themselves, the type of the teaching aids, and the other educational facilities.
- The nature and quality of instruction the student receives, the conditions of practice, guidance, mode of presentation, feedback, and other teaching dimensions.
- Situational or environmental variables that may be either direct or indirect in their influence on learning outcomes, i.e., conditions affecting learning process including those as simple as class size and those as complex as the various forms of reinforcement and interaction.

Summing up, the major components in a learning process system may be classified as shown in table 1. Apparently, the items in the first column have a relative tendency to have a role in the input side of the system while those in the second and third columns have relative tendencies to have roles in process and output sides respectively.

Table 1
The major components in a learning system

Learning resources	Rate of learning process	Learning outcomes
Prior knowledge of subject	Motivational factors	Amount learned
Background knowledge	Learning style	Learning development
Student abilities & aptitude	Nature & quality of instruction	Current knowledge
Effort (time & energy to act)	Course structure & content	Achievement
Student perception of task value	Study skill	Assessment
Environmental parameters	Comfort	Target knowledge
• Teaching parameters	Demand	Student performance
• Subject matter parameters	Student productivity	
• Administrative parameters		

Mechanism of a learning process

To understand the mechanism of a learning process, two major sets of components should be discussed in the first place. These are: 'ability to learn' and 'desire to learn'. Consequently, this requires study on models of mind and models of student motivation (values) respectively.

Levels of processing in the memory

The idea of different levels of processing is already well established in the psychological literature on human memory and information processing (Entwistle and Ramsden, 1983). Models of human memory have described generally three distinct types of memory: a sensory register (which holds incoming perceptions only briefly), a short-term memory (STM - which holds a limited amount of information for up to about 20 seconds), and a long-term memory (LTM) which itself can be divided into episodic (storing episodes of experience) and semantic (storing and relating concepts). Information can be held in store for longer periods by internal repetition (rehearsal) and if repeated sufficiently often (over learning) it will become a permanent memory trace, presumably in episodic LTM. This process is what would normally be called rote memorization or surface level processing. But much incoming information is reassessed and categorized in STM before being passed to semantic LTM. This is the process that is involved in deep level processing (figure 3).

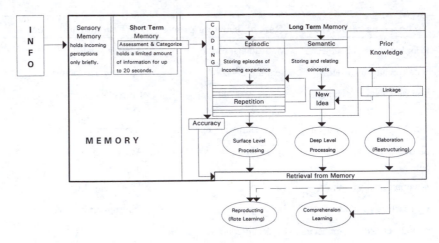

Figure 3   Levels of information processing in the memory

Retrieval from memory depends on the accuracy of a coding process which determines where the incoming information will be stored, and hence where it is expected subsequently to be found. Concepts are built up by repeated comparisons of incoming perceptions or information with pre-existing concepts or linkages between images. If the coding system is to be effective and recall easy, it is essential that the data base should contain a large number of clearly defined and well differentiated concepts which also carry a large number of connecting links with other concepts, ideas or events. The ability to think divergently or creatively will presumably depend on the extent to which the memory has developed a multiplicity of unusual, but valid, interconnections. An orientation towards understanding (deep processing) depends on a deep level of processing and elaboration. Reproducing (surface approach) is more likely to involve over learning by repetition at a shallow level of processing with little use of elaboration.

Student motivation

Motivation is defined in a general way by educators and psychologists as the processes that initiate and sustain behaviour. Motivation is defined more specifically for learning in university courses as purposeful engagement in classroom tasks and study, to master concepts or skills. Although there are many models of motivation that may be relevant to student learning (Weiner, 1992), this study looks at motivation in a way that gives answer to a fundamental question: What do theories of motivation offer to a learning system to enhance the process? On this basis, we have developed a model to organize what are the most important influences of one's personal motivations on learning. The model is based on the premises that student's motivation is heavily influenced by their thinking about what they perceive as important and what they believe they can accomplish. According to this model, 'desire to learn' comprises of values that represents a student's perception of the task value. So the model first tries to recognize these values and, second, identifies the external factors that promote student learning behaviour. These two categories of parameters and their sub-categories have been shown in figure 4. Note that the subsequent progression of the motivation, that is the effort a student puts into the learning task is shown as well. The adjustment feedback loop indicates that if students see little value in what they are learning or in the results of their effort, their motivation will be lessened, even if they believe that they are capable of success.

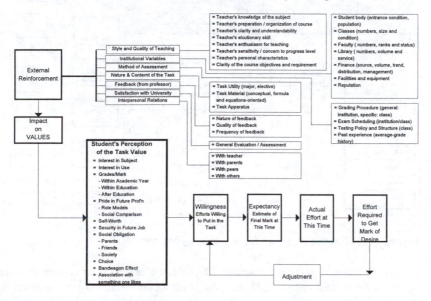

Figure 4   Model of student's 'desire to learn'

Model of a learning process

By combining one's learning wishes and abilities, we can conclude that if students see value in what they are learning, and if they believe that they are able to succeed with reasonable effort, then a typical learning performance will take place. Figure 5 demonstrates how these two major components can interact with each other. The diagram consists of four main blocks: a block for external reinforcement (including different type and quality of the teaching system, instructional material and other

111

Nassereddin Eftekhar et al.

factors), a block for student's values (including ten different studied values), a block for amount of effort that student puts into the task, and finally a block for the amount learned. Learning reinforcers are sub-sets of 'external reinforcement'. In fact external reinforcement has its direct impact on both student desire and ability.

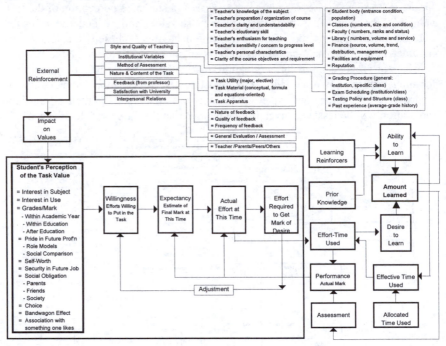

Figure 5   Influence diagram for a learning process

The diagram is an influence diagram. The impact of any of external reinforcement on any of the student values has a consequent effect on the amount of the effort that student puts into the learning task. This, subsequently influences the level of desire to learn and finally the amount learned by the student. This is apparently a cause and effect mechanism that drives the learning process. Thus, the next step is to convert this diagram into a STELLA stock level and flow diagram.

Future work

The current mapping step will be completed by working it out for the block dealing with the amount learned by the student. Then, the completed mapping will be converted into a sound system flow diagram (stock level and flow diagram) by using the purpose-built software (STELLA). At this stage, a series of simulations to demonstrate the effect of different policy actions on the behaviour of the system will be conducted. The results in terms of the structure of the system will be interpreted and the best re-engineered shape for the system will be determined.

References

Entwistle, N. J. & Ramsden, P.(1983) *Understanding Student Learning.* Croom Helm Ltd.: London, UK.

Feldman, K.A. and Paulsen, M.B. (1994) *Teaching and Learning in the College Classroom.* Ashe Reader Series: GINN Press, MA.

Forrester, Jay W. (1994) 'System Dynamics, System Thinking, and Soft OR'. *System Dynamics Review,* Vol.10, Nos.2-3.

Paterson, S & Richmond, B. (1994) *Stella II Technical Documentation.* High Performance Systems Inc: Hanover NH.

Weiner, B. (1992) *Human Motivation: Metaphors, Theories, and Research.* Sage Publications: Newbury Park, CA.

15 Learning statistics: a high level cognitive skill

Tay Wilson
Laurentian University, Ontario, Canada

Abstract

Statistical analysis is one of the most important high level cognitive skills that has to be mastered in many fields. Yet the attainment of this skill is difficult for many. Three tools to assist this mastery (appropriate use of verbal, imaginal and spatial material, recourse to errorless learning and use of a 'meaty' textbook are here examined.

Verbal, imaginal and spatial representations

How can students best learn to be able to 'talk' the subject with comprehension and with comfort? Consider some relevant findings. Paivio (1971) found additive effects on memory when imaging and the verbal systems could be assumed to be operating together; moreover, concrete words, those readily evoking spontaneous images, were retrieved more easily than so-called abstract words, those not so readily evoking spontaneous images. Bower (1970) noted that interactive imagery of items to be remembered was superior, for memory, to both separate imagery and to memorization by rote. Paivio and Csapo (1973) found superior recall when concrete nouns were alternately imaged and then pronounced. Finally, Baddeley, Grant, Wight and Thomson (1975) found that the recall of easily visualizable messages (auditory description of location of numbers in a matrix) was interfered with by a concomitant spatial-visual task (following a pursuit rotor), a concomitant spatial only task (blindfolded pointing to a moving pendulum on basis of auditory feedback) but not by a concomitant visual only task (judgement of brightness).

Re-modelling the statistics course

Apply these findings to statistics teaching in terms of formulae, core definitions and figures. Present key statistics formulae and figures in both verbal and image form. In

Tay Wilson

texts ensure that formulae and figures have clear, precise verbal descriptions of what is meant (right in the 'blue boxes') and parsimonious but clear *spatial* representations of concepts where appropriate. In teaching do several rapid fire alternations of image and verbalization, with layered elaboration where appropriate. Instruct students, in reading the book and studying the formulae, to alternate making the 'image' with saying the explanatory words. Insist that students memorize these formulae and spatial representations and their accompanying verbal descriptions. Test with closed book exams in which the material learned has to be reported in the form in which it is learned. Avoid the 'entertainment approach', whereby concepts are imbedded in complex and hence potentially confusing but supposedly entertaining, visual and computational presentations; but do use bare spatial presentations.

Applying the model: results and conclusions

At Laurentian, fourth year psychology thesis students orally defend their own research project. Sadly but unsurprisingly, achievement is overall quite low in answering such questions as: 'define statistical interaction' and 'explain the logic of the t-test'. However, in 1993, four out of six students receiving some version of the above re-designed statistics course averaged 75 per cent or higher, while only one out of 18 receiving some other type of statistics course obtained such a score (χ^2 = 10.18, df = 1, p < .01).

'Errorless' learning or 'multiple guess'

Some teach statistics courses by means of computer based programmes in which students are given a series of multiple choice questions, instructed to 'figure out' and/or 'guess' the answers. Recent findings regarding the failure, among amnesiacs, of implicit learning techniques and success of 'errorless' learning techniques contra-indicate this type of teaching.

Tulving (1972) distinguished semantic de-contextualized memory for facts about entities and relationships between them and episodic memory about events that happen at a particular time. Graf and Schachter (1985) distinguished implicit memory involving absence of conscious recollection of original learning experience and explicit memory involving conscious recollection. Terrace (1963) distinguished errorless learning allowing no opportunity for subjects to make incorrect responses during initial learning trials and errorful learning, giving ample opportunity to make incorrect responses during initial learning.

Consider now amnesiacs. For them implicit, but not explicit, learning appears to be preserved (Brooks and Baddeley, 1976). Moreover, when young 'normals', elderly 'normals' and severely memory impaired subjects were compared, under errorful learning (e.g. guessing a word beginning with QU) and errorless learning (e.g. 'I am thinking of a five letter word beginning with QU and the word is QUOTE.

Please write that word down.') Baddeley and Wilson (1994) found that amnesiacs demonstrated significantly less learning and more forgetting under errorful than under errorless learning while elderly controls showed no condition differences. They reasoned that implicit memory, the sole resource of many amnesiacs, typically is based upon emitting the strongest response, which if erroneous, leads, upon repetition, to cul-de-sac strengthening of incorrect responses. On the other hand, recourse to explicit episodic memory, available to normals, allows for the elimination of such errors on subsequent trials. Errorless learning techniques were later found to be superior for retraining picture recognition in an agnosic subject and spelling in a dyslexic subject.

Consider now statistics students who might well describe themselves as weak and anxious. Make a new distinction between *merely implicit* (i.e. merely free floating semantic, such as 'virtue is good'), which is opposed to *cognitive explicit* memory/learning, on one hand, and *external explicit* memory/learning, on the other hand. It is recognized first, that both of the latter types of explicit memory/learning are internal; and second, that both involve space-time categories in the Kantian sense. However, in external explicit memory, the space time aspects are somehow dominantly real and importantly existing in the outside or extra-mental world (e.g. my detailed memory of events, times and locations involved in my vacation in Greece) Whereas, in cognitively explicit learning/memory, space-time events, though present, are not mapped importantly to the outside or extra-mental world. Rather is it that they form part of the 'mental glue' binding a coherent, well-organized and highly elaborated set of mental events (e.g. my time and space linked memory of learning the logical steps involved in obtaining the median for grouped data).

It is contended here that a considerable number of weak and anxious statistics students are deficient in their cognitive explicit memory and learning just as are amnesiacs deficient in both types of explicit memory and learning. Two differences exist between amnesiacs and these students however. First, they have, and so recognize, intact external event explicit memory as amnesiacs do not. Second, their deficits in external explicit memory, being in some strong measure, anxiety and social environment induced, can be removed by appropriate teaching techniques, as they can not in the case of many amnesiacs.

What is implied for statistics teaching by combining my model of weak, anxious students with the major results of Baddeley and Wilson's study? First, teaching techniques which encourage, during learning, the emission of wrong answers (errorful learning) will be much less effective than those teaching techniques which avoid, in so far as is possible, the emission of errors by students. Second, prime among the to-be-avoided teaching techniques are computer-style learning techniques in which students may more or less 'guess' correct answers to multiple choice questions. Weak students, by simply guessing on early trials, produce many incorrect responses which can yield pro-active inhibition on later trials. Yet, it is likely to be these very anxious students who will opt for such a counter-productive technique, when given the opportunity. Third, teaching and grading mindless 'cookbook'

117

assignments are, at best, merely neutral for these students; for although they do not induce incorrect answers, they do not either, encourage the development of comprehending, organised and elaborated explicit learning. At worst, combined with multiple 'guessing' assessment they can be negative; deluding already anxious and not highly reality oriented students into believing that they have cognitively mastered the material. Fourth, techniques in which, questions are rapidly, iteratively posed and rhetorically answered before students can produce incorrect responses are likely to be best particularly when combined with an alternating verbal/image presentation. (For some cognitive therapy suggestions see Wilson and Mottin, 1992.)

Testing the model

Evidence bearing upon this model of teaching falls into three categories: interview based material, data from a first year class and from a fourth year thesis class. Consider interview data. Over four years of interviews a common pattern has emerged among students identified as deficient in their mastery of statistical material and as anxious in this regard. First, they seek out those courses involving the most opportunity for guessing and cook-book work and often receive quite high grades. Second, they often convince themselves that they understand the material quite well despite great deficiencies revealed in the most perfunctory interview. Third, they freely admit to being unable to memorize or remember the concepts and formulae necessary for minimal acceptable mastery of the subject. Probing reveals that, generally, although they do not recognize it, their memories are weak because they do not to even engage in the attempt.

Consider data from a fourth year thesis class. Design/analysis presentations of 49 students were ranked half by two professors and half by two other professors (the author was one). Of students who had taken either the present authors perception or his statistics course (in which errorless learning techniques were employed) and obtained a grade above 50 per cent , 11 fell above and two below the median for the thesis group ($\chi^2 = 7.7$, df $= 1$, p < 0.01). Furthermore, when only students known to be weak in statistics were examined, the corresponding frequencies above and below the median were five and two for those receiving 'errorless' teaching versus one and 12 for those receiving other learning ($\chi^2 = 8.8$, df $= 1$, p < 0.01).

Perhaps the purest exemplar of teaching by errorless learning was used in a first year psychology class of 149 students. Recently, Laurentian University has had about 4000 students, of which some 700 are registered as majors in psychology, all of whom must pass an elementary statistics/research design course. However, the standard of entering 'arts' students is not high. About 50 per cent have a high school grade average of 70 per cent or less and about 25 per cent have less than 65 per cent , (compared with 18 per cent and five per cent respectively for all Ontario universities). Persinger and Tiller (1995) found a random sample of first year psychology students to be not much different from random samples of the population at large on several measures (e.g. mean $= 104$ and standard deviation $= 13$ for the

WAIS-R intelligence scale). Finally, for 54 females and 40 males in a Laurentian University introductory psychology class the reported weekly consumption of alcohol was the equivalent of 43, 34 and 22 bottles of beer for male students living off-campus, on-campus and with parents respectively, the corresponding values for females were ten, ten and six (Valliant and Scanlan (1996). Unsurprisingly, large numbers of such students see themselves to be weak in mathematics.

About 20 statistics concepts were taught to a first year class (e.g. measures of central tendency and variability, Z-scores, logic and calculation of t-test for two independent groups and Pearson product moment correlation). Errorless learning was used for some weeks, e.g. three measures of central tendency were stated (mean, median and mode) and then the rhetorical question asked 'what are the three measures of central tendency?' and then without delay the answer was provided while trying to get as many students as possible to say it out loud. The material was tested by closed-book, non-multiple choice questions which required memorization of relevant formulae. This module was well beyond other first year sections in coverage and rigour of examination technique. For 149 students, marks (percentages) on the statistics questions almost doubled from midterm to final (mean = 33, standard deviation = 16, to mean = 59, standard deviation = 23; t = 12.3, p < 0.001). Moreover, the class average marks on the statistics parts of the final exam (mean = 59) were almost the same as the overall class average for the course (mean = 57). It was clear that Laurentian University first year social science students could learn this material despite the fact that in some other first year psychology sections the material was deemed to be too difficult to even present.

A good 'meaty' textbook might help

Can a good meaty textbook help? Ethics make it impossible to assign different text to parts of the same class but in 1995, an opportunity arose to assess, within a class, the value of a textbook when the author took over a class for a sick colleague. The students already had a textbook (Heiman, 1992) which was adequate for the colleague whose teaching was largely based upon an intensive set of personally developed and detailed assignments but not for the model of teaching described above e.g. it did not cover basic concepts, confused theorems with principles, went 55 pages sans formula or even a symbol and then began with a most awkward, useless and difficult to memorize one (i.e. grouped data percentile calculation). The author therefore, informed the class that he would base his teaching upon a much more meaty and rigorous book (McClave and Dietrich, 1994) which was twice the bulk of the Heiman book and much more thorough. The mid-term was closed book and covered, for the most part, basic notions in probability (general and special laws of multiplication and addition of probability, derivation of Bayes theorem from definition of conditional probability, permutations, combinations binomial and Poisson distributions). This material was covered thoroughly in lectures two or three

119

times and almost all of it was covered well in the McClave and Dietrich book. However, there was not one word about this material in the text proper of the Heiman book and only the briefest mention in the appendix. Of the 31/47 students collecting their exam the next week, the mean and standard deviation percent score for the 13 people who bought the McClave and Dietrich book were 73.4 and 16.3 respectively and 59.9 and 20.9 respectively for the 18 students not buying the book (t = 1.95, df = 29, p < .03). (In order to ameliorate non-random assignment of student to book, those students not immediately picking up their exam - almost all failures who did not buy the book - were not considered, thus making it more difficult book buyers to be significantly better than non-book buyers.)

References

Baddeley, A.D., Grant, S., Wight, E., & Thomson, N. (1975). 'Imagery and visual working memory'. In, P.M.A. Rabbit & S. Dornic (eds.), *Attention and performance*, Vol. V. London: Academic Press.

Baddeley, A.D and Wilson D. (1994). 'When implicit learning fails: amnesia and the problem of error elimination'. *Neuropsychologia*. Vol 32, pp. 53 - 68.

Bower, G.H. (1970). 'Imagery as a relational organiser in associative learning'. *Journal of Verbal Learning and Verbal Behaviour*, Vol. 9, p. 529-533.

Graf, P. & Schachter, D.L. (1985). 'Implicit and explicit memory for new associations in normal and amnesic subjects'. *Journal of Experimental Psychology: Learning, Memory, and Cognition*, Vol. 11, pp. 501-518.

Heiman, G. W. (1992) *Basic Statistics for the Behavioural Sciences*. Houghton-Mifflin: Boston.

McClave, J. T. and Dietrich, F. H. (1994) *Statistics, 6th Edition*, Macmillan: New York.

Paivio, A. (1971). *Imagery and verbal processes*. New York: Holt, Rhinehart, and Winston (reprinted by Lawrence Erlbaum Associates Inc. in 1979).

Paivio, A., & Csapo, K. (1973). 'Picture superiority in free recall: imagery or dual coding?' *Cognitive Psychology*, Vol. 5, pp. 176-206.

Persinger, M. A. and Tiller, S. G. (1995). *Faculty paper presentation*, Psychology Department, Laurentian University, Feb, 1995.

Terrace, H. S. (1963). 'Discrimination learning with and without 'errors'. *Journal of Experimental Anal. Behaviour*, Vol. 6, pp. 1-27.

Valliant, P. M. and Scanlan, P. (1996) 'Personality, living arrangements, and alcohol use by first year university students'. *Social Behavior and Personality* Vol. 24, pp. 151 - 156.

Wilson W.T. and Mottin, J. 'Teaching statistics as cognitive psychotherapy'. *World Congress of Cognitive Therapy*. June, 1992.

16 Perceptual learning in inspection tasks

Penny Roling, Paul Sowden, Ian Davies,
Emre Özgen and Margaret Lawler
University of Surrey, UK

Abstract

In many inspection tasks such as examining medical images, acquisition of skill can be explained either by 'low-level' sensory learning, or by higher level conceptual learning, or by both. We report three studies requiring the detection of low contrast features, that investigated the extent to which perceptual learning in inspection tasks can be accounted for in terms of low-level processes alone. Experiment one examined transfer of learning across contrast level, experiment two investigated the importance of attention for learning, and experiment three studied transfer across direction of contrast. The findings support the idea that both low-level perceptual and higher level conceptual skills are significant components underlying detection of low contrast features in inspection tasks.

Introduction

Recent research has indicated that the perception of adults may be more 'plastic' than previously thought (Sagi and Tanne, 1994). Improvements in perceptual judgements as a result of practise have been termed perceptual learning. A distinction can be made between learning localised at early or 'low' levels of visual processing which is highly stimulus specific (e.g. Fahle and Edelman, 1993), and more general learning occurring at later stages of processing, for instance in cognitive processes (e.g. Sowden, Davies and Rose, in press).

The performance exhibited by experts on many inspection tasks learned as adults may, in part, result from perceptual learning. In the present research we concentrate on one such type of inspection task, the inspection of medical images. It is well established that extensive training is required to achieve expert performance on this task, but there is, as yet, no adequate theory of the processes underlying the learning

121

involved. The present series of studies address one part of this issue. Specifically, they examine the extent to which learning to discriminate low-contrast features in X-ray images can be accounted for by low-level processes alone.

Experiment one

This experiment examined whether perceptual learning for the detection of low contrast targets transfers across contrast level. Lack of transfer would be taken as a 'marker' for low-level learning.

Method

Sample, apparatus and stimuli There were twenty four subjects and all had normal or corrected to normal vision.

The stimuli were radiographs of perspex blocks (25mm by 25mm) positioned in a matrix of five by five squares displayed on a light box viewed from 30cm. Each square had a hole either exactly in the centre or midway along one of the four hemi-diagonals. The hole diameter was 0.35mm and the depth was either 0.50mm or 0.75mm. The deeper holes showed up as darker dots on the resulting radiograph. The five possible locations were used equally often for each hole depth. A schematic diagram of one radiograph is presented in figure 1.

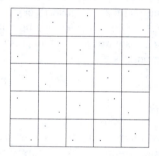

Figure 1   A schematic representation of the radiographs used

Design and procedure   Subjects were assigned to one of two groups and attended five experimental sessions. On days one to four, group one saw only the 0.50mm stimuli, and group two the 0.75mm stimuli. Subjects completed eight grids on the first four days and ten on day five. In each grid they were required to examine each square and decide in which location the target dot was located (five-alternative spatial forced-choice). The subjects recorded their decisions on a response sheet, and also measured the time taken to complete each grid. After each grid was completed the subjects were informed of their score for that grid. On day five group one viewed the 0.75mm stimuli (eight presentations), and group two observed the 0.50mm targets (eight presentations). Additionally, their performance was assessed for two of the grids they had trained on. Each subject received a token payment for participating in the experiment, plus an additional performance related payment.

Results

The following results are all from mixed design analyses of variance. The first stage of analysis examined the training days. Subjects' accuracy increased across days ($F_{3,66}=12.19$, p<0.001) and trials ($F_{7,154}=3.57$, p=0.001); see figure 2.

Subjects' inspection times decreased across days ($F_{3,66}=30.39$, p<0.009) and trials ($F_{7,154}=22$, p<0.001); see figure 3. These results suggest that the improvement in accuracy was not the consequence of a speed accuracy trade-off.

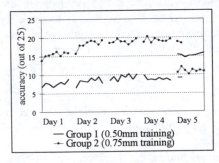

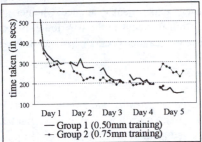

Figure 2   Mean accuracy scores   **Figure 3   Mean time scores**

The second stage of analysis compared the accuracy and speed measures for day one and day five (the 'transfer' day). There was an interaction between 'day' and 'group' ($F_{1,22}=38.54$, p<0.001). The difference in accuracy on day one and day five varies for the two groups in terms of both magnitude and direction; group ones' score is doubled, whilst group twos' decreases. Interestingly, group twos' performance on the 0.50mm stimuli is on average better on day five than group ones' is on day one, whereas for the 0.75mm stimuli there is little difference between the groups (figure 2).

Discussion

Overall the results from experiment one indicate that perceptual learning can occur through frequent exposure to stimuli. Further, they suggest that in training schedules for tasks such as medical image inspection, initial training on easier detection tasks (i.e. high contrast targets) will both improve performance on those tasks and transfer to ability in more difficult discriminations.

The asymmetry of transfer leaves open the question of how much of the learning was low-level. If perceptual learning for both stimulus contrasts was low-level then no transfer would be expected. Yet if the learning occurs at later stages of processing, then why is the transfer only in one direction? Consequently, experiment two attempted to establish the degree to which learning of dot detection is low-level through the use of a different marker for low-level learning.

Experiment two

One of the markers for low-level learning is that it occurs as a function of the number of targets to which a subject is exposed. However, it is not clear from the perceptual learning literature whether attention is required for learning to occur or whether mere exposure to the stimuli is sufficient. Consequently, using the same type of stimuli, the present experiment examined whether attention to the target dots was required for learning to occur in the way found in experiment one. Here, we assume attention to the target features occurs when the observer has knowledge of their presence.

Method

Sample, apparatus and stimuli   Forty-eight subjects were randomly allocated to one of three groups. They were paid £5 for participating and, in addition, they received a small performance related payment.

The stimuli were the same as in experiment one except that there was a hole in the centre of each square (to provide an example) in addition to an identical hole in one of the four corners, and there were four hole depths (0.1, 0.25, 0.5, 0.75 mm) with equal numbers of holes at each depth, in each grid. The task was thus a four-alternative spatial forced-choice.

Design and procedure   For all three groups of subjects the experiment was completed over two consecutive days. On day one the 'explicit learners' practised detecting the dots for eight grids (25 decisions per grid); the 'incidental learners' were required to examine the same images and rate which quadrant of each square was the 'streakiest' (the background of an X-ray is streaky), but they were not told anything about the dots; the 'control group' were required to complete the streakiness task on a set of images that were identical except that they had no dots in them. On day two all three groups completed the dot-detection task as for group one on day one.

Results and discussion

All of the following results are based on the findings of mixed design analyses of variance with repeated measures for the day of the experiment. A graph of the main results can be seen in figure 4.

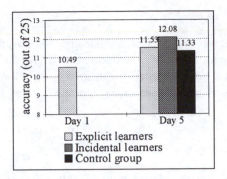

Figure 4   Mean accuracy scores

Do the explicit learners learn? The explicit learners detection accuracy improved across the two days ($F_{1,15}$=9.47, p=0.008) and there was no significant change in their search times. Thus, learning occurred which was not the result of a simple speed accuracy trade-off.

Do the incidental learners learn without attention? The incidental learners were more accurate at the dot detection task on day two than the explicit learners were on day one ($F_{1,30}$=6.31, p=0.018) and there was no significant difference between the two groups on day two. These results suggest the incidental learners have learned as much as the explicit learners as a result of simple exposure to the stimuli.

Do the control group learn? The control group were not significantly more accurate at the dot detection task on day two than the explicit learners were on day one. However, there was also no significant difference between the two groups on day two. Examination of the mean scores shown in figure 4 suggests that this group have learnt almost, but not quite, as much as the other two groups. This suggests that perhaps the learning that occurred in the present experiment was for the most part a general learning process, such as learning about the appearance of X-ray images. However, the fact that the control group may not have learned quite as much, suggests that there may have been a small amount of stimulus-specific learning for the other groups, which could occur incidentally, and which is consistent with, although not conclusive of, a low-level learning process.

Experiment three

Early in the visual pathway many cells are selective for direction of contrast (Kuffler, 1953). Consequently, this experiment used degree of transfer across direction of contrast as a marker for level of learning. A lack of transfer from targets at one direction of contrast to another may indicate learning at a low-level of processing.

Method

Sample, apparatus and stimuli   There were 12 subjects. All had normal or corrected to normal vision.

The stimulus was a digitised version of the Nijmegen CDMAM-phantom (Thijssen, 1992) depicted in figure 5. In each square of the grid are two discs, one in the centre and one in a corner. On one axis of the grid discs vary in size and on the other in contrast. Both discs in a square are identical. Positive and negative contrast versions of the image were created, and were displayed on a computer monitor.

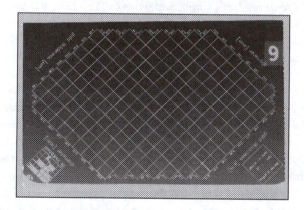

Figure 5   A diagram of the Nijmegen CDMAM-phantom

Design and procedure   The subjects were assigned to one of two groups, and attended five experimental sessions on consecutive days. On days one to four group one saw only positive contrast stimuli and group two negative contrast stimuli. On day five subjects inspected stimuli of the opposite contrast to those they had trained on. Subjects were required to examine each square and decide in which of the four possible corners the target disc was located (four-alternative spatial forced-choice).

Feedback was provided in terms of their total accuracy and detection speed. Each subject received a token payment for participating in the experiment, plus an extra performance related incentive.

Results

The following results are all from mixed design analyses of variance and covariance. Subjects' accuracy increased and detection time decreased across the four days of training ($F_{1,10}$=4.19, p=0.014): learning occurred, and it was not due to a speed accuracy trade-off (figures 6 and 7).

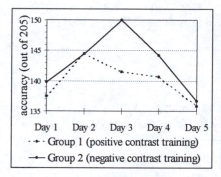

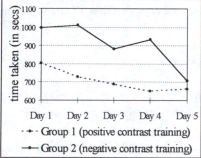

Figure 7   Mean time scores   **Figure 6   Mean accuracy scores**

In the analysis of transfer there was a significant decrease in detection time between day one and day five ($F_{1,10}$=6.03, p=0.034). There was no significant change in accuracy. This could indicate that subjects are trading detection accuracy for a considerable improvement on detection speed. But the integration of time and accuracy in the analysis of covariance made no difference to the effects observed in the separate analyses of accuracy and time.

Discussion

In summary, an improvement in this task occurs with training, but any gains in accuracy do not transfer across direction of contrast. Possibly this is an indication of learning at a low-level of processing, where channels are tuned for direction of contrast. Alternatively an explanation may be found in the idea of 'cognitive set' - subjects repeatedly inspect stimuli at one level of contrast and may find it difficult to change to the opposite direction of contrast.

Penny Roling et al.

General discussion

We have demonstrated in three experiments that perceptual learning occurs in the task of searching for low contrast targets presented against a noisy background. Experiments one and three suggest that part of the learning is low-level as indicated by the lack of transfer across contrast level and across direction of contrast. Experiment two supports this also, but shows that considerable learning which is not related to specific target features can occur. Further research will be required if we are to establish more clearly the relative contributions of these different levels of learning. To the extent that improvement in detection of features in medical images rests on low-level perceptual learning it may be advantageous to modify existing training programmes to incorporate a larger number of practice trials in addition to the tutorial approach that is currently adopted (Sowden and Davies, 1995).

References

Fahle, M. and Edelman, S. (1993) 'Long-term learning in vernier acuity: effects of stimulus orientation, range and of feedback'. *Vision Research*, Vol. 33, pp. 397-412.

Kuffler, S.W. (1953) 'Discharge patterns and functional organization of the mollusc eye'. *Journal of Neurophysiology*, Vol.16, pp. 37-68.

Sagi, D. and Tanne, D. (1994) 'Perceptual learning: learning to see'. *Current Opinion in Neurobiology*, Vol. 4, pp. 195-199.

Sowden, P.T. and Davies, I.R.L. (1995) 'The nature of perceptual skills in screening mammography: implications for training'. *Proceedings of the International Society for Optical Engineering*, Vol. 2436, pp. 143-154.

Sowden, P.T., Davies, I.R.L. and Rose, D. (in press) 'Perceptual learning of stereoacuity'. *Perception*.

Thijssen, M.A.O., Bijkerk, K.R., & Lindeijer J.M. (1992) *Handleiding CDMAM-phantom type 3.2, Project Kwaliteitsbewaking Mammografie - Sectie Fysica en Informatica*, Instituut voor Radiodiagnostiek, Academisch Ziekenhuis Nijmegen St. Radboud.

17 The operator's analysis of the structure of a multi-dimensional video image of a mosaic subject area given the effects of hidden regularities

Anna Molotova, Igor Schukin and Tatiana Ekonomova
Scientific and Technical Centre of System Modelling
Moscow, Russia

Introduction

The problem of the analysis of complex organized patterns of information represented as images to an operator is very real for ergonomic, scientific and technical systems, that solve intellectual problems (management, examination, data interpretation, diagnostics, monitoring, etc). It is related to the visualization of multidimensional data bulks obtained in the modelling of the systems specified.

The typologies of visually complex organized information are many fold and includes such characteristic signs as pattern dimension, its static or dynamic nature, colour and gradational properties and several others (e.g. Grishin, 1982). The analysis of pattern video information is undertaken by an operator, as a rule, in conditions of incomplete and unclear information and a deficiency of decision making time to ascertain the depth of understanding required to ascertain the pattern's structure. In addition, sometimes, as the investigation sometimes show, the analysis of patterns of video information is impeded by the effects of hidden general rules (e.g. Iskhakova, Molotova and Schukin, 1985). Lately the effect hidden regularities has become widely known thanks to the 'magic eye' technique (N.E. Thing Enterprises, 1993).

Effective training of operators in the analysis of complex organized patterns is possible only with due regard for indicated features of working conditions.

Model of pattern information

The extreme variety of visual patterns makes it necessary to have an image of some universal structure in the training system, that allows the researcher to adapt it practically to any subject area. We selected a dotty model as such an image. This universal image is a pattern symbolic model, a syntactic form of conceptions linked with the presentation of complex multidimensional space and time related structure.

The dotty model with a great quantity of dots (between 100-1000) presents enough pattern information to represent the structure of pattern information found in such areas of science and engineering as economical geography, astronomy and fluid dynamics.

In the general case, the origin of structural peculiarities in information patterns may have its roots both in the pattern element's interaction and in specific external limitations (impact) on a set of pattern elements (the theory of Ramsey) (e.g. Graham and Spencer, 1990).

If the operator visually detects some structural peculiarity, then the training process is linked with the development of skills in using the known technical means for a more detailed study of this peculiarity. The situation significantly changes if the operator does not visually detect structural peculiarity of pattern . It should be noted that we generally mean the case where the structural peculiarity objectively and absolutely distinctly shows itself in the information pattern. Its non-detection is linked with the mechanisms of human vision. It is precisely this fact that explains disorder illusion (e.g. Iskhakova, Molotova and Schukin, 1985). The origin of disorder illusion is linked with the fact that pattern elements widely separated within the range of parameters can correspond to the same object (the interval of parameters values is multi-linked). It concerns the problem of identification of the objects during their evolution, to which much attention has been paid when developing the concepts of time.[1]

Let's refer to figure 1 for more details. figure shows the pattern of information with disarrangement of elements, figure 2(a) shows a pattern with a hidden structural peculiarity: the image is a set of pairs of dots with a fixed distance between the pairs. Such an image is a pattern model of information about the parameters of the movement of an aggregate of objects (the pairs of dots conform to the spatial location of an object at two different times). The image from the figure 2(a) may be interpreted as an object pattern, which was subjected to the simplest structural modification.

The example of structural features in figure 2(a) is the simplest, the pattern is a compound of dotty groups. However, the structure of information patterns can be much more complex. The patterns can contain associations (groups of groups), groups of associations, etc, and the elements of groups can be different. In figure 2(b), the groups contain dark and light elements.

---

[1] We suppose that the disorder illusion may also take place for acoustic and tactile patterns.

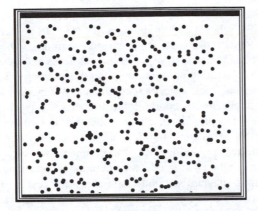

Figure 1   The dotty picture of pattern information

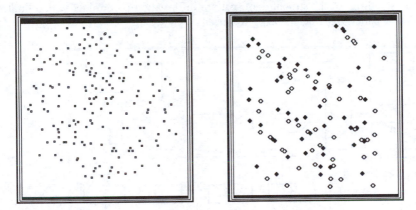

Figure 2(a & b)   Models that have structural regularities

To describe the whole variety of the structural versions, it is common practice to use statistical and morphological methods, and present the structure as graph, which is based on the introduction of relationships of order for the set of structural components of the pattern. With the statistical approach the pattern structure is defined by the set of S-dotty correlation functions, that allows us to analyse space-and-time related regular and stochastic dynamics and the fractal nature of pattern.

Description of the system

Training in the recognition of complex organized pattern information analysis (interpretation, recognition and 'understanding'), under conditions where there are

131

hidden regularities, is undertaken in accordance with conceptual scheme shown in figure 3 (e.g. Molotova, Schukin and Ekonomova, 1994). The system developed on this basis provides intellectual support for the person trained ('the student') to widen the possibilities of visual analysis by technical tools and other additional ones (e.g. Bohr, 1958). The program module of dotty pattern spectrum analysis serves as an 'additional' tool. Parameters of spectrum analysis module are specified by the student. The intellectual support of the trainer ('the teacher') includes controlling program tools that provide: planning of the training script to cover all the area of change in pattern parameters; limiting the number of pattern parameters under investigation; decreasing the number of experiments while simultaneously increasing statistical reliability; taking into consideration the influence of abilities of the person's training (having best and worst performances); and taking into account the complexity of decisions. During the training process records of the student's answers, including the time for decision-making, are kept. According to the results of the automated processing of the records, a model of student's understanding of the structure of pattern information is forming, with a limited value of pattern parameters being specified.

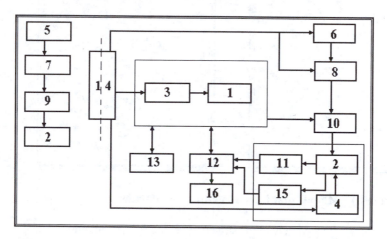

Figure 3   The structural scheme of the system

Key: 1-researcher; 2-operator; 3-intellectual support for researcher; 4-intellectual support for operator: methods for the image structure analysis; 5-real scene; 6-the image of the real scene; 7-means to observe the real scene; 8-model of the observation and reflection means ; 9-means for reflection of information; 10- image generator; 11-presentation of the image structure by operator; 12-analysis of results; 13-forming results; 14-expert; 15 -operator's actions; 16 -model of the perception of pattern information by operator.

Some results of the research

Let us offer some information about the manifestation of the effect of hidden regularities.

In the absence of a priori information about a structural peculiarity, the simplest structural peculiarity relating to the availability of pairs can be revealed by the operator at $l/lo \leq 0,2$, where $l =$ the size of the pair, $lo =$ the average distance between the centres of the pairs. At $l/lo > 0,2$ the regularity of the lay-out of dots which is related to the availability of pairs, cannot be revealed (disorder illusion). This conclusion also holds true for more complicated groups.

If the operator is aware of the presence of a structural peculiarity, for instance, in the following form: 'this picture consists of the pairs of dots (or triplets of dots, or quadruplets of dots)', the likelihood of revealing the groups of dots diminished in a monotonic sequence from 0,9 at $l/lo = 0,2$ to 0,0 at $l/lo = 1$.

The formation of data bulk patterns using the method proposed is performed on the basis of the inter-supplementary results of the cognitive actions of the operator within direct and reverse (supplementary) spaces. It is of importance that the operator interacts with a video pattern exactly within the two spaces, even though he/she previously revealed a distinct structural peculiarity in one of them.

As an example we refer to figure 4 demonstrating a visualized result of cognitive actions of the operator in the Fourier space and is concerned with the video pattern in figure 2(a). The stripes in the Fourier spectrum picture (supplementary, reverse space) mean that the video pattern in figure 2(a) contains a hidden structural regularity: vertically oriented pairs of dots.

The methods proposed for the analysis of the structure of multidimensional video patterns have found applications in:

- investigations into turbulent flows using the method of repeated exposures;
- the analysis of the functioning of electronic systems;
- the analysis of the structure of micro objects in medicine and biology;
- the analysis of the structure of pictures in astronomy.

Let us consider some examples of two of the above mentioned areas of applications.

In fluid dynamics of two-phase flows, there is a method of measuring the speed of the flow of particles based on a two-exposure photographic or holographic picture of the flow. The field of the speeds of the flow of particles is presented in intervals between the pictures of particles taken in the course of the first and second exposures, i.e. by the distances between certain (two-exposure) pairs of particles. When the concentration of the particles in the flow is great enough, the structure of the two-exposure picture is rather complicated even with a simple field of speeds, significantly hindering the realization of trustworthy results in visual analysis. The exterior of such two-exposure pictures of real flows closely resembles those shown in figure 2(a and b). The proposed system of the pattern structure analysis has found an application in creating an automated test bench for measuring a speed of the flow of particles.

133

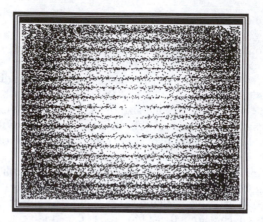

Figure 4   Fourier spectrum

The above method was also used for getting an integrated representation of a radio electronic environment generated by the aggregate of interacting sources of radiation, each radiator being a dot in multidimensional space of parameters of the signal.

References

Bohr, N. (1958), *Atomic physics and human knowledge.* Wiley: New York.

Graham R., & Spencer J.(1990), 'Ramsey theory'. *Scientific American*, Vol.1, p.236.

Grishin, V. (1982), *The image analysis of experiment data.* Nauka: Moscow.

Iskhakova, L., Molotova, A., & Schukin, I. (1985), 'Research of some distinction in perception of dotty pictures'. *Autometry*, Vol. 4, pp. 94-96.

Molotova, A., Schukin, I., & Ekonomova T. (1994), *Proceedings of the 12th Triennial Congress of International Ergonomics Association.* Vol. 4, pp. 313-314.

N.E. Thing Enterprises (1993), *Magic eye.* Michael Joseph: London.

18 Target recognition performance following whole-views, part-views, and both-views training

Sehchang Hah, Deborah A. Reisweber, Jose A. Picart
and Harry Zwick*
United States Military Academy
*United States Army Medical Research Detachment

Abstract

This study compared participants' target recognition performance after training with three different views of target stimuli. In experiment 1 target recognition training was conducted using whole-views or both whole- and part-views of armoured vehicles. Participants then completed a whole-view target recognition test. Participants' target recognition time and accuracy were measured. Recognition times for both training conditions were similar. However, the whole-view group committed significantly fewer target identification errors than the both-views group at the visual ranges of 104, 146, and 264 metres. In experiment 2, each picture was presented one at a time and a part-view group was added. The mean recognition times of the whole-view and the both-views groups were significantly better than that of the part-view only group. There was an interaction effect between visual ranges and vehicle images. There was no statistically significant difference in accuracy among the three groups except at the 264 metre visual range, where the part-view group committed more errors than the other groups. These results suggest that target recognition training for armoured vehicle images should use only whole-view images at different visual ranges.

Introduction

The objective of this study was to test the hypothesis that presenting part-views in addition to whole-views of armoured vehicles images during training would improve the recognition speed and accuracy of whole-view targets.

135

Rensink and Enns (1995) proposed that the initial pre-attentive processes in visual processing are driven by certain grouping mechanisms. They concluded that observers scanned stimuli based on the 'assemblies' of the whole image. Such perceptual processing is fast and automatic and does not access the primitive features or elements in the images (Treisman, 1980; Marr, 1982). In contrast, Reed and Johnson (1975) asked participants to identify part-images imbedded in a larger object. The part-images had been presented earlier during training sessions. They concluded that part-views of an image may be processed separately if the part has a distinct functional or configurational role in the whole-view image. Similarly, Farah, Tanaka, and Drain (1995) presented data to suggest that memorizing part images influences target identification performance. They presented evidence that memorizing part-views of faces helped observers identify the inverted faces better than memorizing whole-views of faces.

During combat, anti-tank gunners are often confronted with enemy targets that on a global level may appear similar to friendly vehicles. Consequently, anti-tank gunners must conduct more detailed processing of the enemy target to identify parts of the vehicle that differentiate it from friendly vehicles. In this study, we used armoured vehicles with distinctive components or parts, such as the turret and gun barrel, that have a functional role in the whole image. Although observers may not pay attention to the parts of images during the pre-attentive processes, they will process the detailed parts of an object only if viewing the whole image does not result in target recognition (Cave and Kosslyn, 1993).

Experiment 1

Method

Participants Sixty cadets enrolled in an introductory psychology course volunteered to participate in this experiment for research participation credit. Half of the cadets were assigned to the Both-views training group and half to the Whole-view training group. All participants had normal or corrected-to-normal vision. Their ages were from 17 to 22.

Equipment An IBM PC 386 Compatible with a customized image analysis board installed was used to run this experiment and collect performance data. The equipment captured and digitized images at a 512 x 512 resolution.

Stimuli Images of six armoured vehicle models of 1/35 scale were captured and converted into digital data files. The armoured vehicles were the Merkava, Challenger, M1, Leopard, Bradley, and T-72 (figure 1). For the part-view group the vehicle images were segmented into three parts as shown in figure 2. The model images were taken to simulate the visual distances of 56 m, 104 m, 146 m, 185 m,

224 m, and 264 m (figure 3). The simulated visual range of images in figure 1 was 56 m. Participants observed the images on a monitor screen at a distance of two metres. A chin rest at the table was used. The luminance of a tank at the 56 m visual range was about 3.5 Ft Lambert and the background at the monitor screen was about 9.2 Ft Lambert at a three-degree aperture.

Figure 1   Whole-view stimuli. They are T72 (Russia), Challenger (England), M1 (U.S.A.), Bradley (U.S.A.), Merkava (Israel), and Leopard (Germany) from the top-right clockwise

Procedure   During training for the both-views group, participants observed a whole-view and three partial views (figure 2). The whole-view group observed four identical whole-view images of their targets. Twenty-four target-image displays (six visual ranges x four repetitions) were presented to both groups (figure 3). Each display remained on the screen for 10 seconds.

During test sessions participants were asked to identify the target image by selecting one of two whole-view images displayed side by side on the monitor screen. Following presentation, participants were required to press a response key and state orally which of the images 'left,' 'right,' 'both,' or 'none' was the target image. There were 100 test trials. A target image appeared 10 times on both sides of the display and five distractor images appeared two times on both sides of the

137

display. This same procedure was used for all simulated visual ranges except the 56m range.

Figure 2 Sample both-views of M1 stimuli   **Figure 3 M1 image at 224m**

Results

The mean recognition times for both groups were similar as shown in figure 4. The recognition time at the distance of 104 m for the whole-view group was faster than the both-views group, but the difference was not significant. The chi-square (χ^2) test on the correctness of the two groups showed significant results at the distances of 104 m (χ^2=7.34; df=1; n=1200; p< 0.01), 146 m (χ^2=7.43; df=1; n=1200, p< 0.01), and 264 m (χ^2=4.90; df=1; n=1200; p< 0.05), (figure 5).

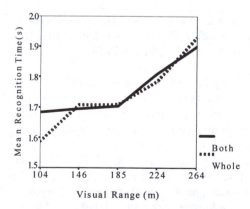

Figure 4 Mean recognition time for the whole-view group and the both-views group across simulated visual ranges in experiment 1

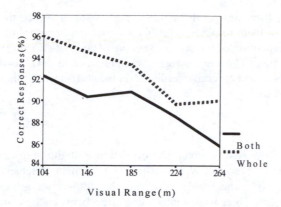

Figure 5   Percentage of correct responses for the both-views and the whole-view groups of experiment 1

Experiment 2

Method

Participants   Sixty cadets enrolled in an introductory psychology course volunteered to participate in the experiment and received research participation credit. In this experiment participants were assigned to three different training groups: whole-view, part-view, and both-views groups. Twenty participants were randomly assigned to each group.

Equipment   Same as in experiment 1.

Stimuli   The same stimuli used in experiment 1 were used except images of the Bradley Fighting Vehicle were not used in experiment 2.

Procedure   For all training groups one of the five armoured vehicle images was randomly selected and assigned to observers as their target image. A total of five sessions were conducted. The second, third, and fourth sessions were training sessions and the fifth session was the main data collection session. In the first session, participants performed a simple choice reaction time task of identifying a circle or a square displayed on a monitor screen. In the second session they observed target images one at a time, presented as either part-views, whole-views, or both-views depending on the group the participant was assigned to. In the third session, they were tested with all of the target and non-target images presented in the same view format as in the second session one at a time. They received feedback on the

139

Sehchang Hah et al.

correctness of their responses. If the participants were incorrect, the image was displayed again for them to observe further without time constraint. The fourth session was the repetition of the second session. The final session was the data-collecting test session. The target images were presented in a whole-view one at a time and participants did not receive feedback on the correctness of their responses. There were 30 test trials.

Results

The repeated measures ANOVA on recognition time with the simple reaction time described earlier as a covariance was significant on the main effect ($F_{2, 44} = 6.41$, $p < 0.005$), (figure 6). The whole-view and the both-views groups were not significantly different. There was an interaction effect between the distance and the non-target armoured tank images. The chi-square test showed significant difference only at the visual range of 264 m ($\chi^2=6.78$; df=1; n=300; p< 0.05). The part-view group had significantly more errors than the other groups. At other visual ranges, there was no significant difference.

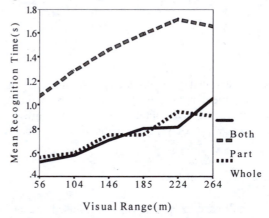

Figure 6 **Mean correct recognition time for the part-view, whole-view and both-view groups across different visual ranges**

Conclusion and discussion

The results of this study suggest that:
(i) Training with whole-views resulted in better target recognition performance relative to training with part-views or both views.
(ii) Participants could not or did not extract invariant characteristics of images across different visual ranges.

140

The results suggest that when participants are trained with whole-view stimuli they form stronger schemas that allow more efficient processing of target images.

References

Cave, C. B. and Kosslyn, S. M. (1993). 'The role of parts and special relations in object identification', *Perception*, Vol. 22, pp. 229-248.

Farah, M. J., Tanaka, J. W., and Drain, H. M. (1995). 'What causes the face inversion effect?' *Journal of Experimental Psychology: Human Perception and Performance,* Vol. 21, pp. 628-634.

Marr, D. (1982). *Vision*. New York: Freeman.

Reed, S. K., and Johnson, J. A. (1975). 'Detection of parts in patterns and images'. *Memory and Cognition,* Vol. 3, pp. 569-575.

Rensink, R. A. and Enns, J. T. (1995). 'Preemption effects in visual search: Evidence for low-level grouping'. *Psychological Review,* Vol. 102, pp. 101-130.

Treisman, A. and Gerald, G . (1980). 'A feature integration theory of attention'. *Cognitive Psychology,* Vol. 12, pp. 97-136.

Acknowledgements

The authors wish to express their thanks to Maj. Benjamin A. Kirkland for help in running experiments. Also, they appreciate the administrative and technical support provided by Ms. Mary J. Ward and Mr. David L. Haack, and are indebted to Ms. Shirley Bonsell and Dr. Stephen Landowne at the Office of the Dean, Academic Research Division, for their continuous encouragement, and administrative and financial support for the research. Finally, the authors wish to thank for Mr. Dan Monroe at Delta Technologies, Colorado Springs, Colorado for his hardware and software support and Mr. Jerry Molchany at the US Army Medical Research Detachment at Brooks Air Force Base, Texas for his software support.

Part Three
MEDICAL ERGONOMICS

19 Depth perception and indirect viewing: reflections on keyhole surgery

Anthony H. Reinhardt-Rutland, Judith M. Annett
and Mervyn Gifford*
University of Ulster at Jordanstown, UK
*Eastern Health and Social Services Board, Belfast, UK

Abstract

In keyhole surgery, the site of operation is viewed at a TV monitor. Depth perception is based on pictorial information, perhaps enhanced by motion, while monocular and binocular information convey the monitor's flatness. Only relative depth can be conveyed and pictorial information can mislead. However, depth perception may be adequate if target tissue is well-separated, with well-defined edges and familiar form. Stereoscopic viewing systems now exist, but are problematic because binocular disparity conflicts with convergence and monocular information. Another strategy to improve precision is to employ individuals lacking binocular function: since there is redundancy in depth information, such individuals seem to compensate.

Introduction

Keyhole surgery is performed remotely. Trocars, narrow-bore tubes containing the camera and instruments, are inserted in the patient to reach the site of operation, which is viewed at a TV monitor. Compared with conventional surgery, incisions are minimal: pain, infection and post-operative care may be reduced. However, the development of keyhole surgery has been technology-driven with little consideration for human information processing. Compared with conventional surgery, seven-fold increases in complication rates following keyhole surgery have been reported (Antia, 1994). The most popular procedure, cholecystectomy (gall-bladder removal), presents a risk of potentially fatal rupture of the bile duct (Treacy & Johnson, 1995).

Among information-processing problems is the loss of kinesthetic information in remote manipulation of instruments; this may contribute to muscular disorders among

145

practitioners (Crombie & Graves, 1996). Also, depth perception is likely to be affected. This is considered in the present paper.

Depth information in normal viewing conditions

Depth information can be classified as *monocular, binocular, motion* and *pictorial*. The first three types are physiological - consequences of inborn design-features; pictorial information refers to depth conveyed in two-dimensional representations. In normal viewing, the various types of information are in accord, so there is redundancy. Hence, depth perception is feasible during attenuated viewing. Note, however, that keyhole surgery entails conflict between types of depth information, because of the TV monitor's flatness. The investigation of depth perception often entails such conflict, as exemplified by stereograms (Julesz, 1971). Another means of investigation is to exclude types of information, except that under consideration. In fact, this is not straightforward. For example, binocular distance adjustments may affect monocular viewing (Predebon, 1994).

Monocular information arises from distance adjustments such as accommodation, the adjustment of lens curvature to maintain a sharp retinal image. Given the facility with which monocular adjustments are performed, monocular information might be expected to influence depth perception strongly. This can best be tested in highly attenuated conditions - static-monocular viewing of simplified stimuli, such as bright points in the dark: they are so small that change in their visual size with distance is not discernible. In fact, such conditions elicit the *equidistance tendency*: the differences in depth are hardly discerned (Reinhardt-Rutland, 1996a,b). Although monocular information in itself barely affects depth perception, it does seem to interact with pictorial information and probably contributes to problems in stereoscopic viewing (see below); such interactions are pertinent to keyhole surgery.

Binocular information includes convergence - rotation of the eyes to avoid diplopia of the fixated object - and binocular disparity - the two retinal images differ because of the separation of the eyes in the head. Binocular information is highly effective for closely viewed objects (Reinhardt-Rutland, 1990), so its loss in keyhole surgery is likely to be deleterious. However, binocular depth perception can be much influenced by pictorial information (see below). Convergence and binocular disparity have been investigated separately. Although convergence is performed effortlessly, it is generally believed not to convey depth (Logvinenko & Belopolskii, 1994). Nonetheless, convergence, like monocular information, seems to interact with other information (Predebon, 1994). Binocular disparity is important in depth perception, as is evident from the stereograms developed last century by Wheatstone and the more recent random-dot anaglyphs, paired patterns of densely-spaced dots (Julesz, 1971). The conflict in depth information in stereoscopic viewing leads to a generally delayed depth effect; furthermore, long periods of stereoscopic viewing are tiring. These points are considered later.

As the observer moves with respect to static objects, the objects elicit systematic *motion information* (motion parallax) at the retina: rates of visual motion are greater for near objects than for distant objects. Related information arises for a surface slanted in depth to the frontal plane: the visual geometry transforms with the observer's motion, according to the degree of slant. Although motion information is believed to be important in depth perception (Simpson, 1993), empirical evidence is equivocal. Evidence suggesting that motion information is important arises from depth-from-motion simulations: dots presented on a VDU screen move systematically as the monocular observer makes side-to-side head motions. Even minimal head motion elicits full depth perception (Rogers & Graham, 1982; Rogers & Rogers, 1992).

In contrast, studies in which moving-monocular observers view *real* stimuli suggest that motion information is rather ineffective, because of the pictorial information that real stimuli contain (Reinhardt-Rutland, 1995). An inherent limitation with motion information is that it accumulates as the observer moves: other types of information are in principle available to perception *immediately*. Also, visual motion is ambiguous, since it may be due to object motion rather than observer motion (Reinhardt-Rutland, 1988). Motion available in keyhole surgery is probably too restricted to be effective, but it may enhance pictorial information (see below).

A simple form of *pictorial information* is an edge: this indicates discontinuity in depth. Higher-order examples exploit edges: occlusion - a nearer object obscures a more distant object along the line of sight - and relative visual size - two objects of similar physical size but at different distances differ in visual size. A surface's orientation-in-depth can be determined if the surface's shape is known; for example, a slanted rectangular surface elicits a trapezoidal image the angles of which depend on the degree and direction of slant. However, pictorial information can mislead: different visual sizes may arise from objects of different physical sizes at the same distance from the observer, while a trapezoidal visual image may arise from a frontal trapezoidal surface. Despite this, pictorial information is often crucial in depth perception (Reinhardt-Rutland, 1995; Stevens & Brookes, 1988). Furthermore, pictorial information can be subtle. Observers judged the orientations-in-depth of unpatterned triangular surfaces of fixed height and variable length. In contrast with rectangular surfaces, orientation-in-depth is not in principle computable: visual length of a triangular surface only conveys *difference* in horizontal orientation-in-depth when triangular surfaces are compared. In fact, significant differences in judgments occurred without comparison: observers apparently employ internalised models of triangular surfaces (Reinhardt-Rutland, 1996a,b).

Depth-from-motion simulations may rely on pictorial information, rather than on motion parallax. For example, discontinuity in motion of dots conveys an edge, denoting difference in depth. Motion information should convey which side of the edge is closer, but pictorially the difference is ambiguous. Rogers and Rogers (1992) report the latter: additional information must be supplied to disambiguate the depth difference. Thus, motion may enhance pictorial information. In *kinetic* occlusion, a relatively distant object undergoes varying occlusion and disocclusion by a relatively close object, as the observer moves with respect to the objects (Gibson, 1979). This may be important in keyhole surgery as an instrument is manipulated around target tissue.

Depth information in keyhole surgery

The range of depth information in keyhole surgery is restricted: binocular information and monocular information convey the flatness of the TV monitor's screen. Motion parallax is not feasible, because motion is likely to be restricted. Therefore, keyhole surgery depends mainly on pictorial information, perhaps elaborated by motion contributing to occlusion, for example. Pictorial information is important and subtle during normal viewing, although this can mislead.

In principle, most depth information can convey *absolute* depth - the observer can determine the precise distance of a given point - but this requires scaling of depth information. For example, the visual size of an object can convey its absolute distance pictorially, if the observer can exploit the relationship between visual size and known physical size of the object. In keyhole surgery, this may be difficult, because visual size is dependent not only on physical size, but also on the precise distance of the camera from the target tissue. This distance will need to vary: there are opposing requirements for a sizeable field of view - requiring 'zooming out' of the site of operation - and of magnification - requiring 'zooming in' to the site of operation. Given this issue and the other points made above, only a degree of *relative* depth between two or more points is plausible in keyhole surgery.

The feasibility of keyhole surgery requires consideration on a case-by-case basis. Pictorial information may be adequate when the site of operation consists of well-separated tissue offering well-defined edges and familiar shapes. In cholecystectomy, pressurised gas is applied to separate the gall-bladder from surrounding tissue, but even here there are worrying problems, as noted earlier (Antia, 1994; Treacy & Johnson, 1995).

Stereoscopic viewing

Since binocular disparity is important in normal depth perception, stereoscopic viewing systems - in effect, real-time equivalents of Wheatstone stereograms - have been developed. In one system, the crucial feature is rapid switching between the eyes of two views of the operation; to exploit the stereoscopic information, spectacles employing liquid-crystal technology are worn. One eye views one camera's output at one instant and the other eye views the other camera's output at the next instant: the switching rate is fast enough to permit stable perception (Wenzl, Lehner, Vry, Pateisky, Sevelda, & Hussein, 1994).

148

However, as indicated earlier, stereoscopic viewing differs in important ways from normal viewing: monocular information and convergence convey the flatness of the TV monitor's screen, which conflicts with binocular disparity conveying depth (Reinhardt-Rutland & Ehrenstein, 1996). One of the outcomes is the fact that stereoscopic depth can take a while to achieve - important if critical stages of operation require switching between normal and stereoscopic viewing. Also, prolonged stereoscopic viewing is tiring: the duration of operations may need to be short. Wenzl et al's (1994) comments concur with these observations. The requirement to zoom in and zoom out of the site of operation exacerbates these problems. The changes in binocular disparity from zooming in and out are much the same as if the observer viewing normally were moving towards and away from the site of operation. However, the latter would entail a systematic relationship between changing binocular disparity and changing monocular information and convergence - not possible in keyhole surgery since the operator is essentially static.

Development of stereoscopic systems continues: a new system projects images direct to each eye (Coghlan, 1995). As in systems relying on liquid-crystal spectacles, the conflict between binocular disparity, convergence and monocular information can be uncomfortable (Regan & Price, 1994).

Operators lacking binocular function

It is worth exploring the capacity of the 10% of the general population without normal binocular function (Sachsenweger & Sachsenweger, 1991). Such individuals are rarely reported as being seriously handicapped in accurate depth judgments. Thus, permanently monocular drivers do not suffer higher casualty-rates than binocular drivers (McKnight, Shinar, & Hilburn, 1991). Because visual depth can be conveyed by each of the different types of information, adequate depth perception may be maintained if one type of depth information is lost (Marotta, Perrot, Nicolle, Servos, & Goodale, 1995).

For normally-sighted operators viewing at a TV monitor conflicts with normal binocular viewing: such operators may never adapt fully to the loss of binocular depth information at TV monitors. In contrast, permanently monocular individuals *always* rely on non-binocular information. Therefore, they should not have to adjust to viewing TV monitors to the same degree.

Concluding summary

Keyhole surgery depends on pictorial information, perhaps enhanced by motion. Its effectiveness is reduced by the flatness of the TV monitor and scaling for absolute depth is a problem: only a degree of relative depth perception is feasible. Also, pictorial information can mislead. Therefore, each case of keyhole surgery should be considered carefully; it may be adequate in cases of well-defined and well-spaced tissue with familiar visual characteristics. The introduction of stereoscopic viewing must be regarded with caution, given that it differs from normal vision: it can be delayed and uncomfortable. Alternatively, it may be worth considering operators without binocular function: they seem able to compensate for this loss and may be better performers in keyhole surgery than normally-sighted individuals.

References

Antia, N. H. (1994). 'Keyhole surgery'. *Lancet,* No. 344, pp. 596-597.

Coghlan, A. (1995). 'Keyhole surgeons enter new dimension'. *New Scientist, No. 48. pp. 2007-*2027.

Crombie, N. A.-M., & Graves, R. J. (1996). 'Ergonomics of keyhole surgical instruments - patient friendly, but surgeon unfriendly?' In, S. A. Robsertson (ed.), *Contemporary Ergonomics 1996.* Taylor & Francis: London.

Gibson, J. J. (1979). *The ecological approach to visual perception.* Houghton-Mifflin: Boston MA.

Julesz, B. 1971, *Foundations of Cyclopean Perception.* Chicago University Press; Chicago.

Logvinenko, A. D., & Belopolskii, V. I. (1994). 'Convergence as a cue for distance', *Perception,* Vol. 23, pp. 207-217.

Marotta, J. J., Perrot, T. S., Nicolle, D., Servos, P., & Goodale, M. A. (1995). 'Adapting to monocular vision: Grasping with one eye'. *Experimental Brain Research,* Vol. 104, pp. 107-114.

McKnight, A. J., Shinar, D. & Hilburn, B. (1991). 'The visual and driving performance of monocular and binocular heavy-duty truck drivers'. *Accident Analysis and Prevention,* Vol. 23, pp. 225-237.

Predebon, J. (1994). 'Convergence responses to monocularly viewed objects: Implications for distance perception'. *Perception,* Vol. 23, p. 303-319.

Regan, E. C., & Price, K. R. (1994). 'Some side effects of immersion Virtual Reality'. *Aviation, Space and Environmental Medicine,* Vol. 65, p. 527-530.

Reinhardt-Rutland, A. H. (1988). 'Induced movement in the visual modality: an overview'. *Psychological Bulletin,* Vol. 103, pp. 57-71.

Reinhardt-Rutland, A. H. (1990). 'Detecting orientation of a surface: The rectangularity postulate and primary depth cues'. *Journal of General Psychology,* Vol. 117, pp. 391-401.

Reinhardt-Rutland, A. H. (1995). 'Perceiving the orientation in depth of real surfaces: Background pattern affects motion and pictorial information'. *Perception,* Vol. 24, pp. 405-414.

Reinhardt-Rutland, A. H. (1996a). 'Depth judgments of triangular surfaces during moving monocular viewing'. *Perception,* Vol. 25, pp. 27-35.

Reinhardt-Rutland, A. H. (1996b). 'Perceiving the orientation-in-depth of triangular surfaces: Static-Monocular, moving-monocular, and static-binocular viewing'. *Journal of General Psychology,* Vol. 123, pp. 19-28.

Reinhardt-Rutland, A. H., & Ehrenstein, W. H. (1996). 'Depth perception and stereoscopic systems for minimally invasive surgery'. In, S. A. Robertson (ed.), *Contemporary Ergonomics 1996.* Taylor & Francis: London.

Rogers, B., & Graham, M. (1982). 'Similarities between motion parallax and stereopsis in human depth perception'. *Vision Research, Vol. 22,* pp. 261-270.

Rogers, S., & Rogers, B. (1992). 'Visual and nonvisual information disambiguate surfaces specified by motion parallax'. *Perception and Psychophysics,* Vol. 52, pp. 446-452.

Sachsenweger, M., & Sachsenweger, U. (1991). 'Stereoscopic acuity in ocular pursuit of moving objects'. *Documenta Opthalmologica,* Vol. 78(1-2), pp. 1-133.

Simpson, W. A. (1993). 'Optic flow and depth perception'. *Spatial Vision,* Vol. 7, pp. 35-75.

Stevens, K. A., & Brookes, A. (1988). 'Integrating stereopsis with monocular interpretations of planar surfaces'. *Vision Research,* Vol. 28, pp. 371-386.

Treacy, P. J., & Johnson, A. G. (1995). 'Is the laparoscopic bubble bursting?' *Lancet,* No. 346 (suppl.), p. 23.

Wenzl, R., Lehner, R., Vry, U., Pateisky, N., Sevelda, P., & Hussein, P. (1994). 'Three-dimensional video-endoscopy: clinical use in gynaecological laparoscopy'. *Lancet,* No. 344, pp. 1621-1622.

20 Construction and validation of a model for decision making in anaesthesia

Philip M.A. de Graaf
Safety Science Group, Delft University of Technology,
The Netherlands

Abstract

The anaesthesia process is becoming more and more complex as a result of the need for continuous improvement of anaesthesia techniques and monitoring equipment. Because of this, the process is not always manageable for the anaesthetist without support. This paper describes the research aimed at finding out which, when, and how information should be presented to the anaesthetist. We have developed a cognitive model of the decision making process of the anaesthetist, which is based on models of decision making in industrial settings and in anaesthesia. The model states that the decision making process of the anaesthetist is guided by goals and expectations, and is primarily influenced by its context. An observation study proved the face validity of the model, but further research will have to show whether the model can be used for finding information requirements in anaesthesia.

Introduction

Anaesthesia monitoring

Improving the anaesthesia process has been subject of research ever since the first reported anaesthesia in 1846. These improvements have resulted in a much safer process, but have also increased complexity considerably. As a result, the role of human error in the incidents that do occur is considerable (Chopra, Bovil, Spierdijk and Koornneef, 1992). Under certain circumstances managing this complex process can become extremely difficult with the limited support of current monitoring devices (Kestin, Miller and Lockart, 1988). An important contributing factor to this

153

problem is the limited capacity and reliability of human data and information processing. We therefore chose to support the anaesthetist by extracting only relevant information from all available data provided.

We suggest here that there is a difference between data and information, although they are often used as synonyms. We define data as the collection of all observations, measurements and knowledge available in the current situation. Information is defined as everything contained in the available data that is relevant for answering the questions that are (or should be) raised by the current situation.

To achieve this goal we need to solve two problems. First we must develop methods that can extract possibly relevant information from the available data. Second we will have to find out which information is needed in all possible situations. This paper describes the research done to solve the latter problem.

Cognitive modelling

To know which information is relevant to the anaesthetist we need to understand the anaesthesia process. To this end we can either model the process directly (patient model), or we can model the anaesthetist (cognitive model). The latter approach has two advantages: first, the anaesthesia process is more complex and variable than the decision making process of the anaesthetist. Second, it seems to be only natural to model the cognitive process of the anaesthetist, since that is the process we want to support.

Although cognitive models are being developed for operators in industrial settings for some time now, they are only beginning to find application in anaesthesia. De Keyser (de Keyser and Nyssen, 1993) applied methods which have been developed for studying human error in industrial process control, to anaesthesia. Another application of decision making models in anaesthesia by Gaba (Gaba, Fish and Howard, 1994) involved the development of training methods for improving crisis management by anaesthetists. Finally Coiera (1994) used a classification scheme for activities of the anaesthetist. Coiera uses two classification criteria. The first classifies an action as strategic or reactive. The second involves three categories: monitoring, diagnosis or control. The implications of a certain category for the type of information required were not reported. None of these models, however, covered all aspects of the process we consider relevant, so we needed to construct one ourselves.

Cognitive modelling in industrial settings has led to general design specification for human decision making models (Hollnagel, 1993 and Bainbridge, 1993). We incorporated these general design considerations in our model design. We also incorporated concepts form methods developed specifically for finding information requirements in supervisory control tasks. The FIKA modelling approach developed by Sundström (1993) and Sundström and Salvador (1995) is based on a decomposition of the cognitive task of the operator in three cognitive activities: (i) situation assessment, (ii) choice of action, and (iii) evaluation of impact of actions. These activities are initiated by information processing goals, which are initiated by violations of functional goals concerning the process. Each of the cognitive activities can be analysed further to obtain the information requirements. This analysis is done by a decomposition of each activity in three steps: i) relevant information identifier, ii) qualitative analyser, and iii) information evaluator. A different approach is followed by Shepherd (Shepherd, 1993). Shepherd proposes a decomposition of the human decision making process in standard tasks requiring standard information. However, this approach is based on a hierarchical task analysis, which is rather difficult to perform for a complex task like delivering anaesthesia.

Cognitive activity flow model

Model design

Based on the modelling considerations described in the previous section, and observations of the anaesthesia process we develop a model for decision making in anaesthesia. The cognitive activity flow (CAF) model, will be the basis for further analysis of the anaesthetist's information requirements.

The model is based on three assumptions: first we assume that the decision making process of the anaesthetist can be decomposed in a number of distinct cognitive activities. Second we assume that such a basic cognitive activity uses external resources to complete its function. Third we assume that the nature of a basic cognitive activity is influenced by a number of autonomous external influencing factors.

Figure 1 gives a schematic view of the CAF model, which we will use to describe each of the elements of the CAF model in more detail.

Flow chart The flow chart forming the basis for our model seems to imply a strict sequence of cognitive activities (see figure 1). The sequence indicated in the flowchart however, is not intended as a predictor for the sequence of cognitive activities performed by the anaesthetist. The links between the different cognitive activities indicate a functional dependency between them, which means that the cognitive activities attributing to the same decision will be executed in this order. Since different decision making cycles may be initiated in parallel, the next activity can in principle be any of the four activities in the model, even if the current activity is known.

We will start our explanation of the flow chart with the *monitor/evaluate* activity. The difference between monitoring and evaluation is that the first is done always, whereas the latter is specifically called for by a previous decision which generates its own goals and expectations. The *monitor/evaluate* activity should result in a trigger for further action if a undesired or unexpected state change occurs. We call these

Philip M.A. de Graaf

changes 'violations' of goals or expectations analogue to Sundström's concept of 'goal-violations'.

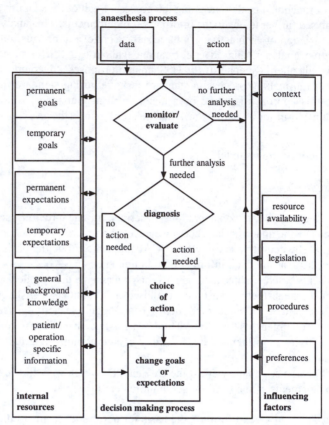

Figure 1   Schematic view of the CAF model of decision making in anaesthesia

The *monitor/evaluate* activity will trigger the *diagnosis* activity which searches for the cause of the detected undesired or unexpected change in patient state. The resulting decision will be a diagnosis which either indicates a need for an intervention or the adjustment of goals or expectations.

If an intervention is needed the *choice of action* activity is triggered which is aimed at the weighing of intervention possibilities. In general one problem can be treated in different ways depending of the anomalies of the specific case. The best alternative is of course implemented.

If an intervention is chosen or no intervention was deemed necessary in the diagnosis stage the *change goals or expectations* activity is triggered. In this stage

156

expectations based on the planned intervention or diagnosis are generated. If the diagnosis process has indicated that goals or expectations are invalid or inaccurate they will be adjusted or eliminated.

Internal resources Each of the cognitive activities has access to any of six internal resources. The first resource contains *permanent goals* which are formulated implicitly or explicitly before the operation and remain valid for the entire operation. The second internal resource contains *temporary goals*. These goals are only generated for a limited period of time. They are often generated in response to temporary (unexpected) states of the process and by decision of the anaesthetist. They are eliminated when the reason for their existence disappears. The third internal resource contains *permanent expectations*. They are also generated before the operation and valid for the entire operation. They can be adjusted or eliminated when they are considered to be no longer valid. The fourth resource contains *temporary expectations*. These expectations are generated and treated in the same way as *temporary goals*. The fifth resource contains *general background knowledge*. This resource consists of all knowledge and experience the anaesthetist has gathered until now. The sixth and final resource contains *patient/operation specific information*. This resource can include all possible data about the patient, since both pre-operative data and perio-operative data can be stored internally by the anaesthetist. Further facts stored in this resource can include interventions and the patient's reaction to them.

Data Besides internal resources the anaesthesiologist has access external resources for his/her decision making. This includes data coming from the patient-monitor, data from the anaesthesia record, comments or answers to questions of operating room personnel, and observation of either patient, equipment, or surgical field. Data is used by cognitive activities in the same way as internal resources.

Action If the decision of the anaesthetist requires some kind of action this will have to be implemented. This is the action that is depicted in the top of figure 1. Although this activity is not included in the decision making process it does require data from the process and other resources.

Influencing factors The interactions between internal resources, data, and cognitive activities are determined by five influencing factors. As we already stated *context* is considered to be an important factor influencing the decision making process. We define context as those characteristics of the current situation that are independent of the type of undesired or unexpected state of the anaesthesia process. This is implemented through five criteria defining the current context-class:
   (i)   *procedural* or *state related* activities
   (ii)   *foreseen* or *unforeseen* activities
   (iii) *experienced* or *inexperienced* activities

(iv) *proactive* or *reactive* activities

(v) *simple* or *multiple* underlying causes.

Other influencing factors are: *resource availability, legislation, procedures,* and personal *preferences* which all speak more or less for themselves.

Model validation

We validated the model by means of an observation study of the anaesthetist during regular task execution. The number of procedures observed in a structured manner was limited to eight. This is a very small number which would not be sufficient by itself. However, the structured observations for validation of the model, were preceded about twenty observed procedures for building the model. Based on this previous experience we did not see any reason to extend the number of procedures.

The model presented here is the second iteration of our modelling effort, since the first model was invalidated by the first part of our observation study. This study showed that the model was lacking expectations as a resource in the model. Furthermore the complexity of the situation was not included as a context characteristic. This model also did not include resource availability as an influencing factor.

The results of the observation study show that both visible and invisible activities occur. The context characteristics make sense to the anaesthetist, and different contexts seem to result in different decision making processes. Answers to questions about the decision making process underlying a decision showed, that all elements in the flowchart represent part of the anaesthetist's decision making process. We found no activities that are not covered in the flowchart. We also found that the motivation for an action of the anaesthetist came from 'violations' of goals or expectations.

Conclusion and discussion

The research described in this paper concerned the design and validation of a model for decision making in anaesthesia. An observation study proved the face-validity of the model and proved the usefulness of the model to find information requirements. Goals and expectations proved to be crucial factors in the decision making process. The context class determines the type of support needed. This can vary from offering only the right measurement data at the right time to supplying diagnosis hypothesis or complete diagnosis. Further research will be aimed at finding relevant goals and expectations since these seem to be the most important factors determining the information requirements in a given situation.

158

References

Bainbridge, L. (1993), 'Types of hierarchy imply types of models', *Ergonomics*, Vol. 36, pp. 1399-1412.

Chopra, V., Bovill, J.G., Spierdijk, J., Koornneef, F. (1992), 'Reported significant observations during anaesthesia: a prospective analysis over an 18 month period', *British Journal of Anaesthesia*, Vol. 68, pp. 13-17.

Coiera, E. (1994), 'Designing for decision support in a clinical monitoring environment', *Proceedings of the International Conference on Medical Physics and Biomedical Engineering - MPBE '94*, 5-7 May, Nicosia, Cyprus, pp. 130-142.

De Keyser, V. & Nyssen, A.S. (1993), 'Les erreur humaines en anesthesie', *Le travail humain*, Vol. 56, pp. 243-266.

Gaba, D.M., Fish, K.J., Howard, S.K. (1994), *Crisis management in anaesthesiology*. Churchill Livingstone: New York.

Hollnagel E. (1993), 'Models of cognition: procedural prototypes and contextual control', *Le Travail Humain*, Vol. 56, pp. 27-51.

Kestin, I.G., Miller, B.R., Lockart, C.H. (1988), 'Auditory Alarms during Anaesthesia Monitoring', *Anaesthesiology*, Vol. 69, pp. 106-109.

Shepherd, A. (1993), 'An approach to information requirements specification for process control tasks', *Ergonomics*, Vol. 36, pp. 1425-1437.

Sundström, G.A. (1993), 'Towards models of tasks and task complexity in supervisory control applications', *Ergonomics*, Vol. 36, pp. 1413-1423.

Sundström, G.A. & Salvador, A.C. (1995), 'Integrating field work in system design: A methodology and two case studies', *IEEE Trans. Syst. Man Cybern.*, Vol.25, pp. 385-399.

Acknowledgements

This research was possible thanks to the hospitality of the anaesthesiology department of the Academic Medical Centre in Amsterdam. We would especially like to thank Dr Cor Kalkman for his contribution.

21 Anaesthesiology and aviation: using the analogy

Carole D.B. Deighton and Wendy Morgan
Cranfield University, UK

Abstract

The similarities in the *workload profile* of the anaesthetist and civil airline pilot provided a basic rationale for investigating the anaesthetist's workload using a subjective technique developed traditionally for the piloted environment. However, the aviation-anaesthesiology analogy cannot be used to assume similarities in the *types* of workload experienced by the two professional groups (e.g. mental, physical, temporal workload). An investigation of the *applicability* of a subjective measure of pilot workload (i.e. the NASA bi-polar scale) was therefore conducted. The technique was completed by 17 anaesthetists from three surgical specialities (general, neurosurgery and cardiothoracic surgery) at three prescribed intervals during an operation (induction, pre-maintenance and pre-recovery). Technique applicability was assessed using a debriefing questionnaire. Results indicated that the dimensions of the NASA bi-polar technique are generally relevant to the work of the anaesthetist but modifications to the titles of three dimensions are recommended to better describe the work of the anaesthetist.

Introduction

Hi-technology, automation and expert decision support systems are becoming an integral part of the working environment of the civil airline pilot and health professional (i.e. anaesthetist, doctor, nurse), (Chambers and Nagel, 1985; Sugg, 1991). Experimental and survey research conducted in the aviation environment has highlighted the need to control the implementation of hi-technology and automation on the flight deck to avoid pilot underload; the erosion of professional skills; and the use of humans as system's monitors (Wiener, 1988; Braune and Fadden, 1987; Braby, Muir and Harris, 1991). These human factors may account for a proportion of the 74% of anaesthetic mishaps reported by Schneider (1988).

In the field of aviation psychology, or human factors, a vast array of subjective, objective and physiological indicators of flight crew workload have been developed to assess the benefits and disbenefits of new flight deck technology and operating procedures (Corwin, Sandry-Garza, Biferno, Boucek, Jonsson and Metalis, 1989). These techniques *may* provide one way of controlling the appropriate introduction and use of hi-technology in the operating theatre. The similarities or 'analogy' between the workload profile of the anaesthetist and civil airline pilot supports this assertion (see figure 1).

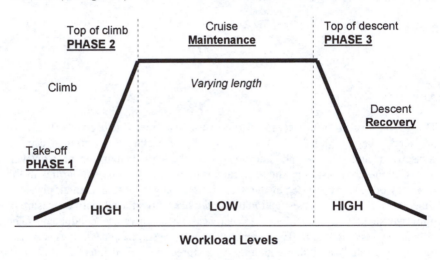

Figure 1   Workload profile of the anaesthetist and civil airline pilot

In this analogy the induction, or putting under phase of the anaesthetist's work has been compared to the high workload take-off phase of flight, when a large number of readings and calculations need to be taken. Induction is followed by a period of maintenance which, similar to the cruise phase of flight, may give rise to a comparatively lower workload and vary in duration from a few minutes to several hours. The final phase, recovery, imposes a comparatively higher workload and is similar to the 'step change' in workload experienced by the pilot during landing.

Research objective

Fundamental research was conducted to test the hypothesis that pilot workload assessment techniques can be used to assess the workload of the anaesthetist. This was investigated by assessing the applicability and sensitivity of a subjective method of pilot workload (NASA bi-polar technique) to the work of the anaesthetist. Applicability refers to the relevance of the *types* of workload (e.g. physical, mental, temporal) which are measured by the technique to the workload of the target group. Sensitivity is defined as the extent to which a technique can detect changes in the amount or *intensity of* workload experienced during the performance of a task. The results reported in this paper will focus on the *qualitative findings* of the debriefing questionnaire which was used to assess the applicability of the technique.

Method

Workload assessment intervals

The following three *event* limited assessment intervals were identified for evaluation and are marked as phases one to three on figure 1.

Phase one	While the anaesthesia was being administered (induction).
Phase two	From when the patient first entered the operating theatre to when the surgeon made the first incision (pre-maintenance).
Phase three	From when the first dressing was applied to when the patient left the operating theatre (pre-recovery).

Phase two may be considered analogous to the top-of-climb where workload is moderate and phase three similar to the end of cruise/top of descent.

Materials

NASA bi-polar scale The NASA Bi-polar technique is a multi-dimensional rating scale which consists of ten subscales: 'overall workload'; 'task difficulty'; 'time pressure'; mental/sensory effort'; 'physical effort'; 'frustration level'; 'stress level'; 'fatigue level'; and 'activity type' (Hart and Staveland, 1988). End-points on each scale are defined by numerical descriptors and values range from one to 100.

Debriefing questionnaire The debriefing questionnaire was semi-structured and designed for self-completion. Questions were presented to elicit information about the applicability of the NASA bi-polar subscales according to the following three sub-criteria:

- *Relevance* Degree of match between the dimensions on the bi-polar scale and the type of workload experienced by the anaesthetist;
- *Sufficiency* Other types of workload unique to the profession which are not described by the NASA bi-polar scale;
- *Language* Appropriateness of the terminology used to describe the dimensions.

Procedure

Participants who volunteered to take part in the study completed the NASA bi-polar scale at the end of each workload assessment interval defined above, i.e. on three

Carole D.B. Deighton and Wendy Morgan

occasions. Operations for evaluation were selected by the participant. The debriefing questionnaire was filled-in at a convenient point after the operation. This procedure ensured that participants were able to base their evaluation of the technique applicability on their experience of completing the instrument in the applied environment.

Participants

A total of 17 anaesthetists from three specialities, (general, neuro and cardiothoracic surgery), took part in the study and included five consultants, six senior registrars and six registrars from Papworth and Addenbrooke's Hospitals in Cambridge, UK. Experience ranged from three to 21 years.

Results

The brief results reported in this paper focus on the *relevance* of the workload dimensions to the work of the anaesthetist; the *sufficiency* of the dimensions included on the technique and the appropriateness of the *terminology* associated with each dimension.

Participants evaluated the *relevance* of each dimension according to a five-point scale with end points one being 'highly applicable'; and five equivalent to 'not applicable' to the work of the anaesthetist. Group ratings for each dimension are presented in table 1 and ranged from 1.42 for 'time pressure' and 'performance' to a mean rating of 2.83 for 'physical effort'. This data indicates that, on average, all dimensions were considered relevant to the work of the anaesthetist.

Table 1
Relevance of dimensions to the work of the anaesthetist
1=Highly applicable and 5=Not applicable

Dimension	Mean (s.d)		Dimension	Mean (s.d)	
Time pressure	1.42	(0.7)	Stress	1.92	(1.4)
Performance	1.42	(0.7)	Fatigue	2.08	(1.2)
Mental/sensory effort	1.50	(0.9)	Overall workload	2.80	(0.8)
			Physical effort	2.83	(0.9)
Task demand	1.83	(1.2)			
Frustration	1.83	(1.2)			

Sufficiency was measured on a five-point scale with descriptors: 'very comprehensive'; 'fairly comprehensive'; 'reasonably comprehensive'; 'dimensions missing' and 'many dimensions missing'. The majority of respondents, 67 per cent, considered the range of dimensions as 'fairly comprehensive'; 25 per cent checked 'very comprehensive' and the remaining 8 per cent ticked 'reasonably comprehensive'.

The suitability of the wording and phrasing of each dimension was assessed using a three point scale with descriptors: 'terminology doesn't need changing; 'needs changing'; 'don't know'. The majority of respondents, 75-80 per cent, indicated that, in general the terminology for all dimensions was generic. Supporting comments, however, provided the following suggestions for modifications primarily to the titles of the dimensions.

- Mental/sensory effort to be replaced by the title 'clinical challenge'.
- Performance to be renamed 'success'.
- Task difficulty to be defined for 'manual dexterity' and 'intellectual difficulty'.

Summary and conclusions

The long term objective of the reported research was to identify a battery of human factors techniques, to include workload assessment methodologies, which can be used to assess the benefits and disbenefits of new technology in the operating theatre.

The similarities in the *workload profile* of the anaesthetist and civil airline pilot provided a basic rationale for investigating the anaesthetists workload using techniques developed traditionally for the piloted environment. Although similar patterns of workload might be evident between the two professions it could not be assumed that the *types* of workload which gave rise to comparable profiles were the same. An investigation of the *applicability* of a subjective measure of pilot workload (i.e. the NASA bi-polar scale) was therefore conducted.

The investigation was undertaken as part of a larger study which considered the sensitivity of the subjective workload technique to the types of workload experienced at event defined points in an operation (induction, pre-maintenance, and pre-recovery).

The anaesthetist's assessment of the applicability of the NASA bi-polar scale was recorded by a self-completion, semi-structured debriefing questionnaire. Results collected from the debriefing questionnaire indicated that, in general, the NASA bi-polar technique is an applicable measure of the types of workload experienced by anaesthetists during the 'induction' 'pre-maintenance' and 'pre-recovery' phases of general, neuro and cardiothoracic surgery. However, minor modifications to the titles of the three bi-polar scales labelled: mental/sensory effort; performance and task difficulty should be undertaken prior to further implementation of the measure in the clinical environment.

The analogy between the workload profile of the anaesthetist and the civil airline pilot provides an *initial* rationale, *only* for using the design philosophies, human factors assessment tools and training methods developed in the aviation environment, in the operating theatre or on the wards. Caution, must be exercised by the enthusiastic human factors researcher who is determined to apply the methodologies developed in the aviation industry to other safety critical environments.

Carole D.B. Deighton and Wendy Morgan

Further research

Three areas of further investigation are proposed.
(i) Investigation of the acceptance and applicability of other subjective and objective methods of workload and situation awareness, developed in the aviation context, to the work of the anaesthetist.
(ii) Evaluation of the relevance of cockpit resource management (CRM) training to the operating theatre.
(iii) Investigation of methods to select health professional and workers in other safety critical industries who are most able to cope with operating in hi-technology environments for extended periods.

References

Braby, C.D., Muir, H.C. & Harris, D. (1991), 'The development of a working model of flight crew underload', in E. Farmer (ed.), *Stress and Error in Aviation*, Avebury Technical: Aldershot.

Braune, R. & Fadden, D.M. (1987), 'Flight deck automation: Is there a useful role for the pilot?'. *Australian Aviation Symposium, Innervate or Ennervate.*

Chambers, A.B. & Nagel, D.C. (1995), 'Pilot of the future: human or computer?'. *Communications of the ACM*, Vol. 28, pp. 1187-1199.

Corwin, , W.H., Sandry-Garza, D.L., Biferno, M.H., Boucek, G.P., Logan, A.L. & Jonsson (1989), 'Assessment of crew workload measurement methods, techniques and procedures'. *Report no. WRDC-TR-89-7006*, Vol. 1.

Hart, S.G. & Staveland, L.E. (1988), 'Development of the NASA-TLX (NASA Task Load Index): results of empirical and theoretical research'. In, Hancock, P.A. & Meshkati, N. (eds.), *Human Mental Workload*. Elsevier: Amsterdam.

Schneider, A.J.L. (1988), 'Regulation of anaesthetic devices in the USA', *Ballieres Clinical Anaesthesiology*, Vol. 2, pp. 353-66.

Sugg, R. (1991), 'Sound the alarm on signals standards inside health care, Sept 7-8. Cited by Greenbaum, R. (1995), 'Design of equipment for safety', in J.S Walker (ed.), *Quality and Safety in Anaesthesia*. BMJ Publishing Group: London.

Wiener, E.L. (1988), 'Cockpit automation', in E.L. Weiner & D.C. Nagel (eds.), *Human Factors in Aviation*. Academic Press Inc: New York.

Acknowledgement

Our thanks are extended to the anaesthetists at Addenbrooke's and Papworth Hospitals in Cambridge, UK who volunteered to take part in the study.

22 Medical cognition and computer support in the intensive care unit: a cognitive engineering approach

Robert Logie, Jim Hunter, Neil McIntosh,*
Ken Gilhooly, Eugenio Alberdi and Jan Reiss*
University of Aberdeen, UK
*University of Edinburgh, UK

Introduction

Computerised aids for data collection, interpretation, and display in the hospital intensive care unit (ICU) offer considerable potential for improving the quality of medical and nursing care. However in a wide variety of health care domains it has been shown repeatedly that computerized aids in medicine may not be readily accepted or widely used by medical or nursing staff (Green, Gilhooly, Logie & Ross, 1991). Even where staff are positive about the utility of the computerized system, there may be no impact on clinical outcome (McIntosh, Cunningham & Elton, 1994). The most common reason given for these difficulties has been a failure in system design to incorporate an adequate knowledge of the cognitions and working practices of the eventual users. In this paper we discuss means to acquire such knowledge and how it might be used to inform system design. First we discuss computerized monitoring of physiological functions in adult and neonatal intensive care. This is followed by a brief review of the literature on human decision making, with specific reference to the medical domain. Third, we discuss possible methods for studying working practices and cognition in the ICU and describe findings from the application of these methods. Finally we propose that this approach to cognitive engineering offers mutual benefits for both cognitive theory and design practice.

Physiological monitoring in intensive care

The clinical monitoring of patients in the ICU has three objectives: one is to allow confirmation that the patient is stable or is responding appropriately to treatment. A second objective is the early detection of physiological events which occur spontaneously, with a view to rectifying problems before they become too established. The third is to detect situations in which the patient fails to respond to a particular therapeutic intervention, thereby requiring alternative action. Information technology is intended to assist in the achievement of these objectives, and intensive care wards for both adults and infants have seen a rapid increase in the data available to the clinical staff. Cardio-vascular data (e.g. heart rate, systemic arterial pressures, central venous pressure, and temperatures) have been available for monitoring on a continuous basis for some time. In addition, sensors are now capable of providing measures of cardiac output and the extent of oxygen saturation in the blood. However, physiological conditions can be indicated by changes in several of these parameters. Each may be displayed on a separate monitor in a different format, resulting in complications for the physician or nurse scanning and assimilating the data.

Computers for monitoring and archiving data

An important development in the last decade has been to use computers to collect data from different monitors and to display them in a more uniform format (e.g. Ambroso et al., 1992; Bass, Badger & McIntosh, 1991; Green, Logie, Gilhooly, Ross & Ronald, 1995).

Computer systems offer a means to avoid some of the information overload arising from multiple monitors through use of integrated and flexible displays. Unfortunately the flexibility of computers and rapid advancements in computer technology can also greatly increase their complexity. For example, increasing the range of options in display format, data interpretation, and other facilities increases the time required for training staff in their use. More complex computer systems often require the employment of computer support staff, and the retraining of staff on the ward when software is upgraded. In addition it becomes necessary to devise procedures for differential levels of access to the computer facilities by different grades of staff.

Whether a system is complex or simple, legal considerations and the perceived or actual reliability of a system may require paper records to be kept. This parallel recording, coupled with training requirements results in the computer adding to rather than easing the workload of ward staff. Medicine of course is not the only area in which investment in information technology has failed to deliver improvements in service provision or cost savings (Landauer, 1995). Despite these difficulties there is a widespread belief within the medical and nursing professions that computers have significant potential in patient care if the system is designed and implemented appropriately (Shortliffe, Perrault, Fagan & Weiderhold, 1990).

Computers as medical decision aids

Computers also have the potential to support medical decision making by optimizing the display content and format for the physiological condition of the patient, by detecting patterns of change or stability in several different parameters, and by recording parameter values for cumulative displays. The major difference between a computerized monitoring system and a decision support system is in the level of interpretation, organisation and selection of available data. The medical decision support system in the ICU has to meet all of the objectives of the monitoring system, but also has to make data available in a form which facilitates decision making. This requires both an understanding of medical decision making and development of the computational algorithms, techniques and interface necessary for organising and presenting the data.

A major issue is whether physicians and/or nursing staff can effectively use the data displayed to spot trends and to take appropriate action. For example, physicians tend to visit each of a number of patients rather than continually monitor a given patient. They may rely on 'snapshot' samples of each patient's physiological condition rather than trends which have been developing over a period. Nursing staff may not have the requisite medical knowledge to interpret physiological trends as they emerge, nor see it as their responsibility to do so. Therefore if trends start to develop on screen these may be ignored or require interpretation to derive an indication as to the current physiological state of the patient.

Computerised monitoring systems may be designed through consultation with a panel of medical experts. However typically it is the more junior physicians and the nursing staff who are the main users of the systems, with nurses having the minute by minute responsibility for checking on the well-being of the patient and detecting problems which arise. The experts may not be fully aware of the cognitions in nursing or junior clinical staff, how or if they interact with the available data, or how the presence of the computer affects the working environment and practices. Moreover, the intuitions among the expert medical staff as to their own cognitive processes on the ward may not necessarily reflect their functional cognition. Experts often rely on compiled knowledge which may not be available to conscious inspection or verbal report (Nisbett & Wilson, 1977).

Medical reasoning and decision making

It is well established that human decision making is prone to a range of biases (Evans, 1989). For example, once an individual forms an hypothesis there is a tendency to seek evidence which confirms that hypothesis rather than to seek disconfirmatory evidence. Another weakness of human cognition is the tendency to select inappropriate base rates when making probability judgements or assessing risk. For example, if a test to detect a disease whose prevalence is 1/1000 has a false-positive rate of five per cent, then what is the chance that a person found to have a positive result actually has the disease? Most of a sample of 60 Harvard Medical School students and staff gave the response 95 per cent. But this answer fails to take into account the very low base rate of the disease, and the correct answer is two per cent (Cascells, Schoenberger & Grayboys, 1978). It is possible to improve correct response rates if the figures are given as frequencies (e.g. 50 out of 1000) rather than as probabilities (e.g. five per cent) (cited in Gilhooly, 1996, pp 188-189).

Qualified medical practitioners are apparently no less prone to faulty probabilistic reasoning than are medical students or other adults (Christensen-Szalanski & Bushyhead, 1981). Moreover, the diagnostic decisions of junior medical staff appear to rely heavily on incomplete textbook knowledge in their physiological reasoning, which may lead to erroneous decisions. There is also evidence that inexperienced staff use over simplified analogies which are derived from teaching practices in medical training (Feltovich, Spiro & Coulson, 1989). The decisions of experienced physicians appear to be driven largely by their clinical experience rather than physiological reasoning, and neither expert nor novice physicians appear to rely on systematic evaluation of evidence (Evans & Patel, 1989).

Notably the vast majority of studies in medical reasoning and decision making have involved simulated patient scenarios, either using actors in the role of patients, or vignettes comprising a medical history and sets of symptoms (Gilhooly, 1990). Rarely have studies of medical decision making taken place with genuine patients or genuine patient data (Koehler, in press). If medical decision making in practice were found to be prone to the biases demonstrated in laboratory simulations this would have important implications for the design of a computerised medical decision support system. A system would have severely limited utility if the system designer assumed that expert clinicians systematically evaluate evidence, or if the system failed to take account of possible biases in decision making.

Methodologies for studying clinical decision making in the ICU

Even if decision biases are found in the real life setting, it is important to consider (i) what factors medical and nursing practitioners *perceive* to be those which affect their decision making; (ii) whether the major factors which practitioners identify are those which actually do affect their decision making; (iii) whether biases identified in laboratory studies have any impact on genuine medical decision making in the complex context of the ICU.

Our approach has been to use a range of methodologies, specifically questionnaires, semi-structured interviews, systematic observation of staff on the ward, and experimental techniques. Often in applied settings, the methodologies developed in the laboratory are inappropriate for addressing practical problems, including aspects of design. However the medical domain, and specifically neo-natal

ICU, offers an environment and a set of applied problems which lend themselves to objective experimental methodologies as well as interview and observation.

Questionnaires, interviews and observation

Interviews with staff yield a subjective view of working practices, staff attitudes and self-perceived expertise. Interviews also can focus on the clinicians' reports as to how they interpret data and the information sources on which they depend. Clearly in order to make decisions regarding diagnosis, prognosis and treatment, medical staff need access to data sets which are specific to that decision. The interview may establish what these data sets are, and whether the data are derived from clinical observation of the patient, written or computerized case notes, discussion with colleagues, test results, or from standard or computerized monitors.

In some of our previous studies (Ambroso et al., 1992; Gilhooly, Logie, Ross, Ramayya & Green, 1991) questionnaires and interviews were used to investigate the ease with which various grades of staff reported being able to carry out routine activities before and after introduction of a computerised monitoring system (but without explicit decision support). The ICUs involved were sampled from a number of sites in the UK and in mainland Europe. Broadly staff had generally good impressions about the computer systems on their wards, had largely accepted their presence, and reported using them with reasonable frequency. Notably, the majority of respondents felt that the computer system allowed for a better understanding of the state of the patient, as well as providing a single source for patient information, improving legibility of case notes, and providing an archived data base for research and teaching. Negative remarks about the systems included the additional loads of training in system use, parallel recording on paper and computer, system reliability, and the omission of key features. Also the positive attitude among staff was not matched by a detailed knowledge of the system functions, or in many cases effective use of the systems. Moreover some of the benefits were viewed by many staff as *potential* outcomes. Impact on clinical outcome was assessed in one neo-natal ICU (McIntosh et al., 1994) in which the effect of the computers was neutral with respect to survival of the infants or their length of stay on the ward.

With the exception of the clinical impact measures, much of the information above was based on the interviewee's view of what they do and how they do it. Their responses may be affected by who conducts the interview, by what scenarios they consider at the time, or the series of events and actions in recently experienced clinical cases. For these reasons it is crucial to seek other sources of evidence. Information about actual working practice can be obtained by carrying out extended periods of observation and recording of daily activities in the working environment. However observational data reveal little of the cognitions of the individuals involved.

171

Experimental approaches

One important characteristic of computerised monitoring in intensive care is that the physiological data are recorded and archived. This offers a rich source of stimulus material for use in experimental studies with the staff concerned. One fruitful technique is to ask individuals with varying levels of expertise to 'think aloud' as they solve a problem, interpret data, form hypothesis or make decisions (Ericsson & Simon, 1984). Our current approach in examining the cognitions of physicians and nurses is to present staff with data patterns recorded from previous real patients, and then ask them to 'think aloud' during their interpretation of the data. This is the focus of an ongoing project concerned primarily with decision making in neo-natal intensive care. In this work we also plan to run a limited number of studies where clinicians at different grades will be asked to think aloud while dealing on-line with real patients. Think aloud protocols are difficult to collect when real adult patients are involved. In the neo-natal ICU there is no danger of the patient overhearing the content of the protocols as they are generated. This will allow a direct comparison between the 'off-line' and 'on-line' decision making. The think aloud protocols are transcribed, and analysed with respect to the formation and exploration of hypotheses, the ability to detect key features of the physiological data patterns both at the onset of a spontaneous physiological trend and in assessing the impact of some therapeutic intervention. This form of analysis then allows an assessment of the decision making off ward and on ward in terms of the incidence of decision making biases, for example confirmation bias, base rates of probability, and so on. The insight gained into expert clinical interpretation of physiological data patterns will then be used to inform the design of computational algorithms in computerized decision support (Haimowitz & Kohane, 1993).

Cognition and engineering design or cognitive engineering

Our approach draws on laboratory based findings on human decision making and is exploring how these findings might inform the design of a computerised decision support and patient monitoring system. The extent to which these laboratory findings may be found in real medical decision making also will test the generality of the original findings and inform theories of human decision making. This symbiosis between theory in cognitive psychology and its application has been highly successful in a range of other domains. For example, the use of cognitive theories in the study of brain damaged adults has provided significant insight into the nature of those deficits, has informed the design of neuropsychological rehabilitation programmes, and has led to significant advances in theories of cognition and in mapping brain structure to cognitive function. Studies of human face recognition have led to the design of electronic photofit systems and are now informing the design of automated face recognition systems. The drive to develop such systems has forced questions on the theories which informed the development. Studies and theories of the functioning of the human auditory system has led to the development of auditory warnings in aircraft, both in terms of their acoustic properties and in terms of human learning of the association between particular auditory warnings and the nature of the problems which they indicate. This list is by no means comprehensive, but indicates the benefits to be gained from using theories and methodologies developed in the laboratory to solving practical problems of system design. So too in the design of medical decision aids, experimental techniques and tests of the generality of biases in human thinking offer significant potential for the development of decision aids that will genuinely assist clinical and nursing care.

References

Ambroso, C., Bowes, C., Chambrin, M-C., Gilhooly, K., Green, C., Kari, A., Logie, R., Marraro, G. Mereu, M., Rembold, P. & Reynolds, M. (1992). 'INFORM: European survey of computers in intensive care units'. *International Journal of Clinical Monitoring and Computing*, Vol. 9, pp. 53-61.

Bass, C.A., Badger, P. & McIntosh, N. (1991). 'Mary 3: A new generation computer monitoring system'. *Fetal and Neonatal Physiological Measurements,* pp. 187-190.

Cascells, W., Schoenberger, A. & Grayboys, T. (1978). 'Interpretation by physicians of clinical laboratory results'. *New England Journal of Medicine*, Vol. 299, p. 999-1000.

Christensen-Szalanski, J. & Bushyhead, J. (1981). 'Physicians' use of probabilistic information in a real clinical setting'. *Journal of Experimental Psychology: Human Perception and Performance*, Vol. 7, pp. 928-935.

Ericsson K.A. & Simon H. (1984). *Protocol Analysis: Verbal Reports as Data*. MIT Press: Cambridge, M.A.

Evans D.A. & Patel V.L. (1989). *Cognitive Science in Medicine*. MIT Press: Cambridge, M.A.

Evans, J.St.B.T. (1989). *Bias in human reasoning: causes and consequences*. Lawrence Erlbaum Associates: Hove, UK.

Feltovich, P.J., Spiro, R.J. & Coulson, R.L. (1989). 'The nature of conceptual understanding in biomedicine: the deep structure of complex ideas and the development of misconceptions'. In, D.A. Evans & V.L. Patel (eds.) *Cognitive Science in Medicine*. MIT Press: Cambridge, M.A.

Gilhooly, K.J. (1990). 'Cognitive psychology and medical diagnosis'. *Applied Cognitive Psychology*, Vol. 4, pp. 261-272.

Gilhooly, K.J. (1996). *Thinking: directed, undirected and creative*. Third edition. Academic Press: London.

Gilhooly, K.J., Logie, R.H., Ross, D., Ramayya, P. & Green, C. (1991). 'User's perceptions of a computerised medical information system in intensive care (ABICUS) on introduction and after two months use'. *International Journal of Clinical Monitoring and Computing*, Vol. 8, pp.101-106.

Green C.A., Gilhooly K.J., Logie R.H. & Ross D.G. (1991). 'Human factors and computerisation in intensive care units: a review'. *International Journal of Clinical Monitoring and Computing*, Vol 8, pp. 167-178.

Green, C.A. Logie, R.H., Gilhooly, K.J., Ross, D.G. & Ronald, A. (1996) 'Aberdeen polygons: computer displays of physiological profiles for intensive care'. *Ergonomics,* Vol. 39, pp. 412-428.

Haimowitz I.J. & Kohane I.S. (1993). 'Automatic trend detection with multiple temporal hypotheses'. *Proceedings of the 13th International Joint conference on Artificial Intelligence.* Morgan Kaufmann: San Mateo.

Koehler, J.J. (in press). 'The base rate fallacy reconsidered: descriptive, normative and methodological challenges'. *Brain and Behavioral Sciences.*

Landauer, T.K. (1995). *The trouble with computers.* MIT Press: Cambridge, MA.

McIntosh, N., Cunningham, S. & Elton, R.A. (1994). 'Computerised trend monitoring'. *Pediatric Research,* Vol 36, pp. 28 *et seq.*

Nisbett, R.E. & Wilson, T.D. (1977). 'Telling more than we can know: verbal reports on mental processes'. *Psychological Review*, Vol. 84, pp. 231-259.

Shortliffe, E.H, Perrault, L.E., Fagan, L.M. & Wiederhold, G. (eds.) (1990). *Medical informatics: computer applications in health care.* Addison-Wesley: New York.

Acknowledgements

The authors would like to acknowledge the support of the UK Economic and Social Research Council, grant number L127251019.

23 The patient-monitor system in intensive care: eliciting nurses' mental models

Amanda Gilbert
University of Sussex, UK

Abstract

Intensive care nurses behave analogously to users of other complex systems in their interactions with the patient-monitor system. Based on Moray's (1992) assertion that transitions of sampling between elements of a system reveal the underlying cognitive representation of that system, nurses' mental models of the patient-monitor system were elicited. Nurses with different levels of expertise assessed a series of cases presented on computer. Their behaviour in sampling the cases was measured using a withholding technique in which all system data were kept hidden unless selected by means of a mouse movement. Pattern differences between nurses with different amounts of experience revealed that expert nurses' causal understanding allowed them to consider many more links between elements than inexperienced nurses. In addition, by making explicit the patterns of behaviour underlying expertise, the withholding technique provided a valuable aid to training.

Introduction

Nurses working in intensive care units (ICUs) behave analogously to users of other complex systems. As well as providing general nursing care, an intensive care nurse is responsible for maintaining the patient's stability, avoiding massive fluctuations in variables such as heart rate and arterial blood pressure. The nurse must continually monitor patient signs, administer fluids and drugs and observe their effects on objective and subjective measures of patient status (from cardiac output through to skin colour). Thus, in common with other complex control systems, such as those found in nuclear power plants, large amounts of information must be integrated in order for the nurse to maintain an accurate representation of the patient's status on which to base their nursing actions. In addition, these systems share a common factor of high cost associated with failure to recognize salient changes.

Although the nursing literature acknowledges the importance of nursing knowledge both as a description of nursing skill and as a foundation of theory and, hence, a basis for the institution of nursing as a profession (Smith, 1991), the methodologies used to explore the psychology of nursing do not in general reflect this. Indeed, the preponderance of studies grounded in the view of intensive care nurses as carers (Smith, 1991) and of nursing as a highly stressful, basically palliative process (Bailey & Clarke, 1989) perpetuates the notion of nurses as doctors' passive assistants. By adopting a different description of the intensive care nursing role, i.e. considering nurses as operators of complex systems, a new agenda for future research is set which provides an appreciation of nurses as active participants in patient treatment and recovery.

In his assessment of the impact of technology on nursing, Fitter (1987) states that nurses must have a representation in the form of a mental model of the nursing task allowing for manipulation and regulation of information associated with the technology. In this study, a rigorous definition of mental models (Moray, 1990; 1992) has been used to explore the ways in which such models affect nurses' reasoning about the patient-monitor system.

From novice to expert

Benner (1984) describes the types of skills which distinguish between nurses at different stages of development from novice to expert. Using intensive care nurses' introspections on their own interactions with patients as data to illustrate these stages, she identifies five stages of proficiency to which she ascribes the characteristics listed in table 1.

Though valuable to nurses concerned with evaluating their own performance, Benner's work is purely descriptive and provides no information about how expertise develops. Her reference to experts' use of mental models derives from a model of skill acquisition which implies that experts can perform in a way that novices can not, and gives an 'on top of it all' picture of expertise. This has been superseded by models in which experts are held to work harder, plan more and engage in continual revision of goals and methods (Scardamalia & Bereiter, 1991). However, Benner's detailed descriptions do present a useful framework on which to base studies of developing knowledge and for the comparison of mental models.

Table 1
Benner's (1984) five levels of proficiency and their characteristics

Proficiency	Characteristics
Novice	No experience of situations likely to be encountered. Limited, rule-governed behaviour.
Advanced Beginner	Able to note meaningful aspects of a situation as a result of experience in similar cases. Has difficulty in assessing the relative importance of different aspects and tends to focus on one thing in isolation. Stimulus-response approach to events.
Competent	Actions seen in terms of long-range goals. Assessment of relative importance of different aspects of current and anticipated situation. Some organisation of ideas.
Proficient	Situations perceived as wholes rather than in terms of aspects. Experience provides perspective; fewer options are considered as the nurse identifies salient aspects of a problem. Maxims are used to reflect nuances of a situation. Nurses can reach this level of competence after 3 to 5 years.
Expert	No reliance on rules, guidelines or maxims. Reasoning is more holistic. The nurse has an intuitive grasp of the situation and locates the source of a problem easily.

Mental models

The term 'mental model' has been used in a number of different contexts and to refer to a variety of different types of mental representation. Definitions vary; however, for the purpose of this project, a specific definition, Moray's (1990) lattice theory of mental models, has been selected.

In the most general terms, mental models can be considered as structural analogues of the world (Johnson-Laird, 1983). They allow for the internal simulation of a particular system or situation from which judgements might be made. Thus, they also allow for the prediction of future system states. Based on this notion, Moray (1990) presents a much more constrained definition. He describes mental models of complex control systems as hierarchical lattices of causality. Lattices are constructed through homomorphic (or many to one)

177

mappings from the physical system and contain descriptions of the system at different levels of abstraction. Moray (1990) requires that reasoning about the causal relationships between the elements which make up the system can happen only between levels of abstraction, that is, up and down the hierarchy. Thus, causal relationships between system elements can only be understood if they are linked at a higher level.

Moray's approach has a great deal to recommend it in that he provides a formalism by which users' models can be described and which therefore has application for both system design and training. In addition, he makes a number of predictions for the formalism which form the basis of its test.

Following on from Rasmussen (1986), Moray (1992) suggests that, given that individuals will apply their past experience to new problems, experienced system users will display lattices of increasing complexity. Thus, nurses with greater levels of experience are likely to show differences in their reported understanding of the causal relationships within the patient- monitor system.

Another prediction arises from some work by Lee & Moray (1992). They found that causal reasoning about the system could be inferred from shifts of attention between its elements, the user's mental model controlling the ways in which information about the system is sampled. Thus, the structure of the mental model was present in the user's sampling behaviour and its measurement would reveal the lattice (Moray, 1992).

Measuring nurses' mental models

The aim of this study was to elicit and compare intensive care nurses' mental models of the patient-monitor system by measuring the ways in which nurses' sampling behaviour changed with experience. Detailed analyses of the nursing task and of nurses' reported understanding of the causal relationships between the system's components which form the basis of this work are presented in Gilbert (1996).

In this study, nurses' interactions with the patient-monitor system were collected using a method proposed by Lee & Moray (1992). They argued that a withholding technique, in which operators moved a mouse in order to gather information about a system, would approximate to the behaviour of operators scanning a system. Such a method would not require the complex measurement of eye movements and, by making each movement more explicit, avoid a great deal of the controversy surrounding eye gaze studies.

The withholding technique

The withholding technique was implemented using a Hypercard 2.1 program running on an Apple Macintosh portable computer. Four cases were presented, each of which contained data from 14 discrete system elements including ECG traces and recent nursing actions. In order to assess each patient's current condition, data could be accessed by moving the mouse pointer into a labelled section of the screen. Moving the mouse into the section causes the information to appear; moving out of the section causes the information to disappear. Thus, a nurses' movements through the system could be mapped by recording the time spent at every location and the order in which the elements were sampled.

Method

Twenty-one nurses took part in the study. All were qualified nurses, ranging in intensive care experience from two months to 16 years. Subsequently, they were assigned to three groups; Experts, Competent and Advanced Beginners.

Nurses were asked to assess each of the four patients with a view to planning their ongoing care. Detailed instructions were provided about the method of obtaining data but nurses were not informed that their movements through the system would be recorded. Having been given the opportunity to practice moving the mouse in order to obtain patient data, they were then presented with each of the four cases in a random order. They were encouraged to comment on their thoughts about the cases as they assessed them and to write any notes they required. They were also free to ask questions and to speculate on the patient's medical condition.

Results

Pattern differences revealed differences in the complexity of the nurses' mental models. These differences are best revealed by considering the possible patterns of search employed by members of each group. In figures 1 and 2, links between elements identified by five or more nurses in two groups have been represented in networks. Transitions between elements, and therefore causal links in Moray's terms, are indicated by the connecting lines. Thus, the thickest lines represent the possible first transitions and each subsequent transition is represented by successively thinner lines. Figure 1 shows the first two possible transitions used by nurses in the expert group and figure 2 those for the advanced beginners. Note that, with a starting point of 'arterial blood pressure', a key element for all groups, the commonly used links allow the expert nurses to cover the entire system in these two moves, whereas advanced beginners covered only half. Competent nurses showed a similar pattern of behaviour to the expert group, though the group as a whole showed less consensus.

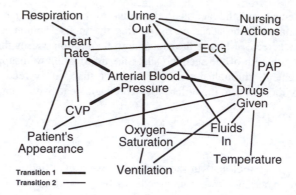

Figure 1 **Network of possible transitions made by experts in their first two moves**

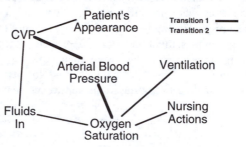

Figure 2 **Network of possible transitions made by advanced beginners in their first two moves**

Discussion

These patterns provide some support for Moray's predictions in that they indicate a difference in complexity of causal understanding of the patient-monitor system. However, construction of Moray's lattices of causality as described earlier in this chapter, proved to be inappropriate and, for any system containing more than a few discrete components, unwieldy. Thus, we must consider whether Moray's theory of mental models has any functional application and whether his lattices of causality can provide any useful information other than a visual comparison of the effects of expertise.

However, both the theory and the methodology by which it is tested have application in the development of nursing expertise and this issue will be discussed in the final section of this chapter.

Implications for training

Mental models are often argued to have a role to play in training. Indeed, a considerable amount of research has been carried out which demonstrates the value of mental models in the development of skilled behaviour (e.g. Kieras & Bovair, 1984). However, many such studies lack a clear description of the mental model and this means that, in practice, there is little information available to the trainer as to what might be the most suitable model to optimise development of expertise.

The approach presented here may provide a solution to this problem. The computer based task provides a method by which patterns of sampling behaviour and, hence, causal understanding can be described. Thus, there is a direct application to training. Moreover, the withholding technique is extremely versatile as it allows for training at all levels of expertise. In her descriptions of levels of proficiency (table 1), Benner (1984) also provides a detailed analysis of the different training requirements for nurses during their progression from novice to expert.

For example, she suggests that training of advanced beginners should focus on the recognition of aspects of the situation, that is, content-specific features of the patient's condition which can be related to previous experience. In addition, advanced beginners need help in setting priorities for care. The case studies in the program can be assessed in these terms by incorporating discussion about aspects in common with cases met on the unit.

In the case of experts, Benner (1984) advocates a much more systematic and introspective approach to training. Thus, the case studies could form the focus of detailed discussion between two nurses of equal experience and the issues presented by the case and points of view arising from it could be compared. This type of exchange has value for expert nurses because it allows them to introspect on the knowledge which guides their practice. In addition, it gives them an insight into the nursing task which they can apply in training of less experienced nurses.

Thus, differences in patterns of behaviour between nurses with varying levels of expertise provide evidence of the types of mental model differences predicted by Moray (1992). Experienced nurses' more complex understanding of the causal relationships between the elements of the patient-monitor system, demonstrated by their more efficient coverage of the system when assessing patients, indicates how Benner's (1984) findings might be explained. Furthermore, the application of the withholding technique in training provides a valuable, theoretically grounded resource in the development of nursing skill.

References

Bailey, R. & Clarke, M. (1989) *Stress and Coping in Nursing.* Chapman and Hall: London.

Benner, P. (1984) *From Novice to Expert.* Addison-Wesley: Menlo Park, CA.

Fitter, M. (1987), 'The impact of new technology on nurses and patients', in R. Payne & J. Firth-Cozens (eds.), *Stress in Health Professionals.* John Wiley & Sons: Chichester.

Gilbert, A.K. (1996) *The Role of Technology in Intensive Care Nursing: Mental Models of the Patient-Monitor System.* Unpublished PhD Thesis: University of Sheffield.

Johnson-Laird, P.N. (1983). *Mental Models.* Cambridge University Press: Cambridge.

Kieras, D.E. & Bovair, S. (1984), 'The role of a mental model in learning to operate a device'. *Cognitive Science,* Vol. 8, pp. 255-273.

Lee, J.D. & Moray, N. (1992), 'Operators monitoring patterns and fault recovery in the supervisory control of a semi-automatic process'. *Proceedings of the Human Factors Society 36th Annual Meeting,* Vol. II, pp.1143-1147.

Moray, N. (1990), 'A lattice theory approach to the structure of mental models'. *Philosophical Transcripts of the Royal Society of London, Series B,* Vol. 327, pp. 577-583.

Moray, N. (1992), Mental models of Complex Dynamic Systems. *Proceedings of the Second Interdisciplinary Workshop on Mental Models,* Cambridge, UK, 23-25 March 1992.

Rasmussen, J. (1986) *Information Processing and Human-Machine Interaction: An Approach to Cognitive Engineering.* Elsevier: North Holland.

Scardamalia, M & Bereiter, C. (1991), 'Literate Expertise', in K.A. Ericsson & J. Smith (eds.), *Toward a General Theory of Expertise: Prospects and Limits.* Cambridge University Press: Cambridge.

Part Four
APPLIED COGNITIVE PSYCHOLOGY

24 Audiovisual links in attention: implications for interface design

Charles Spence and Jon Driver*
University of Cambridge, UK
*Birkbeck College, University of London, UK

Abstract

In recent years interface operators have been presented with increasingly complex visual working environments. This has led many human factors researchers to resort to the auditory channel as an alternative, or supplementary, means of information transfer. However, little consideration has been given to possible limits on an operator's ability to process information presented simultaneously to different sensory modalities (e.g. to audition and vision). We highlight several recent studies from cognitive psychology which help to elucidate and quantify the nature of these limitations on multimodal information processing. The main findings are that: (i) people respond more slowly to visual stimuli when required simultaneously to monitor, or attend to, the auditory channel; (ii) people find it easier to process concurrent auditory and visual streams of information when they are presented from the same location; and (iii) auditory warning signals are more effective at attracting attention to positions than visual signals.

Introduction

Human factors researchers are increasingly using the auditory channel to present information to pilots and other operators working with complex visual displays (Edworthy, 1994). The development of auditory virtual reality seems certain to ensure that this trend continues. The inherently greater alerting effects of auditory cues (Posner, 1978), and the ability to present such stimuli out of the current field of view (which may be necessary when the operator is required to move around), means that they may provide more effective warning signals than visual stimuli. Auditory cues can also be used to facilitate the detection and foveation of significant visual stimuli in both empty and cluttered visual environments (e.g. Perrott, Sadralodabai, Saberi, & Strybel, 1991).

185

However, despite the increasing requirements placed on interface operators to monitor or process information presented simultaneously in audition and vision, few studies have attempted to investigate systematically the nature of any constraints which may limit our ability to attend to information presented in different modalities (Selcon, Taylor, & McKenna, 1995). Indeed, the common assumption seems to have been that people can process information presented to the eye and ear independently (e.g. Wogalter, Kalsher, & Racicot, 1993). However, several recent studies have shown that there are 'hard-wired' links between auditory and visual attentional systems which place significant limitations on an operator's ability to process information presented in different modalities.

The experimental study of attention

Our senses are constantly bombarded by information emanating from the distal events which normally fill our environments. These events are typically specified by information which is available to several sensory systems simultaneously (e.g. as when we both see and hear something moving). We are, however, severely limited in the amount of information we can fully process at any one time. Mechanisms of selective attention allow us to process preferentially just those stimuli which may be of particular interest to us. In the last two decades cognitive psychologists have conducted numerous studies in an attempt to elucidate the underlying mechanisms which control attention. However, the majority of this research has been directed at issues related to selection within just unimodal *visual* scenes (see Klein, Kingstone, & Pontefract, 1992, for a recent review).

The most frequently used research tool for the study of attention has been the cuing paradigm devised by Posner (1978) for studying *covert* shifts of attention, which occur in the absence of overt realignments of the peripheral receptors (i.e. without movements of the eyes and the ears). In a typical study, participants make a simple reaction to the onset of a visual target which may appear at any one of several positions. The participant's covert attention is directed to a particular location before the onset of each target, by cues such as a peripheral flash, or a central arrow pointing to the likely position of the target. Target detection is normally better at the cued location relative to uncued locations, even when participants do not move their eyes toward the cued locus. This result has been attributed to a beneficial shift in covert visual attention toward the cued position.

The cuing paradigm has been used to highlight a distinction between exogenous and endogenous attentional mechanisms. Exogenous (or automatic) orienting refers to the bottom-up control of attention by salient peripheral events (such as uninformative peripheral auditory or visual cues), and this has been contrasted with the endogenous (or voluntary) orienting mechanisms which are thought to control strategic shifts of attention. These occur as a result of the participant's expectancies (typically induced by informative symbolic cues, as when a central arrow indicates that a target is likely in a particular direction). Several qualitative differences between these forms of covert visual orienting have been demonstrated in vision (e.g. Klein, 1994). Recent studies have shown that covert shifts of *auditory* attention may also occur both exogenously and endogenously (e.g. Spence & Driver, 1994).

Given that both exogenous and endogenous mechanisms of covert selective attention operate within hearing and vision, the question arises as to how they may be linked across the modalities. In the following sections we will highlight several recent findings from our laboratory which were directed at this particular problem. The three issues which we will focus on are: (i) whether the attentional resources available to process auditory and visual information are independent; (ii) whether there are *spatial* links in the allocation of auditory and visual attention; and (iii) whether there are any asymmetries in how attention-capturing auditory and visual events are.

Experimental findings

Dividing attention between ear and eye

Interface operators must divide their attention between vision and audition in order to process efficiently the information presented by audiovisual displays. There is a large body of research devoted to the issue of whether attentional resources in audition and vision are entirely independent, or whether it takes time to shift attention from one modality to another. Many researchers have claimed to show that there is a significant cost associated with endogenously shifting attention between audition and vision. However, Spence and Driver (in press-a) recently highlighted a number of potential confounds in the results of the majority of these previous studies.

Spence and Driver (in press-a) reported four experiments designed to examine whether endogenous attention-shifting costs could still be demonstrated when the confounds inherent in the previous studies were removed. A random sequence of auditory and visual targets were presented to participants from one of four positions arranged in a rectangle around fixation. An informative precue (80 per cent valid with respect to the actual target modality) was presented prior to target onset, and participants were instructed to attend to the modality indicated by this symbolic cue. Significant costs were associated with shifting attention between audition and vision, and vice versa, across a range of tasks which included simple detection, colour/loudness discrimination, and localization. Reaction times were increased by approximately eight per cent on those trials where participants were required to shift their attention from the expected modality to another prior to responding. These findings show that the resources available for the processing of auditory and visual information are not independent. Operators benefit from accurate expectations of the likely target modality, and show substantial costs if their expectations are not fulfilled.

187

Charles Spence and Jon Driver

Spatial constraints in the cross-modal allocation of attention

Several researchers have suggested that attention operates on a supramodal representation of space in the human brain (e.g. Farah, Wong, Monheit, & Morrow, 1989; Ward, 1994). One implication of this claim would be that auditory and visual attention can only be allocated to one common location at a time. In other words, operators should find it impossible to process visual information presented in one location and auditory information presented from another simultaneously. However, Driver and Spence (1994; Spence & Driver, 1996) were able to demonstrate that auditory and visual endogenous attention can be allocated to different regions under the appropriate conditions, albeit with some difficulty, and they proposed an alternative 'separable-but-linked' hypothesis to account for the cross-modal interactions controlling attention.

Participants in Spence and Driver's (1996) studies were required to judge the elevation (up vs. down) of auditory and visual targets presented from either the left or right of fixation. In some experiments participants were instructed to direct just their auditory or just their visual attention to one side. Directing attention to the left or right in an up/down discrimination task is known as the 'orthogonal cuing' procedure, and has several methodological advantages when studying covert spatial attention, as Spence and Driver (1996) discuss. Results showed that when targets were expected on a particular side in just *one* modality, corresponding shifts of attention also took place in the other modality, as evidenced by faster elevation judgments on that side. In another experiment, participants were instructed to direct their auditory attention to one side, and their visual attention to the other side for a whole block of trials. Results showed that participants could 'split' auditory and visual endogenous attention to some extent when targets in the two modalities were expected on constant but opposite sides, albeit with reduced efficiency compared to elevation performance when auditory and visual targets were expected on the same side.

Similar results were reported by Driver and Spence (1994) in a series of continuous monitoring studies, where participants were required to repeat (shadow) one of two verbal messages (one auditory stream was presented from either side of the participant's midline). In one experiment participants were given lip-read information which matched the auditory stream which they were trying to shadow. This visual information produced a larger improvement in performance when presented on the same side as the target sounds rather than the opposite side, supporting the claim that directing auditory and visual attention in different directions induces a performance cost. Furthermore, this difficulty cannot be attributed to the direction of the participant's gaze, as there was no effect of passively fixating meaningless lip-movements on the same versus opposite side as the target sounds. Similar results were also reported under conditions where the visual task was changed to monitoring for a specified target in a stream of visual characters appearing successively at a single location (i.e. where the auditory and visual tasks were unrelated), and even occurred when the irrelevant auditory stream was removed (i.e. to produce a conventional dual task scenario, with no distracting information).

These results show that auditory and visual attention are linked, such that an endogenous shift of either just auditory or just visual attention in one direction tends to elicit a concomitant shift of attention in the other modality. This makes it hard to direct auditory and visual attention in different locations simultaneously. However, contrary to previous claims (e.g. Farah et al., 1989; Ward, 1994), attention does not operate on a supramodal representation of space. Instead, it seems that endogenous auditory and visual attention can be focussed on different positions under the appropriate circumstances, albeit with a cost in performance.

Warning signals and attentional capture

One function of warning signals is to capture an operator's attention and make him or her aware of pressing or urgent information (Woods, 1995). Although it is commonly assumed that auditory stimuli provide the most effective warning signals (e.g. Edworthy, 1994; Wogalter et al., 1993), there have been few empirical studies of this issue. Furthermore, there has been a lack of consensus in the literature regarding the existence of cross-modal links in exogenous spatial orienting. Some researchers have argued that the presentation of spatially-uninformative peripheral auditory stimuli results in the cross-modal exogenous orienting of visual attention to the cued location (e.g. Buchtel & Butter, 1988; Farah et al., 1989; Klein, Brennan, & Gilani, 1987), but others have failed to find any such effects (Ward, 1994). Similarly, there has been some controversy over whether visual events attract auditory attention, with positive results reported by Ward, but not by others (e.g. Buchtel & Butter, 1988; Klein et al., 1987). Unfortunately, all these prior studies are open to alternative non-attentional explanations in terms of criterion shifting, response priming, or the use of auditory detection tasks that are insensitive to the distribution of attention (see Spence & Driver, 1994; Spence & Driver, in press-b, for a critical review).

Spence and Driver (in press-b) recently adapted their orthogonal-cuing paradigm to investigate cross-modal links in exogenous (i.e. automatic) spatial orienting, by presenting spatially-uninformative peripheral cues (auditory or visual) from either the left or right of participant's fixation, shortly (100 - 700 ms) before auditory or visual targets requiring an elevation (up/down) discrimination. Judgments were faster and more accurate for targets in either modality when preceded by an auditory cue on the same rather than opposite side as the target, even though the cue was spatially-uninformative with regard to the likely target location. This suggests that peripheral sounds summon exogenous covert orienting in both hearing and vision, resulting in better spatial localization within the attended region in both modalities. Several further studies revealed that, in contrast to auditory cues, spatially-uninformative visual cues only reliably affected visual judgments, having no effect on hearing across a wide range of parameters. These results suggest a one-way cross-modal dependence in the control of exogenous spatial orienting, with auditory orienting leading to concomitant visual orienting, but not vice versa. These results provide an empirical basis for claims that auditory warning signals are more effective in capturing attention, and also provide a reliable paradigm for measuring the effectiveness of various warning signals in producing orienting. The method can be adapted to examine exactly how spatially-specific such warning effects are.

Conclusions

The results of the experiments reported here clearly show that auditory and visual information-processing do not occur independently. Instead, audiovisual attentional resources are constrained by various cross-modal links (both exogenous and endogenous) between hearing and vision, which limit an operator's ability to process auditory and visual information simultaneously. Our main findings were, firstly, that visual information-processing performance decreases when people are required to attend to the auditory channel (and vice versa), even if they only *expect* a sound which subsequently does not occur. Second, people can attend more effectively to auditory and visual stimuli when they are presented from the same perceived distal location, and if they shift their attention endogenously in one modality, the other modality tends to follow. Finally, studies of exogenous cross-modal orienting reveal that auditory warning signals are more effective at automatically attracting spatial attention than visual signals.

These results may help to provide some preliminary guidelines for the design and evaluation of future multimodal interfaces. They highlight the fact that the addition of an auditory information channel to a visual interface leads to a significant trade-off in performance unless carefully considered. The benefits to be accrued from increasing the potential rate of information-transfer in cluttered visual working environments, and from the greater alerting properties of auditory stimuli, must be weighed against possible visual performance decrements attributed to the simultaneous division of attention between different sensory modalities. Our results also show that careful consideration should be given to the perceived source from which information in different modalities is presented, because decrements in performance caused by dividing attention can be significantly reduced simply by presenting stimuli from the same perceived distal location. Presumably, the development of auditory virtual reality will make this easier to achieve in the coming years. Finally, our orthogonal cuing paradigm provides an effective means of assessing the automatic 'attention-grabbing' properties of various warning signals for inducing appropriate exogenous spatial orienting.

References

Buchtel, H.A., & Butter, C.M. (1988). 'Spatial attention shifts: Implications for the role of polysensory mechanisms'. *Neuropsychologia*, Vol. 26, pp. 499-509.

Driver, J., & Spence, C.J. (1994). 'Spatial synergies between auditory and visual attention', in C. Umiltà & M. Moscovitch (eds.), *Attention and performance: Conscious and nonconscious information processing,* MIT Press: Cambridge, MA.

Edworthy, J. (1994). 'The design and implementation of non-verbal auditory warnings'. *Applied Ergonomics*, Vol. 25, pp. 202-210.

Farah, M.J., Wong, A.B., Monheit, M.A., & Morrow, L.A. (1989). 'Parietal lobe mechanisms of spatial attention: modality-specific or supramodal?' *Neuropsychologia*, Vol. 27, pp. 461-470.

Klein, R.M. (1994). 'Perceptual-motor expectancies interact with covert visual orienting under conditions of endogenous but not exogenous control'. *Canadian Journal of Experimental Psychology*, Vol. 48, pp. 167-181.

Klein, R.M., Brennan, M., & Gilani, A. (1987, November). 'Covert cross-modality orienting of attention in space'. Paper presented at the annual meeting of the Psychonomics Society, Seattle.

Klein, R.M., Kingstone, A., & Pontefract, A. (1992). 'orienting of visual attention'. In K. Rayner (ed.) *Eye movements and visual cognition: Scene perception and reading.* Springer-Verlag: New York.

Perrott, D.R., Sadralodabai, T., Saberi, K., & Strybel, T.Z. (1991). 'Aurally aided visual search in the central visual field: Effects of visual load and visual enhancement of the target'. *Human Factors*, Vol. 33, pp. 389-400.

Posner, M.I. (1978). *Chronometric explorations of mind.* Erlbaum: Hillsdale, NJ.

Selcon, S.J., Taylor, R.M., & McKenna, F.P. (1995). 'Integrating multiple information sources: using redundancy in the design of warnings'. *Ergonomics*, Vol. 38, pp. 2362-2370.

Spence, C.J., & Driver, J. (1994). 'Covert spatial orienting in audition: exogenous and endogenous mechanisms'. *Journal of Experimental Psychology: Human Perception and Performance*, Vol. 20, pp. 555-574.

Spence, C., & Driver, J. (1996). 'Audiovisual links in endogenous covert spatial attention'. *Journal of Experimental Psychology: Human Perception and Performance*, Vol. 22, pp. 1005-1030.

Spence, C., & Driver, J. (in press-a). 'On measuring selective attention to an expected sensory modality'. *Perception & Psychophysics.*

Spence, C., & Driver, J. (in press-b). 'Audiovisual links in exogenous covert spatial orienting'. *Perception & Psychophysics.*

Ward, L.M. (1994). 'Supramodal and modality-specific mechanisms for stimulus-driven shifts of auditory and visual attention'. *Canadian Journal of Experimental Psychology*, Vol. 48, pp. 242-259.

Wogalter, M.S., Kalsher, M.J., & Racicot, B.M. (1993). 'Behavioral compliance with warnings: effects of voice, context, and location'. *Safety Science*, Vol. 16, pp. 637-654.

Woods, D.D. (1995). 'The alarm problem and directed attention in dynamic fault management'. *Ergonomics*, Vol. 38, pp. 2371-2393.

Acknowledgements

This work was supported by a Junior Research Fellowship to the first author from St. John's College, Cambridge, and by grants from the MRC (UK).

25 A parallel distributed processing model of redundant information integration

Matthew Jackson and Steven J. Selcon
Defence Evaluation & Research Agency, Farnborough, UK

Abstract

A parallel distributed processing model of cross-modal, multiple information source integration was developed from a conceptual model by Selcon, Taylor and McKenna (1995) with the aim of developing a tool for display design. Quantitative data from the study were used to train a multilayer perceptron which was then used to predict the 11 other possible combinations of integrated information. Simulation one examined a network trained using primed and unprimed pathways and measured responses in absolute and forced choice conditions. Both conditions produced significant correlation with the Selcon et al (1995) empirical data.

Simulation two manipulated the integration rate of the visual verbal stimulus and improved the performance of the model to explain 92% of the variance. Results to date strongly support Selcon et al's (1995) conceptual model of redundancy gain and suggest that future development of the model may prove useful in display design.

Introduction

The applicability of redundant information source integration, in terms of either interference or facilitation, is important in the area of design for time-critical systems. One such obvious system is the human-machine interface of a fighter aircraft where time critical decisions are required. In addition, modern technology has made it possible to present auditory information spatially, necessitating research into the use of multi-modal information sources.

Cognitive information source integration is an area of investigation originated from the classic Stroop effect (Stroop, 1935), where incongruent word names and ink colours produce interference. Furthermore, Stroop facilitation showed that congruent stimuli produce an improvement in reaction time. Redundancy gains usually refer to the reduction in reaction time (RT) for a recognition experiment due to multiple presentations of the target (Grice and Canham, 1990). The term redundancy is used to describe this effect as it is the addition of extra stimuli, over that sufficient to complete the task, that produces the reduction in RT. Selcon, Taylor and McKenna (1995) examined whether performance could be improved by the presentation of multiple redundant sources of information. In the experiment, a simulated missile approach warning system used various combinations of stimuli presented across modalities to indicate the direction, either from the left or right, of an approaching missile. Four sources of information were presented independently and in all possible congruent, concurrent combinations (table 1). Significant redundancy gains were observed representing an overall reduction in RT of 30 percent. Selcon et al (1995) describe a conceptual PDP model of redundant information integration. Their model states that, provided the information pathways access a common neurone, the addition of more than one concurrent, congruent source of information will result in a reduced time to reach the activation criterion of that neurone.

The aim of this study was to take Selcon et al's (1995) conceptual model and produce a PDP implementation on computer. The model was trained using the RT data for the unintegrated, baseline stimuli. These individual pathways were then activated simultaneously to integrate the information sources and predict integrated RT data. This data could then be correlated against the quantitative data from the Selcon et al (1995) study. If validated, the model may, once fully developed, provide a useful tool for predicting operator performance on novel displays that utilise redundancy gain effects in their design. Within this framework it is further possible to examine priming effects on cognitive information source integration by examining the model with and without information about the individual stimuli primed into the pathway strengths.

Method

PDP models are constructed from a series of processing units called neurones that are inter-connected via pathways used to transfer information. The quality and speed of processing is dependent on the flow of information which in turn is dependent on the strength or ability of the appropriate pathways to transfer this information. The strength of a pathway is referred to as its weight ,w which may have either excitatory (+ve) or inhibitory (-ve) values. In a PDP network information is represented by the particular pattern of activation of neurones across the network. During processing the neurones are required to take up the appropriate pattern of activation that will translate or match the pattern of sensory inputs to the appropriate response at the output layer.

Table 1
Stimuli combinations from Selcon et al (1995)

COND-ITION	STIMULUS	INFORMATION CONTENT
C1	*Visual Verbal (Vv)*	Written word in centre of display
C2	*Visual Spatial (Vs)*	Row of Xs at one side of display
C3	*Auditory Verbal (Av)*	Spoken word equally to both ears
C4	*Auditory Spatial (As)*	Tone to one ear only
C5	*Vv + Vs*	Written word at one side of display
C6	*Vv + Av*	Written word in centre of display, spoken word to both ears
C7	*Vv + As*	Written word in centre of display, tone to one ear
C8	*Vs + Av*	Xs on one side of display, spoken word to both ears
C9	*Vs + As*	Xs on one side of display, tone to one ear
C10	*Av + As*	Spoken word to one ear only
C11	*Vv + Vs + Av*	Written word on one side of display, spoken word to both ears
C12	*Vv + Vs + As*	Written word on one side of display, tone to one ear
C13	*Vv + Av + As*	Written word in centre of display, spoken word in one ear
C14	*Vs + Av + As*	Xs on one side of display, spoken word to one ear
C15	*Vv + Vs + Av + As*	Written word on one side of display, spoken word to one ear.

The PDP model developed here has eight input neurones corresponding to the individual stimuli of the Selcon et al (1995) experiment, four requiring a left response and four requiring a right response. Two hidden neurones are fully connected to the input layer. These neurones act as the common neurone that must be accessed by the multiple pathways to produce the redundancy gains predicted by the conceptual model. The hidden neurones are in turn fully connected to two output neurones representing a left and right response. The model employs Rumelhart's (1986) back propagation learning algorithm with McClelland's (1979) cascade model to allow the model to learn the appropriate patterns of activation and to

195

provide a mechanism for the modelling of RT data. Repeated forward and backward passes of information (iterations) are designed to gradually reduce the overall difference between required and actual output to a value whereby presentation of an input pattern produces an approximation to the desired activations at the output. Simulated RT will be proportional to the number of forward passes during testing, required for the output activation to accumulatively exceed a fixed threshold.

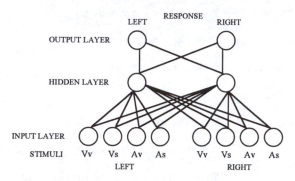

Figure 1   Model architecture

Simulation one

Training   Each subject's results were presented to the network and modelled individually. Eight training patterns were generated for each subject based on only one of the eight possible input stimuli being on at any one time. Hence the network learnt the pattern of activation for the individual stimuli which were then integrated in the testing phase.

For the unprimed condition the value of the input forced into the input layer was proportional to the appropriate empirical RT value from Selcon et al (1995) for that subject and each training pattern was presented an equal number of times. In the primed condition the inputs were given a unitary value and the pathways were trained a varying number of times proportional to the empirical RT data. Increased training strengthens the pathways hence information about the individual stimuli was being primed into the network.

Testing   For testing, patterns of inputs are used to indicate the presence or absence of a stimulus by activating the appropriate input neurone. The active pathways pass information forward through the common hidden neurone and on to the output layer to produce an output activation.

For the forced choice condition accumulative activation was calculated by summing the difference between the most active and least active output neurones.

For the absolute condition accumulative activation was calculated by summing the activation of the most active output neurone only.

After training on an individual subject's baseline data, the model was interrogated to provide all possible combinations of the baseline stimuli ie C1-C15. The stimuli required either a left or right response so two sets of C1-C15 were produced. The left/right responses were then averaged. All 18 subject's mean simulated responses were then averaged to produce an overall value for each condition for correlation against the empirical data.

Results

The table below shows the correlation for each condition between the subject's mean simulation and empirical data for conditions C5-C15.

Table 2
Results for simulation one

	Absolute response	Forced choice response
Primed	$r = 0.757$, prob<0.001, 10 df	$r = 0.735$, prob<0.001, 10 df
Un-primed	$r = 0.835$, prob<0.001, 10 df	$r = 0.807$, prob<0.001 , 10 df

The training conditions, C1-C4 , are not included in the correlation.

All results are highly significant, explaining between 54% of the variance for the primed forced choice condition and 69% for the unprimed absolute response condition.

Discussion

From the correlation values it is clear that the model explains the variance of the empirical data well in both primed and unprimed conditions. The unprimed, absolute response condition has the highest significant correlation of 0.835 explaining 70 percent of the variance in the data. In the simulation a redundancy gain is produced by two or more congruent neurones simultaneously being activated. The congruent input neurones pass on an increased amount of activation to the common hidden neurone and on to the appropriate output neurone. The increased output activation means that the number of forward passes required for the accumulated output activation (absolute or forced choice) to exceed the fixed response threshold is reduced ie simulated RT is reduced.

The common factor in the large simulated redundancy gains that do not fit the empirical data is the C1, Visual verbal (Vv), condition where a written word (left/right) was presented in the centre of the display. It may be that the difference in the results is due to an insensitivity in the design of the Selcon et al (1995) experiment to C1 or that the stimulus itself is not effectively integrating with other stimuli in a manner not explained by the conceptual model. To examine the latter suggestion, another simulation was conducted.

Simulation two

There may be a number of reasons why the Vv stimulus did not integrate well with other stimuli that are not contained in our model. One possibility is that the Vv stimulus, which produced the slowest RT, is too slow/weak to integrate effectively with the other, faster stimuli. This slowness translates to a low information transfer rate which may be insufficient to produce redundancy gains. Another possibility is that the Vv stimulus has irrelevant semantic connections associated with the words 'left' and 'right' relating to non-position meanings e.g. 'left behind', 'left over', correct, agreed, OK, etc. The reduced number of relevant semantic connections may result in the appropriate response neurone being activated too few times, or too weakly, to produce a significant redundancy effect.

The previous simulations showed a large redundancy gain for the Vv stimulus, consistent with the PDP model put forward by Selcon et al (1995) but not shown in the empirical data. In simulation two the ability of the Vv stimulus to integrate with other stimuli was manipulated to examine whether the hypothesis that Vv was not integrating effectively is a characteristic of the human system for the Vv stimulus, not incorporated into the original conceptual model. This should be reflected in an improvement in the performance of the model.

Training and testing The most successful simulation thus far, the unprimed absolute condition, was trained in the same manner and using the same empirical data as that used in simulation one. The main difference in the simulation came in the test phase where the strength of the pathway associated with Vv was randomly degraded during the multiple forward passes that generate the RT data. This degrading of the pathway could be assumed to be mathematically analogous to the effect of either reducing the ability of the common neurone to integrate a slow stimulus or of reducing the number of connections to the common node (due to a sharing of semantic connections).

Results

A Pearson's correlation gave a significant correlation $r = 0.959$, prob<0.001, 10 df).

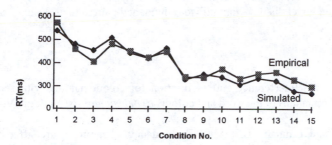

Figure 2   Results for simulation two

Discussion

The performance of the model was improved by limiting the ability of the Vv stimulus to integrate with other stimuli. It is impossible to discriminate from the model between the two suggested hypotheses for the effect as, at this level of examination, both can be reduced to be mathematically similar in nature.

We have shown that the original conceptual model is limited in that it assumes equal integration of stimuli. This experiment has indicated that different stimuli can have different rates of integration, highlighted by the improvements in performance of simulation two.

General discussion

Although the model successfully explained 90% of the variance in the empirical data its limitations need to be addressed before assessing its potential as a display design tool. The Selcon et al (1995) study was a single task design where attentional allocation had been assumed. If the effects of attentional priority can be introduced into the model   it would allow more effective modelling of complex MMI environments.

The question of usefulness as a predictive tool rests on later empirical experiments to establish whether the original empirical results robustly reflect redundant information source integration or whether the non-significant findings associated with the visual verbal stimuli were the result of an experimental insensitivity. *A priori* verification of the model is therefore required.

The conceptual model of information source integration by Selcon et al (1995) has been robustly supported by the performance of the PDP model, however refinement of the model indicated that differing rates of information integration need to be addressed. With further development it may be possible to predict a user's performance on novel displays that utilise redundancy gain in their design.

References

Dyer, F.N. (1973) Interference and facilitation for colour naming with separate bilateral presentations of the word and colour. *Experimental Psychology*, Vol. 99, pp. 314-317.

Grice, G.R., and Canham, L. (1990) Redundancy Phenomena are affected by Response Requirements. *Perception and Psychophysics*, Vol. 48, pp. 209-213.

McClelland, J.L. and Rumelhart, D.E. and the PDP research group (1986) *Parallel Distributed Processing*, Vols 1 and 2. Cambridge University Press: Cambridge.

McClelland, J.L. (1979) On the time relations of Mental Processes: An examination of Systems of Processes in Cascade. *Psychological Review*, Vol. 86, pp. 287-330.

Rumelhart, D.E., Hinton, G.E., and Williams, R.J. (1986). 'Learning internal representations by error propagation'. In, McClelland, J.L. and Rumelhart, D.E. and the PDP research group (eds.) *Parallel Distributed Processing*, Vols 1 and 2. Cambridge University Press: Cambridge.

Selcon, S.J., Taylor, R.M. and McKenna, F.P. (1995) 'Integrating multiple information sources: using redundancy in the design of warnings'. *Ergonomics*, Vol 2, pp. 190-200.

Stroop, J.R. (1935) Studies of Interference in Serial Verbal Reactions. *Journal of Experimental Psychology*, Vol. 84, pp. 127-190.

26 The magical name Miller, plus or minus the umlaut

Derek J. Smith
University of Wales Institute, Cardiff, UK

Abstract

Models of cognitive processing traditionally fail when they address higher mental processes such as consciousness and volition. Due in part to the lack of suitable diagramming methods, and despite pioneering work by Miller (1956), attempts to determine the channel capacities of information pathways in the mind have had only restricted success. Reasons for this are discussed, and suggestions for improvement made.

Millers, milling, and control systems

It is now more than 40 years since George Miller gave us 'The Magical Number Seven, Plus or Minus Two', and in that intervening period the cognitive approach has progressively established itself as one of the major theoretical orientations of modern psychology. However, the specific concepts the Miller paper introduced us to - concepts such as channel capacity, subitizing, and 'chunking' - have not shared that success. For example, in a sample of five recent cognitive textbooks only 18 out of a total of 2311 pages dealt in any way with these concepts, and the count for unquantified versus quantified information flow diagrams was 42 - nil.

What we believe these facts illustrate is that the Miller paper helped fuel cognitive psychology's appetite for information processing terminology and diagrams, but failed to persuade it to quantify the boxes and arrows used in those diagrams. Cognitive psychologists have accordingly been getting away all these years with a soft, common sense, *hydraulic,* definition of information, namely that it is knowledge of a sort, and seems to flow down axon tracts (or arrows) the way water flows down pipes.

Not that measuring information flow was ever going to be easy. Even the Miller paper was forced to apply its hypothetical flow meter (see figure 1) across the

Derek J. Smith

cognitive system as an unanalysed whole, obtaining by so doing an end-to-end channel capacity of around 2.8 bits. Which is interesting enough in its own right, but tells us nothing about the internal modular organization of the mind. And that is a serious failing, given that both modern cognitive modelling and the far older study of the localization of mental function are frequently brought to grief by the modularity problem. Indeed, even at the cutting edge of modern artificial intelligence research, the development of modular neural network architectures is beginning to place a hefty premium on the ability to analyse the flow of information between the separate nodes of a multi-noded problem solver (e.g. Norris, 1991). And why? Because we still do not really understand how a mind is put together. We recognize that it is basically a glorified control system, but the principles of its architecture are little better understood today than they were a century ago. Above all, we are still unable to place the age-old mysteries of will, consciousness, memory, skill, and knowledge on our diagrams, because we have no mathematical method to locate such phenomena with any precision. To put it bluntly, the soft option - the unquantified information flow diagram - has become a luxury we can no longer afford. Nowadays, we need models which specify internal information transfer rates. We need, in other words, to return to the sort of numbers which so persecuted Miller in the 1950s.[1]

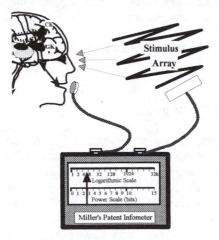

Figure 1   An information flow meter

---

[1] We give due credit to one of the few models to stray from the hydraulic view of information, namely Helmar Frank's Organogramm (Frank, 1963). However, even though this model specifies internal information capacities and transfer rates, it is rarely cited and takes a more simplistic definition of LTM than is now in vogue - see subsequent discussion.

With all this in mind, the originally conceived purpose of the present paper was to preview the type of model this tightening of the discipline might spawn. However, when in the summer of 1995 we began to flesh out our arguments, we started to feel a little persecuted ourselves - by the name Miller. For just as George Miller was plagued in his time by the magical number seven, so, too, is the history of control systems plagued by a recurrent theme. As coincidence would have it, many of the formative uses of control technology had to do with millers!

The Miller (1956) paper applied a hypothetical information flow meter across the cognitive system *as a whole*, thus measuring its end-to-end transmission capacity (in this case for a spoken response to a visual stimulus). This gave the magical number seven on the upper, natural numbers, scale, or 2.8 bits on the lower, powers of two, scale. The internal modularity shown on this occasion is that suggested by the 19th century 'diagram maker' Henry Bastian.

Now the story of milling begins approximately 10,000 years ago, with the discovery that two suitably shaped stones could be used as a primitive pestle and mortar to crush up grass seeds. And so versatile and nutritious was the resulting food source that as a species we turned from our nomadic hunter-gatherer lifestyle to one based instead on settlement dwelling and the cultivation and processing of grain. Without exaggeration, it was grain and the ability to mill it which put the 'new' into the new stone age and the *civis* into civilization. It was a truly epoch-making invention, and subsequent developments in the technology have merely improved upon the basic two-stone system. Here is the main evolutionary sequence:

by 3000 BC	**saddle quern:** a large flat bedstone with a smaller topstone.	
by 500 BC	**rotary quern:** a pair of round stones with an annular common face.	
by 0 AD	**watermill:** a rotary quern driven by a waterwheel.	
by 700 AD	**'Persian' windmill:** a vertically axled windmill.	
by 1200 AD	**postmill:** a horizontally axled windmill; pivoted on a central post.	
by 1400 AD	**'Dutch' mill:** the 'classic' windmill; only the cap, or 'tower', rotates.	
by 1800 AD	**advanced Dutch mill:** with automatic control processes (see next).	

So where does the control technology come in? Well, after the invention of the postmill, for example, one of the miller's chores was to manhandle the mill tower - several tons of it - round into a new position every time the wind direction changed. In 1745, however, Edward Lee perfected his *fantail mechanism,* a small rotor mounted at a right angle to the main sails and geared down onto a circular track. Whenever the wind shifted off the main sails, it would drive the fantail instead, thus cranking the tower back into the wind again (and the fantail back out of it). Another common problem was how to maintain the quality of the grind when gusting made the topstone turn so quickly that it 'bounced' and coarsened the flour. Millers traditionally had to spend a lot of time trimming their sails and making adjustments to the height of their topstones to compensate. Until 1787, that is, when Thomas Mead introduced his *centrifugal governor* as a means of making these adjustments automatically and from some distance away via a complex set of link rods, pivots, and springs.

Negative feedback mechanisms such as Lee's and Mead's - where action is taken to counteract some observed error - have been widely used in mechanical engineering ever since. Nevertheless, they are only capable of maintaining a preset turning speed, so you still need a miller to do the presetting. There are thus two basic flows of command and feedback: on the one hand there is a continuous flow of information *within* the control mechanism itself, and on the other there is a more intermittent flow between the mechanism and the miller. And this is where the name Miller begins to persecute, for this particular distinction goes back at least to R.B. Miller (1953, cited in Annett, 1969), who contrasted *action feedback* - that which is required internally by a device - and *learning feedback* - that which is required by that device's higher-order control processes.

So we now have two Millers to contend with: G.A. telling us that the total amount of information the mind can cope with is highly restricted, and R.B. telling us to expect a hierarchy of control processes in all complex systems. Indeed, there is precisely such a hierarchy in the mind, as is shown diagrammatically by circuits I to III in figure 2. Moreover, it is possible that by measuring the information flows within and between such circuits we could learn something special about the miller in the mental mill - that is to say, about the phenomenon of consciousness. But to expand upon that possibility, we need to introduce yet another Miller!

Max Müller and the search for semantic absolutes

Our third miller - the 19th century professor of linguistics, Max Müller - was one of the first to recognize that word meanings are constantly evolving, and spent a lifetime studying the etymologies of words in a variety of languages with a view to tracking down their derivations (Müller, 1887). Working in this way, he reduced all languages to much smaller pools of word roots and fundamental concepts. To give but one example, the Greek words for lift, compare, tribute, spread, delay, bury, madness, endure, recover, reproach, help, and excel (to name but a few) all derive in various ways from φερ, 'to bear'. Müller's central argument goes as follows:

'Give us about 800 roots, and we can explain the largest dictionary; give us about 121 concepts, and we can account for the 800 roots. Even these 121 concepts might be reduced to a much smaller number, if we cared to do so'. (op. cit., p551.)

But not all authorities agree on where to draw the line. Whereas Müller chose a pool of 121 'original concepts', Saban (1993) chooses 31 basic 'semantic fields', and in the original 1852 edition of his renowned thesaurus Peter Roget went for 1,000 'related ideas'. So why the disagreement? Well insofar as it was responsible for importing the concept of the bit from engineering into psychology, the answer lies in George Miller's paper. This is because the logarithmic nature of the bit renders 31, 121, and 1,000 not so different after all: to be precise, they might just represent three points on the *powers of two* dimension.[2] That is to say, we need *five bits* of information to specify a single one of Saban's 31 semantic fields, *seven bits* of information to specify a single one of Müller's 121 original concepts, and *ten bits* of information to specify a single one of Roget's 1000 related ideas. Could we, therefore, be looking at a semantic memory which somehow operates according to a binary chop principle?

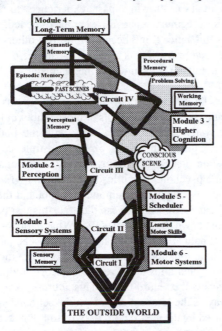

This six-module flow diagram has been simplified from Smith (1993), and is compatible with a host of earlier diagrams, notably Frank (1963) and Lehrl and Fischer (1988). Sensory information ascends from module 1 to module 3, where it becomes conscious, and a corresponding motor pathway descends from module 3 to module 6. The main LTM complex is Module 4 (top left). Four major information flow circuits link the modules. Circuits I and II constitute the *action feedback* system, by which the sensory systems monitor the effect the motor systems are having on the outside world. Circuit III is the *learning feedback* system, by which behaviour is consciously directed. Circuit IV is the *LTM system* as described in the text. [Diagram from Smith (1996:97), by permission of University of Wales Institute, Cardiff.]

Figure 2 The four mental control circuits

---

[2] Thus 2^5 is 32, 2^7 is 12^8, and 2^{10} is 1024. The relationship between the linear and logarithmic measures of information can be seen on the upper and lower scales of the flow meter shown in figure 1.

Derek J. Smith

Now to see how this might be of use to engineering psychologists, we need a model which differentiates between the various subtypes of knowledge, and it so happens that these are clearly separated in our own six-module model of cognition (Smith, 1993). The layout of this model is shown in figure 2, and semantic memory can be seen to be a major subcomponent of module 4. Note also the three basic subsystems. Firstly there is an action feedback system (circuits I and II), then there is a learning feedback system (circuit III), and finally there is a long term memory (LTM) system (circuit IV) allowing past experience to be fed back into consciousness (as acts of memory retrieval) whenever needed. And it is semantic memory which drives this latter flow, because it allows otherwise random acts of recollection to become *declarative*, that is to say, propositions of truth. It is semantic memory which, by organizing and indexing mere imagery, allows it to become knowledge.

The point about these three fundamentally different subsystems is that they require fundamentally different backgrounds and skills of those who would understand them. The action feedback system, for example, deals with the body's biomechanical systems and therefore requires the skills of the real-time control engineer, the learning feedback system deals with the mystery of consciousness and therefore requires the skills of the psychologist-philosopher, and the LTM system deals with the safe distribution and indexing of large amounts of data and therefore requires the skills of the database designer. Indeed, we can illustrate this last point by considering the database mechanism known as *currency of set*. What happens in many databases is that large volumes of data are organized into indexed sets, and when that data is accessed for the first time looking for a specific record, the index is scanned by a binary chop technique. This allows the required record address to be extracted, which is then used to access the record itself. This address - known as the *database key* - is then stored away as the 'current record' in the set concerned, and it remains safely stored until replaced by the next record drawn from that set. In the meantime, however, many other records in many other sets can be processed, and the benefit comes in the (extremely common) event that this subsequent processing wants to see the original record a second time. This is because the database software can now access it directly using the stored database key,[3] *without the overhead of re-reading the set index*.

Now you need only to imagine a body of data indexed on several dimensions simultaneously, to see how the benefit of such a contrivance can accumulate, and you need only to look at the growing preference for 'domain' theories of memory organization (e.g. Allport, 1985) to see how easy it is to view biological memory as indexed on several dimensions simultaneously. The set currency approach would also go a long way towards explaining the powers of two relationship linking Müller's, Roget's, and Saban's notions of semantic absolutes. On some occasions

---

[3] Using an instruction which (in pseudocode) would take the form OBTAIN CURRENT OF <SET-NAME>.

broad semantic statements need to be made (requiring bit counts in the range one to five), on other occasions mid-range statements need to be made (in the range six to ten), and on yet other occasions very precise concept identification is needed (in the range 11 to 18, or so). There is, in short, no absolute absolute. Nor ever was. It is all a matter of how much semantic information needs to be 'kept current' to support the processing at hand, and that will vary widely from task to task.

Conclusion

In summary, we hope we have demonstrated that Millers have played (and continue to play) a vital part in analysing the deepest mysteries of mental life. In addition to harnessing one of nature's seriously impressive pieces of wisdom, the seed, they invented mechanisms to tame the forces of earth, wind, and fire as well, and even provided us (in the form of the miller-mill relationship) with a perfect metaphor for the mind-brain relationship. Moreover, we have been forced by space constraints to ignore a host of lesser contributions, such as the fact that P. Müller's (1963) *Lernmatrizen* helped fashion the modern neural network, or that R. Miller provides us with a comprehensive set of neuronal circuit diagrams for a host of learning phenomena (Miller, 1981). And to cap it all, millers were even amongst the first to use flow diagrams to map out their processes, with Storck and Teague (1952) describing these as having been 'regularly used' (and - reassuringly - much argued about) in their trade magazines from 1883 onwards. Millers, and yet more millers! Of course it might all be pernicious coincidence; an act of cosmic vengeance for some long-forgotten peccadillo. Or then again it might be that there is something deep and profound about Millers themselves, as well as their magical numbers.

References

Allport, D.A. (1985). 'Distributed memory, modular systems and dysphasia.' In S.K. Newman,. & R. Epstein (eds.) *Current perspectives in dysphasia.* Churchill Livingstone: Edinburgh.

Annett, J. (1969). *Feedback and Human Behaviour.* Penguin: Harmondsworth.

Frank, H. (1963). 'Informationspsychologie und Nachrichtentechnik', in N. Wiener, & J.P. Schadé, (eds.), *Nerve, Brain and Memory Models.* Elsevier: Amsterdam.

Lehrl, S. & Fischer, B. (1988). 'The basic parameters of human information processing'. *Personality and Individual Differences,* Vol. 9, pp. 883-896.

Miller, G.A. (1956). 'The magical number seven, plus or minus two'. *Psychological Review,* Vol. 63, pp. 81-96.

Miller, R. (1981). *Meaning and Purpose in the Intact Brain.* Clarendon: Oxford.

Müller, F.M. (1887). *The Science of Thought.* Longmans: London.

Derek J. Smith

Müller, P. (1963). 'Klassen und Eigenschaften von Lernmatrizen', in N. Wiener, & J.P. Schadé (eds.), *Nerve, Brain and Memory Models.* Elsevier: Amsterdam.

Norris, D. (1991). 'The constraints on connectionism'. *The Psychologist*, Vol. 4, pp. 293-296.

Saban, R. (1993). *Aux Sources du Langage Articulé.* Masson: Paris.

Smith, D.J. (1993). 'The psychology of effective college governance. Part 2 - The cognitive skills'. *Journal of Further and Higher Education*, Vol. 17, pp. 77-85.

Smith, D.J. (1996). *Brain and Communication.* UWIC: Cardiff.

Storck, J. & Teague, W.D. (1952). *Flour for Man's Bread: A History of Milling.* University of Minnesota: Minneapolis, MN.

27 A partial theory and engineering model of human information-seeking tasks

James R. Buck and Steven M. Zellers
Department of Industrial Engineering
The University of Iowa, USA

Abstract

A partial theory and associated engineering model of human performance for a select group of lower order cognitive tasks is presented. The theory builds on an accepted taxonomy of task types based on Miller (1984) and the partial collection of tasks used here are called, 'information-seeking tasks'. Also, some properties needed for a prediction model are described. The theory and model presented are consistent with much of the literature. A series of empirical results are analysed. Applications include extensions to: task and task-timeline analysis, synthetic time predicting systems, and modelling human behaviour for computer and operator-in-the-loop simulations, human reliability analysis, learning curve analysis, and concurrent engineering. Implications of this theory and model to these applications of industrial engineering practice are discussed.

Introduction

Information-seeking tasks are those tasks that involve the visual and or auditory acquisition of a target stimulus and the corresponding conversion of the stimulus to a specific skill or knowledge. Therefore, the information processing steps involve lower order search processing operations, semantic or contextual coding of information, and response behaviour. The information-seeking tasks can be described more precisely a sequence of cognitive sub-tasks that define pre-response processing, i.e., those steps which lead to a calculated response behaviour. Such information-seeking tasks are generally initiated by a self-terminating visual search within static field. Upon search termination, the information-seeking task sequence may then proceed with other lower-order processing operations such as *compare, classify, verify, enumerate,* and *compute.* Miller (1984) presents a taxonomy of such tasks which are consistent with many identified types in the application literature Edwards & Lees, 1974; Rassmussen, 1986; Berliner et al., 1964; Christensen & Mills, 1967; Coffey, 1961; Hitt, 1961; Bainbridge, 1974). The information-seeking sequence then proceeds with a calculated psychomotor response.

The information seeking task generally incorporates a variety of cognitive activities and motor responses. The precise program of task operations is known here as a *micromethod* (Wang, 1986). That program specifies the path and spread of attention, rates of performing these activities, etc. that creates the timing of component activities in the task (Posner & Mitchell, 1967).

A partial theory and model

Human information processing tasks are also distinguished by *complexity* differences. With the motor activity of reaching, distance and the shape of the reach path are complexity variables that require more resources and affect performance speed and accuracy (Nieber, 1988; Buck et al., 1988). Cognitive tasks which require the individual to acquire a target within a visual field may be described with complexity variables of spatial, visual, and cognitive dimension. Variables in information-seeking activities include: visual search distances, memory demands of target referent, density of visual field, semantic cohesion of visual field, etc. For example, we may define the basis micromethod of a two dimensional visual search as a one dimensional search (row search) for a simplified, standardized object referent. Complexity differences may also cause *behavioural* changes (i.e. differences in what one does) that result in greater or lesser exerted *effort.* These behaviour-effort features, in turn, affect human *performance* (i.e. differences in how well one does) as measured by time and accuracy. Thus, the amount of required component activity associated with sensory, information-processing, and motor tasks is a function of the type of task and the condition of the complexity variables associated with each task type. We therefore define a set of *basis micromethod*s for a given sequence. These basis micromethods define a basis set of sub-tasks for the activity, and define a subspace of the micromethod space. We may then relate the task micromethod to the elemental micromethod in terms of the complexity function. This function describes the relative complexity of the micromethod in terms of the desired performance measure.

Two important aspects of task flow are the *composition* and *flow* characteristics. Composition aspects of this stream consists of: (i) the numbers of different types of tasks in the stream, (ii) relative frequencies of each type, and (iii) the sequencing pattern of these task types and complexities. The Hick-Hyman theory (Hick, 1952; Hyman, 1953) describes human reaction time increases with greater degrees of uncertainty in the information theory sense of the word uncertainty. According to this theory, one should expect greater performance times with external generation of more different types of tasks in a task stream.

For many tasks, performance is greatly dependent on the micromethod sequence or ordering, Take for example the case of component assembly. In such cases, simplifying assumptions of stream independence are not valid; i.e., component assembly order is highly inflexible. Dependence effects are often highly non-linear. For example, Buck et al.(1988) showed that reaction times for informationally independent micromethod sequences were less than those of dependent sequences. However, a linear approximation of such order effects can be readily achieved using elementary statistical results such as the least squares approximation.

Finally, we must account for potential *concurrency* of multiple micromethod sequences. Many tasks can be performed concurrently but some pairs involve much more interference than others. Tasks that use different senses tend to be less interfering (Hick, 1952). Some mental and motor tasks can be performed concurrently with small amounts of interference. Still many features of concurrent tasking are uncertain.

We present a mathematical model that accounts for both the Hick-Hyman uncertainty and sequence effects. Assume that task completion time **T** is the performance variable of interest. Then, **T** may be described as:

$$\mathbf{T} = M(N) \cdot \frac{\sum\limits_{i=1}^{N} \mathbf{s}_i \cdot \mathbf{o}_i}{T_{ave}} \cdot \sum\limits_{i=1}^{N} \overline{\mathbf{C}}_i \cdot \overline{\mathbf{H}}_i \qquad (1)$$

Where:

$M(N)$ = Global memory effect based on total number of tasks

$\mathbf{C}$ = A complexity function for the basis micromethod n based on set factors as size and dimension of data field, size of symbol set, number of different types of symbols etc.

$E_m(n)$ = Expected completion time for base micromethod element n

$\mathbf{H} = A\ln(\frac{1}{\rho_n})$ = the Hick-Hyman uncertainty of the micromethod

$\mathbf{S}_j$ = microtask sequence vector

o = order effect coefficient vector

Let $E(n)$ be the task completion time for an elemental micromethod n. We define the complexity function most simply as:

$$C(n) = \alpha \cdot E(n)^{\beta}$$

(2)

where a and b are the task time multipliers and exponents, respectively. $C(n)$ then defines the task completion time for the general micromethod n.

If we assume that stream frequency dependence exists in the task sequence, then the Hick Hyman law may be used to relate reaction time effects to task uncertainty. The Hick Hyman law states that response time for choice n tasks increases linearly with respect to the entropy of the micromethod. Entropy of the task is defined as:

$$H(n) = A\log\frac{1}{p_n}$$

(3)

where p_n is the probabilistic uncertainty of the micromethod.

Sequence effects may be approximated from order samples using the least squares approximation. Assume that O is a time-order matrix of at least rank N, where N is the total number of sub-tasks. Then:

$$\mathbf{T}_i = \sum_{j=1}^{N} S_{ij} \cdot \mathbf{o}_j$$

(4)

converting S to matrix notation and solving for the order effect coefficients $\mathbf{o}$ yields:

$$\mathbf{o} = \mathbf{S}^{-1} \cdot \mathbf{T}$$

(5)

The sequence $\mathbf{S}$ may not be invertible, however, we are guaranteed that it is positive semi-definite from this definition. Therefore, a least squares estimate of $\mathbf{o}$ may be achieved using the singular value decomposition form:

$$\mathbf{o} = svd\,\{\mathbf{S}\} \cdot \mathbf{T}$$

(6)

Therefore, given any task sequence $\mathbf{s}$, the totals task time can be estimated as:

$$\mathbf{T} = \sum_{i=1}^{N} \mathbf{s}_i \cdot \mathbf{o}_i$$

(7)

Therefore, the total task model, with sequence effect scaling, becomes:

$$\mathbf{T} = M(N) \cdot \frac{\sum\limits_{i=1}^{N} \mathbf{s}_i \cdot \mathbf{o}_i}{T_{ave}} \cdot \sum_{i=1}^{N} \overline{\mathbf{C}}_i \cdot \overline{\mathbf{H}}_i \qquad (8)$$

Conclusion

The creation of synthetic prediction methods for lower-order cognitive task performance appears to be feasible. A preliminary, simplified mathematical model is offered. The obvious implications to engineering practice is that existing synthetic systems for motor tasks may be extended to cognitive tasks. Studies which attempt to validate the strength of the predictive models are ongoing.

References

Bainbridge, L. (1974), 'Analysis of verbal protocol from a process control task', in E.Edwards and F. P. Lees (eds.), *The Human Operator in Process Control*. Taylor & Francis, Ltd: London.

Berliner, C., Angell, D. and Shearer, J. W. (1964), 'Behaviors, measures, and instruments for performance evaluation in simulated environments'. *Symposium and Workshop on the Quantification of Human Performance*. Albuquerque, NM.

Buck, J. R., Badarinath, N. B., and Kachitvichyanukul, V. (1988), Cognitive task performance time and accuracy in supervisory process control'. *IIE Transactions*, Vol. 20, pp. 349-358.

Card, S., Moran, T. and Newell, A. (1986), 'The model human processor: an engineering model of human performance', in K. R. Boff (ed.) *Handbook of Perceptual and Human Performance*. J. P. Thomas editors.

Christensen, J.M. and Mills, R.G. (1967), 'What does the operator do in complex systems?'. *Human Factors*, Vol. 4 , pp. 329-340.

Coffey, J.L. (1961), 'A Comparison of vertical and horizontal arrangements of alpha-numeric material'. *Human Factors*, Vol. 3, pp. 93-98.

Edwards, E. and Lees, F. P. (1974) *The Human operator in process control*. Taylor & Francis Ltd: London.

Goldman, J. & Hart, L. W. Jr. (1965), 'Information theory and industrial learning', *The Journal of Industrial Engineering*, Vol. 16, pp. 306-362.

Hick, W.E. (1952), 'On the rate of gain of information'. *Quarterly Journal of Experimental Psychology*, Vol. 4, pp. 11-26.

Hitt, W.D. (1961), 'An Evaluation of Five Different Abstract Coding Methods'. *Human Factors,* Vol. 2, pp. 11-26.

Hyman, R. (1953), 'Stimulus information as a determinant of reaction time', *Experimental Psychology*, Vol. 80, pp. 423-432.

Jain, A.K. (1989) *Fundamentals of Digital Image Processing.* Prentice Hall: New York.

Miller, R. B. (1984), 'Miller's terminology: definitions for the 25 task functions involved in a generalized information-processing system', in R.B. Miller (ed.),*Taxonomies of Human Performance.* Academic Press: Orlando, FL.

Nieber, B. W. (1988) *Motion and Time Study.* R. /D. Irwin Inc: Homewood, IL.

Posner, M.I. & Mitchell, R.F. (1967), 'Chronometric Analysis of Classification'. Psychological Review, Vol. 74, pp. 392-409.

Rassmussen, J. (1986) *Information processing and human-machine interaction: an approach to cognitive engineering.* North-Holland Press: New York.

Rosenstein, A.B. (1955), 'The industrial engineering application of communications-information theory'. *The Journal of Industrial Engineering,* pp. 10-21.

Ross, E. K. (1960) 'Information Content Analysis', Unpublished Doctoral thesis. Washington University: St. Louis, MO.

Sage, A.P. (1981), 'Behavioural and organizational considerations in the design of information systems and processes for planning and decision support', *IEEE Transactions on Systems, Man, and Cybernetics*, Vol. 11, pp. 640-678.

Sternberg, S. (1969), 'Memory scanning: mental processes revealed by reaction time experiments'. *American Scientist*, Vol. 57, pp. 421-457.

Wang, M.I. (1986) *Cognitive Tasks, Micromethods and Simulations.* Unpublished Master's thesis. The University of Iowa: Iowa City, IA.

28 Model-computer interaction: implementing the action perception loop for cognitive models

Gordon D. Baxter and Frank E. Ritter
University of Nottingham, UK

Abstract

Cognitive models which interact with their environment are comparatively scarce. The speed of a model's task performance is therefore governed by the speed of cognition, with the rate at which data can be exchanged with the external world simply being ignored. Typically, the accuracy of task performance is also too high: no slips of action can occur because no external actions are ever performed. To investigate ways of solving these problems, simulations of visual perception and motor action have been developed and integrated with two cognitive models. When visual perception and motor action are used, the speed of task performance is reduced to more realistic levels. Implementing plausible simulations of visual perception and motor action requires a wide range of skills, including advanced programming techniques. The utility of the simulated perceptual capabilities is being demonstrated by reimplementing them for integration with another cognitive model, using a commercially available interface toolkit.

Modelling human task performance

Human task performance generally involves the construction of an internal representation of the task at hand (Craik, 1967). The generation of this representation often depends on the use of external cues, which are utilized in the selection of relevant stored information. The representation is then mentally manipulated to yield results that can be used in doing the task.

The tasks being considered here involve the use of a computer application system. In this type of task, vision is the dominant sense for receiving input data.

Gordon D. Baxter and Frank E. Ritter

The outcome of these tasks also usually requires some physical motor activity, such as pressing a key on a keyboard, or using the mouse. Task performance is thus governed by four basic factors:

(i) The data that is available in the task environment.
(ii) The input data that is received.
(iii) The processing of the received data, along with any appropriate stored data.
(iv) The output data that is produced.

Ultimately, any model of human task performance must take account of all of these factors, since they all affect the speed, and the accuracy of performance. The models of task performance that have been built to date do not yet fully address all of these requirements.

Several models have been created by researchers in the psychological sciences (see Ritter & Larkin, 1994 for a review). Most of these models were limited in that they only simulated the cognitive aspects of single tasks. Any information the models required to do the task was often instantaneously available, and the results of performing the task were only ever accessible by cognition. These models suffer from two main failings. First, they carry out the task too quickly, and take an unfeasibly short time to learn how to do the task. Second, they often perform the task perfectly: they never make the action slips that are evident in human task performance, because they never perform any external actions.

Cognitive systems engineering has also yielded a number of performance models (see Cacciabue & Hollnagel, 1995 for a review). In general these models have tried to take account of the human, the computer system, *and* the interaction between the two. One of the best known models, the Cognitive Simulation Model (COSIMO), simulates the performance of nuclear power plant operators (Cacciabue, Decortis, Drozdowicz, Masson & Norvik, 1992). Perception is implemented in COSIMO using a selective filtering mechanism. COSIMO was relatively successful: it models some of the erroneous actions that are made by real operators, and exhibits a rate of task performance comparable to that of real operators. The main identified failing of COSIMO, however, is that it does not model inferential reasoning.

Towards task performance models

Any model of task performance must take account of the context in which the task takes place, since context plays an important role in all but the simplest of tasks (Hollnagel, 1993; Hutchins, 1995; Nardi, 1996). The most obvious way of doing this is by utilising the available senses, and then allowing perception to interpret the incoming signals they produce. The use of the term 'cognitive modelling' is thus somewhat misleading, since it implies that only the cognitive

216

aspects of the task are being modelled. In reality, what should be modelled is the whole of human task performance.

The importance of perception in task performance has been noted elsewhere (e.g. Lesgold, Glaser, Rubinson, Klopfer, Feltovich, & Wang, 1988; Larkin, 1989). In the tasks considered here, visual perception provides the basis for generating mental representations. Since visual perception and higher level cognition are intrinsically linked (Chalmers, French, & Hofstadter, 1995), task performance models must include simulation of visual perception.

The exact nature of the relationship between sensations and cognition, however, remains largely undefined. Theories of task performance tend to concentrate on one to the exclusion of the other. Where theories have attempted to account for both sensations and cognition, the computational details have often been omitted (Shrager, 1990).

One of the earliest attempts at developing a model that considered both sensation and cognition was HOS, the human operator simulator (Wherry, 1976). HOS utilized a number of subroutines which calculated the times required to perform actions such as looking at a display, and reaching out to grasp some control device. These calculations were based on the results of existing studies. Although HOS did not do any physical actions as such, it could be used to generate timeline analyses that closely matched human performance across a number of tasks.

The need for interaction with the environment is tacitly acknowledged in cognitive architectures, such as ACT (Anderson, 1993), and Soar (Newell, 1990), which are employed in the development of cognitive models. The details of how this interaction happens, however, are fairly sketchy, although this situation is now being addressed (e.g. Anderson, Matessa, & Douglas, 1995).

In general, models that have incorporated external interaction have ignored the psychological plausibility of those interactions. If complete models of human task performance are to be created, any interaction that is involved has to be subject to the same psychological (and physiological) constraints as it is in humans. The model's performance should then match human performance more closely in terms of speed and accuracy.

Implementing the senses

In order to interact with the task environment, models require some means of transmitting information to, and receiving information from that environment. For the tasks considered here, this is done by providing simulations of visual perception and motor action which operate at a relatively abstract level of detail. The need to simulate the more intricate aspects of interaction, such as physical

Gordon D. Baxter and Frank E. Ritter

sensation, is deferred until the adequacy of the proposed mechanisms can be demonstrated.

The key to success initially lies in determining where to locate the implementations of visual perception and motor action. There are two basic choices: they can either form part of the cognitive model, or they can be part of the application simulation. It is immediately apparent that visual perception and motor action are not part of cognition although they can be controlled and influenced by it. Since the level of abstraction being used relates to task interface objects (widgets), the visual perception and motor action mechanisms are located *within* the task simulation interface. In this way they can directly access the data structures that implement the widgets.

It is also important that the implementations of the perceptual mechanisms are task independent. There is a set of functions that cognition can use to control them, but at the task application end, all that is required is access to a declarative representation of the interface objects.

Finally, there has to be some way of observing the model's interaction behaviour as it carries out the task. This effect is achieved by generating visible representations of the perceptual mechanisms - a model eye, and a model hand - which appear on the application display screen. The model's eye is shown as a transparent object enclosing the part of the display that the model is currently looking at; the model's hand appears as a mouse pointer.

Models that interact with their environment

Two models which incorporate interaction with their application have been built to date. These models were implemented using the Soar cognitive architecture. The simulations of the tasks, and the perceptual mechanisms, were developed using Garnet (Myers, Giuse, Dannenberg, Vander Zanden, Kosbie, Pervin, Mickish, & Marchal, 1990). The first application was a simulation of a simplified Air Traffic Control (ATC) task. The second simulation was a simple tabletop on which a number of blocks were located.

A third Soar model is currently being built for a simplified ship based electronic warfare (EW) task. The task simulation is written in Lisp (Ramsay, 1995); the application interface and perceptual mechanisms have been developed using SL-GMS (Sherrill-Lubinski Corporation, 1994).

The ATC task model

A simplified ATC-like task was generated with an interactive interface that could be used by real users as well as models (Bass, Baxter, & Ritter, 1995). The task involved directing a plane around a fixed flight path to the point where it could be handed over to ground control. Included in the task interface was a visual perception capability, which the model used to perceive information already present on the display. The model could also track the plane object's movements on the screen, and change the plane's heading at the appropriate way markers.

In order to implement the interaction between the model and the task simulation, the visual perception mechanism had to have access to the data structures used to represent the objects on the screen. Since the model operates at a symbolic level, it was provided with access to objects at that level. So, for example, the model perceives a radio button as a radio button, rather than as a number of separate shaded boxes.

The tabletop model

A simulated mouse was created in order to provide models with a motor action capability (Rassouli, 1995). The model was tested by creating a simple task application which allowed the model to move the simulated mouse around the application window, and perform mouse button operations. In this way the model was able to perform a rudimentary level of interaction. The model was able to move the mouse over items on the menu bar, and click on them to pull down that menu. The model was unable to select items from menus, however, due to windowing constraints.

Within Garnet, interface objects such as the model's mouse, have to be attached to a specific window; pull down menus are implemented as windows. When a menu is selected, its window appears on top of the window where the simulated mouse pointer is located. It is thus impossible to select menu items: the mouse pointer cannot be positioned over menu items, because it is not in the menu's window. The problem cannot be simply resolved by placing a clear window, with the mouse pointer in it, on top of the other windows, since the X windowing system does not support the creation of transparent windows.

Once the motor action simulation was available, it was included in the ATC task model. Modelling detailed interaction between the perceptual mechanisms - hand eye co-ordination - was prevented by the limitations of the implemented motor action mechanism.

The EW task model

Experiences with the models described above helped us to refine ideas about how to design the perceptual mechanisms for models in a more general way (Baxter & Ritter, 1996). Based on a modified specification of requirements, the perceptual mechanisms are currently being implemented in SL-GMS for inclusion in the interface to a ship based EW task simulation. The basic limitations of the target system (X windows) are being circumvented by effectively adding an extra level to the windowing system.

Lessons learned

Creating models that can routinely interact with their environment is hard work. It requires a diverse range of skills: an understanding of visual perception, motor action, and cognition; the ability to build cognitive models; and a detailed knowledge of windowing systems.

The time that the model takes to perform the task is increased when visual perception and motor action are used. The task also becomes more involved, since there are aspects to the interaction that can be learned by the model as it does the task. Performance still remains too fast, however.

The intricate nature of hand eye co-ordination adds further complications to the interaction. A cursory glance at the task of changing the aircraft heading in the ATC simulation suggests that all that is required is to select the desired option from the appropriate menu, and then click on the desired radio button. On closer inspection, however, it turns out that at least twelve operations are needed to perform this apparently simple operation, due to the level of hand eye co-ordination involved in selecting individual objects.

Task performance in the cases presented here not only depends on domain knowledge, but also depends on human-computer interaction knowledge. In order to select items from a pull down menu, the model has to know which behaviours are associated with which task interface objects. So, for example, the model has to know that command buttons can be clicked.

Finally, adding physical interaction to the models should eventually give rise to a range of erroneous actions. Although this improves the degree of correspondence with real task performance, it also adds another level of complexity to the models, since error detection and recovery will also have to be accounted for.

References

Anderson, J.R. (1993) *Rules of the Mind.* Lawrence Erlbaum Associates: Hillsdale, NJ.

Anderson, J.R., Matessa, M., & Douglas, S. (1995), 'The ACT-R theory of visual attention', in *Proceedings of the Seventeenth Annual Conference of the Cognitive Science Society.* Lawrence Erlbaum Associates: Hillsdale, NJ.

Bass, E.J., Baxter, G.D., & Ritter, F.E. (1995), 'Creating models to control simulations: A generic approach'. *AISB Quarterly*, Vol. 93, pp. 18-25.

Baxter, G.D., & Ritter, F.E. (1996), *Designing Abstract Visual Perceptual and Motor Capabilities for Use by Cognitive Models* (Technical Report No. 36). University of Nottingham: ESRC Centre for Research in Development, Instruction, and Training.

Cacciabue, P.C. & Hollnagel, E. (1995), 'Simulation of cognition: Applications' in J-M. Hoc, P.C. Cacciabue, & E. Hollnagel (eds.), *Expertise and Technology: Cognition & Human-Computer Cooperation*. Lawrence Erlbaum Associates: Hillsdale, NJ.

Cacciabue, P.C., Decortis, F., Drozdowicz, B., Masson, M., & Norvik, J-P. (1992), 'COSIMO: A cognitive simulation model of human decision making and behavior in accident management of complex plants'. *IEEE Transactions on Systems, Man, and Cybernetics*, Vol. 22, pp. 1058-1074.

Chalmers, D., French, R., & Hofstadter, D. (1995), 'High-level perception: Representation, and analogy', in D. Hofstadter (ed.), *Fluid Concepts & Creative Analogies*. Basic Books: New York, NY.

Craik, K.J.W. (1967) *The Nature of Explanation*. Cambridge University Press: Cambridge, UK.

Hofstadter, D., & French, R. (1995), 'Tabletop, battleOp, ob-Platte, potelbat, belpatto, platobet', in D. Hofstadter (ed.), *Fluid Concepts & Creative Analogies*. Basic Books: New York, NY.

Hollnagel, E. (1993) *Human Reliability Analysis: Context and Control*. Academic Press: London, UK.

Larkin, J.H. (1989), 'Display-based problem solving', in D. Klahr & K. Kotovsky (eds.), *Complex Information Processing: The Impact of Herbert A. Simon*. Lawrence Erlbaum Associates: Hillsdale, NJ.

Lesgold, A., Glaser, R., Rubinson, H., Klopfer, D., Feltovich, P., & Wang, Y. (1988), 'Expertise in a complex skill: Diagnosing x-ray pictures', in M. Chi, R. Glaser, & M. Farr (eds.), *The Nature of Expertise*. Lawrence Erlbaum Associates: Hillsdale, NJ.

Myers, B., Giuse, D., Dannenberg, R., Vander Zanden, V., Kosbie, D., Pervin, E., Mickish, A., & Marchal, P. (1990), 'Garnet: Comprehensive support for graphical, highly interactive user interfaces'. *IEEE Computer*, Vol. 23, pp. 71-85.

Newell, A. (1990) *Unified Theories of Cognition*. Harvard University Press: Cambridge, MA.

Ramsay, A. F. (1995), *OOPSDG Modelling Environment for the Centre for Human Sciences* (Technical Report No. DRA/CIS(SS5)/1026/9/2). DRA: Portsdown.

Rassouli, J. (1995), *Steps Towards a Process Model of Mouse-based Interaction*. University of Nottingham: Unpublished M.Sc. thesis.

Ritter, F.E., & Larkin, J.H. (1994), 'Developing process models as summaries of HCI sequences'. *Human-Computer Interaction*, Vol. 9, pp. 345-383.

Gordon D. Baxter and Frank E. Ritter

Sherrill-Lubinski Corporation (1994) *SL-GMS Technical Overview*. Sherrill-Lubinski Corporation: Corte Madera, CA.

Shrager, J. (1990), 'Commonsense perception and the psychology of theory formation', in J. Shrager & P. Langley (eds.), *Computational Models of Scientific Discovery and Theory Formation*. Morgan Kaufmann: San Mateo, CA.

Wherry, R.J. (1976), 'The human operator simulator - HOS', in T. B. Sheridan & G. Johannsen (eds.), *Monitoring Behavior and Supervisory Control*. Plenum Press: New York, NY.

Acknowledgement

The research described in this paper was supported by the DERA, and the ESRC Centre for Research in Development, Instruction, and Training. The views expressed in the paper are those of the authors and should not necessarily be attributed to the Ministry of Defence.

29 Predicting transaction time for dual-tasks using critical path

Chris Baber and Brian Mellor*
Industrial Ergonomics Group,
University of Birmingham, UK
*Speech Research Unit, DERA (Malvern), UK

Abstract

Critical path analysis (CPA) is a project management technique which allows consideration of the effects of multiple tasks on overall performance time. CPA has been used as a means of modelling user performance. In this paper, CPA is used for performance modelling, predicting transaction time and as a means of generating hypotheses concerning human performance. Predictions are shown to lie within 12% of times obtained from experimentation (at the 5% significance level). CPA models allow inspection of the effects of different tasks on performance.

Predicting transaction time

Transaction time is a useful, unambiguous metric of system performance and, while one might debate the relative speed-accuracy trade-off for unit-tasks, a system which permits fast, efficient transactions is likely to lead to all manner of savings in comparison with a slower device; the human factors question which should be raised is, to what cost would be fast system incur, in terms of error and workload? Research following the keystroke level model (KLM) of Card et al. (1980; 1983) has sought to develop or refine the timings used in predictions (Olson and Olson, 1990).

While the work of Card et al. (1983) presents a significant first step in performance modelling, it also leads to questions concerning parallel activity, strategy and workload. To an extent, these problems can be addressed by considering the manner in which times are combined.

Schweickert (1980) reports the use of critical path analysis as a means of extrapolating times in choice-reaction tasks. Schweickert's (1980) work was directed at the question of whether changes in reaction time were due to a general increase in all unit-tasks or whether some unit-tasks were more subject to change than others. This work leads to two assumptions: first, changes in task demands, e.g., as a result of additional tasks, will not affect all tasks to the same extent; second, some tasks can be performed in parallel. More recently, research has been directed at the possibility of using critical path modelling as a means of extending the work of Card et al. (1983). For example, Olson and Olson (1990) conclude their paper with a discussion of critical path modelling, Gray et al. (1993) have demonstrated the potential of such an approach in predicting transactions time in the design of a telephone operator workstation, and Lawrence et al. (1995) use the approach to demonstrate how telephone operators successfully performed the 'social' task of call handling with the 'technological' task of using a computer database. Indeed, the Gray et al. (1993) and Lawrence et al. (1995) work demonstrates the benefit of considering parallel activity in system design; a new telephone operator assistance system had been developed, based on a model of serial task performance and, rather than the anticipated saving in time, led to an increase in transaction time. The explanation for the counter-intuitive results were that the redesign of system had focused on computer-based tasks which were not on the critical path, i.e., which were being performed in parallel with other activities.

Method

In this paper, a version of critical path analysis (CPA) is presented and predictions are compared with actual task performance obtained from laboratory studies. CPA is used both to predict transaction time and as a means of describing human performance and workload distribution. The approach used in this paper is part of a broader design method.

The first step is to develop an application description using a simple, standard format:

DO(task) WITH(modality) USING (device)
WHILE(other tasks)
IN(environment)

For example, one study employed the primary task of target classification with the secondary task of mental arithmetic. Target classification could be performed using trackball, cursor keys or automatic speech recognition (ASR), while the secondary task was performed using auditory presentation and spoken response. If we consider the ASR (target classification) condition, the application description is:

DO[classify target] WITH[speech] USING[ASR]
WHILE
DO[mental arithmetic] WITH[auditory] USING[speech]
IN[laboratory]

From this description, it is possible to generate a conflict matrix as shown in table 1. The idea for a conflict matrix is developed from the underlying model of human information processing employed in this work. Following multiple resource theory (Wickens, 1992) we assume discrete channels of information processing, i.e., visuo-spatial and verbal. These channels are of limited capacity and will become overloaded when the capacity is exceeded. Furthermore, the processing of information is most efficient when minimal translation is required, e.g., response to a verbal message will be fastest when spoken. There will be tasks which are limited due to resource capacity (resource-limited) and which will have reduce performance when capacity is exceeded, and tasks which are limited due to attentional limits (data-limited) and which will have reduced performance irrespective of resource.

Table 1
Conflict matrix for ASR condition

Code	Input	Processing	Output
Visual/Manual	Acquire target	Classify target	
Auditory/Spoken	Receive sum	Mental arithmetic	Position cursor
		Generate report	Enter data
			Speak answer

It is assumed that there will be high levels of conflict in the auditory / speech modality, but it is not clear from table 1 how this conflict will affect performance, e.g., the conflict could prevent performance of one of the tasks (the person might simply not perform the mental arithmetic task), performance could impair performance of one of the tasks (report generation could be slowed or the mental arithmetic task could be error-prone), performance could be maintained at the expense of increasing perceived levels of workload. The obvious way to investigate which explanation will hold will be to run user-trials. However, it is proposed that developing a model of performance could be beneficial in that it would allow hypotheses to be scoped and would allow likely effects to be considered prior to running trials (this would be beneficial when the trials require equipment to be purpose-built).

Having produced an application description, the next step is to develop a performance description. In the current state of the method, hierarchical task analysis (HTA) is employed. The level of detail given in the HTA will depend on the nature of application. However, this is a useful exercise in that it focuses attention during design on the range of tasks required. It might seem odd to draw an HTA for a system that has not been built. However, the benefits of the approach are that it allows designers to consider what goals will be important to task performance, how these goals will be met and what tasks ought to be supported. Furthermore, once tasks have been defined, the designer can consider possible devices to support the tasks, e.g., in this study, we were interested in speech recognition, trackball and cursor keys are interaction devices, with a visual display unit to present information and feedback to the users.

Having established a description of the tasks which will be performed in the condition, the next step is to determine their temporal relationships. From both working memory and multiple resource theories it is plausible for tasks to be performed in parallel (particularly if they draw on different codes). Step three develops a critical path diagram from the previous steps. The critical path diagram is constructed by asking questions such as, which tasks need to be completed before a given task can commence?

In order to complete the critical path diagram, it is necessary to assign times to tasks. Olson and Olson (1990) provide a set of times which can be used off-the-shelf. Unfortunately, this set of times has little relating to speech. Baber and Hone (1993) produced a task-network model of spoken dialogues using assumptions about phoneme length. The first pass through the diagram will use times taken from literature. This provides an initial estimate of transaction time. For the ASR condition, we further assume different levels of recognition accuracy to provide a set of times. However, critical path analysis offers a useful means of deriving unknown times. In this work, the time to speak a command and the time to perform mental arithmetic were defined as unknown. From working through the critical path analysis diagram, and calculating unknown times using the backward pass, it was possible to generate predicted transaction times and to produce models of task performance, by considering the relative critical paths.

Results

Experiments were conducted, in which people performed both tasks, and full details of these are reported in Baber et al. (1996). For the trackball condition, the critical path analysis method generated a prediction of 13.2 seconds. This is illustrated by figure 1, in which it is clear that some parallel activity is possible. From the experiment, the mean transaction time was 13.2 (+/-3.1) seconds.

For the first pass of the ASR condition (using standard times from Baber and Hone, 1993), the predicted time was 31.1 seconds (assuming a recognition accuracy of 70%). From the experiment, the mean transaction time was 34.71 (+/- 11) seconds. Thus, the predicted time was 3.61 seconds less than the actual. The error is around 10% of the experimental time. Given that the experimental time had a 30% error (standard deviation), the prediction was deemed to be acceptable.

Predicting transaction time for dual-tasks using critical path

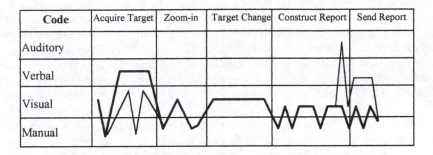

Code	Acquire Target	Zoom-in	Target Change	Construct Report	Send Report
Auditory					
Verbal					
Visual					
Manual					

Figure 1   Critical path diagram for trackball condition

Model validation

Liao and Milgram (1991) propose that validating predictions from human performance models is tantamount to test whether or not to accept the null hypothesis. They present a simple method for calculating the validity of the prediction, based on defining the acceptable level of type II error (beta) and on the acceptable difference between observed and predicted times. From this calculation, we see that, at the 5% significance level, the model predicts observed transaction time (providing we are prepared to accept 10% chance of making a type II error). Thus, we can accept H_0 and say that there is no significant difference between the observed and predicted times, providing difference of 12% is considered acceptable. Repeating the procedure with the trackball data, we find that we can accept H_0 and say there is no difference between observed and predicted times. However, the observed data were collected from a small sample (only six people). This reduces the power of the result (to around only 10%). If we wish to ensure an acceptable power (say 80%), then we would require 72 observations. Thus, further work is necessary before the model can be said to be validated.

From this validation, we can say that initial analysis suggests that the model has a reasonable output validity, i.e., the predicted times are within acceptable range of observed times. However, to ensure that the model is useful it is necessary to examine the conceptual validity of the model. One way to do this is to examine the effects and to consider whether the effects found in running the model can be described in terms of the underlying theory.

Exploration of effects

The second pass of the ASR condition employed a backward pass to derive times for speech. Taking a transaction time of 34.71 seconds, and assuming the times to speak each command were related to Baber and Hone's timings, the derived times were around 1.4 times greater than proposed times, i.e., for the zoom-in task, the proposed

227

time was 1.07 seconds and the derived times was 1.54 seconds. This equates to an accuracy of around 60%. Thus, performance of the ASR system was a significant factor in transaction time. Finally, the predicted times lie within 10% of the mean observed times only when two assumptions are met: the ASR condition has one more arithmetic task than the trackball condition; the ASR condition uses two words for each target description in the report stage. Both conditions were observed from analysis of DAT recordings of user speech. The arithmetic task was presented at set time intervals: the longer the study took, the more likely another arithmetic task would be played. The report could be completed by either speaking a single word, e.g., red, or by speaking the menu heading and then the word, e.g., colour, red. The model predicted that, with the same number of arithmetic tasks, with 99% accuracy and with single words for report completion, transaction time for ASR would be 19 seconds. One participant did complete the task in 19 seconds, and was observed to follow the conditions outlined above. Of particular interest to our work was the relationship between workload and transaction time. Assuming a simple relationship between level of workload and transaction time, such that transaction time for no workload is treated as a base-line, the following table can be defined.

Table 2
Increase in predicted time across workload

Phase	Time		% Increase	
	ASR	Trackball	ASR	Trackball
Acquire target				
No workload	9.68	1.18	0	0
Medium workload	11.83	1.77	22	50
High workload	14.03	2.12	45	80
Zoom -in				
No workload	1.48	1.47	0	0
Medium workload	1.5	1.88	1	28
High workload	1.64	1.67	11	14
Construct Report				
No workload	12.23	8.36	0	0
Medium workload	15.06	9.64	23	15
High workload	16.28	10.87	33	30

From table 2, it is apparent that high workload (i.e., mental arithmetic with no carry-over) has a less impact on the third than the first phases for ASR and for trackball (with moderate impact on the zoom-in phase). The pattern of results are somewhat different for the medium workload (mental arithmetic with carry-over). This raises interesting questions concerning the nature of task difficulty and human performance. The acquire target phase is much faster using trackball than ASR (in all conditions). The principle explanation of this result lies in the nature of the tasks (with ASR being inappropriate for cursor manipulation). There was little difference between conditions for the zoom-in phase (although medium workload appears to have an impact on the trackball; perhaps this was due to the timing of presentation of the mental arithmetic task). Finally, the relative difference in times for the construct report phase was less than for the acquire target phase (and workload appears to have a similar impact on performance for the two devices). It is proposed that report construction is a verbal task and best supported by ASR; the relatively poor performance of the ASR has skewed the performance times in this phase.

Discussion

In this paper we report the use of critical path analysis as a tool for modelling dual-task performance. The method serves a number of purposes. As a design aid, it allows for user-centred design specifications to be developed and tested. This was not evaluated in this study. As a prediction technique, it allows for transaction time to be predicted on the basis of appropriate task description. The results show that predicted transactions time lie within 10% of times obtained from experiment. Further work is required to validate these times. As a means of describing user performance, the approach allows for the development of questions, e.g., relating measures of task difficulty to workload under different performance conditions.

References

Baber, C. (1996) *Beyond the Desktop: designing and using interaction devices.* Academic Press: London.

Baber, C. & Hone, K.S. (1993) 'Modelling error recovery and repair in automatic speech recognition'. *International Journal of Man-Machine Studies,* Vol. 39, pp. 495-515.

Baber, C., Mellor, B., Graham, R., Noyes, J.M. & Tunley, C. (1996) 'Workload and the use of automatic speech recognition: the effects of time and resource demands'. *Speech Communication,* Vol. 20, pp. 37-53.

Card, S.K., Moran, T.P. & Newell, A. (1980). 'The keystroke level model for user performance time with interactive systems'. *Communications of the ACM,* Vol. 23, pp. 396-410.

Card, S.K., Moran, T.P. & Newell, A. (1983) *The Psychology of Human-Computer Interaction.* Lawrence Erlbaum: Hillsdale, NJ.

Gray, W.D., John, B.E. & Atwood, M.E. (1993). 'Project Ernestine: validating a GOMS analysis for predicting and explaining real-world task performance', *Human-Computer Interaction,* Vol. 8, pp. 237-309.

Lawrence, D., Atwood, M.E., Dews, S. & Turner, T. (1995). 'Social interaction in the use and design of a workstation: two contexts of interaction' in P.J. Thomas (ed.), *The Social and Interactional Dimensions of Human-Computer Interfaces,* Cambridge University Press: Cambridge, pp. 240-260.

Liao, J. & Milgram, P. (1991) 'On validating human performance simulation models', *Proceedings of the Human Factors Society 35th Annual Meeting.* Human Factors Society: Santa Monica, CA, pp.1260-126.

Olson, J.R. & Olson, G.M. (1990) 'The growth of cognitive modelling in human-computer interaction since GOMS', *Human-Computer Interaction,* Vol. 5, pp. 221-265.

Schweickert, R. (1980) 'Critical path scheduling of mental processes in a dual task', *Science,* Vol. 209, pp. 704-706.

Wickens, C.D. (1992) *Engineering Psychology and Human Performance* (2nd. Edition) New York: Harper Collins.

30 Engineering psychology: the hidden psychologist - a case study on the evaluation of the Safer Cities programme using a geographical information system

Ho Law
Home Office Research & Statistics Directorate
Operational Research Unit, London, UK

Abstract

Psychologists have been practising engineering psychology long before it became a recognised discipline. For example, between 1988-1994 the Safer Cities programme implemented over 3,000 crime prevention schemes in 20 cities in England. The large-scale evaluation of the programme's impact on crime, fear etc demonstrates how a psychologist applying his skill in engineering psychology to implement the evaluation design using a geographical information system. This includes rapid prototyping of user interface design and system development within the dual requirements of both human-computer interaction and software engineering disciplines. Many psychologists working in a similar situation are called hidden psychologists as they are neither identified as psychologists in their teams nor recognized as psychologists by their own professional societies. It is hoped that this paper will open the debate about the role of engineering psychology within the profession, and argue the case for its recognition by the Society.

Introduction

This paper has been written as a response to MacLeod's (1994) call for creating a new special interest group (SIG) in engineering psychology in the UK. On 4 July 1996 at the kick-off meeting of the British Psychological Society (BPS) SIG in Engineering Psychology at the Centre for Human Sciences, DERA, Farnborough, I took on the role as a member of the Working Action Group and Communication Group to help to develop and promote engineering psychology within the BPS's Occupational Psychology Division and Section.

I share MacLeod's concern that occupational psychology as a discipline should face the real competitive world by a dual approach of both breadth and specialization. From my own experience, psychologists have been practising engineering psychology long before it became a recognised discipline. These psychologists (like myself) are very often employed as scientists (say, in operational research) or researchers in the field, working with other professions within a multi-disciplinary team on real world problems. These psychologists, in this sense, are hidden, for they are neither identified as psychologists in their teams nor recognized as psychologists by their own professional societies (such as the BPS). This explains why the decreasing evidence of any active and manifest relationships of the discipline to the broad multidisciplinary field of human factors and software engineering as observed by MacLeod (1994).

MacLeod (1994) argues that if the BPS is to meet the 'challenge for change' described by Lindsay & Lunt, (1993), all specialized subsets of psychology should be recognized and supported. This includes engineering psychology in contrast to its existing 'undercover' nature in the UK. Using the evaluation of the Safer Cities Programme (SCP) as a case study, this paper aims to expand further the 'undercover' nature of engineering psychology and at the same time review how a psychologist applying his skill in engineering psychology to implement the evaluation design using a geographical information system (GIS). The SCP is a good example as its evaluation calls for psychologists' full 'gamut of skills and experience'. This includes rapid prototyping of user interface design and system development within the dual requirements of both human-computer interaction (HCI) and software engineering disciplines. Next section provides the context of the SCP evaluation. Section three describes some of the facets of engineering psychology - some of which is highlighted in detail in section four. Section five discusses, from the engineering psychology's perspective, the conclusions so far, and the lessons learnt.

Safer Cities programme evaluation

Phase one of the Safer Cities programme (SCP) was inaugurated in 1988 and wound up in Autumn 1995. Altogether, it implemented over 3,000 highly diverse and geographically scattered crime preventive schemes in 20 cities and cost about £30 million, including £8 million administrative costs. Safer Cities was set up as part of 'Action for Cities', the Government's wider programme to deal with the multiple social, physical and economic problems of some of our larger urban areas. The objectives of Safer Cities were to reduce crime, lessen fear of crime, and create Safer Cities within which economic enterprise and community life could flourish (Home Office, 1993). Safer Cities initiatives were locally-based, reflecting an understanding developed since the 1980s that crime is best tackled at the local level. The initiative also adopted a 'partnership' or multi-agency approach to crime prevention. The Programme impact evaluation by the Home Office Research and Statistics Directorate (RSD), seeks to answer two key questions: i) was there any change in crime and fear in the Safer Cities project cities? ii) if so, to what extent can this change be attributed to the effects of Safer Cities action, as opposed to other causes? (See Ekblom, 1992.)

The evaluation requires combining diverse sources of data covering different territorial units (1981 and 1991 enumeration districts (EDs), beats, 'neighbourhoods') using a GIS and its associated relational database. For example, *action data* from coordinators' entries on SCP's management information system, showing details of nearly 3,000 individual schemes in terms of timing, financial input, target crime problem etc. (Law & Ekblom, 1996).

The various datasets are linked relationally, most through a database called INFO within ARC/INFO GIS (Law & Ekblom, 1994). The relations are described using the so-called EAR (entity-attribute-relationship) model (Everest, 1986), in which composite keys - attributes common to different datasets - enable action, outcome and context data to be linked. Scoping and scoring was carried out within ARC/INFO GIS and all the data were brought together for statistical modelling using the ML3E software on another PC. (For action and outcome measures using the scoping and scoring principles, see Ekblom, Sutton and Wiggins, 1993; Ekblom, Howes; and Law, 1994.)

From knowledge to data representation and storage

For the purpose of this paper, I would focus on the data transformation process which was necessary to support the classification task here. All the 3000 schemes of the Safer Cities programme had to be classified into different categories on a wide range of variables according to the nature of the action on the basis of free-text description of each scheme in the management information system. The categories were designed in-house (Ekblom, 1994; Law & Ekblom, 1996) and they were applied by a specially trained coder who had previously collaborated in the development of the classification categories. The structure of the classification was hierarchical in nature which had to be represented in a relational database structure and stored in INFO accordingly.

Each entity was linked by a common key, SCHEME-ID. The values of the schemes could be represented by a set of TRUE tables. The hierarchical structure of the tree (branch-nodes) was represented by the entity-attribute relationship. The relationship was recursed by defining the attribute as an entity for next branch down if there were any, and so on. Thus the tree structure A-B,C; B-D,E can be represented by the following logical schema: A(scheme-ID, B, C); B(scheme-ID, D, E).

A menu-driven user interface was rapidly developed to enable the end-user to select the classification options with ease by simply clicking with a mouse pointing device. The structure of the menu again was hierarchical to reflect the structure of the categories. The design of the user interface can be explained in terms of the so called GOMS model of Card, Moran and Newell (1983).

Discussion and lessons learnt

The first batch of results on burglary prevention shows that Safer Cities programme was a success and so was its evaluation (Ekblom, Law & Sutton, 1996; Law 1996), but let us not forget the success was directly due to the contribution of psychologists' expertise, particularly in engineering psychology. This section will highlight some of these contributions:

Top-down software engineering approach vs rapid prototyping

From the software engineering perspective (Sommerville, 1992), it is desirable to take an engineering approach to get all the user requirement, design specification right from the start and implement a large scale GIS just like any other software project. In practice, however especially in research application, this is unlikely to be feasible as users may not know what they want from the start, even if they do, they may change their mind (as in this project). A more robust - rapid prototyping approach seems to be more appropriate. Unfortunately, owing to the nature of GIS (with a large data base system as one of its parts), it is not robust enough to adopt such an approach entirely. A realistic application is most likely a half-way house between the two approaches (as demonstrated in this case study).

Learning curve effect

The learning curve of information technology is typically long (Leenders & Henderson, 1980). However, with the design and development of the user friendly interface, the learning curve can be rapid for the 'end-user' - for example, the input of the classification (Law & Ekblom, 1994). The time to do a task decreases with practice according to power law of practice. The time T_n to perform a task on the nth trial follows a power law (Card, Moran, & Newell, 1983):

$$T_n = T_1 n^{-a} \text{ or:} \tag{1}$$

$$\log T_n = \log T_1 - a \log n \tag{2}$$

where T_1 is the time to do the first trial.

A time-log was kept by the coder during the coding process (Law & Ekblom, 1996). Applying the above equation to our records, we found approximately: a = 0.17 (unusually short for this kind of task.); T_1 = 15 minutes; T_{3000} = 3.8 minutes - this predicted value is indeed close to our recorded value (3.5 minutes). This shows that power law is valid. The above results support psychologists' recommendation that continuous improvement of user interface is important as it increases productivity and efficiency of computer system applications and GIS is no exception.

Spatial expert system

As demonstrated in this project, research applications are usually knowledge intensive. The process of system development represents a process of eliciting knowledge from the user (who is also a domain 'expert') and transforming the knowledge into a computer storage schema - a classic expert system approach (Johnson & Keravnou 1985; Waterman, 1986). Although expert system techniques have been mature for some time, unfortunately no tools have been provided within GIS. Users are left to develop their own (for example, Brunsden, 1989; Cross, Openshaw, and Waugh, 1992). Some kind of intelligent front end attached to GIS may be desirable for the future. This is the area within which engineering psychologists can have a significant contribution.

Error modelling

One key question remains - what is it that makes GIS so different from other computer systems? The answer of course lies in the 'G' within GIS - it manipulates spatial data. This leads to all sorts of problems in terms of spatial and non-spatial data transformation such as over-lay operation which creates a range of errors. Furthermore the errors may propagate along the data transformation process, and the end-users may not even be aware of this (Goodchild & Gopal, 1989). While GIS has not provided any tool to address data accuracy issues, research in this area is also rare (in comparison with the above two research topics). Thus the issues on error modelling on spatial data increasingly becomes one of the most important and urgent research issues on our agenda. Research is under way to investigate the error modelling of spatial data used in the evaluation of the Safer Cities programme (Law & Fisher, 1995). However, human error in the process of spatial data transformation has so far been poorly addressed.

Conclusion

Owing to the impact of technologies as exemplified by the information super-highway and GIS technology described in this paper, the world in which we live is increasingly shrinking and interdependent. It therefore seems vital that engineering psychology explores the influence that information technologies have upon their users and their everyday life. The very future of our society depends increasingly upon how we re-engineer these powerful technologies. If occupational psychology were to make authoritative pronouncements on whether or not these various technological implementations have any implication on safety and efficacy, it is vital for the Society to accept engineering psychology as an important but inseparable part of occupational psychology. Engineering psychologists can thus put themselves in a position to give an informed advice upon the issues such as safety and efficacy of these technologies in producing technological change. The creation of the Special Interest Group in engineering psychology within the British Psychological Society, the Division and Section for occupational psychology is an encouraging first step. The engineering psychologists have remained hidden for so long, the time has come for them to find a home to which they feel belong. This paper has demonstrated (with an example of the large scale evaluation of the Safer Cities programme by psychologists) that engineering psychologists can have a significant contribution in many areas of multidisciplines. It is hoped that this paper will open the debate about the role of engineering psychology within the profession.

References

Brunsden C. (1989) *Spatial analysis techniques applied to the local crime pattern analysis*, PhD thesis. Newcastle University.

Card, S.K., Moran, T.P. & Newell, A. (1983) *The psychology of Human-Computer Interaction*, Lawrence Erlbaum: Hillsdale NJ.

Cross, A., S. Openshaw and D. Waugh. (1992) ARC/CRIME: A crime pattern analysis add-on for ARC/INFO. Paper presented at *ARC/INFO User's Conference*, Nottingham.

Ekblom, P. (1988) *Getting the best out of crime analysis*. Crime Prevention Unit Paper 10. Home Office: London.

Ekblom, P. (1992) 'The Safer Cities Programme impact evaluation: problems and progress'. *Studies on Crime and Crime Prevention*, Vol. 1, pp. 35-51.

Ekblom, P. (1994) 'Proximal circumstances: a theory-based classification of crime prevention'. *Crime Prevention Studies*, Vol 2.

Ekblom, P., M. Sutton and R. Wiggins. (1993) 'Scoping, scoring and modelling: linking measures of crime preventive action to measures of outcome in a large, multi-site evaluation'. Paper presented to *Royal Statistical Society*, London, December.

Ekblom, P., Howes D; and Law H.C. (1994) 'Scoping, scoring and modelling: linking measures of crime preventive action to measures of outcome in a large, multi-site evaluation using GIS and multilevel modelling', pp. 123-132. *Proceedings of the GISRUK.*

Ekblom, P., Law H.C. and Sutton, M. (in press) *Safer Cities and Residential Burglary.* Home Office Research Study. HMSO: London.

Everest, G. (1986) *Database Management - Objectives, System Functions and Administration.* McGraw-Hill: New York.

Goodchild M.F. & Gopal S. (eds.) (1989) *Accuracy of Spatial Databases.* Taylor & Francis: London.

Home Office (1993). *Safer Cities Progress Report, 1991-1992.* Home Office: London.

Johnson L. & Keravnou E.T. (1985) *Expert systems technology - a guide.* Abacus Press.

Law, H. C. (1996) *Geographical Information for governments - seminar report.* Home Office: London.

Law, H. C. & Ekblom, P. (1994) 'Application of GIS: Evaluation of Safer Programme'. *Proceedings of the AGI '94.*

Law, H. C. & Fisher, P. F. (1995) 'Error modelling in areal interpolation: a case study on the data precision of the Safer Cities Evaluation'. *Proceedings of the GIS Research UK*, GISRUK'95.

Leenders M.R. & Henderson R (1980) 'Startup research presents purchasing problems and opportunities', in E. Rhodes & D. Wield (eds.) *Implementing New Technologies.* Open University: Milton Keynes.

Lindsay, G., & & Lunt, I. (1993) 'The challenge of change'. *The Psychologist*, Vol. 6, pp. 210-213.

Macleod, I. (1994) 'The case for an SIG in engineering psychology'. *The Occupational Psychologist*, No 22, April.

Sommerville, I. (1992) *Software Engineering.* Addison-Wesley: Wokingham.

Waterman, D.A. (1986) *A guide to Expert Systems.* Addison-Wesley: Wokingham

Acknowledgements

The case study described in this paper was part of a large scale research project on Safer Cities programme evaluation by the Home Office Research & Statistics Directorate between 1988-1995. I am indebted to Dr Paul Ekblom for his scoping

237

and scoring principle in the evaluation design; and wish to thank him for his support and encouragement throughout this project.

Disclaimer

The views expressed are those of the author and do not necessarily represent those of the Home Office or any other government department

31 Rewritable routines in human interaction with public technology

Chris Baber and Neville Stanton*
Industrial Ergonomics Group,
University of Birmingham, UK
*Department of Psychology,
University of Southampton, UK

Abstract

In this paper we are concerned with problem solving in human interaction with public technology. Ideas from the problem solving literature are considered in terms of task analysis for error identification (TAFEI). Human interaction with public technology is viewed as comprising variations on means-ends analysis problem solving. Following Newell and Simon's pioneering work, we consider the relationship between states in the human-machine interaction and the planning requirements and working memory load on users. We introduce the notion of rewritable routines to describe this relationship.

Introduction

We have been developing a method for predicting user error in human-interaction with machines. This method is called task analysis for error identification (TAFEI) and is reported in detail elsewhere (e.g., Baber and Stanton, 1992; 1994; Stanton and Baber, 1996). TAFEI combines hierarchical task analysis with state space diagrams to provide a description of human-machine interaction. It is important to capture the interaction between human and machine at this state level in order to consider the types of errors which can arise. Error identification has been the focus of the initial work with TAFEI and the method can allow up to 80% of user errors to be identified (Baber and Stanton, 1996). However, the majority of the errors captured can be described as 'slips', or aberrations of physical activity. In order to develop the method further, it is necessary to have some explanation of 'mistakes', i.e., aberrations at a cognitive level.

Considering interaction as progressing between states has led us to assume that human-machine interaction employs plans relevant for each specific state. This assumption is shared with Simon and Young (1988), who propose '...users engage only in simple forms of planning, [and] we can predict certain errors in user behaviour due to the characteristics of a particular interface design.' (p.591). The idea of state-dependent planning is not intended to rule out planning on a more global scale. However, these global plans can be defined as goals, and the goals will be decomposed and modified as users progress through the interaction states. The modification of goals in each state will depend on immediate information received from the machine and the match between this information and the current set of goals. This borrows from the notion of situated action (Suchman, 1988).

In studies of people using a ticket vending machine, it has been observed that performance is faster on second and third trials than on the initial trial (Baber and Parker, 1994). These findings are also apparent in studies on automated-teller machine (ATM) use (Hatta and Iiyama, 1991). This suggests that people develop *ad hoc* routines for using public technology, and that the routines can be held in working memory during the course of a string of transactions. However, Baber and Parker (1994) show that people make similar errors irrespective of level of experience, which suggests that the storage of routines will be fragile and easily disrupted.

Thus, it is suggested that routines will be influenced by the developing interaction between user and machine (an assumption which underlies TAFEI). On the other hand, patterns of automated-teller machine (ATM) use suggest that people tend to perform a limited range of transactions in their interaction with public technology (Burford and Baber, 1994). This could either suggest that people will have well-rehearsed routines for these transactions (and overcome the storage fragility problems), or that people deliberately limit the number of routines they employ in order to simplify human-machine interaction by minimising the planning requirements. Studies of ATM use suggest that people tend to withdraw cash and check their balance more often than other transactions (indeed, the frequency with which these two transactions are used appears to be greater than the sum of other transactions). Thus, we can find evidence for limiting number of routines. By way of illustration of well-rehearsed routines, consider the mundane task of inserting a card into an ATM; there are four orientations for the card and the orientations can differ across machines. Observations suggest that users insert the card with little regard for printed instructions or labels on the machines. This implies a robust 'card insertion routine' for ATM use. However, the fact that insertion errors are common (at least when people use an unfamiliar machine) suggests that the routines are not flexible. Our concern in this paper is to develop an explanatory model of the extent to which a user's routines need to be learned and retained (possibly through stereotypes) and the extent to which they can be shaped during human-machine interaction.

Relevant states

We assume that use of public technology will be goal-directed (Stanton and Baber, 1996). This means that there will be a specific end-state of the interaction, e.g., obtaining a valid ticket from a ticket vending machine, withdrawing cash from an automated-teller machine etc. Possession of a goal does not necessarily imply possession of plans to achieve that goal. However, the range of possible actions will be constrained by the design of the machine and the user's interpretation of the machine. TAFEI is based on the assumption that for each state in human-machine interaction, there will be a finite number of following states. The number of states can be limited by the design of the machine and the goals of the user. In this paper we introduce the notion, adapted from Hayes-Roth and Hayes-Roth (1979), of 'relevant states'. Relevant states are those states from which a path to the goal can be seen. Assuming the existence of relevant states makes human-machine interaction a form of the means-ends analysis approach to problem solving presented by Newell and Simon (1972). People tend to employ means-ends analysis in problem solving, particularly when they lack more sophisticated strategies (Baron, 1994). Interaction with public technology is performed on an intermittent basis and people are unlikely to try to develop sophisticated strategies. Thus, it is assumed that human-machine interaction for public technology will employ mean-ends analysis.

Further, we assume that a goal can be reached via a number of relevant states, and the design of the machine could lead to states which appear relevant. In using public technology, the user will attempt to move from current state to the goal via relevant states. This is known in the problem solving literature as hill climbing. Actions are selected by comparing the current state with the goal, and the action which looks likely to lead to the goal will be chosen. This means that errors can arise when people reject correct actions which do not look as if they will reach the goal, or select actions which appear to lead to a goal but do not. We assume that users will interpret the relevance of actions in terms of the relationship between the current state and the goal. This is known in the literature as back chaining, where people create subgoals which are achievable in the current state to allow progression to the goal (Larkin et al., 1980). This means that the user has to work forwards to the goal (to consider possible states) and backwards from the goal (to determine relevant states). As Duncan (1993) says, 'Thus, the stimulus actually selected for control of behaviour is not simply the best match to a preexisting specification of what is needed in pursuit of a current goal. The goal itself may change; the selected stimulus is the one most relevant to the selected goal.' (p.63).

We assume that the user will seek relevant information during the interaction, where relevance is determined by goal definition, machine state and previous actions. The activity of seeking information is not intended to imply exhaustive search; rather the user will be defining a new problem space in each state. Chi et al. (1981) demonstrate that problem classification can have a bearing on solution strategy and will vary between novice and expert. We assume that interaction with public technology involves a continuous process of problem classification.

Thus, we have an initial description of human-machine interaction which retains the state-based description used in TAFEI and allows the introduction of some cognitive operations. Before proceeding, there is an obvious criticism of the assumptions which needs to be dealt with; given that people will interpret each state in a transaction in terms of problem space, seek a means of relating the state to a goal, and perform an action to move closer to the goal, it can be assumed that transaction times will be extreme. However, there are three points to bear in mind. First, only classifying the state in sufficient detail to allow an action to be formulated will reduce time (i.e., a variation on the theme of 'satisficing'). Second, the notion of 'compatibility' implies that people have stereotyped actions which can be applied to different situations. Oddly enough, despite many papers published on the topic of compatibility, there is little by way of theoretical explanation of the phenomena, particularly with reference to contemporary cognitive theory. Third, users will develop a repertoire of routines on the basis of information extracted from an interface (Kempton, 1986) - c.f., the use of mental models.

Rewritable routines

In order to move from current to relevant states, eliminating other possible states, the user needs to retain some record of the interaction and to have some means of assigning relevance to states. At each state, this record will be modified. Thus, it will need to be rewritable. We assume that the record will be held in working memory, presumably in the articulatory loop which has a limited duration. As the record will also guide the next action, we see this as a rewritable routine. There might be common features for parts of the interaction which can maintain the routine across several states. For example, consider using a ticket vending machine. There are two possible high-level routines which could be applied:

(i)   in the 'vending machine routine', the user inserts money and then makes a selection;

(ii) in the 'ticket clerk routine', the user requests a ticket and then pays.

Depending on which routine is used, the first action will be either to insert money or select a ticket. Previous observations suggest that, in error-prone interactions, errors at initial points are very common, i.e., determining which action to perform first. We suspect that other errors might occur at 'planning' boundaries, i.e., points at which significant changes of routine arise, although have no evidence of this to date.

The routine which is likely to be used can be influenced by the design of the machine. Figure 1 presents a simple schematic of this process. The possible states (interpreted by the user from the machine) are compared against states which could lead to the goal. The comparator has a two-way connection to the rewritable routines (with the routines both influencing the comparator, i.e., by defining relevance, and taking the output to define action).

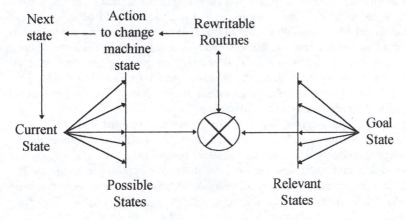

Figure 1   Simple schematic of rewritable routines

The routines will be rewritable in that they will need to be updated or modified at each state in the interaction. Assuming that the routines could be held in the articulatory loop of working memory would give a duration of around two seconds without rehearsal. Furthermore, assuming that the design of the machine can capture aspects of the routines (i.e., through affordance or compatibility) would reduce the memory issue by pairing a routine with machine state to provide a direct action (when there is no direct pairing then some form of routine formulation will be required, perhaps through translation). Next we assume that routines can vary in detail, with a hierarchy of detail from abstract (i.e., vague goals) to concise (i.e., explicit plans) to concrete (i.e., specific actions). Finally, we assume that the routines will exhibit inheritance at different levels. This would allow a link to made with some of the research into mental models.

Running the description

Baber and Parker (1994) observed a number of errors which people make when using a ticket vending machine. Around 80% of these errors could be predicted by TAFEI (Baber and Stanton, 1996). The main errors were related to the mode of the machine, i.e., change given, exact money only, closed, waiting. Observations indicated that people tended to use a machine as if it was always in change given mode. This either suggests that state indication on the machine was sufficiently poor to allow confusion or that users were only employing some of the information. The machine studied had a display positioned around one metre above the machine to indicate mode, with a further display on a LED on the machine. Thus, the mode state is indicated. The fact that users missed the indications suggests that the comparator was operating on limited information, either because the users did not see the indicators or because the users took no notice of them. Not seeing the indicators would be a function of conspicuity (and this is certainly a possible explanation). Not noticing the indicators would be a function of relevance; users would hold a definition of relevance in their rewritable routines which would not require mode indication. This explanation is plausible when one assumes that machine mode was not important until the final stages of the transaction when the user had to insert money. Thus, mode was not important in the initial states of the interaction.

There were errors observed in button use. This could be attributed to slips, with a large number of buttons in close proximity being likely to lead to the wrong button being pressed. While no data was collected on the buttons used, it seems unlikely that slips would account for all of these errors. An alternative explanation lies in the fact that the button errors were often attributable to errors in sequence rather than operation. This suggests that users were working to a routine which differed from that anticipated by the machine.

TAFEI failed to predict some of the observed errors. These were lose place in interaction, lose ticket exit, confusion due to options not available. It is proposed that each of these errors can be attributed to the description illustrated in figure 1. If the progression through states is not indicated, then the routine might not be updated appropriately. This would leave the user with a gap in the routine. Lose ticket exit referred to occasions when users were unable to locate the tray in which the ticket appeared. One explanation of this was that the ticket tray also served as the coin return tray; assuming that coin return and ticket dispensing were separate functions could lead to user seeking the ticket dispenser in another location. Confused by operations not available relates current state to users interpretation of relevance, i.e., users could be seeking information which was either not present or was presented in another form.

Conclusions

Our aim in writing this paper has been to relate theories from cognitive psychology to the TAFEI method. We have taken ideas from problem solving and related these to the use of machines. While the notion that using machines can be considered as a form of problem solving is in no way novel, the relationship of the ideas to TAFEI suggests that state-based descriptions of human-machine interaction can be developed to incorporate a cognitive dimension. Research being undertaken at present is investigating the relationship between interface design and user error, with a view to predicting cognitive error in human-machine interaction.

References

Baber, C. & Parker, A. (1994), 'Buying a ticket on the Underground', in S.A. Robertson (ed.), *Contemporary Ergonomics 1994*. Taylor and Francis: London, pp. 46-51.

Baber, C. & Stanton, N.A. (1994), 'Task analysis for error identification',*Ergonomics*, Vol. 37, pp. 1923-1942.

Baber, C. & Stanton. N.A. (1996), 'Human error identification techniques applied to public technology: predictions compared with observed use'. *Applied Ergonomics*, Vol. 27, pp. 119-131

Baron, J. (1994) *'Thinking and Deciding'*. Cambridge University Press: Cambridge.

Burford, B.C. & Baber, C. (1994). 'A user-centred evaluation of a simulated adaptive autoteller', in, S.A. Robertson (ed.) *Contemporary Ergonomics 1994*. Taylor and Francis: London, pp. 64 - 69.

Chi, M.T.H., Feltovich, P.J., & Glaser, R. (1981). 'Categorization and representation of physics knowledge by experts and novices'. *Cognitive Science*, Vol. 5 pp. 121-152.

Duncan, J. (1993) 'Selection of input and goal in the control of behaviour', in A. Baddeley & L. Weiskrantz (eds.) Attention Selection Awareness. Clarendon Press: Oxford.

Hatta, K. & Iiyama, Y. (1991), 'Ergonomic study of automatic-teller machine operability'. *International Journal of Human-Computer Interaction*, Vol. 3, pp. 295-309.

Hayes Roth, B. & Hayes Roth, F. (1979) 'A cognitive model of planning'. *Cognitive Science*, Vol. 3, pp. 275-310.

Kempton, W. (1986), 'Two theories used of home heat control' *Cognitive Science*, Vol. 10, pp. 75-91.

Larkin, J.H., McDermott, D., Simon, D.P. & Simon, H.A. (1980). 'Expert and novice performance in solving physics problems'. *Science*, Vol. 208, pp. 1335-1342.

Newell, A. & Simon, H.A. (1972). *Human Problem Solving*. Prentice Hall Englewood Cliffs, NJ.

Simon, T. & Young, R.M. (1988). 'GOMS meets STRIPS: the integration of planning with skilled procedure execution in human-computer interaction', in, D.M. Jones & R. Winder (eds.), *People and Computers IV*. Cambridge University Press: Cambridge.

Stanton, N.A. & Baber, C. (1996). 'A systems approach to human error identification'. *Safety Science*, Vol. 22, pp. 215-228.

Suchman, L. (1988) *'Plans and Situated Actions'*. Cambridge University Press: Cambridge.

32 The function and effectiveness of dynamic task allocation

Andrew J. Tattersall and Catherine A. Morgan
University of Wales Cardiff, UK

Abstract

Dynamic (or adaptive) control of task allocation in complex human-machine systems refers to the flexible allocation of tasks or functions between the operator and the system. Two studies are described that examined the impact of explicit task allocation on performance, subjective workload and situation awareness in a complex multiple-task environment. Participants were asked to control four tasks simultaneously: a monitoring task involving the detection of different types of visual signal, a tracking task involving manual control and visual input, a communications task involving the detection and response to auditory signals, and a resource management task involving maintenance of water levels and flow in a set of tanks. At relatively low levels of task demands there were few differences in performance and workload between the control group and operators who had explicit control over task allocation. The benefits of explicit task allocation became clearer at higher levels of task demands.

Introduction

Traditionally there have been two major options for the designers of complex human-machine systems. The first is to leave the human operator in control of all the tasks, but in increasingly complex and demanding situations there are clear implications for impaired performance and loss of control. The second is to use automation, but this does not always lead to improved system performance. The reduction in operator control over the system may also lead to impaired operator performance, particularly in critical situations, as well as increased levels of frustration and anxiety. An alternative is to introduce a more flexible method for allocating responsibility for performing sub-tasks between the human and the

247

system in which some of the advantages of automation are gained whilst maintaining operator involvement in the system. Four clear advantages of dynamic task allocation (DTA) have been proposed.

(i)   The resources of the system are used more fully.

(ii) Operator workload is maintained at a relatively constant level. Lemoine, Crevits, Debernard and Millot (1995) showed that compared to a no aid condition, both implicit (computer control of task allocation) and explicit (operator control) modes of DTA improved system and human performance on a heavy workload ATC task and reduced the global workload experienced by controllers.

(iii) It enables the human to have a relatively flexible role in the system and as the human operator is maintained in the 'system loop' the operator is able to gain a coherent view of the system's functions (Rouse, 1981). Theoretically, therefore, DTA will not only enhance the operator's situation awareness (SA) within the system but also prevent, to some extent, skill decay (Lockhart, Strub, Hawley and Tapia, 1993). If the AI system does breakdown or make an error, the operator should be familiar with the system and so is more likely to be able to diagnose failures and to make corrective procedures or take over the computer's role.

(iv) DTA will not only improve system performance but also be more acceptable to operators than static automation (Greenstein, Arnaut and Revesman, 1986).

Broadly there are two main types of method for controlling the allocation of tasks in a complex system operating in a dynamic task allocation mode. The first is explicit allocation, in which the operator has control over when and for how long tasks are to be performed manually or automatically. The second method is implicit task allocation, in which the computer or AI system allocates the tasks either to the human or computer. However, implicit DTA is relatively difficult to implement and it is also difficult to define appropriate allocation criteria for dynamic adaptation. A further problem is that methods for on-line use of data to inform the decision-making system are not easily obtainable. Explicit task allocation may be a more practical alternative, at least in the short term, although there are concerns that giving operators an option to switch tasks between automated and manual control may result in additional, perhaps unwanted, workload. It is clear that more research is necessary to investigate and compare the effectiveness of implicit and explicit modes of task allocation. The two experiments reported here were carried out to compare explicit control of task allocation and static task allocation with respect to multiple task performance, subjective workload ratings and situation awareness in medium (experiment one) and high (experiment two) task load environments.

Experimental methods

Measures

Performance was assessed using the multi-attribute task battery (MAT) (Comstock and Arnegard, 1992). This comprises four task elements: monitoring, tracking, communications and resource management. Performance data are generated for each task element and they can be performed singly or simultaneously in any combination. The task was presented and controlled using a Minstrel PC-Compatible computer with a 13 inch screen. A joystick and keyboard were used for control inputs. The four tasks are described below and a representation of the computer screen is presented in figure 1.

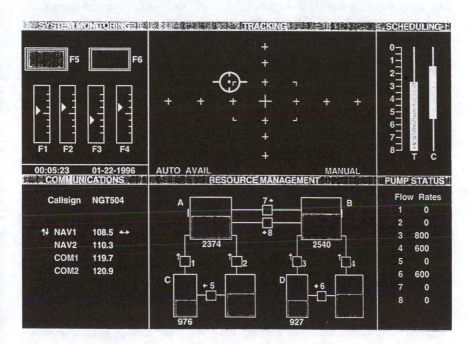

Figure 1 Illustration of MAT battery screen

The monitoring task requires subjects to monitor and correct deviations in the level of four gauges and to detect the absence of a green warning light (which is normally on) and the presence of a red warning light (which is normally off). Performance was recorded in terms of subjects' response time (ms) to correct gauge and light deviations and the number of incorrect responses (false alarms and misses) made during the task.

249

The tracking task is a two-dimensional compensatory tracking task that requires subjects to maintain a target in the central area of the tracking window using a joystick. Data were recorded in terms of root mean square error (RMS error) of the target from the centre.

The communications task simulates the presentation of auditory air traffic control messages. Each message consists of a six-digit call sign followed by a command. On the identification of a target call sign, operators change the frequency of one of four channels, using the up and down arrow keys to move the cursor to the frequency channel that needs to be changed and the left and right arrow keys to the change the frequency. Performance was measured in terms of number of errors and mean response time (ms).

The resource management task requires operators to maintain the water level of two main tanks (A and B) at a specified level (2500 units) by transferring water from four supply tasks. This is achieved by pressing appropriate keys on the numeric pad to turn any of the eight pumps on or off. Pump failures can be initiated, which are indicated by a red light in the square on the pump. Water cannot then be transferred through that pump until the fault is corrected. Performance was recorded as the mean absolute deviation of water in tanks A and B from the criterion level and the number of pump activations and deactivations made during the task.

In addition to the performance measures, subjective workload (WL) and situation awareness (SA) ratings were collected for each phase of task performance. WL was assessed using a computerised version of the NASA TLX (Hart and Staveland, 1988). The TLX includes six dimensions: mental demand, physical demand, temporal demand, performance, effort and frustration. After each ten minute phase participants were required to rate each dimension on a scale from 1-100. Overall WL scores were calculated as the mean ratings on the six scales. SA was assessed using the situation awareness rating technique (SART) (Taylor, 1989). The 14-item SART was used, which includes items relating to the instability, complexity, variability and familiarity of the situation, arousal, concentration and division of attention, spare mental capacity, information quantity and quality gained and gives scores on the primary dimensions of demand on attentional resources, supply of attentional resources, and understanding of the situation. Ratings were given for each item on a ten-point Likert scale from one (low) to ten (high).

Participants

There were thirty-six participants in each of the experiments, aged between 18 and 30 years. None had any previous experience of the MAT battery. In each experiment, 12 participants were randomly allocated to the control group (static task allocation) and 24 were allocated to the explicit task allocation group.

Procedure

After receiving detailed instructions regarding the function of each sub-task comprising the MAT battery, participants were given five minutes practice/familiarisation on each task. In the experimental phase participants were required to perform all four tasks simultaneously for 40 minutes. This phase was divided into four ten minute blocks, each separated by completion of the subjective ratings. The procedure was the same for all participants, except that the explicit group received additional information informing them that the control of the tracking task and the resource management task could be switched between automatic and manual control at any stage during the experiment.

The task load of all four tasks remained roughly constant throughout each experiment. The tracking task was set at the low difficulty setting in each experiment and a continuous string of call-signs were presented, giving 86 call signs per ten minute block with a ratio of own to other call-signs of 1:2. In experiment one there were 32 light or gauge deviations in each ten minute block and six pump failures on the resource management task. The number of events in the monitoring and resource management tasks was increased by 50 per cent in experiment two, with 48 light or gauge deviations and nine pump failures every ten minutes.

Results

There were significant differences in levels of performance and subjective workload between the control groups of the two experiments indicating that the manipulation of task load had the desired effect. Of the 24 subjects in the explicit condition of experiment one, seven did not automate either the tracking or resource management task in the 40 minute experimental session. The tracking task was automated for an average of 1126 seconds and the resource management task for 343 seconds. In experiment two, six participants did not use the opportunity to automate either of the tasks. The mean duration of automated tracking was 1081 seconds and the mean duration of automated resource management was 1042 seconds. Participants using automation made an average of three switches between automatic and manual modes in experiment one and just over two switches in experiment two.

In experiment one, no significant differences were found between the control and explicit groups in monitoring, communication and tracking task performance, although the control group showed less variable and slightly better tracking performance than the explicit group. On the resource management task, the explicit group maintained the water in tanks A and B closer to the criterion level and also made more pump activations and deactivations throughout the experiment compared to the control condition. The control group did, however, achieve a comparable level of performance on this task by the end of the 40 minute experimental period.

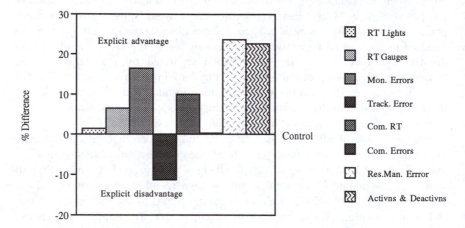

Figure 2   Performance differences between control and explicit conditions in experiment one

There was no significant difference in overall workload between the control and explicit groups although the control group rated their performance to be better than the explicit group. No other differences were found between the two groups for specific dimensions of workload. In terms of SA, the control group rated the tasks as being less variable and unstable than the explicit group. They also reported having more spare mental capacity available when performing the tasks and less demand on attentional resources.

The data were examined further to compare those participants in the explicit condition who had used the opportunity to change the allocation of tasks during the experiment (i.e. those subjects who had automated either the tracking task or resource management task or both at some point during the experiment) with those subjects who did not take the opportunity to automate either task. No significant differences were found between the performance of the two sub-groups on the monitoring task. However, those using automation were found to make significantly more errors on the resource management task. They also showed poorer tracking performance and were slower at responding to call-signs in the communications task than those who did not use automation. Furthermore, participants using the opportunity to automate reported higher levels of overall workload than those that did not automate either task. They reported having to put more effort into achieving the level of performance attained on the tasks and also found the tasks to be less complex and unstable than those that did automate.

They also reported having more spare mental capacity and increased levels of concentration during the experiment.

In experiment two the explicit group were found to respond more rapidly to the warning lights and gauge deviations and made fewer errors on the monitoring task than the control group. The explicit group also generally performed better on the tracking task than the control group, particularly in the first half of the experiment. There was no main effect of group on the communications task, but the explicit group made significantly less error on the resource management task. In achieving their better level of performance, however, they did not make significantly more control inputs (see figure 3).

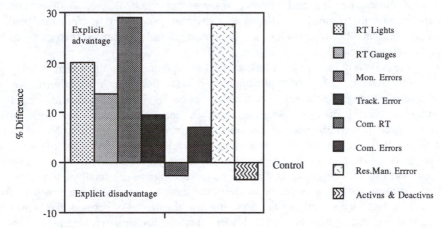

Figure 3   Performance differences between control and explicit conditions in experiment two

The workload ratings indicated that the explicit group experienced less mental and physical demand than the control group throughout the experiment. The explicit group also reported lower levels of instability, complexity, variability and demand than the control group as well as enhanced levels of quantity and quality of information gained.

The comparisons between those who did and did not use automation in the explicit group revealed that those who switched task control were generally better on the monitoring task in terms of both response times and errors than those subjects that did not automate either task during the experiment. Tracking error and communication task error were also greater for those subjects that did not automate either task. In summary, the performance results suggest that, in general, participants who took advantage of the opportunity to automate performed better than those participants who decided not to switch task control. There was no difference between the two sub-groups in terms of perceived workload, although non-automating subjects experienced greater instability of tasks and greater demands on concentration.

Discussion

The primary aim of these experiments was to evaluate the effects of explicit task control on performance and subjective measures of workload and situation awareness. Of particular note is the finding that at least 25 per cent of participants in the explicit control conditions actually did not take the opportunity to reallocate the control of the tracking and resource management tasks. Further analyses and experiments are planned to investigate individual patterns of performance and subjective state that might allow the prediction of task allocation strategies and performance difficulties.

At the relatively low levels of task demand in experiment one there were actually very few benefits, if any, of explicit control of task allocation. In experiment two, with relatively higher task demands, there do appear to be clear benefits associated with the control of task allocation, both in comparison with the levels of performance, perceived workload and situation awareness of a control group and of a group that did not use the opportunity to switch control of the tasks. This is extremely interesting as it suggests that dynamic task allocation, in this case controlled explicitly by subjects, has the potential to improve overall performance. Perhaps more interesting is the implication from these two studies that the particular model or algorithm underlying the decisions to reallocate tasks between the human operator and the system is crucial. Under relatively low load conditions explicit control does not appear to be beneficial and may in fact have detrimental effects in some cases. Under higher load conditions, the benefits of automating one or two of the tasks become more apparent.

References

Comstock, J.R., & Arnegard, R.J. (1992). *The Multi-Attribute Task Battery for Human Operator Workload and Strategic Behavior Research.* NASA Langley Research Center: Hampton, Virginia.

Greenstein, J.S., Arnaut, L.Y., & Revesman, M.E. (1986). 'An empirical comparison of model-based and explicit communication for dynamic human-computer task allocation'. *International Journal of Man-Machine Studies*, Vol. 24, pp. 355-363.

Hart, S.G., & Staveland, L.E. (1988). 'Development of a NASA TLX (Task Load Index): Results of empirical and theoretical research'. In, P. Hancock & N. Meshkati (eds.), *Human Mental Workload.* Elsevier: Amsterdam.

Lemoine, M.P., Crevits, I., Debernard, S., & Millot, P. (1995). 'Men-Machines Co-operation: Toward an Experimentation of a Multi-Level Co-operative Organisation in Air Traffic Control'. *International Workshop on the Design of Co-operative Systems*, Antibes, France.

Lockhart, J.M., Strub, M.H., Hawley, J.K. & Tapia, L.A. (1993). 'Automation and supervisory control: a perspective on human performance, training, and performance aiding'. *Proceedings of the Human Factors and Ergonomics Society 37th Annual Meeting.*

Rouse, W.B. (1981). 'Human-computer interaction in the control of dynamic systems'. *ACM Computing Surveys*, Vol. 13, pp. 71-99.

Taylor, R.M. (1989). 'Situational Awareness Rating Technique (SART): The development of a tool for aircrew systems design'. In *Proceedings of the AGARD AMP Symposium on Situational Awareness in Aerospace Operations, CP478.* NATO AGARD: Seuilly-sur Seine.

Acknowledgements

This work has been carried out with the support of the Defence Research Agency Centre for Human Sciences. The views expressed in the paper are those of the authors and should not necessarily be attributed to the Defence Research Agency.

33 Implicit memory: new procedures for cognitive load investigations in work situations

Patrice Terrier, Michel Neboit* and Jean-Marie Collier
Toulouse II University, France
*INES-EDI, Vandoeuvre, France

Abstract

This selective review suggests opportunities for mental load assessment in industrial settings. Considering the well-known difficulties encountered by the usual methods, we first review data acquired through current developments of implicit memory research for (i) measuring the contribution of types of processing within a task, (ii) isolating the influence of basic resources from constructs, and (iii) contrasting automatic and controlled processing. The ecological value of these approaches is then highlighted. First, a non-intrusive but precise method has been developed in each case. Second, there is no longer a need to ask the operator to think back to a study episode when analysing memory. Experiments conducted in a process control situation have helped support several of these points, and confirm the rationality of a position: an ecological analysis of memory does not require abandoning conventional laboratory paradigms, but rather demands the use of paradigms that fit natural functioning.

What effective cognitive load assessment should be

Mental workload measurements have been extensively documented in the last two decades (Moray, 1979; Hancock and Meshkati, 1988). However, when one considers their effective application to industrial settings, it is seen to be fraught with difficulties. For an ergonomist, a valuable method should (i) be non-intrusive, with no modification of current activity, and should be used with minimum apparatus, (ii) be able to be adapted to different contexts, (iii) provide information on processing operations.

Combine practical criteria and cognitive sensitivity

Although there is strong evidence that the usual methods can be mapped on to one or two of these properties, the well-known difficulty is that none of them have all three properties simultaneously. When the method is quite informative on processing operations (dual task methods) it is also highly intrusive. When the method is completely non-intrusive, with minimum apparatus, there is no information on cognitive operations (subjective workload measurements). Even the regulatory approach, relying on the study of operative modes is faced with this problem. The problem with such an approach revolves around the possibility of generalizing the technique, and time constraints for the practitioner.

On the other hand, the use of memory tasks can easily handle these three constraints simultaneously. First, memory tasks are non-intrusive and require minimal apparatus. Second, they can be adapted to the variety of working materials and activities, in that memory for words, images, and motor acts, can be studied. Third, and more important, there is little doubt about the fact that memory performance reflects prior information processing operations.

Start from often-neglected evidence

On the theoretical side, the core problem for cognitive load assessment also assumes a study of memory literature: automaticity (Leplat, 1988; Strayer and Kramer, 1990; Hasher and Zachs, 1979; Logan, 1988a). Distinctions relying on processes representing different degrees of effort are sufficiently entrenched in human factors literature that one may simply search this literature for methods that could give access to cognitive operations that are supposed to differ in cost: automatic versus effortful, conceptually-driven versus perceptually-driven, etc. Unfortunately, recent research has shown that experimental psychologists have been significantly wrong in their effort to create pure process conditions (Logan, 1988a, 1988b; Myers and Fisk, 1987).

An important point has often been neglected: task performance always represents a blend between conceptually-driven and perceptually-driven operations, between controlled and automatic operations (Bargh, 1992; Jacoby, 1991). As a result, a valuable procedure for accessing mental operations in natural environments should start from this point. This starting point was endorsed in recent research (Terrier, 1996). The thesis is that cognitive load analysis can effectively be developed on the basis of a particular tool kit: dissociation between measurements of retention.

Implicit memory: some facts

In recent years, entire books have been devoted to the study of implicit memory, that is to the study of dissociation between explicit and implicit measurements of retention (e.g. Lewandowsky, Dunn and Kirsner, 1989; Graf and Masson, 1993; Schacter and Tulving, 1994).

Tasks and processes

Explicit measurements of retention are those that involve conscious recollection. Recall and recognition are typical examples of explicit tests in that, although subjects either reconstruct or select a response, they are always asked to 'think back' to study episodes. Implicit measurements of retention are those in which no act of conscious recollection is necessary to accomplish the task (Graf and Schacter, 1985). Subjects are instructed to perform the task at hand as well as possible and they are not instructed to think back to prior episodes. For example, when having studied a word (DISPLAY), subjects can be given a stem completion test (DIS____) or a word fragment completion test (D_S__A_) in which they are simply told to complete the missing letters in order to form a word. Since studied and non-studied words are intermixed during the test, memory can be revealed by an ease in performance that is attributable to information processing during the prior episodes. Stem completion and fragment completion are two examples of implicit tests of memory.

Yet experimental factors that affect performance for one type of test often have a negligible impact on performance for the other type of test. Level of processing has little influence on implicit tests although its influence on explicit tests is largely known (e.g. Jacoby, 1983; Jacoby and Dallas, 1981; Light and Singh, 1987; Schacter and McGlynn, 1989; Roediger, Weldon, Stadler and Riegler, 1992; Light, La Voie, Valencia-Laver, Albertson Owens and Mead, 1992). On the other hand, modality shifts between study and test phases have a negligible influence on explicit tests but a great impact on implicit tests (e.g. Bassili, Smith and MacLeod, 1989; Jacoby and Dallas, 1981; Light, et al., 1992; Roediger and Srinivas, 1993). For example, in an implicit test, performance is not found to be better when information is processed at a deep level rather than at a shallow level during study, and performance is found to be better when study and test modalities correspond rather than when they differ. In addition, and in order to (apparently) complicate the matter, dissociation also exists within the same class of tests.

A transfer-appropriate-processing (TAP) explanation, placing an emphasis on the consistency (or compatibility) of mental operations between study and test phases can handle a vast majority of such data. The basic point of the TAP framework (Morris, Brandsford and Franks, 1977; Roediger, Weldon and Challis, 1989) is the following: most explicit tests of memory basically recruit conceptual processing operations conducted at study. They are consistent with top-down or conceptually-driven operations, whence their sensitivity to a level of processing manipulation and their insensitivity to surface variations between study and test episodes. On the other hand, most implicit tests are essentially perceptually-driven. Here, data-driven operations conducted during the study phase are primarily recruited, whence the observed sensitivity to surface variations (e.g. modality) and the relative insensitivity to a level of processing manipulation or other conceptual manipulations. This simple and testable assumption has now proven its ability to explain dissociation between and within classes of tests, and its direct consequence on accessing mental operations should now appear.

Practical implications

Measuring the contribution of types of processes within a task Of particular interest are studies in which a conceptual test and a perceptual memory test have been compared as a function of a level of processing manipulation (for a review, see Roediger, et al., 1989). Some studies have simultaneously observed that (i) an increase in conceptual demands during the study phase produced increased performance for a (putative) conceptual test but decreased performance for a (putative) perceptual test, whereas (ii) an increase in perceptual demands produced an increase in the putative perceptual test and a decrease in the conceptual test.

The conclusion is that these studies have provided a clear and direct illustration of the fact that the 'cognitive load' concept has now some justification in respect to processing operations: when strain was varied in terms of cognitive operations, stress also varied in terms of corresponding cognitive operations. The implications are straightforward for human factors practitioners because they can now readily test classical assumptions in work settings: when are we so often entitled to call a driving task or an inspection task a perceptive task? We see no need here to tell the reader what should be observed with a couple of memory tests (one mostly perceptive, the other mostly conceptual) in order to test this very frequent yet probably false assumption. To summarize, the relative balance between conceptual and perceptual operations can be analysed by manipulating the sort of memory task once the real task being investigated has been completed.

Separating the effects of basic resources from those of constructed resources We have just discussed a general characteristic of most implicit tests that shows their perceptive nature. Surface manipulations, such as modality variations, affect these tests: when presentation modalities for both study and test correspond (auditive-auditive, visual-visual), performance is better than when they differ (auditive-visual, visual-auditive).

A second property thus immediately follows in that the effect of basic resources can be isolated within memory performance. Since the effect of codes, modalities, or encoding formats constitute important topics in human factors literature (see Wickens and Liu, 1988), it might be useful to be able to remove the effect of higher cognitive functions from observed performance. For other studies, for example when two interfaces are compared as a function of memory performance (e.g. Vicente, 1992; Moray, 1993) the effect of the encoding format represents a disturbing factor because access to meaning must be assessed above all (Vicente, 1992). It might thus be useful to remove the effect of encoding formats. In each of these cases, the observer can develop a suitable design for an experiment or observations in that the compatibility between resources can be manipulated with respect to the particular objective: measurements that remove the contribution of codes and modalities in performance, thus reflecting cognitive resources; measurements that primarily recruit their contribution; and measurements that compare situations with respect to the relative importance of basic versus higher order resources by systematically varying compatibility between resources.

Contrasting controlled and automatic effects Another set of studies has provided a new procedure for studying automatic and controlled processing operations. Because such literature specifically deals with the nature of operations occurring at retrieval, it is of less interest to us. We only evoke an initial presentation of this procedure in order to show that it can easily be adapted to work situations, contrary to conventional interference paradigms.

Jacoby (Jacoby, 1991) has developed a paradigm devoted to the study of cognitive control in retrieval operations. After a study phase, the subject is tested alternatively in two conditions that are labelled inclusion and exclusion conditions. For example, in a stem completion test, the subject is alternately asked to complete the stems with previous study words (inclusion condition) or to complete them with unstudied words (exclusion condition). With the proportion of stems that are completed with studied words in each condition, the observer has two probabilities of completing a stem with a studied word that reflect cognitive control in retrieval. If cognitive control is perfect, the subject will (i) systematically complete stems with a studied word in the inclusion condition, (ii) never complete with a studied word in the exclusion condition. Subtracting the second probability from the first gives the cognitive control. For example, .70-0= .70 is a score representing perfect cognitive control. On the contrary, if cognitive control is null, the two probabilities will be equal to each other (.70-.70= 0). The degree of cognitive control is thus obtained by a simple subtraction between 'trying to do' and 'trying not to do' the same thing, in accordance with the logic used in several classical paradigms of interference. This paradigm, known as the process-dissociation procedure, is of interest in an ecological context because if it conveys the same logic as that used in usual interference paradigms (stroop, flanker, etc.), it is clearly usable in work settings: there is no need to modify the studied activity.

Toward an ecological approach to processing operations in work settings

A task typology based on cognitive operations and their context of occurrence represents a major challenge for cognitive disciplines. We have just seen that such a project is currently being actively developed, at least for tasks that can be used after a given activity: memory tasks. Several ecological characteristics should be emphasized, and implicit memory should be tested in a complex situation.

Ecological advantages

First, in each case, a non-intrusive but precise method has been developed. The method is non-intrusive because it makes use of the fact that initial activities (study phase) can be accessed in a precise mode by means of a subsequent memory test. If we contrast the proposed rationale with rationales still used in ergonomics literature, it appears that the use of memory tasks in work analysis is still restricted to recall or recognition, hence restricted to methods that recruit conceptual processing operations conducted during the study phase (e.g. Vicente, 1992, Moray, 1993). It is also quite possible that frameworks focussing on ecological psychology should also use memory tasks that are essentially perceptive in nature.

Second, any use of memory tasks in natural environments should answer the following questions: assuming that operators continuously use their past experience to identify current information (memory processes), what is the usual form of retrieval used, and consequently, what form of retrieval should I provoke? Because conceptual and perceptual memory tests can be developed, either tapping explicit or implicit modes of retrieval, the point is that a general contribution to work analysis is now possible because it is no longer necessary to ask the operator to think back to previous episodes when analysing processing activities.

Implicit memory in process control

These ideas have been tested with experts controlling a pressurized water reactor (Terrier, 1996). As a team of work psychologists and ergonomists, we were interested in the analysis of initial activities, so we neglected the process-dissociation procedure and concentrated our efforts on (i) the possibility of using memory tasks that fit natural functioning rather than tasks that systematically impose a recollective experience, (ii) the possibility of accessing both conceptual and perceptual activities by means of appropriate memory tests.

Three experiments supported the hypotheses, and demonstrated the possibility of implicit memory techniques being adapted to practical ergonomics issues. For example, in an initial experiment we used an implicit measure of memory for the colour coding of warning labels in order to test the relevance of the colour coding for severity functions. The implicit nature of retrieval was studied more carefully in two subsequent experiments which adapted fragment completion techniques to warning labels. These two experiments provided additional evidence of the (real) implicit nature of retrieval when operators are simply asked to do a task at hand, and replicated dissociation between memory tests as a function of level of processing (severity judgments versus abbreviation judgments), thus providing evidence that the practitioner may use methods that primarily recruit conceptual operations or perceptual operations.

Concluding remarks

Effective cognitive load analysis in work situations should consider both practical and scientific criteria. Memory tasks are compatible with practitioners' constraints (time, adaptability, non intrusiveness) and also present, as revealed by recent advances in the field of implicit memory, interesting properties for an interactive study of processing operations, an isolation of the effects of basic resources in performance, and the study of cognitive control.

Since the major cause of lack of progress in the workload area is the lack of generality of results (Wierwille, 1988), memory tests are useful task analysis techniques because the systematic delineating of cognitive operations is seen as a less ambitious and more achievable objective in this case. Far from neglecting experiments that have focussed on determining interactive effects in dual or triple tasks, we argue for the development of this logic by endorsing the important problem of generalizability of results. By suggesting that implicit measurements of retention have an ecological advantage over explicit measurements for work settings, thus providing 'operative memory tasks', we simply consider some advice (Lockhart and Craik, 1990): an ecological analysis of memory does not require abandoning conventional laboratory paradigms, but rather demands the use of paradigms that fit natural functioning.

References

Bargh, J.A. (1992), 'The ecology of automaticity: toward establishing the conditions needed to produce automatic processing effects'. *American Journal of Psychology*, Vol. 105, pp. 181-201.

Bassili, J.N., Smith, M.C. & MacLeod, C.M. (1989), 'Auditory and visual word-stem completion: separating data-driven and conceptually driven processes'. *Quarterly Journal of Experimental Psychology*, Vol. 41A, pp. 439-453.

Graf, P. & Masson, M.E.J. (1993) *Implicit memory: new directions in cognition, development, and neuropsychology*. Laurence Erlbaum Associates: Hillsdale, NJ.

Graf, P. & Schacter, D.L. (1985), 'Implicit and explicit memory for new associations in normal and amnesic subjects'. *Journal of Experimental Psychology: Learning, Memory, and Cognition*, Vol. 11, pp. 501-518.

Hancock, P. & Meshkati, N. (1988) *Human mental workload*. North-Holland: Amsterdam.

Hasher, L.M. & Zachs, R. (1979), 'Automatic and effortful processes in memory'. *Journal of Experimental Psychology: General*, Vol. 108, pp. 356-388.

Jacoby, L.L. (1983), 'Remembering the data: analysing interactive processes in reading'. *Journal of Verbal Learning and Verbal Behavior*, Vol. 22, pp. 485-508.

Jacoby, L.L. (1991), 'A process-dissociation framework: separating automatic and intentional uses of memory'. *Journal of Memory and Language*, Vol. 30, pp. 513-541.

Jacoby, L.L. & Dallas, M. (1981), 'On the relationship between autobiographical memory and perceptual learning'. *Journal of Experimental Psychology: General*, Vol. 110, pp. 306-340.

Leplat, J. (1988), 'Les habileté cognitives dans le travail', in P. Perruchet (ed.), *Les automatismes cognitifs*. Mardaga: Liège.

Lewandowsky, S., Dunn, J.C. & Kirsner, K. (1989) *Implicit memory: theoretical issues*. Laurence Erlbaum Associates: Hillsdale, NJ.

Light, L.L., La Voie, D., Valencia-Laver, D., Albertson Owens, S.A. & Mead, G. (1992), 'Direct and indirect measures of memory for modality in young and older adults'. *Journal of Experimental Psychology: Learning, Memory, and Cognition*, Vol. 18, pp. 1284-1297.

Light, L.L. & Singh, A. (1987), 'Implicit and explicit memory for young and older adults'. *Journal of Experimental Psychology: Learning, Memory, and Cognition*, Vol. 13, pp. 531-541.

Lockhart, R.S. & Craik F.I.M. (1990), 'Levels of processing: a retrospective commentary on a framework for memory research'. *Canadian Journal of Psychology*, Vol. 44, pp. 87-112.

Logan, G.D. (1988a), 'Automaticity, resources, and memory: theoretical controversies and practical implications'. *Human Factors*, Vol. 30, pp. 583-598.

Logan, G.D. (1988b), 'Toward an instance theory of automatisation'. *Psychological Review*, Vol. 95, pp. 492-528.

MacLeod, C.M. & Bassili, J.N. (1989), 'Are implicit and explicit tests differentially sensitive to item-specific versus relational information?', in S. Lewandowsky, J.C., Dunn & K. Kirsner (eds.), *Implicit memory: theoretical issues*. Erlbaum: Hillsdale, N.J.

Moray, N. (1979) *Mental Workload. Its theory and measurement*. NATO Conference Series, Series III: Human Factors, Vol. 8. Plenum Press: New York.

Moray, N. (1993), 'Direct perception interfaces for nuclear power plants', in *Proceedings of the 4th European Conference on Cognitive Science Approaches to Process Control*. August 25-27, Fredensborg, Denmark.

Morris, C.D., Brandsford, J.D. & Franks, J.J. (1977), 'Level of processing versus transfer appropriate processing'. *Journal of Verbal Learning and Verbal Behavior*, Vol. 16, pp. 519-533.

Myers, G.L. & Fisk, A.D. (1987), 'Training consistent task components: application of automatic and controlled processing theory to industrial task training'. *Human Factors*, Vol. 29, pp. 492-528.

Roediger, H.L., III, Weldon, M.S. & Challis, B.H. (1989), 'Explaining dissociations between implicit and explicit measures of retention: a processing account', in H.L. Roediger III & F.I.M. Craik (eds.), *Varieties of memory and consciousness: essays in honour of Endel Tulving*. Erlbaum: Hillsdale, NJ.

Roediger, H.L., Weldon, S., Stadler, M.L. & Riegler, G.L. (1992), 'Direct comparison of two implicit memory tests: word fragment and word stem completion'. *Journal of Experimental Psychology: Learning, Memory, and Cognition,* Vol. 18, pp. 1251-1269.

Schacter, D.L. & McGlynn, S.M.(1989), 'Implicit memory: effects of elaboration depend on unitization'. *American Journal of Psychology,* Vol. 102, pp. 151-181.

Schacter, D.L. & Tulving, E. (1994) *Memory systems 1994.* MIT Press: Cambridge MA.

Strayer, D.L. & Kramer, A.F. (1990), 'An analysis of memory based theories of automaticity'. *Journal of Experimental Psychology: Learning, Memory, and Cognition,* Vol. 16, pp. 291-304.

Terrier, P. (1996), 'Mémoire implicite et étude opérative des traitements. Exploration dans le contexte de l'évaluation d'interfaces'. *Les Notes Scientifiques et Techniques de l'INRS, 143.*

Vicente, K.J. (1992), 'Memory recall in process control: a measure of expertise and display effectiveness'. *Memory & Cognition,* Vol. 20, pp. 356-373.

Wickens, C.D. & Liu, Y. (1988), 'Codes and modalities in multiple resources: a success and a qualification'. *Human Factors,* Vol. 30, pp. 599-616.

Wierwille, W.W. (1988), 'Important remaining issues in mental workload estimation', in P. Hancock & N. Meshkati (eds.), *Human mental workload .* North-Holland: Amsterdam.

34 Duration estimates: a potentially useful tool for cognitive ergonomists

Alex R. Carmichael
University of Manchester, UK

Abstract

Following a general overview of some of the cognitive theories of duration estimation (as distinct from perception) some of their fundamental limitations are identified. A variety of studies, generally of an applied nature, are briefly described and factors that have been found to affect the extent and direction (overestimation/underestimation) of duration estimates are indicated. These are related to findings from a recent study by the author, involving duration estimates. It is then argued that duration estimates can be reasonably viewed as an (albeit indirect) index of cognitive overload that can be mediated by a variety of motivational and affective factors, making them a potentially useful for tool for cognitive ergonomists.

Introduction

Over the years, people's ability to perceive and judge various aspects of the passage of time have been examined both from a broad range of perspectives and in a broad range of contexts. In general, this corpus can be divided into two approaches. One is guided by the assumption that the processes involved are fundamentally perceptual and the other assumes somewhat 'higher order' cognitive processes are the key.

These approaches often appear to be in conflict. However, this is not necessarily problematic as it can be argued that each approach functions at a different level of enquiry. The distinction can be characterised in the following way. The perceptual approach is mainly concerned with relatively short durations of less than around five seconds which can be encompassed by what Fraisse (1984) calls 'the psychological present'. While, periods of time beyond 'the psychological present' by definition rely on cognitive processes such as memory to be apprehended. Fraisse (1984) labels

267

Alex R. Carmichael

these processes as 'perception' and 'estimation' of duration, respectively. While it is believed that this is a useful distinction, no claim is made here that these processes are, in any absolute sense, mutually independent only that they are not in direct conflict. The present paper focuses on the cognitive level and thus refers to 'duration estimates' (DE).

Cognitive theories of DE

The brief review which follows is not intended as exhaustive rather it provides exemplars of the main themes and perspectives relevant to the present discussion. Further, work covered below is not concerned with 'prospective' DE. A significant amount of research into DE uses a 'prospective' paradigm, wherein subjects are made aware in advance of the requirement to estimate some period of time. Awareness of the salience of duration during the period in question limits the relevance of such findings to the present discussion. Thus, the work referred to below has used retrospective paradigms such that the requirement for a DE is only made apparent after the period in question.

One example comes from a series of experiments carried out by Ornstein (1969) and is generally referred to as the 'storage size' hypothesis. As the name suggests, this view proposes that a DE is made on the basis of the amount of information stored in memory during the period in question. This is based on experimental findings such that, given equal durations, subjects presented with 20 items will give larger estimates of the duration than those presented with only ten items. Also, given equal numbers of stimuli, shorter estimations can be elicited if a framework for 'chunking' the items into fewer units is provided. Findings from other researchers have generally supported this view, but many of these can also be interpreted to support Block's 'contextual change' theory (e.g. Block & Reed, 1978; Block, 1982).

Block's view emphasises the amount of changes in 'process context' that occur during a particular interval. For example, he found that subjects presented with a list of letters and numbers to be memorised estimated the duration as longer than those presented with (same size) lists of letters *or* numbers. In general it can be seen that the main distinction between these two views is one of terminology. That is say, each view indicates DE as based on some (retrospective) 'count' of the processing 'steps' undertaken during the period in question and they differ mainly in the definition of (the important aspects of) those 'steps'.

Underwood and Swain (1973) offer a third view in which DE is based on (rather than a 'count') a judgement of the amount of attentional capacity expended during a period. This is based on findings such that a period during which a word list is presented aurally will be estimated as longer if the stimuli is accompanied by white noise than if it is not. Again, it can be seen that this emphasis does not uniquely distinguish this view and it is perhaps not surprising that findings offered in support

268

of this view are often claimed to support the other two outlined above (and vice versa).

Studies aimed at directly pitting these (and similar) views against each other (e.g. Poynter, 1983) fail to unambiguously support any one over the others. This suggests that (at present, at least) purely cognitive views of DE are limited in some fundamental way. Hogan (1978) indicates two aspects not addressed by the above views which could plausibly relate to this limitation. The first relates to the fact that they tend to be couched in terms which imply a linear relationship between the preferred cognitive variable (e.g. storage size, contextual change etc.) and DE. Whereas, in general terms, it seems equally likely that the relationship may be more complicated. This contention is strengthened by the second aspect, which is the lack of consideration of (non-cognitive) individual differences (in Hogan's particular study this was extroversion-introversion). These criticisms are strengthened by a variety of data from research beyond the purely cognitive.

Other variables found to affect DE

One example is provided by Hornik (1992) who found that subjects in a positive mood state underestimated and those in a negative mood state overestimated a period in which they were involved in simulated shopping exercise (which echoes the old adage that 'time flies when you're having fun'). This study differs from those below in that the objective 'task' carried out by all subjects was the same and only there transient mood differed. Whereas, the following studies tend to manipulate some aspect of the 'task' with the aim of affecting DE. Also, unlike the Hornik study, the following studies explicitly orient subjects toward some episode (e.g. video or tape recording etc.) for the purpose of a subsequent test of some kind. In this context the general finding is of varying degrees of over- rather than under-estimation (e.g. Loftus, Schooler, Boone & Kline, 1987, experiment one) who also criticise the cognitive theories for emphasising the input (i.e. stimuli) in their operational definitions rather than the output (i.e. actual performance) such that when DE is related solely to the latter, predicted effects tend to disappear.

Troutwine (1984), for example found that of two five minute narratives a 'boring' one ('a mundane passage from an ethics text') was overestimated to greater extent than an 'interesting' one ('a tale of mythological adventure'). A similar effect was found by Lopez & Malhotra (1991) for 'most preferred' compared to 'least preferred' excerpts of music, with the latter overestimated to a greater extent.

Using video recordings of a simulated bank robbery, Loftus et al (1987, experiment three) manipulated the extent to which the episodes would be 'stressful' to the viewers. This distinction is described in the following way, "A 'low stress' version depicted the robber entering the bank and handing a note to the teller. A 'high stress' version depicted the robber displaying an automatic pistol, and using profane and threatening language."(p.8). They found that the duration of both versions were overestimated, the 'high stress' version significantly more so. They also found that self ratings of 'arousal' did differ between the two versions (in the predicted direction) but did not themselves differentiate DE.

In general, the above findings (albeit a limited set of exemplars) indicate that DE can be variously affected by cognitive, affective and subjective preference variables. They also offer reason to speculate that DE are affected non-linearly (e.g. a 'boring' narrative overestimated more than an 'interesting' one, compared to a 'low stress' [boring?] video overestimated *less* than a 'high stress' [interesting?] one). That is to say, labels such as 'low stress' and 'high stress' are wholly relative, such that for one person a 'high stress' episode may be just that, but for another person, the same episode could be considered no more than 'interesting'. An example of this comes from Loftus et al (1987, experiment three) who found that the over-estimations of the 'high stress' version were more pronounced for the female subjects, which they interpret on the grounds that the male subjects were (due to cultural role differences) less affected by the manipulation, suggesting that the males effectively watched a 'moderate stress' version.

Taken together, the above suggests that durations which are 'not interesting enough' will be overestimated *more* than episodes which are 'optimally interesting' which, in turn, will be overestimated *less* than episodes which are 'too interesting'. This idea that deviation from the 'optimally interesting' will lead to overestimation of duration was postulated some years ago by Fraisse (1964) who stated 'Satisfaction and unconsciousness of duration are two concomitant effects of an activity which is exactly adequate to the present motivation. Inversely, dissatisfaction and a feeling of duration are both consequences of frustration'(p 207), again this has echoes of 'time flies when you're having fun'. Knowledge of this latter work prompted the present author to include DE in an assessment of an audio-description of television service (AUDETEL, funded by the EC TIDE programme) with a sighted elderly sample.

Audio-description and DE

As part of a series of experiments examining the utility of this service for the sighted elderly population, one study examined the effects (on comprehension, enjoyment etc.) of increasing the amount of audio-description presented. Simply stated it was found that 'minimum' and 'maximum' versions improved comprehension compared to an 'original' (no description) condition (F(2,58) = 15.326, p < 0.0001). However, comparison of the two description conditions showed no overall difference in the level of the comprehension measure, although analyses of variance indicated that performance in the 'maximum' condition was more variable, regarding the effects of age (see figure 1) and also IQ score and various other individual difference variables.

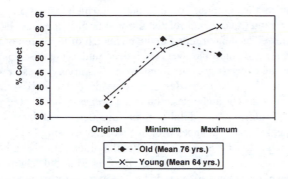

Figure 1   Performance on a composite memory measure by age group and description type

Similar analysis of DE showed the general tendency for all subjects to overestimate but also showed an interaction between age and condition ($F(2,56) = 3.389$, $p = 0.041$, see figure 2). Such that, age did not differentiate overestimation in the 'original' and 'minimum' conditions ($F(1,28) = 1.637$, $p = 0.211$ and $F(1,28) = 1.282$, $p = 0.267$, respectively) but did significantly affect the extent of over-estimation in the 'maximum' condition ($F(1,28) = 7.535$, $p = 0.011$).

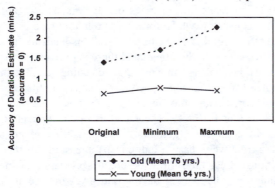

Figure 2   DE (overestimation) by age group and description type

Discussion

It is accepted that the findings of the audio-description study do not, in themselves, take us any closer to indicating the specific processes involved in DE. Nonetheless, it is hoped that when they are considered along with the other findings presented above they will support a view of DE that suggests it as potentially useful measure in a variety of cognitive ergonomic contexts. That is to say, DE is undoubtedly related in some way to the 'amount' of information which passes through the cognitive system. But, rather than being related to input or output per se, DE seems more appropriately viewed as being related to the mismatch of input and output. In other words DE is related to cognitive over- (or indeed under-) load. This view is generally supported by the over-estimations found in studies involving 'study' of the content of a duration, which tend to be designed to produce cognitive overload in order to avoid ceiling effects. The audio-description data suggest that for the younger volunteers, the increased information available in the 'maximum' condition could be utilised to improve memory performance, with this extra processing (and increased performance) not relating to any difference in DE. For the older volunteers, however, the same additional information did not improve performance but did relate to longer DE. Assuming that the older volunteers attended to the extra information (but could not adequately process and utilise it), this suggests that the relatively greater cognitive overload experienced by this group in this condition was the cause of the relatively greater over-estimations.

Other findings presented above strongly indicate that DE is also related to more than just the cognitive processing dimension. These studies showed effects of 'stress' 'mood' and 'interest' upon DE, all of which can be important factors in various applied settings. It is also apparent that none of these variables can reasonably be claimed to *cause* the others but it does seem reasonable to accept that they are all interrelated.

So, accepting that DE is related to these various factors (and regardless of the specific details of the mechanisms which form these relations) we do know that its *not* (solely determined by) any of them. On the one hand this leads to the age old call for more research into this area. On the other hand there is potential for DE to index overload in the cognitive domain. Also, in more applied settings there is the potential for DE to capture some of the variance not, as yet, explained by the experimenter's knowledge (or assumptions) about the 'input', nor by measures of the 'output', subjective preferences and/or feelings. There are also two other major points in favour of using DE in cognitive ergonomics. First is that given appropriate circumstances it is a relatively easy (and cheap) measure to incorporate in experimental evaluations. Secondly, the widespread acceptance of the 'truth' of concepts, such as 'time flies when you're having fun' gives the use of this measure substantial face validity.

References

Block, R. A. (1982). 'Temporal judgements and contextual change' *Journal of Experimental Psychology Learning, Memory, and Cognition*; Vol. 8, pp. 530-544.
Block, R. A., & Reed, M. A. (1978). 'Remembered duration: Evidence for a contextual-change hypothesis' *Journal of Experimental Psychology Human Learning and Memory*, Vol. 4, pp. 656-665.

Fraisse, P. (1964). *The Psychology of Time* (Leith, Jennifer, Trans.). Eyre & Spottiswoode Ltd: London.

Fraisse, P. (1984). 'Perception and Estimation of Time' *Annual Review of Psychology*, Vol. 35, pp. 1-36.

Hogan, H. W. (1978). 'A theoretical reconciliation of competing views of time perception' *American Journal of Psychology*, Vol. 91, pp. 417-428.

Hornik, J. (1992). 'Time estimation and orientation mediated by transient mood' *Journal of Socio-Economics*, Vol. 21, pp. 209-227.

Loftus, E. F., Schooler, J. W., Boone, S. M., & Kline, D. (1987). 'Time Went By So Slowly: Overestimation of Event Duration by Males and Females' *Applied Cognitive Psychology*, Vol. 1, pp. 3-13.

Lopez, L., & Malhotra, R. (1991). 'Estimation of time intervals with most preferred and least preferred music' *Psychological Studies*, Vol. 36, pp. 203-209.

Ornstein, R., E. (1969). *On the Experience of Time*. Penguin Books Ltd: Harmondsworth.

Poynter, W. D. (1983). 'Duration judgement and the segmentation of experience' *Memory and Cognition*, Vol. 11, pp. 77-82.

Troutwine, R. (1984). 'Perceived Task Quality and Estimated Interval: Foundation for Temporal Attributions' *Perceptual and Motor Skills*, Vol. 58, pp. 100-102.

Underwood, G., & Swain, R. A. (1973). 'Selectivity of attention and the perception of duration' *Perception*, Vol. 2, pp. 101-105.

35 Research on auditory comfort by EEG measurement

Min Cheol Whang*, Ji Eun Kim† and Chul Jung Kim*
* Ergonomics Laboratory,
Korea Research Institute of Standards and Science
†Department of Psychology,
ChungNam National University, Korea

Abstract

EEG parameters, measured with respect to auditory emotion were observed in this study. EEG was observed in 21 localized areas. The auditory stimuli were natural sounds, such as a creek, crashes, and machining noise, etc. These can cause both positive and negative emotions. The behaviour of EEG according to positive and negative auditory stimuli showed significant differences. The results showed that differences between positive and negative response existed depending on the localized area and qualitative variations in the respective waves, such as delta, theta, alpha, beta.

Introduction

Research on human comfort leads manufacturers to pursue future directions in product technology. It has been attempted to measure human psychological states via physiological signals such as EEG, EP, ECG, EOG, and GSR, etc. However, it is not clear the mechanisms by which variations in the physiological signal are caused by external stimuli. Partial observations by psychophysiological, ergonomic, and cognitive engineering researchers have shown that physiological responses to external stimuli are indicative of human psychological states.

Psychological activity causes changes in the electric potential of brain and results in an EEG (electroencephalogram). EEG is generally considered as a measurement for determining human psychological state. There have been many observations of EEG related to psychological states when external stimulus are transmitted to brain via the five sensory modes, which are visual, auditory, olfactory, tactile and gustatory sense. Physiological responses to auditory stimuli can be related to auditory emotion. It is assumed that EEG is a measure defining auditory emotion.

Psychologists have differentiated between tasks that require attention to stimuli so they can be processed (intake) and contrast them with tasks that require the exclusion of environmental stimuli for their effective completion (rejection). EEG patterns for intake and rejection of auditory tasks was compared by Ray and Cole (1985). During rejection tasks alpha power was greater in the right than the left hemisphere. Auditory arousal is affective parameter determining auditory perception. In a comparison of a high vigilance performance group with low vigilance subjects, it was found that the high group had less posterior theta and alpha activity than the low group (Valentino, et al., 1993). In addition, the high performance group had greater amounts of beta than the low performers. Therefore, good performers can be distinguished from poor performers by the greater EEG arousal levels, as defined by higher levels of beta activity and lower levels of alpha and posterior theta.

EEG laterality exists according to auditory emotional mode. A more positive emotional state was found to be associated with desynchrony of alpha over the left frontal region (indicating high left frontal activation), while right frontal activity was found for a more negative emotional state (Davidson, 1979). Perceptual discrimination of music stimuli appears to be accompanied by EEG changes in the direction of alpha desynchronization (Walker, 1980). The right hemisphere is involved to a greater extent than the left in the performance of musical tasks, whereas verbal tasks primarily involve the left hemisphere. Exceptions may occur, as in the case of musically trained individuals in whom the analytic information processing of music may transform music related activities into a left hemisphere function (Rugg & Dickins, 1982; Davidson, et al., 1990).

The significance of words is a parameter of auditory psychological states. When subjects recalled events that made them feel badly, or they received a negative emotion-evoking word, there was a decrease in right frontal alpha activity (Davidson, et al., 1979). When subjects recalled events that made them feel good, or they received positive emotion-evoking words, there was a decrease in left frontal alpha activity (Ahern & Schwartz, 1985; Davidson, et al, 1981; Davidson, et al., 1979; Fox & Davidson, 1986).

While a number of studies in the EEG literature have reported interhemisphere differences consistent with the hypothesis that music or word processing involves the right more than the left hemisphere, in this study the relationship between EEG response and emotional auditory stimuli occurring as natural sounds which we can frequently listen in our life such as a creek, crashing, machining noise etc, is investigated. Therefore EEG is measured to determine auditory emotional responses and states of these natural emotionally-evoked sounds. This study observes the behaviour of EEG according to positive and negative auditory stimuli and to characterize the auditory parameters of EEG such as the relative power of delta, theta, alpha and beta waves and the corresponding local area of brain.

Method

The experimental system constructed for the presentation of the stimuli and physiological data acquisition is shown figure 1. The experimental system consisted of two main systems for the production of the auditory stimulus and the measurement of the physiological signals.

Auditory stimuli should evoke the emotion which is dependent on the subject involvement in the experiment. The involvement is determined by the subject's mental workload during the experiment and the experimental environment. In order to control for the mental workload of the subject, the independence between the subject environment and the measurement environment was necessary. Also, the subject should feel comfortable in the environment. Therefore, the subject chamber was constructed of the dimensions two metres wide, four and a half metres long and three metres high. Inside, the floor was carpeted, the walls papered, evenly illuminated and room temperature was maintained. A reclining chair was provided and adjusted into a comfortable position for the subject.

The auditory stimulus was presented by an InKel 100Kw Audio System (Inkel, AVP-8500G). The amplifier was located outside and the dual speakers inside the chamber. A CD player (Inkel, AVP-8500G) was used for the presentation of the stimuli. The volume of sound was constant during the experiment. The stimulus was prepared as a both a negative and a positive one. The sounds used were the sound of a creek, a cathedral bell, a sea wave, a car crash, a factory noise, and jet engine noise. The stimulus sounds were selected from an sound effects CD which was commercially available.

A Spectrum 32 D/P EEG measurement system was used for this study. This is a modular instrument, providing a full range of EEG, quantitative EEG measurements, evoked potentials and brain map function. The system consists of an amplifier, PC, 32 channel data acquisition system, A/D convertor, 650MB optical disc, and a colour monitor.

University students participated in this study. They were healthy and did not have any auditory sensory problems. They consisted of 10 males and 10 females. They were all paid after the experiment.

The electrodes (SH-48, Grass) were placed on cerebrum according to International EEG nomenclature. It is referred to as the 10-20 system because the various locations are either 10% or 20% of the distance between the standard points used for measurement. Electrode gel (Elefix, Nihon Koheden) was used for facilitating electrical transmission. The resistance between the active and reference leads was measured by impedance meter conveniently built into the recording device.

277

Recording of EEG was performed when the resistance was less than 5000 Ohms. The resistance level indicates a good attachment of electrodes on the scalp.

It takes some time for subjects to become comfortable due to the electrode placement on the cerebrum. The subject told the experimenter when they were comfortable. After adapting to the electrode placement, the subject sat and relaxed on the chair in the chamber. The EEG of the unstimulus state was measured for two minutes. Then, the stimulus was given for 30 seconds. The subject was then unstimulated for a further two minutes in order to recover from the previous stimulus. Another stimulus was given after recovery.

The presentation of the stimuli took turns of negative and positive sounds. A subjective assessment was performed after experiment was completed. The stimuli were scaled from -5 to +5. If the stimulus was the best, it is scored +5. If the stimulus was the worst, it scored -5.

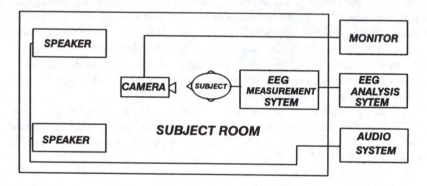

Figure 1   Experimental system

Analysis

EEG information recorded by each individual electrode was analysed for its basic frequencies such as delta, theta, alpha and beta. The EEG spectrum can be segmented on frequency or topographic structure.

The spectral analysis of the EEG requires the choice of epoch length for the EEG, which is usually 2.5 secs per epoch. Artifacts in the EEG recording was identified and eliminated by epoch performance. The epoch length is inversely related to the width and spacing of the frequency bins, and so temporal resolution can only be obtained at the expense of frequency resolution. A fast Fourier transform was used to process the data.

The information gathered from each electrode was processed for relative power. Coherence measures are defined between homologous electrode pairs. Relative power is scaled in percentages, and ranges from 0.00 to +1.00 (100%), therefore only the top half of the scale can be used. Relative power is an index of the power accounted for in one frequency band relative to the total amount of power (summed across all frequency bands). The sum of all power is equal to 100%.

The data analysed in this study consisted of the relative power of four frequencies at 21 electrode points with respect to the positive and negative auditory stimuli. This data included the nonstimulus states before the positive and negative stimuli. Therefore, the data has four, 21 electrode relative powers for four states (rest state before positive stimulus, positive stimulus state, rest state before negative stimulus and negative stimulus state).

Although six auditory stimuli were presented, only two responses were selected based on the results of the subjective test, those to which the results showed the maximum positive score and maximum negative stimulus score.

A particular physiological response to a given stimulus depends on the prestimulus level. This is the law of initial value (Wilder, 1957, 1967, 1976). Therefore, the stimulus state is calculated from a normalized value from the unstimulus state, for example (unstimulus-stimulus)/unstimulus. The normalized value indicates percentage change of the stimulus state from the unstimulus state. It is noted that the unstimulus state is the state before the stimulus. This was used for statistical analysis. The negative response was compared with the positive response at individual electrodes for 20 subjects using the Student paired t-test.

Results

The results are described in figure 2. Figures represent the cerebral top-view. The triangle indicates the subject's nose. Therefore, the cerebral area close to the nose is the frontal area and the other side from the nose is the occipital region. The results of Student t-test are shown in figure 2. The circled symbol indicates that a p value is less than 0.05. These are the comparisons between positive and negative responses in terms of percentage change from baseline, when negative and positive stimuli are presented, respectively. These were for the initial 10 second stimulus period.

Delta wave shows differences at the left frontal (Fz, F3, F7), left central and temporal (Cz, C3, T3), right parietal (Pz, P4, P6), and in one left parietal area (P3). Left anterior and right posterior areas generally show significant differences in delta waves between positive and negative response.

Theta waves shows differences at left parietal (Pz, P3), posterior temporal (T5, T6), occipital (Oz, O1, O2) and one right central area (C4). Most posterior areas shows difference in the theta wave.

Alpha wave shows difference at frontal (Fz, F3, F4), central (Cz, C3, C4), temporal (T3, T4, T5, T6), and parietal areas (Pz, P3, P4). Alpha differences are shown in most areas except some frontal and occipital areas.

279

Min Cheol Whang et al.

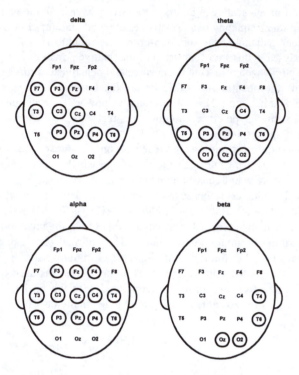

Figure 2   Local brain area variations in normalized positive and negative responses. Circled areas indicates p values less than 0.05 using the Student paired t-test

Beta waves show difference at right temporal (T4, T6) and right occipital areas (Oz, O2).

Figure 3 shows variations in averaged EEG between positive and negative responses. Selected areas in respective EEG waves were based on results of t-tests showing p values less than 0.05. Since normalized value was defined as (stimulus-prestimulus)/prestimulus, the y axis value is positive with an increase from the prestimulus state. Delta increases with positive stimuli but increases less or decreases with negative stimuli. Theta and alpha increase with positive stimuli while they decrease with negative stimuli. Beta increases with negative stimuli but less so with positive stimuli. Therefore, alpha increases with positive responses while delta, theta, and beta increase with negative stimuli.

280

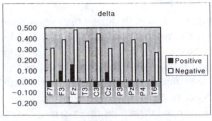
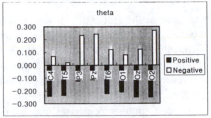

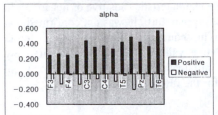
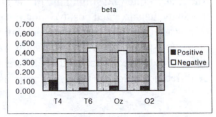

Figure 3   Shown are EEG variations of averaged EEG components for positive and negative responses. Selected areas in the respective EEG wave were based on results of the t-tests showing p values less than 0.05. Longitudinal value are positive with an increase and negative with a decrease

Discussion and conclusion

There are local area variations of brain activity in respect of waves such as delta, theta, alpha and beta between positive and negative responses. For example, Cz has delta and alpha differences between positive and negative responses while T6 has delta, theta, alpha and beta differences. In the consideration of the dominant areas showing significant differences, delta was in the left; theta, posterior; alpha mostly in the central area; and beta, right. Therefore, respective wave differences in the evaluation of emotion may be locally dependent. Qualitative variations in respective waves existed between positive and negative responses. There was an increase in delta, theta, and beta waves but a decrease in alpha with a negative stimulus. Decrease was less in quantity in delta and compared to the increase in alpha. However, this decrease in quantity is comparable to the increase in theta. Beta is different from the other waves and increases with both positive and negative stimuli. Therefore, the dominant parameters may be delta, theta and beta with an increase in negative responses and a theta decrease and alpha increase in positive responses.

This study defines the prestimulus state as a reference state. Most studies collect EEG in rest state which is somewhat stimulated. Then, the stimulus state is compared with the resting state. However, as sequential stimuli were presented, there may be the possibility of the existence of a different reference state in each interval time. That is, if the interval state is fully recovered from the previous stimulus, it is the same as the rest state. However, this state is not certain during the experiment. Therefore, the prestimulus state is used for avoiding resultant fluctuations by different reference states. Of course, it is attempted to free the prestimulus state from the previous stimulus. It is noted that all the results in this study are based on this reference state. The response is higher in the high initial state than in low initial state (Wheeler, et al., 1993). If the prestimulus is activated by incomplete recovery from a previous stimulus, responses may have a chance to become more extreme. This is true if the sequential stimuli are of the same characteristic (positive or negative). In this study, negative and positive stimuli were given in turn. It was not confirmed that responses depended on initial activation in sequential stimuli having different characteristics. These results show relative values. There are quantitatively differences between results from different initial values. Qualitative trends may not be different. Study of this issue remains for the future.

References

Ahern, G., L., Schwartz, G. E., (1985). 'Differential lateralization for positive and negative emotion in the human brain: EEG spectral analysis'. *Neuropsychology*, Vol. 23, pp. 745-755.

Davidson, R.J., (1979). 'Hemispheric specialization for affective processes in normals: Behavioral and electrophysiological studies'. The meeting of the society for Biological Psychiatry, Atlanta, May, 1979.

Davidson, R. J., Schwartz, G. E., Saron, C., Bennett, J., & Goleman, D. J.(1979). 'Frontal versus parietal EEG asymmetry during positive and negative affect' (abstract). *Psychophysiology*, Vol. 16, pp. 202-203.

Davidson, R.J., Champman, J.P., Champman, L.J., & Henriques, J.P., (1990). 'Asymmetrical brain electrical activity discriminates between psychometrically-matched verbal and spatial cognitive tasks'. *Psychophysiology*, Vol. 27, pp. 528-543.

Davidson, R. J.(1992). 'Anterior cerebral asymmetry and the nature of emotion'. *Brain and Cognition*, Vol. 20, pp. 125-151.

Fox, N. A., & Davidson, R. J.(1986). 'Taste-elicited changes in facial signs of emotion and the asymmetry of brain electrical activity in human newborns'. *Neuropsychologia*, Vol. 24, pp. 417-422.

Ray, W. J., & Cole, H. W. (1985). 'EEG alpha activity reflects attentional demands, and beta activity reflects emotional and cognitive processes'. *Science*, Vol. 228, pp. 750-752.

Rugg, M.D., & Dickins, A.M.J.(1982). 'Dissociation of alpha and theta activity as a function of verbal and visuospatial tasks'. *Electroencephalography and Clinical Neurophysiology*, Vol. 53, pp. 201-207.

Valentino, D. A., & Dufresne, R. L. (1991). 'Attention tasks and EEG power spectra'. *International Journal of Psychophysiology*, Vol. 11, pp. 299-302.

Walker, J. L. (1980). 'Alpha EEG correlates of performance on a music recognition test'. *Physiological Psychology*, Vol. 8, pp. 417-420.

Wheeler, R. E., Davidson, R. J., & Tomarken, A. J. (1993). 'Frontal brain asymmetry and emotional reactivity: A biological substrate of affective style'. *Psychophysiology*, Vol. 30, pp. 82-89.

Wilder, J. (1957). 'The law of initial value in neurology and psychiatry'. *Journal of Nervous and Mental Disease*, Vol. 125, pp. 73-86.

Wilder, J., (1976). The 'law of initial value', neglected biological law and its significance for research and practice (1931). In, S. W. Porges & M.G.H. Coles (eds.), Psychophysiology (pp. 38-46). Dowden, Hutchinson & Row: Stroudsberg, PA.

36 Head orientation and binaural depth perception

Peter J. Simpson and Keith J. Nation
University of Surrey, UK

Abstract

This study investigates how direction of gaze, varied by changing head orientation relative to a sound source, effects the estimation of the distance of the sound source. The stimulus materials, consisting of single words, were recorded binaurally using a dummy head in a small reverberant room. The results show that subjects' distance estimation for a transient sound stimulus is accurate up to five metres. Overall, performance was not effected by head orientation. There was some evidence which suggested that subjects overestimated distance when the head 'faced' the sound source and underestimated of distance when the head was turned away from the source. The results suggests that adding binaural information to computer generated visual information, for example in virtual reality systems, can overcome problems of distance scaling in space perception and enhance the perception of location and depth.

Introduction

Developments in computer graphics systems make it possible to generate visual information which results in detailed perception of the visual world. At one level these systems present stimulus information which is equivalent to that used in classic representational art to depict surfaces, form and depth. Computer graphics systems can also be designed to provide information reflecting changes in viewpoint arising from head movement, posture changes and movement through the space depicted (Greenberg, 1991). These systems can be used to simulate actual or possible visual worlds for use in training combined with multimedia features, and in research and design to aid specification and evaluation.

Peter J. Simpson and Keith J. Nation

Adding sound to vision

Computer graphics systems can be used to create visual worlds with high levels of clarity and detail. But in the real world our visual perception is complemented by our perception of the acoustic environment (Lindsay and Norman, 1972). Binaural sound information arising from differences in both the time of arrival at the two ears, and the frequency content and intensity of the sound, can enhance the perception of horizontal and vertical location, and distance for sound emitting objects (Moore, 1989). Adding reverberant information can lead to the perception of the spatial extent and therefore the perceived spaciousness of a location.

In a reverberant environment distance perception depends on the ratio of the intensity of the direct to the reflected sound. The direct and indirect components of the sound stimulus differ in frequency composition due to the selective reflection from surfaces and diffraction of sound round the head. Thus the orientation of the head relative to the location of the sound emitting object, and any bounding surfaces in the auditory space, influences the intensity and frequency content of sound available at each ear. Under natural conditions, the listener can change his/her head orientation to direct gaze at the sound source. This adaptation is difficult to achieve under simulated 'virtual reality' conditions. An experiment was undertaken to investigate how head orientation influences distance judgements under binaural listening conditions.

Method and apparatus

The experimental conditions used in the present study were generated by recording auditory events making up the stimulus set within a physical space using binaural recording equipment mounted on a dummy. Subsequently the experimental stimulus set were presented to the subjects in the original recording space by means of headphones. Subjects had a chance to become familiar with the acoustics of the recording space before starting the testing component of the experiment.

To record the stimulus material we used a JVC HM-200E binaural headset mounted on a dummy head supported on a tripod. The dummy head did not include a torso. The binaural headset incorporated microphones which were mounted in a simple ear like structure which included an analogue of the pinna. The 'ears' were one metre above the floor so the recording head approximated the seated position of the subjects when they were tested in the recording room. The recordings were made in a small 4.5 by 7 metres room. The room had 'bright' acoustics reflecting the hard surfaces of the bounding walls.

Conditions and stimulus set

A stimulus set was prepared using the binaural recording equipment to record the output from a loudspeaker. The loudspeaker was positioned so that it was at one, two, three, four and five metres from the recording head. This was achieved by moving the loudspeaker along the mid line of the long seven metre axis of the recording room. The recording head was positioned so that it was one metre in front of one of the smaller end walls. The room contained no furniture or other objects apart from the dummy recording head on a tripod, loudspeaker, recording and playback apparatus, amplifier and leads. The apparatus was small compared to the dimension of the room. The stimulus set was constructed by using single two and three syllable words generated by a good quality speech synthesizer. The words were chose to provide a wide frequency spectrum sound stimulus with a limited periodic (vowel) component. Eight words were used (kitchen, picture, Washington, twenty, system, voice, Chicago, question) and the synthesizer was adjusted to make the words last approximately 0.5 seconds.

The recordings were made with the dummy head 'looking' straight ahead so that it was aligned to 'face' the loudspeaker and also with the head turned 45 degrees to the right and to the left. These two conditions were included to simulate the condition of the direction of gaze not coinciding with the position of the sound emitting object. The 45 degree turn to the right and to the left conditions were included to allow for the possibility that the reflective properties of the longest side walls in the room were different. Thus the experiment included eight test stimuli, recorded at three head orientations and at five distances. The combination of these three variables yielded a total of 120 distinct stimulus combinations. After recording a presentation order was developed and three test tapes were produced containing 40 stimuli. Each group of 40 was adjusted to contained a balanced set of the experimental conditions. In the main test subjects were presented with a stimulus event at the rate of one every seven seconds for each block of 40 stimuli.

Nature of the task and instructions

After initial familiarisation with the room and the apparatus, subjects were presented with instructions describing the main task. The instructions explained that they were required to listen to sequences of single words presented via headphones. The conditions of the original recordings were explained. Subjects were asked to estimate of the distance of the stimulus event and the orientation of the dummy head when the recording was made. Subjects were then presented with a practice task involving 15 of stimuli events they would hear in the main study. They were given feedback about the accuracy of their response in the practice task. No feedback on the accuracy of responses was offered during the main study.

Subjects

The study reported in this paper is based on six subjects who were undergraduate students on the BSc Psychology degree at the University of Surrey. The study uses a repeated measures procedure. Each subject's data are based on the eight judgements they made for each of the 15 possible combinations of head orientation and distance.

Results

The estimates of distance obtained for each subject involved the use of a five point scale. Given the nature of the judgement task and the restriction on the scale range, it is appropriate to treat the dependent measure as if it were at the ordinal level. The data presented in figure one shows how the median judged distance varied with actual distance for the five distances used.

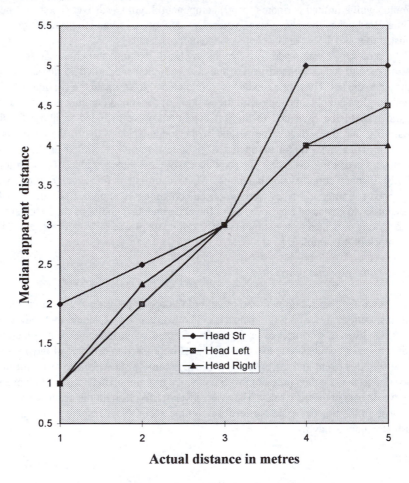

Figure 1   **Apparent distance across three head orientations**

Figure 1 reveals that judged distance increased with actual distance in a linear fashion. The results for the head left and head right conditions are very similar. But there are some differences between the results for these conditions and the head straight condition. Spearman rank correlations carried out on the three sets of results for the head orientation conditions produced coefficients equal to or greater than 0.99, p < 0.01, for all three conditions. In order to determine the effects of distance and head orientation a two-way analysis of variance, involving an extension of the Friedman test, was carried out. The test revealed that the factor distance had a statistically reliable effect on performance (χ^2= 23.1, k = 5, df = 4, p< 0.001) and similarly the factor head orientation (χ^2 = 9.25, k = 3, df = 2, p < 0.008). However there was no evidence of a reliable interaction between the factors distance and head orientation (p > 0.05).

Additional analysis using the Friedman test on the results obtained for the head orientation showed that while there was no difference between the head left and head right conditions, both these conditions reliably differed from the head straight condition.

Discussion

Source of the head orientation effect

Inspection of the results present in figure one suggests that the origins of the reliable effects of head orientation arise from two sources. When the sound source is close to the recording head at one or two metres, subjects judge that the sound source is further away when the recording head is facing the sound source. However when the sound source is at the furthest distance of five metres, the distance is underestimated when the recording head is turned through 45 degrees.

Earlier it was mentioned that sound is diffracted round the human head to produce the head shadowing effect. This effect varies with the orientation of the ears to a sound source. Figure two shows the effects of head shadowing for the recording head used in the present study. This data was obtained by present white noise to the dummy head at one metre and measuring the output from the binaural microphone mounted in the right hand 'ear'. All three curves show a peak at between 2KHz and 4KHz. This feature matches the human ear and reflect the effect of the ear canal. Comparison of the results for the three head orientations show differences among the orientations at 4KHz and above. In essence when the head is turned to the left, the right ear faces the sound source and we see an increased sound pressure level for the higher frequencies. The corresponding effect for when the right ear is turned away from the sound source is to decrease the sound pressure level relative to the head straight condition.

Differences in the relative intensity of sound at the two ear provides reliable information about the orientation of the head. However if the subject is relying on sound intensity to judge distance, the increase in pressure level of the higher frequency components of the sound source may lead subjects to judge an object as closer than its actual distance. A similar argument can be made for the apparent overestimation of distance in the one metre condition when the head is straight. Relative to the head turn left or right conditions, the higher frequency sound pressure levels are lower and thus the sound source could be perceived as further away.

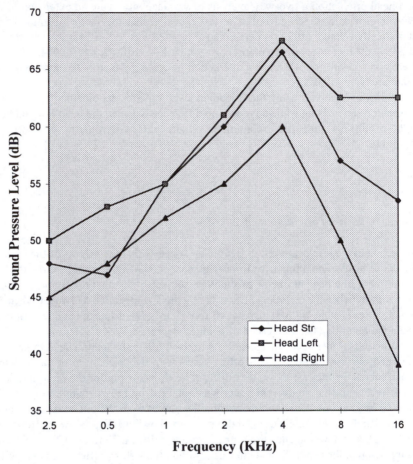

Figure 2   Diffraction effects and head orientation

This explanation assumes that subjects in the present study are making judgements about the apparent distance of a sound source in the context of coping with the changes which results from head shadowing linked to the orientation of the recording head orientation. If subjects rely on intensity as the major criteria, then the pattern of results obtained will follow.

Conclusion

The pattern of results obtained in the present study reveal that under the conditions used subjects are accurate in their judgement of apparent distance. This finding is somewhat at variance with earlier findings. However a key difference in the present study is the use of an information rich environment when creating the stimulus material. Earlier studies have involve anechoic or open field conditions and asked for judgements about distance extending up to tens of metres. While the study did reveal a reliable effect of head orientation, the results suggest that subjects displayed a marked degree of perceptual constancy with respect to distance judgements. Thus when considering how to combine sound to vision in computer graphics and virtual reality environments, while we should ensure that the sound information is both rich and realistically match the acoustic environment depicted, there may be little gain in attempting to allow for the changes linked to head orientation and direction of gaze.

References

Greenberg, D.P. (1991) 'Computers and Architecture' *Scientific American.* February 1991, Vol. 264, pp. 88 to 93.
Lindsay, P.H. & Norman, D.A. (1972) *Human Information Processing.* Academic Press: New York.
Moore, B.J. (1989) *'An Introduction to Hearing'.* Academic Press: London.

37 The perception of spatial layout in telepresence systems

Andy Parton, Mark F. Bradshaw, Bart DeBruyn,
Alison Wheeler, John Pretlove, Jörg Huber
and Ian R.L. Davies
Department of Psychology, University of Surrey, UK

Abstract

The effect of different depth cues presented through a head mounted display (HMD) in a dark (no pictorial cue) environment was investigated. The relative effects of binocular disparity, motion parallax, and a combination of the two, were assessed for a simple nulling task (based on the Howard-Dolman stereo test) at two viewing distances. Performance was best for the two motion conditions which were significantly better than the static monocular condition. There was no further improvement when both binocular disparity and motion parallax was available. In addition, there was no significant difference between the two viewing distances. Performance on the task when the HMD unit was used never attained the levels typical in control conditions where the subjects viewed the stimuli naturally. This included the condition in which many cues to depth were presented through the HMD. It is argued that these results are task specific and may reflect limitations in the viewing equipment although there was large individual differences in performance.

Introduction

Information from a number of different sources is available to the visual system which determine the depth and spatial layout of objects within a scene. These sources include binocular disparities (the differences in the positions of objects in the two eyes' views), the angle of convergence, relative motion (created by observer or object motion), differential accommodation, and pictorial cues (e.g. perspective, occlusion and changes in surface texture density). The type of depth information (e.g. absolute or relative) which can be derived from each source varies. In normal viewing

293

conditions the information specified by the different visual cues is complementary but in more impoverished environments the visual system may become reliant on a specific cue and so its limitations may become more apparent. This may depend on the informational requirements of the visually guided task being performed.

An ideal telepresence system should replicate the information available to an operator in the natural viewing situation. If successful, the operator should be unable to distinguish the real remote environment from the local environment (see Loomis, 1992). To achieve this aim, it is necessary to preserve the different sources of visual information in the system that an operator is sensitive to. This can be problematic with traditional television displays because they often carry impoverished or conflicting information (e.g. a single screen conveys no disparity information). Modern telepresence systems have addressed some of these shortcomings by augmenting the available cues to include binocular disparities and motion information linked to the observer's head movements (see Asbery and Pretlove, 1995). Both cues have been shown psychophysically to be effective cues for depth (see Howard and Rogers, 1995). However the extent to which these improvements have solved this problem in telepresence systems remains open to question. Indeed it may be the case that certain information is sufficient to solve particular tasks (e.g. nulling) but not others (e.g. depth judgements). Undoubtedly certain limitations. remain, for example, operators must accommodate on a fixed distance screen rather than the objects lying in depth within it (see Wann, Rushton, & Mon-Williams, 1995).

The present study assessed the relative benefits afforded by different sources of information within a telepresence environment. The experiment measured performance using a simple nulling task (a variant of the standard Howard-Dolman stereo acuity test - see Howard, 1919) in six experimental conditions defined by the type of visual information available. These included: binocular viewing, motion parallax and a combination of the two sources. Observers viewed three horizontally separated LEDs in a dark environment and were required to adjust the central one so it appeared equi-distant with its two flanking (fixed) LEDs. The subject's mean deviation from zero, expressed in angular terms, was taken as their acuity. Note that the type of information required to perform this task is relatively low. For example, in the binocular conditions there is no need to scale the disparity information to recover relative distances or even to know the sign of the disparity, the magnitude of disparity is sufficient to perform the task correctly. As a result a reliable performance should be achievable even under impoverished viewing conditions. The addition of different depth cues may significantly improve performance but the actual amount and relative benefits of the cues remain to be quantified.

Our experimental paradigm (and dark viewing) was chosen because (i) it readily isolates the sources of information being studied by removing pictorial depth cues, (ii) the potential effects of minification by the HMD (see Lumsden, 1980 for review) is mitigated as the effects of pictorial cues are eliminated and (iii) the luminance of the LEDs (and therefore their perceived sizes) could be varied randomly between trails to obviate any potential artefacts.

The experiment was performed at two viewing distances: 1.5 and 3 meters to assess whether performance interacts with distance within the HMD equipment. Note that disparities vary with absolute viewing distance and therefore only when settings are converted to units of binocular disparity (or their equivalent) can the results from the two viewing distances be compared directly.

Method

Subjects   Five observers participated in this experiment. Four were naive to the purpose of the experiment and had only limited experience of psychophysical experiments in general. All had normal or corrected to normal vision.

Apparatus   The experimental equipment is depicted in figures 1a and 1b.

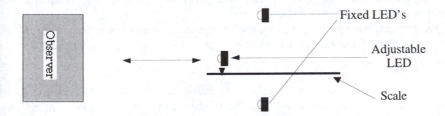

Figure 1a   An aerial view of the layout experimental equipment

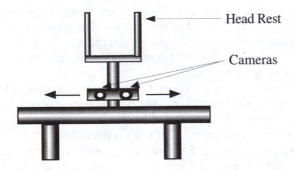

Figure 1b   A front view of the observers head rest

The stimuli were viewed via an EyeGen 3 head mounted display (HMD) manufactured by Virtual Research. This has two CRT displays magnified to subtend 32° horizontally and 24° vertically. The resolution of the screens was 493 by 250 lines. The HMD and cable weighed 37oz (900g).

The images were captured by two Panasonic industrial CCD colour cameras (resolution 681 by 582 pixels) which were mounted in the headrest unit and so were slaved to the observer movement. The headrest could translate horizontally as it was mounted on rollers which moved on a smooth metallic bar. These rollers could be tightened to fix the head rest in place when required. During the head-movement conditions, the observers moved their heads back-and-forth ± 6.5 cm either side of the midline at 1 Hz. The extent of travel was limited by two end-stops.

The stimulus was comprised of three yellow LED lights centred in black cardboard four centimetres square. Two of the lights were fixed in position equidistant from the observer ± 2.5° either side of the midline and at the same vertical height as the cameras (or observers' eyes). The distance of the fixed LEDs to the camera plates was either 1.5 or 3 metres. The third LED was attached to a motor and be could moved backwards and forwards along the midline. The luminance of the adjustable light was fixed. A scale was placed along side it so its position in relation to the fixed LEDs could be recorded.

Experiments were performed in a completely dark room and any reflections from the LEDs were eliminated by a black screen placed between the observer and the stimuli.

Procedure   The observer was required to move the adjustable LED so that it appeared to lie at the same distance as the flanking LEDs (i.e. to make them co-linear). The adjustable LED moved at a constant rate but its direction was under observer control. On each trial the initial position of the light was set randomly although an equal number of trials started behind and in front of the flanking LEDs. Settings were recorded as deviations from the zero point measured in millimetres. A positive score lay in front of this point and a negative score behind it. The task was performed under the six viewing conditions listed below.

(i)   Monocularly via the Head Mounted Display (Mono).
(ii)   Binocularly via the HMD (Bino).
(iii)   Monocularly via the HMD with hor. head movement (Mono-MP).
(iv)   Binocularly via the HMD with hor. head movement (Bino-MP).
(v)   Binocularly via the HMD with the room lights on (Bino-Full).
(vi)   Binocularly looking directly at the lights (Bino-Real).

Each observer completed four settings in each condition for two viewing distances, 1.5 and 3 metres.

Results and discussion

In the real-world viewing condition (direct, natural viewing) the unsigned mean settings were 13 and 65.5 mm at the viewing distances of 1.5 and 3 metres respectively. This was the best performance and suggests that observers were good at this task in these conditions. Performance was worst in the monocular stationary condition. In contrast with the real world condition, the means settings were 221 and 482 mm 1.5 and 3 metres respectively.

In order to compare directly the scores between the two viewing distances it was necessary to convert them into a distance invariant form. The movement of the light was perpendicular to the midpoint of the cameras (and eyes). Therefore, for the binocular condition, the disparity between the central fixated LED and the target null position can be expressed, as the difference between the vergence angles of the eyes at these points. Although the other monocular conditions do not generate binocular disparities they can be converted into units of *equivalent disparity*. For example, whilst translating back-and-forth the observer travels through twice the interocular distance and so the same angular displacements were created in the spatio-temporal domain as in the spatial domain (binocular condition). Consequently the same formulae was applied to this data and by a similar justification to the binocular motion data to convert it into equivalent disparity.

Grouped signed mean data for the different viewing conditions and two distances are shown in figures 2a and 2b. The signed means act as a measure of bias (accuracy) in the responses. The error bars show the standard errors across all settings within that condition.

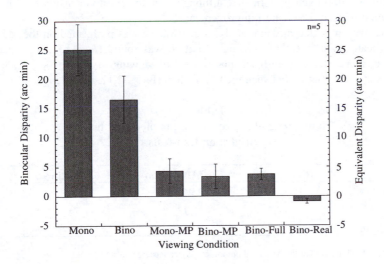

Figure 2a Group signed means (1.5 metres)

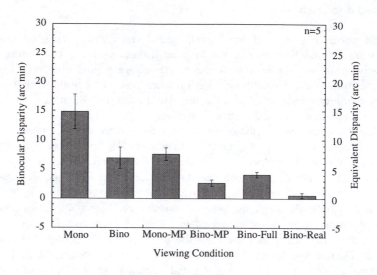

Figure 2b Group signed means (3.0 metres)

The results show a positive bias in all the test conditions (the first four conditions) with only the control (full-cue in the HMD) and the real world viewing conditions being close to zero. The difficulty in the monocular/static condition is attributable to the absence of reliable cues to depth. The addition of distance cues improved performance although it is difficult to clearly state which condition produced the greatest improvement.

A two-way repeated measure analysis of variance was performed on the data. A significant main effect of viewing condition was found ($F_{(3,12)}$=5.20, p <.05). However, there was no significant main effect of viewing distance ($F_{(1,4)}$=3.28, p =.144) nor an interaction between the two factors ($F_{(3,12)}$=2.17, p =.145).

Table 1
Summaries of the results of planned post hoc
paired samples t-tests

	Bino	MP-Mono	MP-Bino
Mono	2.12	2.49*	2.61*
Bino	-	-1.73	-1.74
MP-Mono	-	-	1.54

Note: Results significant at the 0.05 level are indicated by an asterisk; df=4.

The monocular data was tested with a one tailed test as it was hypothesised to be significantly worse (e.g. greater than the other conditions). The other conditions were tested with a two tailed test as no expected direction of difference was predicted.

There appears to be great individual variation (particularly in relation to the relative merits of static binocular, and monocular motion parallax) and so individual subject data is also of interest. The results for the individual observers are shown in figure 3.

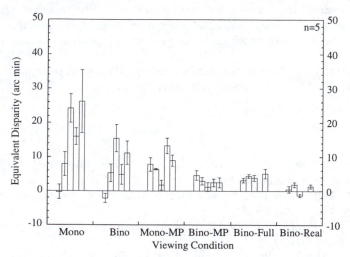

Figure 3   All subjects' individual data (3.0 metres)

Whilst the group data indicates a generally better level of performance for motion parallax (the binocular condition has a far greater bias at 1.5 metres and judgements are less precise at both viewing distances) for certain observers the results indicate that binocular viewing can be equally beneficial.

Further experimentation will be required to assess this fully. It is likely that the relative benefits of binocular and motion parallax are task dependant. As mentioned earlier the actual information requirements of this task was quite low. Performance in a metric task which requires a judgement of absolute distance to properly scale responses is quite different (see Parton, Bradshaw, Pretlove, DeBruyn and Davies, in preparation).

An additional point of interest is that observers perform consistently worse within the lights on (a full cue environment) in the telepresence system than in an impoverished (dark) real environment. This probably reflects the fact that there are limits imposed on performance by the equipment. Although the fact that some observers were able to perform well indicates that in general they had not reached a ceiling in performance and were not restricted by absolute equipment limitations. The noise introduced by the telepresence equipment may well by responsible for much between subject variation. The relative importance of different equipment limitations (e.g. screen resolution and the conflicts from accommodation) is not resolvable from this data.

In summary, the data indicates that under impoverished viewing conditions the use of a telepresence systems can introduce a great deal of noise. As a result between subject variability is high. Performance is improved considerably by the addition of motion depth cues but this is not especially improved by a combination of both binocular disparity information and motion. This may be because the subjects have reached a ceiling level of performance for this particular task.

Whilst it seems likely that theses results are task specific overall performance is probably still limited by the equipment rather than the operator.

References

Asbery, R. & Pretlove, J. (1995). 'Telepresence for remote inspection'. *Service Robot : An International Journal.*, Vol. 1, pp. 20-23.

Howard, H.J. (1919). 'A test for the judgement of distance'. *American Journal of Psychology*, Vol. 2, pp. 656-675.

Howard, I.P. & Rogers, B.J. (1995). *Binocular Vision and Stereopsis.* Oxford University Press: Oxford.

Loomis, J.M. (1992). 'Presence and distal attribution: phenomenology, determinants an assessment'. *Proceedings of SPIE 1666, Human Vision, Visual Processing and Digital Display III.*

Lumsden, E. (1980). 'The problems of magnification and minification: An explanation of the distortions of distance, slant, shape, and velocity', in *The Perception of Pictures*. Academic Press: London.

Parton, A., Bradshaw, M., Pretlove, J., DeBruyn, B. & Davies, I. (in preparation). *'The task dependant use of binocular disparity and motion parallax information in quasi-real and telepresence environments'.*

Wann, J.P., Rushton, S. & Mon-Williams, M. (1995). 'Natural problems for stereoscopic depth perception in virtual environments'. *Vision Research*, Vol. 35, pp. 2731-273.

38 Validation: the best kept secret in Ergonomics!

Neville Stanton and Mark Young
University of Southampton, UK

Abstract

This chapter reviews the lack of validation studies on ergonomics' methods. A review of the literature indicated that there is upward of 60 methods available to the ergonomist. The results of a survey of professional ergonomists indicated that none of the respondents was aware of any documented evidence of the reliability and validity of the methods they were using. This was supported by a review of the literature which shows that validation studies are very sparse. An important goal for future research is to establish the reliability and validity of ergonomics methods.

Ergonomics methods

There appears to be a growing number of texts in recent years describing, illustrating and espousing a plethora of ergonomics methods (Diaper, 1989; Kirwan & Ainsworth, 1992; Kirwan, 1994, Corlett & Clarke, 1995; Wilson & Corlett, 1995; Jordan, Thomas, Weedmeester & McClelland, 1996). The rise in the number of texts reporting on ergonomics methods may be seen as a response to the requirement for more inventive approaches for assessing the user and their requirements. In many ways this may be taken to mean that the call for user-centred design has been a success. This may, however, have resulted in the pragmatic development of methods having priority over scientific rigour. In a recent review of ergonomics' methods, Stanton & Young (1995) identified over 60 methods available to the ergonomist. The abundance of methods might be confusing for the ergonomist. Wilson (1995) suggests that a:

> ...method which to one researcher or practitioner is an invaluable aid
> to all their work may to another be vague or insubstantial in concept,
> difficult to use and variable in its outcome. (p. 21)

Neville Stanton and Mark Young

Despite the proliferation of methods, there are few attempts to validate them. Typically studies are sparse and only applied to a few of the methods covered in the books. None of the texts surveyed contained any description of studies that relate to the acquisition of the method or, apart from Kirwan (1994), the relative merits of one method over another. In a rather critical paper, Kanis (1994) identified the uses and abuses of validation in ergonomics research. He argues that either validation studies are simply not undertaken, or where they are undertaken appropriate measures are not used. Williams (1985) suggests that there are at least five possible reasons why methods are not validated, in his review of human error identification techniques. First, developers may be concerned that the outcome of the studies may not present their technique in a very good light. Second, the costs associated with validation studies may be prohibitive. Third, their may be pressure on the developer not to show the inherent weaknesses of the approach method. Fourth, there may not be enough participants available with sufficient level of skill to conduct validation studies. Finally, developers may be misguided in their understanding of what constitutes an acceptable validation study.

Reliability and validity

Reliability and validity are interdependent concepts, a method cannot be valid if it is not reliable. The reliability of a method may tested in a variety of forms. Essentially it concerns the degree to which the method can be repeated with the same reliability relative to the outcome. Three methods of determining reliability of a method are as follows. Test-retest reliability is the correlation of performance on the method with the performance obtained by the same group of people retested after a period of time. Alternate forms reliability is an estimate of the extent to which different forms of a method measure the same performance. Internal consistency is a means of determining homogeneity of performance by using split-half coefficients resulting from comparative sessions of the method.

Similarly there are a number of methods for establishing validity of method, some more credible than others. Face validity concerns whether the method appears to relate to the task performance it is supposed to capture. Face validity can help the acceptance of the method, but does not necessarily guarantee that is correct. Therefore this can be very misleading. Views on methods can be extreme. The blind acceptance or rejection of a method without recourse to evidence is not recommended. The acceptance of a method without objective validation is termed faith validity. Content validity of a method is the extent to which the method can be rationally related to the activities that make up task performance. Concurrent validity is the relationship between the performance obtained method and some criterion of actual task performance that can be obtained at the same time. Whereas, predictive validity is the extent to which performance captured by the method correlates with some future outcome. This is particularly important if the behaviour cannot be observed concurrently, for example due to its infrequency (such as real emergency events). There may be some considerable delay before validation is complete, but we may still wish to exploit the data. Therefore we would attempt to satisfy other relevant forms of validity, such as content validity and concurrent validity, before we are able to check predictive validity. It can sometimes be difficult to establish comparable measures of performance, and it is also important to have a cross section of performance to avoid suffering from problems related to restricted sample range. Construct validity is more abstract than other forms of validity, and it the extent to which the method is based upon some theoretical construct. For example, we may have a theoretical notion of human information processing and error which we seek to examine. Building up a picture of construct validity is typically a long process.

Validation is an essential part of the development process, without it there is no way of being sure that the method actually captures representative activity of the operational environment. Once this has been established however, it may be possible to use the data derived from the method to predict the success of a particular design in the real environment.

The 'quick and dirty' dozen?

For the purposes of this review, we have selected a dozen methods regularly used by ergonomists, and we ask what evidence exists by which we may judge their reliability and validity? We argue that all but one of the methods (i.e. SHERPA) has no reported evidence of formal validation studies in the ergonomics literature. The methods were:
- guidelines
- heuristics
- checklists
- observation
- interviews
- questionnaires
- link analysis
- layout analysis
- hierarchical task analysis (HTA)
- systematic human error reduction and prediction approach (SHERPA)
- repertory grids
- keystroke level model (KLM).

As mentioned, only SHERPA appears to have undergone some formal validation studies (Kirwan, 1992; Baber & Stanton, 1996). Other methods have been involved where validation may be inferred, e.g. Nielson's (1992) study of heuristics and Baber, Hoyes & Stanton's (1992) study of KLM. However, we feel that validation studies of ergonomics methods need to be conducted with the same rigour as is the norm for psychometric tests.

A survey of professional ergonomists

We decided to question respondents' experience with ergonomics' methods, asking if they had any evidence of validity or reliability. There were no references by the respondents to reported evidence for reliability or validity in the literature which concords with our earlier investigations (Stanton & Young, 1995). Statistical analysis of the respondents' ratings of the techniques revealed three interesting and statistically significant results. First, some methods were rated as easier to use than others (chi-square, corrected for ties, = 33.0595; p<0.0005). Checklists were rated as significantly easier to use than simulation (Z, corrected for ties, = -3.3994; p<0.001), guidelines were rated as significantly easier to use than prototyping (Z, corrected for ties, = -2,578; p<0.01) and interviews were rated as significantly easier to use than mock-ups (Z, corrected for ties, = -2.1381; p<0.05). We noted earlier that only a limited range of methods are used but there is no guarantee that these are the most appropriate. Baber & Mirza (1995) report that product designers tend to restrict their methods to interviews, observation and checklists (which was confirmed in our study). Similar to the report by Baber & Mirza (1995), our finding suggests that this is likely to be due to the ease of applying the methods. Second, the ease with which methods are rated depends upon whether software support is used. The results show that where no software support is used, the method is rated as easier to use than where software support is provided (Z, corrected for ties, = -2.6597; p<0.01). Although perhaps this is a counter-intuitive finding, our own experience suggests that software can make even a relatively easy method quite complex and cumbersome. With some irony we would suggest that developers of ergonomics software cannot afford to ignore ergonomics in the design of their product! However, it is our experience that software can make the ergonomist's activities more efficient in the long term. Finally, the data suggest that users of ergonomics methods perceive differences in ease of use of methods depending upon the level of training they have received (Chi-square, corrected for ties, = 6.0639; p<0.05). Those who have received no training rate the methods as easier to use than those who have received informal training (Z, corrected for ties, = -1.9919; p<0.05). We suggest that this result is probably due to both groups' misconception of the method and would recommend formal training in any approach used.

General discussion

In a recent paper, Stanton & Young (1996) consider the relative merits of ergonomics' methods on the basis of subjective reports from users. The appropriateness of the application of ergonomics' methods to points in the design life cycle of products and devices is one of continuing debate. Obviously some methods depend upon the existence of a device to evaluate (such as observation, link analysis and layout analysis) whereas others do not (such as heuristics, checklists and repertory grids). An interesting picture is painted by the survey which asks what people use the methods for. The responses showed that four main areas of application were highlighted: data collection, design, assessment and validation of design. The interview is directly and indirectly linked to five other methods. This makes the interview an important design method. Given the concern about reliability and validity of the interview in other fields of research (Cook, 1988) we would caution users of this technique to ensure that they employ a semi-structured and situationally focussed approach to the device evaluation interview.

From our studies we have shown that initial training and practice time in ergonomics' methods is quite varied depending upon the technique being addressed (Stanton & Young, 1996). Questionnaires were the quickest to train and practice whilst HTA and PHEA took the longest time of the methods we evaluated. In a similar vein, application times varied between methods. Again, the questionnaire was the quickest to apply whilst HTA and PHEA took longer to apply in a device evaluation study. In assessing the relative benefits of one method we can consider the applicability of the approaches (which would favour interviews and repertory grid as generic approaches) and training (which would favour the questionnaire as a quick approach) and application (which would again favour the questionnaire as a quick approach).

Conclusions

In conclusion, there is clearly little reported evidence in the literature of reliability or validity of ergonomics' methods. This was confirmed by the survey and literature search. The lack of evidence is not, we argue, due to the complexity or vagaries of what validity means. Rather, it is likely to be due to the lack of motivation on behalf of the people who develop and use the methods to ensure they meet with the criteria. If the status of the ergonomics is to be raised to that of a scientific discipline, surely validation of its underpinning methods will be required.

References

Annett, J., Duncan, K. D., Stammers, R. and Grey, M. J. (1971). *Task analysis. Department of Employment Training information,* paper 6. HMSO: London.
Baber, C. (1996) 'Repertory grid theory and its application to product evaluation' in, P. W. Jordan; B. Thomas; B. A. Weerdmeester & I. L. McClelland (eds) *Usability Evaluation in Industry.* Taylor and Francis: London.
Baber, C. and Mirza, M. G. (1996) 'Ergonomics and the evaluation of consumer products: surveys of evaluation practices' in N. A. Stanton (ed.) *Human Factors in Consumer Product Design.* Taylor and Francis: London.

Baber, C. and Stanton, N. A. (1996a) 'Observation as a usability method' in P. W. Jordan; B. Thomas; B. A. Weerdmeester & I. L. McClelland (eds.) *Usability Evaluation in Industry*. Taylor and Francis: London.

Baber, C. and Stanton, N. A. (1996b) 'Human error identification techniques applied to public technology: predictions compared with observed use' *Applied Ergonomics* Vol. 27, pp. 119-131.

Brooke, J. (1996) 'SUS: a 'quick and dirty' usability scale' in P. W. Jordan; B. Thomas; B. A. Weerdmeester & I. L. McClelland (eds.) *Usability Evaluation in Industry*. Taylor and Francis: London.

Card, S. K., Moran, T. P. and Newell, A. (1983) *The Psychology of Human-Computer Interaction*. Erlbaum: Hillsdale NJ.

Cook, M. (1988) *Personnel Selection and Productivity*. Wiley: Chichester.

Corlett, E. N. & Clarke, T. S. (1995) *The Ergonomics of Workspaces and Machines, (2nd Edition)*. Taylor and Francis: London.

Diaper, D. (1989) *Task Analysis in Human Computer Interaction*. Ellis Horwood: Chichester.

Drury, C. G. (1995) 'Methods for direct observation of performance' in J. Wilson and N. Corlett (eds.) *Evaluation of Human Work, (2nd edition)*. Taylor & Francis: London.

Easterby, R. (1984) 'Tasks, processes and display design' in R. Easterby and H. Zwaga (eds.) *Information Design*. Taylor and Francis: London.

Embrey, D. (1983) 'Quantitative and qualitative prediction of human error in safety assessments' in the *Institution of Chemical Engineers symposium Series* No. 130 pp. 329-350.

FormsDesigner (1992) Communication Research Institute, Australia.

Jordan, P. W.; Thomas, B.; Weerdmeester, B. A. & McClelland, I. L. (1996) *Usability Evaluation in Industry*. Taylor and Francis: London.

Kelly, G. A. (1955) *The Psychology of Personal Constructs*. Norton: New York.

Kirwan, B. and Ainsworth, L. (1992) *A Guide to Task Analysis*. Taylor & Francis: London.

Kirwan, B. (1994) *A Guide to Practical Human Reliability Assessment*. Taylor and Francis: London.

Nielsen, J. (1992) 'Finding usability problems through heuristic evaluation' in *Proceedings of the ACM Conference on Human Factors in Computing Systems* ACM Press, Monterey CA.

Ravden, S. J and Johnson, G. I. (1989) *Evaluating Usability of Human-Computer interfaces: a practical method*. Ellis Horwood: Chichester.

Sinclair, M. (1995) 'Subjective assessment' in J. Wilson and N. Corlett (eds.) *Evaluation of Human Work (2nd edition)*. Taylor & Francis: London.

Stammers, R. B. Carey, M. and Astley, J. A. (1990) 'Task analysis' in J. Wilson and N. Corlett (eds.) *Evaluation of Human Work*. Taylor & Francis: London.

Stammers, R. B. and Shepherd, A. (1995) 'Task analysis' in J. Wilson and N. Corlett (eds.) *Evaluation of Human Work (2nd edition).* Taylor & Francis: London.

Stanton, N. A. (1995) 'Analysing worker activity: a new approach to risk assessment' *Health and Safety Bulletin,* No. 240 pp 9-11.

Stanton, N. A. and Baber, C. (1996) 'Factors affecting the selection of methods and techniques prior to conducting a usability evaluation' in P. W. Jordan; B. Thomas; B. A. Weerdmeester & I. L. McClelland (eds.) *Usability Evaluation in Industry.* Taylor and Francis: London.

Stanton, N. A. and Stevenage, S. (1996) 'Learning to predict human error: issues of reliability, validity and acceptability'. Submitted to *Human Factors.*

Stanton, N. A. and Young, M. (1995) Development of a methodology for improving safety in the operation of in-car devices. *EPSRC/DOT LINK Report 1.* University of Southampton: Southampton.

Stanton, N. A. & Young, M. (1996) 'Is utility in the mind of the beholder: a study of ergonomics' methods'. Paper submitted to *Applied Ergonomics.*

Williams, J. (1985). Validation of human reliability assessment techniques. *Reliability Engineering,* Vol. 11, pp. 149-162.

Wilson, J. (1995) 'A framework and context for ergonomics methodology' in J. Wilson and N. Corlett (eds.) *Evaluation of Human Work (2nd edition).* Taylor and Francis: London.

Wilson, J. and Corlett, N. (1995) *Evaluation of Human Work (2nd edition).* Taylor and Francis: London.

Woodson, W. E., Tillman, B. and Tillman, P. (1992) *Human Factors Design Handbook* (2nd edition). McGraw-Hill: New York.

Youngman, M. B. (1982) *Designing and Analysing Questionnaires.* TRC, Maidenhead.

Acknowledgement

This research reported in this paper was supported by the LINK Transport Infrastructure and Operations Programme

39 Performance anxiety and coping strategies for musicians

Sture Brändström and Anna-Karin Gullberg
Luleå University, Sweden

Introduction

Performance anxiety or stage fright is a common problem for musicians. In this paper the more general term performance anxiety is used, because anxiety can occur in off stage playing as well, for example when playing for peers or for a teacher. In the similar way a musician is given a broad definition: it refers to amateurs and professionals of different genres, as well as music students.

There are many factors contributing to performance anxiety, but the increasing demands on technical perfection is probably one of the most important. Many musicians seem to play for the purpose of demonstrating technical skills and they forget that music has a creative and communicating purpose.

According to several studies in music psychology, often more than half of the respondents report that they suffer from performance anxiety (cf. Gabrielson, 1992). This unpleasant experience often contributes to impairments in performance and sometimes makes the musician lose control. The symptoms of performance anxiety are physical and mental.

Physical symptoms are autonomous reactions such as an increase in heart rate and respiration, sweaty palms, excessive muscular tension and others. The annoying thing about these symptoms is that they tend to place themselves in 'wrong' places: the pianist gets cold hands, the violinist a trembling bow hand, the singer a quivering voice, etc. The mental symptoms are fear of failure, loss of concentration, weak self-confidence, defensive conduct, and many more. If the above mentioned stress symptoms are too extensive, it often results in errors and non-communicating performances (cf. Grunwald, 1996).

Coping strategies

Musicians often have developed their own personal coping strategies and you can find a broad repertory such as: careful preparation, relaxation, self-hypnosis, positive

309

thinking, etc. Roland Persson (1994) identified the following four main groups of coping strategies: cognitive, somatic, behavioural, and pharmaceutical interventions (chiefly beta blockers).

Cognitive strategies, such as visualization and different kinds of hypnosis, are aimed at influencing the body through the mentality. The somatic strategies on the other hand work in the different direction: a relaxed body is expected to result in a calm mental condition. Meditation, Alexander Technique, autogen training, are examples on mainly somatic interventions.

Behavioural strategies, often named systematic desensitization, stand for 'unlearning' anxiety, through exposing the musician frequently to concerts or concertlike situations. The more you play for others, the less nervous you will be, is the reasoning behind that strategy. It has to be mentioned, that in most cases combinations of different kinds of strategies are used (c.f. Schéele, 1989).

The relationship between music performance and the sciences of psychology and medicine, is not very strong and established compared with the relationship between sport and psychology/medicine. Nowadays, almost every top level sportsman in the world, is undergoing some kind of mental training beside physical and technical training. In Scandinavia, athletic psychology has had a positive development the last decades (c.f. Jansson,1995; Railo, 1972; Unestähl, 1979).

Many musicians, music educators, researchers in music pedagogy and music psychology (among others present authors), have understood that most of the experiences from the athletic psychology are applicable also to music. There is a lot to learn from the mental preparation and training of sportsmen before an important competition. It is on one hand a question of optimal performance and on the other hand a matter of enjoyment and avoiding injuries. Both of these ambitions are to a high degree relevant for the area of music.

Mental training for musicians

Between 1987-1990 a mental training programme by Lars-Erik Unestähl has been used as an optional part of the project 'self-formulated goals and self-evaluation in music education'. This study was performed within the piano curriculum at the Piteå School of Music (Brändström, 1995). Together with prof. Hans-Ola Eriksson and five diploma students in solo organ playing, present authors carried out a pilot study during 1994. This study together with the above mentioned piano study, confirmed the suspicion that almost every student more or less suffered performance anxiety. In many cases the stress related problems of the students, seemed to be high enough to influence negatively on the quality of playing and affected in many cases even the personal health and well beeing in general.

For that reason it was decided to perform a more extended project in cooperation with Unestähl. His approach could be described as a combination of cognitive, somatic and behavioural strategies - with an apparent emphasis on self-suggestion and self-hypnosis. One of his leading principles for mental training is: our nervous system cannot discriminate between a real experience and a vividly represented inner experience. In the competition or concert situation the optimal achievement will best occur with the attitude: let it happen. At a practical level, the instructions from Uneståhl are in form of tape recordings, and every training occasion takes about ten minutes.

Purpose

An obvious aim with the project was to help students with performance anxiety, but also to improve the education in Piteå School of Music as a whole by implementing mental training. The central research questions at issue can be formulated as:

- What is the effect of a mental training programme on music students' perfomance anxiety?
- Are there any other possitive or negative effects?

The present study has still to be seen as a pilot study and one important purpose is also the development of equipment and methods of measurement. Therefore, the following two questions could be important for the future:

- Which physiological and psychological variables are the most suitable to measure in performance situations?
- What kind of measuring instruments are most effective, reliable and useful in this context?

Method

Subjects

The subjects were nineteen music students. There were four drop-outs during the whole project. From the fifteen subjects who took both the pretest and the posttest and trained at least 20 times, four came from Framnäs Folk High School (in the municipality of Piteå). From School of Music in Piteå there were eight music teacher students, one studied to be a church musician and two were diploma students in organ. Other instruments represented were organ, guitar, piano, trombone, violoncello, flute, and piano. Ten students were selected for the experimental group and five for control group.

Procedure

The design of the study was: pretest - treatment - posttest. The experimental group was told to listen to four different programmes in mental training for four months, preferably once a day. A control group, receiving no training, was used for comparison.

311

9-10 December 1995, (13 December for organists): Pretest All of the participants were instructed to play or sing two pieces: one piece they knew very well and one under rehearsal. Before the performances, finger temperature was measured and survey data of cognitive/emotional variables were collected.

During the performances the physiological variables heart rate and muscle tension by electromyography (EMG), were registrated by a system called PIMEX. The PIMEX system is an interactive system, where the video signal from motion pictures and the analogue physiological signals are mixed and continuously recorded in real time. This function makes it possible to correlate performance with physiological fluctuations. It also gives opportuniy to evaluate performances for visual signs of anxiety. After the performances self-evaluations in the form of survey data were collected.

8th January 1996 Unestähl gave a lecture to the experimental group and delivered two of the tape recorded training programmes, which were originally designed for sportsmen. He also instructed the student group about how to work with the programmes for best results

18 March 1996 Unestähl gave a seminar for the experimental group and delivered one programme called 'Dare to speak' and one called 'Mental training for musicians' constructed by Kjell Fagéus, a Swedish Clarinettist (c.f. Fagéus, 1996).

5 May 1996, (23 May for organists). Posttest: with the same procedure as at the pretest. The following types of data were collected:
- Physological data: heart rate, EMG, finger temperature.
- Psychological data: self evaluations (survey data).
- Videotaped performances.

Preliminary results

At present, most of the data is not analysed. In this last section of the paper some results will be presented in order to touch upon some tendencies and above all, to open up a discussion.

Table 1
Heart rate for experimental group (n= 10) and control group (n=5)

	Mean		Maximum	
	Pre	Post	Pre	Post
Experimental group	128	121	145	135
Control group	104	109	123	122

As the table shows, the experimental group has a generally lower heart rate in the posttest than in the pretest, and that could be considered an indication of a treatment effect. One can not find these differences in the control group. The fact that the control group has lower pulse values in general, could be due to the fact that most of them were more experienced performers, compared with the experimental group.

Data on finger temperature is availible for four subjects (the organ players) and the mean of the differences is 5.5 degrees higher in the posttest. This could also point towards a treatment effect (better blood floowing through the fingertips).

EMG data is at present under analysis and printed measurements from the posttest are available for every participant. In the appendix one organ player is selected to illustrate the form of data in question. Heart rate for the same subject during the pretest and posttest included in the appendix. A comparison between the posttests shows a certain degree of correlation; for example in the middle of the time axis, one can see a stop between two pieces. An important messurement issue for the future is probably to coordinate EMG, heart rate and other parameters along the time axis.

An overarching methodological issue is also the balance between quantitative and qualitative methods. In the view of present authors, much speaks for not forgetting the way the musicians experience performance anxiety and prospective improvements. Phenomenological interviews are perhaps one of the most appropriate methods, to let the subjects give a picture of their thoughts and feelings in connection to performance anxiety. As will be seen from some of the written comments in this study, coping strategies and mental training can even improve the musician's quality of life.

'I have had problems to relax in left shoulder, arm and fingers. This has been improved and also my general ability of concentration. It's also more easy for me to quickly distribute the same weight to the feet.'

'I'm calmer in exposed situations. I have better self-confidence, though I thought it was good before we started the training.'

'Really! I have got an increased inner security and become much happier and more even to my temper.'

References

Bråndström, S. (1995). 'Self-formulated goals and self-evaluation in music education'. *Bulletin for the Council of Research in Music Education*. Vol. 127, pp. 16-21.

Gabrielsson, A. (1992). 'Music Performance'. In J. Deutsch (ed.). *The Psychology of Music*. Academic Press: New York.

Grunwald, D. (1996). *Practical psychology in the curriculum for music teachers in the Netherlands.* Paper presented at the 22nd World Conference of the International Society for Music Education, Amsterdam, July 24th, 1996.

Jansson, L. (1995). *Avspänd teknik*. Farsta: SISU idrottsböcker.

Sture Brändström and Anna-Karin Gullberg

Persson, R. S. (1994). *Psyke, stress och konstnärlig frihet: ansats till en yrkesmusikalisk psykosomatik.* Manuskript. Högskolan för Lärarutbildning & Kommunikation: Jönköping.

Railo, W. (1972). Tränings- och tävlingspsykologi. Riks-idrottsförbundets utbildningssektion: Stockholm.

Schéele, B. von. (1989). *Stresskontrollguiden.* Edition Reimers: Stockholm.

Uneståhl, L.-E. (1979). *Självkontroll genom mental träning.* Veje Förlag: Örebro.

Acknowledgement

For eminent technical support we want to thank Bror Tingvall, Luleå University.

40 Fatigue risk assessment for safety critical staff

Deborah Lucas, Colin Mackay, Nicola Cowell*
and Andrew Livingstone*
Health Directorate, Health and Safety Executive, UK
*WS Atkins Ltd, UK

Abstract

Worker fatigue may increase the probability of an accident. Whilst the hours of work of airline staff and HGV drivers are subject to prescribed limits, recent policy for UK railway safety critical staff adopts a different approach based on risk assessment principles. This means that a suitable and sufficient risk assessment should be carried out by a railway company before changes are made to existing hours or patterns of work.

This paper describes the development of guidance on conducting a fatigue risk assessment. A fatigue index has been proposed based on six key factors: time of day, time on task, rest breaks, shift variability, daily rest, and recovery between blocks of shifts. A simple additive model is used to combine ratings from each factor and the concept of a factor moving into a 'red zone' has been included. Initial feedback on the utility of this method is presented.

Introduction

Today many safety critical operations frequently need around the clock operations and fatigue is increasingly recognised as a significant problem for a wide variety of such industries. In the US the National Transportation Safety Board (NTSB) has found fatigue to be a causal or contributory factor in accidents in every mode of transportation and has issued almost 80 fatigue-related safety recommendations since 1972 (NASA, 1995). In the UK safety critical worker fatigue has been implicated in the Clapham Junction railway accident (Hidden, 1989) and has been addressed through the Railway (Safety Critical Work) Regulations 1994. Regulation 4(1) states that 'The employer should ensure, so far as is reasonably practicable, that no employee carrying out safety critical work is asked to work such hours as would be

315

liable to cause fatigue and therefore could endanger safety'. The RSCW regulations are supported by an approved code of practice (ACoP) which gives practical guidance on how to comply with the duty in regulation four and by descriptive guidance on the features of working patterns which affect fatigue. The ACoP recommends that employers should carry out a suitable and sufficient risk assessment before making certain changes (e.g. significant changes to existing work time patterns) which may increase the risk of fatigue.

The concept of carrying out a risk assessment for fatigue is in accord with the risk assessment principles enshrined in the Management of Health and Safety at Work Regulations (1992). It is a different concept from the prescriptive limits set on working patterns in other industries such as air crews and HGV drivers. There is considerable relevant research and some guidance on, for example, shift work patterns and individual differences in shift tolerance (e.g. Monk and Folkard, 1992; Moore-Ede, 1993). In addition, NASA and the NTSB have recently compiled a fatigue resource directory (1995) which aims to provide transportation-industry members with current, accessible information on the topic. However, no specifically applicable research on risk assessment and fatigue was identified in the published scientific literature. Indeed early attempts to develop an objective test of fatigue funded by the Industrial Fatigue Board set up after World War I concluded that 'the term fatigue be absolutely banished from precise scientific discussion, and consequently that attempts to obtain a fatigue test be abandoned' (Muscio, 1921).

There are problems with the definition and measurement of fatigue, with the meaning assigned to the concept by lay and scientific communities, and with epidemiological data on its prevalence (Lewis and Wessely, 1992). Nelson (1996) has argued that the barrier to society acknowledging the need to take action to counter fatigue in safety critical work contexts is familiarity with the problem. Fatigue happens every day as a part of everyday life. Fatigue may even seem acceptable and be part of 'getting the job done'.

Guidance on fatigue and safety critical working

Definition and symptoms

The guidance on Railway Safety Critical Work (Hours of Work and Fatigue) adopts the subjective definition of fatigue in being a perceived state of weariness caused by prolonged or excessive exertion. Symptoms of fatigue include those of drowsiness and dullness, problems in concentrating, and physical symptoms such as feeling dizzy, muscle tremors (Yoshitake, 1978). The guidance states that 'fatigue is a result of prolonged mental or physical exertion. It reduces people's mental alertness and affects their performance. Errors caused by impaired concentration, perception, judgement or memory will become more likely. People may become impatient. Ultimately there may be drowsiness or involuntary sleep' (HSE, in press).

Causes of fatigue

The guidance recognises that there are many causes of fatigue. In focussing on working time patterns other factors such as the nature of the work, the workload and the working environment are also stated as being relevant. For the working time pattern the guidance recommends consideration of all aspects together. Specific information is provided on performance and length of period of duty, intervals between duties, recovery time, rest breaks during a shift, and variability of shifts.

Fatigue management

Limited guidance is provided on fatigue management including such measures as improvements in the working environment and in work design, and education for shift work. Reference is made to devices which monitor and stimulate alertness.

Sources of information

Some helpful references on shift work are given and appropriate professional societies are listed.

Developing a fatigue risk assessment method

Two stages of fatigue risk assessment

A practicable method of carrying out a fatigue risk assessment for safety critical applications has been developed. The suggested method consists of two stages. Stage one is a method of comparing two working time patterns to establish if one is likely to result in more of less fatigue than the other. A fatigue index has been developed to attempt to do this which is described in more detail below. Stage two is a more in-depth risk assessment for use when stage one has identified that a proposed new working time pattern would be likely to increase fatigue. Stage two involves identifying the errors which increased fatigue would make more likely, together with their consequences; then assessing the increased risk and deciding upon appropriate management methods. Further details of stage two are not given in this paper.

Fatigue index

The stage one fatigue index has been developed as a reasonably practicable method of assessing whether a change to a working time pattern is likely to increase fatigue. It is intended to capture current knowledge on some of the key factors affecting fatigue. The intention is that the method would be quick and simple to use without extensive psychological training. The method has been developed following a review of available literature. It is based on ratings from the literature, from experts' judgement and best estimates and as such must be seen as only one approach to the problem of fatigue risk assessment.

The method gives 'fatigue ratings' for six aspects of working time pattern: length of period of duty, intervals between duties, recovery time, rest breaks, variability of shifts and time of day. Individual factors which may influence fatigue are deliberately excluded from consideration since it is assumed that the assessment will be carried out for groups of safety critical workers. The six fatigue ratings are then added together to give an overall 'fatigue index' for that pattern. Fatigue indices for different working time patterns may then be compared. The model underlying the fatigue index is currently a simple additive one and interactions between factors are not captured at present. For each of the six factors 'red zones' are indicated to help employers focus attention on aspects of a working time pattern which may cause particular difficulty.

The intention is that if the overall fatigue index of a proposed working time pattern is no higher than that of the existing pattern and none or only one of the six individual fatigue ratings is in a 'red zone' then the employer may decide that the result of the risk assessment is satisfactory. Any increase in the fatigue index or two or more fatigue ratings falling in 'red zones' indicates a need to reconsider the proposed working time change or to carry out a more detailed (stage two) risk assessment.

Examples of two of the fatigue ratings are given below. The first is for assessing intervals between duties. Take the length of each daily rest interval, or the average length if it varies, and assess the fatigue rating using table 1 below. In a shift cycle where there are several different blocks of shifts, the average interval for each block should be calculated and the shortest average interval taken. However, if any daily rest interval is less than eight hours, disregard all other intervals and count the fatigue rating as 10. Here a fatigue rating (FR) of eight or more would fall into the 'red zone'.

Table 1
Assessing fatigue rating for intervals between duties

Interval	15 hrs or more	Under 15 but at least 14	Under 14 but at least 13	Under 13 but at least 12	Under 12 but at least 11	Under 11 but at least 10	Under 10 hours
FR	2	3	4	5	6	8	10

The second rating is for assessing the length of a period of duty. Assess the FR for the longest period of duty (including planned overtime) normally worked using table 2 below. 'Period of duty' is defined as consisting wholly or partly of safety critical work and includes overtime and meal or rest breaks.

Table 2
Assess length of period of duty

Time on task	9 hrs or under	Over 9 and up to 11 hrs	Over 11 and up to 12 hrs	Over 12 and up to 13 hrs	Over 13 and up to 14 hrs	Over 14 and up to 16 hrs	Over 16 hrs
FR	2	3	4	7	8	9	10

Review of method

The fatigue index method was subjected to a peer review by asking five external experts in the fields of chronobiology and human performance to consider the following questions: general view of the approach taken, agreement with the six factors selected, comments on the fatigue ratings for each factor, view of the use of 'red zones', comment on the use of an additive model for the six factors. The method was also presented to a number of representatives from the rail industry in the UK.

Four of the five experts were in general agreement with the approach taken and felt that the method and associated guidance were useful and informative. The potential dangers of promoting a quantified method for fatigue risk assessment were mentioned, i.e. that users could become over-reliant on the numbers calculated rather than on a broader assessment of the task being carried out. Some experts suggested additional factors which influence factor and/or different fatigue ratings for existing factors. These suggestions were considered and a number of changes to the fatigue ratings were made as a result. The idea of a 'red zone' was perceived as useful and there was a suggestion that a 'concern/warning zone' could also be helpful. A number of experts made useful suggestions for ways of validating the fatigue index. One expert was not in favour of the method and recommended that a data driven approach using quantitative computer simulation should be developed instead.

The method was trialed by two of the rail industries. Detailed results are not available but the method was reported as being quick and easy to use once the relevant information had been assembled. There were concerns that, as with other numerical assessments, there could be a tendency to manipulate numbers rather than trying to understand the problem of fatigue.

Discussion

With the promising reviews and early trials it has been decided to continue the development of the fatigue index. The next stage will be a contract placed by competitive tender to attempt to validate and, where necessary, further refine or extend the method. The research is expected to compare the fatigue index factors and ratings against a range of actual work patterns in a number of industrial sectors (including the railway sector), to obtain data (either objective or subjective) to enable these work patterns to be assessed as more or less fatiguing, and to then consider the extent to which the fatigue index can be seen as a valid measure for these patterns.

References

Hidden, A. (1989) *Investigation into the Clapham Junction Railway Accident.* HMSO: London.

HSE (1994) *Railway safety critical work:* Guidance on Regulations. HSE Books.

HSE (in press) *Approved code of practice on the hours of work of staff undertaking safety critical work on the railways.* HSE Books.

Lewis, G and Wessely, S. (1992) 'The epidemiology of fatigue: more questions than answers'. *Journal of Epidemiology and Community Health,* Vol. 46, pp. 92-97.

Monk, T.H. and Folkard, S. (1992) *Making Shift work Tolerable.* Taylor and Francis: London.

Moore-Ede, M (1993) *The 24 hour society: the Risks, Costs and Challenges of a World that Never Stops.* Addison-Wesley: London.

Muscio, B. (1921) 'Is a fatigue test possible?' *British Journal of Psychology,* Vol. 12, pp. 31-46.

NASA and NTSB (1995) *Fatigue Resource Directory.* Managing Fatigue in Transportation: Promoting Safety and Productivity. Tysons Corner, Virginia, November 1-2.

Nelson, T.M. (1996) 'Fatigue, the ecology of driving and related matters'. *Second International Conference on Fatigue and Transportation.* Freemantle, Western Australia, February 11-16..

Yoshitake, H. (1978) Three characteristic patterns of subjective fatigue symptoms. *Ergonomics,* Vol. 21, pp. 231-233.

Acknowledgements

We would like to thank the following for all their help in preparing and reviewing the guidance and Fatigue Index: Michael Madeley and Roger Short of HSE, Professor Simon Folkard, Dr Jim Waterhouse, Dr Lawrence Smith, Dr Peter Totterdell and Dr Martin Moore-Ede. We would also like to acknowledge those representatives from the railway industry who made helpful comments on earlier versions of the guidance. The views expressed are those of the authors.

Part Five
PRODUCT DESIGN AND EVALUATION

41 Integrating requirements acquisition and user modelling: things users want, and things users do

Gordon Rugg and Ann Blandford
School of Computing Science, Middlesex University, UK

Abstract

The last few years have seen considerable developments in requirements acquisition and theory-based user modelling (as an approach to usability evaluation). This paper describes an initial framework for integrating these areas. Requirements analysis is needed both to inform system design and to identify potentially problematic areas where user modelling is needed. Conversely, the identification of problems through user modelling raises questions that can only be answered through further requirements acquisition. Appropriate techniques must be selected, particularly in cases where users' knowledge of their tasks may be semi-tacit. The framework is illustrated by reference to a case study taken from the domain of air traffic control.

Introduction

In the development of high-cost, safety-critical, systems involving humans and computers, it is critically important to get the requirements right, and to understand how users will work with the computer systems. Failure to do so can cost money and lives. The last few years have seen considerable developments in requirements acquisition and theory-based user modelling, but although the two areas have clear connections, there has until now been no attempt to integrate them. This paper describes an initial model for integration.

Requirements acquisition

Requirements acquisition arose because traditional techniques such as interviewing and questionnaires were not performing adequately when system requirements were being

323

Gordon Rugg and Ann Blandford

collected and formalised into specifications. More techniques were needed, and requirements acquisition and formalisation needed to be systematised and made more rigorous. Elicitation techniques were imported from a range of disciplines, with the aim of producing a systematic methodology for eliciting, formalising and verifying user requirements for software systems.

Techniques and methods advocated by different workers in the area come from widely disparate sources. Approaches range from the ethnographic approach to highly formalised techniques such as repertory grids. Between these extremes are techniques such as scenarios, structured and unstructured interviews and protocol analysis. An overview of these approaches is given in Maiden & Rugg (1996). Maiden and Rugg present an integrating framework that helps analysts identify which techniques are appropriate for eliciting different types of requirements.

One important activity is to compare front and back versions of behaviour in the domain (Goffman, 1959), to see how well the 'official' version of practice in the domain corresponds with the 'behind the scenes' reality. Traditional techniques for requirements acquisition such as interviews and questionnaires often fail to elicit the 'behind the scenes' reality. If a user model is to have any hope of validity, it needs to be based on the realities of the domain.

A second important issue is detection of tacit and semi-tacit knowledge about relevant domain factors. Tacit knowledge is knowledge which the user has, but which is not accessible to introspection; non-tacit knowledge is knowledge to which the user has full, valid access via introspection. The concept of semi-tacit knowledge is developed within the Maiden & Rugg framework, to handle types of knowledge which (for various reasons) can be accessed via some techniques, but not via others. One example is 'taken for granted' knowledge, which is not mentioned because the listener is assumed to know it already. Unfortunately, domain experts often misjudge what can be taken for granted, and therefore fail to mention important requirements. Other examples are rare events recognised but not recalled when the initial specifications were written, and tasks performed using compiled or implicit knowledge. As illustrated below, user modelling can help with teasing out this semi-tacit knowledge.

Requirements acquisition has concentrated on eliciting and formalising client requirements, with a tendency towards static specification rather than context-sensitive specification. There would, however, be much to gain from having an improved methodology for handling context-sensitive system behaviour. User modelling offers formalised methods for modelling user and system behaviour in a way that takes account of some aspects of the context of use, and there would be clear advantages in integrating it with requirements acquisition.

User modelling

User modelling involves developing a precise description of a prototypical user, as a basis for analysing how such a user is likely to work with a device. Although

324

currently not widely used in design practice, user modelling can complement other approaches to improving usability such as user testing and discount usability evaluation methods (Nielsen & Mack, 1994). Firstly, because it has a theoretical basis, the usability analyst can draw on that theory to develop a deeper understanding of particular usability problems and of how a design might be modified to overcome them. Secondly, appropriate use of theory-based techniques can reduce the need for - and cost of - extensive usability trials with each design prototype. This is particularly important in design contexts where users are specialists with limited time to participate in usability trials. Thirdly, theory-based techniques can support scenario-based design (Carroll, 1995) and introduce user concerns into the design process before it is possible to construct a realistic prototype system that can be tested with users, by which point many design commitments have already be made. This concern is particularly pertinent to the design of high reliability systems, where the initial investment in rigorous formal specification makes the cost of later design changes very high.

Just as different techniques are appropriate for different purposes in requirements acquisition, so different usability techniques, including various approaches to user modelling, are appropriate at different stages in design, and for analysing different aspects of usability. However, for the purposes of this paper we consider just one approach to user modelling - namely programmable user modelling analysis (PUMA; Blandford & Young, 1995b). PUMA involves describing the user's tasks with a proposed, or existing, system in terms of conceptual operations, the user's knowledge about the system and the means by which users select particular operations to perform in various contexts. The user's knowledge of the system will include both static knowledge and context-sensitive knowledge (for example, knowledge derived by looking at the device state). See Blandford and Young (1995a; in press) for more details. If a complete and rigorous description is produced then the resulting model can be run to give a range of modelled behaviours. However, in many situations the process of describing the user's knowledge in particular terms can help to expose hidden assumptions, under-specified aspects of the design, or inconsistencies, without ever getting as far as running the model.

Integrating requirements acquisition and user modelling

The basic framework described here is relatively simple.
(i)   As in standard design practice, requirements are used to guide system design.
(ii) A set of appropriate tasks for user modelling are identified, also through requirements acquisition.
(iii) Initial user and system models are constructed and tested for each appropriate task.
(iv) If the tests reveal that further information is needed for the modelling, then further requirements acquisition is used.

(v) Once the modelling is complete, the results are fed back to the client, so that the initial specification can be changed or formalised as appropriate.

(vi) If the specification is changed, then the process goes through further iterations as necessary.

Illustrative example

We illustrate the framework with an example, taken from an analysis by Blandford and Young (1995b), of the computer entry and readout device (CERD), a component of an air traffic control workstation. The overall design of the workstation is described by Hall (1996).

The CERD is a touch-sensitive panel that allows air traffic control officers (ATCOs) to exchange messages with the national airspace system about flights that are scheduled to land at the local airport. In particular, ATCOs can construct and send messages requesting changes to the landing order of flights. Flights that they need to refer to are available as hot-spots on the panel.

Stage 1

The first step is to design a system to satisfy identified requirements.

To maintain consistency with established practice, flights on the CERD are displayed in a form that is similar to the paper flight strips that ATCOs have traditionally worked with. Up to 12 flights can be displayed at any time; flights are shown in landing order, in blocks of six. By default, these blocks are determined in relation to the Common Approach Point; at the time the screen display is updated, the flights in positions 1-6 (or 7-12, or 13-18, etc.) relative to the Common Approach Point are displayed in the first block, and the following 6 flights in the second block, as shown in figure 1. There are scrolling buttons that allow the ATCO to see flights in adjacent blocks.

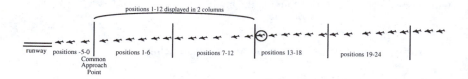

Figure 1   **Flights for display on the CERD are organised into blocks of adjacent flights relative to the common approach point**

As well as the requirement to display flights relative to the common approach point, requirements analysis showed that the CERD display should not change in a continuous manner, so that flight strips were to remain in the same position on the screen while they remained eligible for display on that screen. (Flights become ineligible as they move forward in the landing order (as aircraft land) or if they are diverted to another airport.) Therefore, as well as the scrolling operations to display flights in different positions in the landing order, there is a 'tidy' operation to refresh the display of the current positions.

Stage 2

The task model is then constructed on the basis of information obtained through a requirements analysis of the domain of application, and used as the basis for an initial user model. One task ATCOs perform routinely is to work through the landing order from front (nearest to landing) to back, checking for any problems, such as a light aircraft being scheduled to land immediately behind a jumbo jet. (A large time interval is needed between such landings so that air turbulence is at an acceptable level for the smaller craft when it lands). When such problems are found, the ATCO will typically request a change in the landing order.

Stage 3

The third stage is to construct and test a model. Our modelling involves describing this task in terms of the way ATCOs would work with the device. Since the tasks of checking the landing order and sending messages to request changes to that order are interleaved, and since they have to use the CERD for constructing messages, the ATCOs are likely to choose to use the CERD for the checking task unless there are other factors in the context of use that would guide them to make an alternative choice. We focus on the task of checking the landing order.

This task can be described as iteratively viewing and checking the next block of flights to the left (i.e. further away from landing) until the end of the landing order is reached. The task of viewing the next block of flights to the left was described from both a user and a device perspective. The user-description says, put simply in English, 'If there are more flights further out in the landing order then to view those flights, press the scroll-left key.' The corresponding device description says 'The effect of scroll-left is that the flights in the next six positions in the landing order are displayed'. One question we need to ask as analysts is whether there are contexts of use in which there is a mis-match between the user's intention and the actual change in the device state.

The user modelling highlighted the possibility of there being such a mis-match in situations where the screen was very untidy. For example, if positions 1-12 are currently displayed, but seven of the flights in this region have moved past the common approach point or been diverted, then when the ATCO presses scroll-left, the circled flight in figure 1 is actually in position six, so will not be displayed.

Stage 4

Stage four involves using the appropriate requirements acquisition technique to gather any supplementary information needed to make the task and user models complete. Choice of technique is driven by the type of information needed.

The situation identified above had apparently not been considered by the designers. The user modellers did not have the information necessary to know whether this would actually be a problem. It was necessary to find out whether there were situations in which the display might get this untidy, and whether there might be consequent problems. The answers to these questions would be provided by requirements acquisition. In this example, answering the first question would require direct or indirect observation, rather than interviews, since expert recall of the nature and frequency of particular cases can be surprisingly inaccurate. Answering the second question would require techniques such as scenarios or critical incident analysis to cope with human shortcomings in predicting possible outcomes.

Stages 5 and 6

In stage five, the model of user behaviour is translated into the appropriate formalism for inclusion within the requirements and/or specification document, for feedback to the client to check that the model so far is correct. In addition, the modelling process may reveal unexpected advantages to the proposed system, which the client may wish to use as the basis for changes and enhancements.

If the specification is changed, then the process goes through further iterations as necessary (stage six).

Conclusion and summary

As Green (1990) argues, human-computer interaction is not going to advance by developing one all-encompassing theory of the design and analysis of interactive systems, but by developing a range of localised theories and techniques. The challenge, then, is to scope these localised theories effectively (giving a clear account of when and how to use them, and of what they can deliver), and to develop a good understanding of ways in which they can be used together effectively. In this paper, we present an initial account of relationships between requirements acquisition and user modelling.

While work on requirements acquisition has been conducted largely in industrial design contexts, most developments in user modelling have taken place within the research laboratory. Work has recently started on applying the PUMA technique within natural design settings. As that work progresses, we expect to develop a fuller understanding of the ways in which the techniques discussed in this paper can be used together effectively.

References

Blandford, A. E. & Young, R. M. (1995a) 'Separating user and device descriptions for modelling interactive problem solving'. In, K. Nordby, P. Helmersen, D. J. Gilmore, and S. Arnesen (eds.): *Human-Computer Interaction: Interact'95*. Chapman and Hall, 1995. pp. 91-96.

Blandford, A. & Young, R. (1995b) *Applying programmable user models to real design problems*. Amodeus2 Project Document UM/WP30 (submitted for journal publication).

Blandford, A. E. & Young, R. M. (in press) 'Specifying user knowledge for the design of interactive systems' (to appear in Software Engineering Journal).

Carroll, J. M. (1995) (ed.) *Scenario-Based Design: Envisioning Work and Technology in Systems Development*. Wiley: New York.

Goffman, E. (1955) *The presentation of self in everyday life*. Doubleday: New York.

Green, T. R. G. (1990) 'Limited theories as a framework for Human-Computer Interaction', in D. Ackermann & M. J. Tauber (eds.) *Mental Models and Human-Computer Interaction 1*. Elsevier Science, North-Holland.

Hall, A. (1996) *Using Formal Methods to Develop an ATC Information System IEEE* Software, March. 66-76.

Maiden, N.A.M. & Rugg, G. (1996) 'ACRE: Selecting methods for requirements acquisition'. *Software Engineering Journal*, May 1996.

Nielson, J. & Mack, R. (1994) (eds.) *Usability Inspection Methods*. Wiley: New York.

42 Knowledge needs analysis for complex systems

Philip J.A. Scown and Janice E. Whatley
Manchester Metropolitan University, UK

Abstract

Computer user modelling has been applied in a number of domains, for a range of purposes. Examples include computer assisted learning, industrial processing and text editing. User modelling methods are reviewed. Their applicability to complex systems, such as those found in manufacturing, commerce, aviation, is considered with reference to their ability to cope with real-time situations involving multiple agents.

Interaction framework (I.F.) is briefly described and its application to describing complex systems is considered. The mathematical support for formally describing systems in terms of the agents involved, their objectives and the interaction events required to realise objectives. Links between objectives and interaction events are made explicit as are temporal constraints. Analysis of a model built using I.F. assists with the 'cognitive specification' of a canonical user in a particular rôle with respect to temporal issues. Examples from manufacturing and aviation demonstrate this approach.

Introduction

Computer user modelling has been applied in a number of domains over a number of years. Examples include computer assisted learning (Sleeman & Brown, 1982), industrial processing (Hoc, 1989) and text editing (Young & Abowd, 1994). A variety of static (Rich, 1983; Jerrams-Smith, 1983; Blandford & Young, 1995) and dynamic (Jerrams-Smith, 1983; Dix et al, 1992) techniques have been applied. Purposes range from direct assistance to specific users (Dix et al, 1992; Sleeman, 1982), to the design of more general user interface management systems (Malinowski et al, 1992).

The foci of user modelling have been on improving system performance and making things better for the user. System performance can be improved by giving the user support that is more appropriate to the user than would be the case without the user model. Such support may allow tasks to be carried out in a way that is more efficient and/or more effective. A problem with such approaches is that they do not consider the time constraints that may apply in real-time systems, particularly when other agents are required to make the system work as intended.

A number of these user modelling methods are compared and assessed for their applicability to complex systems, such as those found in manufacturing, commerce, aviation and others. This has been done with reference to their ability to cope with real-time situations involving multiple agents.

The problem environment

The focus of the authors has been on systems that include multiple agents, simultaneously engaged in activity within a real-time environment. Such systems have been termed SMART systems (Scown, 1992). In such systems human or computer agents are engaged in a number of activities some of which are time constrained, requiring real-time responses. Though simultaneously active the agents may be operating synchronously or asynchronously. Delegation and demarcation are frequently found in these situations.

The term agent is not used here in the 'beliefs, desires and intentions' (BDI) sense applied by the 'agent' community. Instead the term is used to represent macro agents, agents that may be delegated to but that do not necessarily have beliefs or intentions in the sense that agents with intelligence are expected to have. Agents within SMART systems may be BDI agents, but they may also be significant mechanistic sub-systems of the larger system under consideration. Compound agents are also permitted. These are collections of individual (or 'atomic') agents that may be regarded as a single agent for some purposes.

Within SMART systems the nature of the time constraints imposed by real-time factors means that the availability of agents to be delegated to may have a significant effect on system performance. Where one agent requires the services of another to achieve a particular objective they are dependant on the availability of that agent if they are to progress and achieve. If the agent to be delegated to is not available then there will be a delay or another method must be found. Various definitions of real-time can be found within the computing literature. Typically they refer to responses following instantly from inputs, or if not instant, then at least with a very short delay. While truly 'instant' responses can be ruled out as literally impossible a 'short delay' requires more consideration. Part of the nature of agents is their great variety, they may be human or computer in nature and may be performing simple tasks or some that are highly complex. A definition of 'short delay' was required to cope with all of these possibilities. It was decided that real-time exists where the acceptable or required response latency was approximately equal to an agent's ability to respond within that time interval. This definition allows for a wide range of situations to be classified as real-time: millisecond responses from computers to days or weeks from a more cumbersome group of individuals or an organisation.

The range of modelling methods

During human-computer interaction it is necessary for the human to know something of the computer being interacted with. The approach of Young et al (Young et al., 1989) is to consider the designer's intended procedure (DIP) for a device and what a user needs to know in order to be able to use the device according to the procedure. This approach was developed into programmable user models (PUMs). While the analytical approach of PUMs can be useful (Young & Abowd, 1994) it has limited application when there is no formal DIP or in SMART situations. What is required is a system modelling approach that supports a PUMs type analysis for SMART systems.

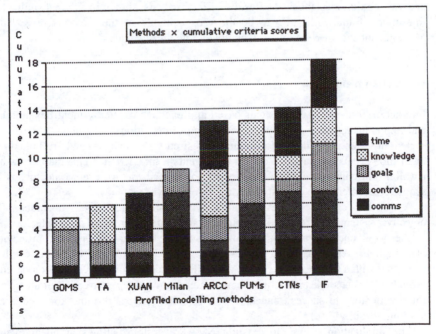

Figure 1   Comparison of subjective scores

A number of modelling methods were considered. A view was taken that an existing method may be usable as it is, or with some modification. This permitted methods with known shortcomings to be considered. The methods considered were:

- Ethnography (Hughes et al, 1994).
- Graphical dialogue environment, GRADIENT (Alty & Ritchie, 1991).
- Interaction framework, I.F. (Blandford et al, 1994 & 1995).
- Executable user action notation, XUAN (Gray et al, 1994).
- Programmable user models, PUMs (Young et al, 1989; Blandford & Young ESPRIT 7040 reports).
- Goals operations methods and selection, GOMS (Card, Moran & Newell, 1983; Dix et al, 1993).
- Abstract reasoning from concrete clues, ARCC (Decortis et al, 1991).
- Dialogue analysis, Milan model (De Michelis & Grasso, 1994).
- Coloured timed petri nets, CTNs (Furuta & Stotts, 1994).
- Hierarchical task analysis, HTA (Shepherd, 1989).
- Task action grammar, TAG (Payne & Green 1989).

Prior to considering any of the methods criteria were established against which each could be measured. A subjective scoring system was devised so that the relative suitability of methods for modelling SMART systems to support knowledge needs analysis could be established. Results of the analysis, shown in figure 1, indicate interaction framework (I.F.) to be the most suitable of the methods reviewed. Methods not shown were found to be unsuitable during analysis.

Interaction framework

Interaction framework is a systems based approach. It explicitly identifies atomic and compound agents engaged within a system of interactions. The objectives of the system are identified (defined in terms of desired state changes) and are linked to interaction events (exchanges between two agents). Interaction events may occur in parallel, allowing multi-agent situations to be described. An event trajectory is a sequence of interaction events achieving an objective.

A number of undesirable trajectory types can be identified: unachievable objective, system reset required, simple interactional detour, blind alley interaction. These occur under a range of conditions, such as the unavailability of an agent, inappropriate event ordering or poor event timing. Thus an 'ideal' trajectory can be compared with a trajectory that is faulty and the outcomes classified and compared. From here it is possible to describe the minimum knowledge requirement of an agent for a trajectory to succeed and the specific consequences if some knowledge is missing or faulty.

The application of I.F. to existing SMART systems allows an ideal event trajectory to be described for any situation we might imagine. This is analogous to the DIP that is developed, or evolves, during the design of devices for non-SMART interactions (e.g. word processing).

Using I.F. to support the cognitive specification of users through knowledge needs analysis

For a given system I.F. may be used to make explicit the relationships between objectives, agents and interaction events. Each of these three facets of I.F. has interesting features that can make them difficult to formalise.

Objectives are derived from system goals. Objectives are achievable items of activity that provide milestones in the assessment of systems performance and the achievement of goals. Objectives are decomposed until, at their lowest level, an objective can be achieved through an identifiable sequence of interaction events. Such a sequence defines an interaction trajectory. One problem with objectives is deciding how to include intangible constraints such as : actions to be performed as safely as possible, or to be performed with the minimum of delay.

As previously stated agents may be atomic or compound. While the definition of atomic agents is relatively straightforward the identification of meaningful compound agents can be more problematic. It is not always clear during the early stages of analysis whether two or more atomic agents (or even two or more clearly defined compound agents) can be grouped together to form a new meaningful compound agent.

The definition of interaction events places emphasis on interaction rather than event. Thus an interaction event is not said to have occurred until it has been perceived and comprehended by the recipient agent. This allows for considerable latencies of for interaction events that are initiated but never completed and thus are not said to have occurred.

The benefit to be gained from an I.F. analysis appears to be twofold. Firstly it supports the formal description of multi-agent systems with significant temporal factors. Secondly, the process of using I.F. forces some aspects of the system description to be clarified or causes specific problem areas to be recognised and scoped if not resolved. This is similar to the gains to be had from a PUMs approach to more simple systems (Young et al, 1989).

Examples of I.F. applied to aviation and process control

To explore the gains to be made in knowledge needs analysis I.F. was used to analyse segments of two different SMART systems. These were from different domains each with their own objectives and temporal characteristics. The first domain is from aviation where time constraints are sometimes quite tight and where there is a wide variety of agent rôles. The second is from process control, specifically the production of iron. In this example though the variation in rôles is less than aviation the temporal characteristics are considered more complex as a result of long response latencies.

The specific aviation situation modelled is the making of an unscheduled turn in order to avoid a converging aircraft near miss. The turn needs to be made promptly if the aircraft are to maintain adequate separation. An I.F. analysis of the situation makes a number of issues explicit. For the turn to be initiated the autopilot may need to be disengaged. Thus the status of the autopilot needs to be available to the flight crew either from its display or by tracking. Also, for the necessary interactions to be executed efficiently there should be no detours or duplication. Members of the flight crew need to know the correct sequence of interaction events if the sub-objectives constituting the main objective are to be achieved. Either the pilot or the co-pilot should disengage the autopilot - but not both. In initiating the turn the air traffic control officer (ATCO) needs to know the amount of time available for making the turn and the time in which it can be made - otherwise some other action is required. Where human and computer agents interact, e.g. with navigational computer or flight management system, a PUMs type analysis of the interaction will assist with identifying specific user knowledge requirements.

In the blast furnace example the controlling agents need to be able to distinguish between normal operation and a range of single or multiple abnormal situations (Hoc, 1989). The various operators have specific responsibilities for aspects of furnace operation. However, the nature of the process is that there can be considerable response latencies. This requires a degree of anticipation of outcome from actions such that a worsening of the situation may be expected to occur temporarily while actions take effect. It is also necessary for each of the agents to know what action has been taken by others. Again this is either by direct display or indirect tracking. Failure to be aware of the actions of others may result in the execution of inappropriate remedial action.

Conclusions

While a number of diverse system modelling techniques exist to support resolution of human factors problems in human-computer systems there are few that deal satisfactorily with temporal aspects of interaction. Interaction framework provides some support through the provision of a relatively easy to use system modelling method. Temporal factors can be made explicit and precise and can be related to the ability of an agent to respond. Parallel system activity is made explicit. Thus it can clearly be seen when an agent's occupation with one task may make the agent unavailable for to support other activity. The duration of unavailability may be known or may be indeterminate. Such knowledge is useful to other agents who may decide on an alternative course of action if a required agent cannot be available within the required time. Having a clear and precise understanding of these knowledge requirements is clearly useful in the design of complex systems in general and SMART systems in particular. Using I.F. to describe the requirements of agent performance supports the cognitive specification of agents by putting boundaries on what an agent will need to know in order to be able to interact effectively within system time constraints.

References

Alty J.L., Ritchie R.A. (1991) 'An algebraic approach to interface specification analysis', in G.R.S. Weir & J.L. Alty. (eds.) *Human Computer Interaction and Complex Systems*. Academic Press: Boston.

Blandford A., Harrison M.D. & Barnard P.J. (1994) 'Understanding the properties of interactions', personal communication.

Blandford A., Harrison M.D. and Barnard P.J. (1995) 'Using Interaction Framework to guide the design of interactive systems', to appear in *International Journal of Human-Computer Studies*.

Blandford A.E., Young R.M. (1994) 'Separating user and device descriptions in PUMs', publication of Amodeus: ESPRIT BRA 7040 (document ID: UM_WP18).

Blandford A.E., Young R.M. (1994) 'PUMs analysis of a prototype media space design', publication of Amodeus: ESPRIT BRA 7040 (document ID: UM_WP 24.

Blandford A.E., Young R.M. (1994) 'A first PUMs analysis of the CERD exemplar' publication of Amodeus: ESPRIT BRA 7040 (document ID: UM_WP 25).

Blandford A.E., Young R.M., (1995) 'Separating user and device descriptions for modelling interactive problem solving', in, K. Nordby, P. Helmersen P., D.J. Gilmore D.J. & S. A. Arnesen S.A. (eds.), *Human-Computer Interaction proceedings of Interact '95*. Lillehammer: Chapman & Hall.

Card S.K., Moran T.P. and Newell A. (1983) *The psychology of human-computer interaction*. Lawrence Erlbaum Associates: Hillsdale, NJ.

Decortis F., de Keyser V., Cacciabue P.C. & Volta G. (1991) 'The temporal dimension of man-machine interaction' in, G.R.S. Weir & J.L. Alty. (eds.) *Human Computer Interaction and Complex Systems*. Academic Press: Boston.

De Michelis G., Grasso A.M. (1994) 'Situating conversations within the language/action perspective: the Milan conversation model', in R. Furuta & C. Neuwirth (eds.) *Proceedings of ACM 1994 conference on CSCW*.

Dix. A., Finlay J., Beale R. (1992), 'Analysis of user behaviour as time series', in Monk A., Diaper D. and Harrison M.D. (eds.), *People and Computers VII, proceedings of the HCI '92 conference, York.*, Cambridge University Press: Cambridge.

Dix A., Finlay J., Abowd G. & Beale R. (1993) 'Human-Computer Interaction' Prentice-Hall: New York.

Furuta R. & Stotts P.D. (1994) 'Interpreted Collaboration protocols and their use in groupware prototyping', in R. Furuta & C. Neuwirth (eds.), *Proceedings of ACM 1994 conference on CSCW*.

Gray P., England D. & McGowan S. (1994) 'XUAN: enhancing UAN to capture temporal relationships among actions' in, G. Cockton, S.W. Draper and G.R.S. Weir (eds.), *People and Computers IX, proceedings of HCI '94*, Glasgow. Cambridge University Press: Cambridge.

Hoc, J-M. (1989), 'Strategies in controlling a continuous process with long response latencies: needs for computer support to diagnosis'. *International Journal of Man-Machine Studies*, Vol. 30, pp 47-67.

Hughes J., King V., Rodden T., Andersen H. (1994) 'Moving out from the control room: ethnography in system design', in R. Furuta & C. Neuwirth (eds.), *Proceedings of ACM 1994 conference on CSCW.*

Jerrams-Smith J. (1987), 'An expert system with a supportive interface for UNIX'. *Behaviour and Information Technology,* Vol. 6, pp 37-41.

Malinowski U., Kühme T., Dietrich H. & Schneider-Hufschmidt M. (1992), 'A taxonomy of adaptive user interfaces', in A. Monk, D. Diaper and M.D. Harrison,. (eds.), *People and Computers VII, proceedings of the HCI '92 conference, York,* Cambridge University Press: Cambridge.

Payne S.J., and Green T.R.G. (1989) 'Task-action grammar: the model and its development' in, D. Diaper (ed.), *Task Analysis for Human-Computer Interaction,* Ellis Horwood.

Rich E. (1983), 'Users are individuals: individualizing user models'. *International Journal of Human-Computer Studies,* Vol. 18, pp.199-214.

Scown P.J.A. (1992) 'Real-time issues in multi-agent computer systems' *Proceedings of joint ACM-ISCTI conference: East-West HCI,* St. Petersburg, Russia, August.

Shepherd A. (1989) 'Analysis and training in information technology tasks' in D. Diaper (ed.) *Task Analysis for Human-Computer Interaction,* Ellis Horwood.

Sleeman D. and Brown J.S. (1982), *Intelligent Tutoring Systems.* Academic Press: Boston.

Sleeman D. (1982), 'Assessing aspects of competence in basic algebra' in, Sleeman D. and Brown J.S. (eds.), *Intelligent Tutoring Systems.* Academic Press: Boston

Young R.M., Green T.R.G. & Simon T. (1989) 'Programmable user models for predictive evaluation of interface designs' in, K. Bice & C. Lewis (eds.) *Proceedings of CHI'89,* ACM.

Young R.M., Abowd G.D. (1994), 'Multi-perspective modelling of interface design issues: undo in a collaborative editor' in, G. Cockton, S.W. Draper and G.R.S. Weir (eds.), *People and Computers IX, proceedings of HCI '94,* Glasgow. Cambridge University Press: Cambridge.

43 Generating user requirements from discount usability evaluations

Hilary Johnson
Department of Computer Science, Queen Mary and
Westfield College,University of London, UK

Abstract

Falzon (1990) argues that cognitive ergonomics is the sub-field of cognitive science especially concerned with human task-oriented activity. Much human task-oriented activity is now undertaken using interactive computer systems and therefore, cognitive ergonomics and human computer interaction have closely related concerns. In HCI evaluations are conducted in order to assess the effectiveness of human task-oriented activity supported by computer. However, the process of evaluation should also provide the basis for improving the design by generating redesign requirements. Unfortunately, a common complaint from practitioners is that while these methods might be good at identifying usability problems, they do not begin to provide solutions to the problems identified. This paper is specifically concerned with the generation of user requirements as a result of conducting discount usability evaluation studies using heuristic evaluation and cognitive walk-through. The requirements generated by the different evaluation methods are outlined and discussed.

Introduction

A number of researchers concerned with the design and use of computers have attempted to demonstrate how cognitive psychology and cognitive ergonomics might contribute to human computer interaction, (e.g. Falzon, 1990; Norman, 1986; Long and Dowell, 1989; and Payne, 1996). Falzon argues that cognitive ergonomics can be defined as the sub-field of cognitive science especially concerned with human task-oriented activity. However, for other researchers, rather than cognitive ergonomics being a sub-field of another (sub)discipline, both cognitive ergonomics and HCI are to be considered as disciplines in their own right, and knowledge and

339

practices should flow both from the 'source' discipline to the 'recipient' discipline, and vice versa. Therefore, HCI should reciprocate the contribution made by other disciplines by contributing knowledge and practices back to those source disciplines, although this is seldom the practice. Payne (1996) for instance, argues persuasively with well-chosen examples that the design of technologies can benefit from cognitive psychology and the science of psychology can benefit from a consideration of technology.

One common feature of the papers is that they talk about notions such as 'effective work', 'action and performance towards goals' and so on. Although not mentioned explicitly, it is the knowledge and practice of evaluation that gives rise to assessments of effectiveness and progress towards goals. The exception is Payne who argues explicitly for theory-based evaluation being one promising area of HCI for the mutual exchange between cognitive psychology and cognitive technology. Whilst agreeing with this sentiment, and presently being engaged in research into theory-based evaluation (with Hamilton, 1996), it is of concern that theory-based evaluation is not more widely used. The consequences of this lack of use means in turn a lack of empirical data to support the theories to be tested and little basis for reciprocity. There is of course a distinction between researchers using evaluation as a testbed for psychological theory and therefore contributing knowledge and practices to the source discipline, and the general practice of HCI which does not have the universally acknowledged goal of 'aiding' psychology or cognitive ergonomics. In particular, industrialists who do engage in evaluation practices have some reluctance to using theory-based evaluation, preferring instead to undertake informal evaluations which are assumed to require few resources, e.g. time and expertise. This reluctance and the need for evaluation to consume few resources provides the rationale for the development of supposed 'discount usability' evaluation methods. These methods include specialist reports, usability and cognitive walk-throughs, (Lewis, Polson, Wharton and Rieman, 1990). Evaluators using these methods can assess design specifications, early mock-ups, prototypes or fully implemented systems. The major characteristic of inspection methods is that they draw on expert knowledge to provide judgements about system usability. Guidelines and heuristic evaluation also belong to this expert analysis group (see Nielsen and Molich, 1990).

One research question to be addressed is whether or not usability evaluations conducted using discount techniques provide any data which can support either theory construction or refinement. The point of conducting evaluations is usually to provide some assessment of usability and also to generate solutions to user problems by devising redesign requirements. Whilst the reciprocal activities of cognitive psychology and cognitive technology are of concern, the main focus of this paper is in generating user requirements from evaluations, as an early stage in a research programme investigating both the reciprocity question, and use of evaluation techniques by designers. At some level, the objectives for researchers and designers are similar, i.e. in predicting user behaviour, ease of use and learning of interactive computer systems. It is the results of the evaluation studies that are put to different use, in the case of researchers for generating or refining theories, and for designers gaining the knowledge to design more usable computer systems.

The activity of generating user requirements is very important to the success of the designed interactive system in supporting users' tasks and which if unsatisfactory leads to high subsequent production costs. The main sources for user requirements for new and redesigned systems are the users of the systems, or their representatives (e.g. HCI evaluators) who either take part in task analyses or evaluations of current systems. However, a common complaint from practitioners is that even those evaluation approaches which are to some degree 'usable' while satisfactory at identifying usability problems, they provide no help whatsoever in deciding how to utilize the evaluation study results. Identifying that a problem exists may be construed as part of the requirements process, but the next step of generating a solution to those problems is largely unsupported.

Dutt, Johnson and Johnson (1994) conducted a meta-evaluation study which evaluated different approaches to evaluation against a number of criteria. The underlying theme for the paper, frequently overlooked by readers looking for data to compare discount usability methods, was that evaluation generally was very difficult and that discount usability methods, as is the case with theory-based evaluation, were hard to use. The evaluation techniques chosen, heuristic evaluation and cognitive walk-through differed in the time it took to carry them out, the expertise necessary, the number, type and severity of usability problems identified and also in how easy they were to use, with the cognitive walk-through in particular placing a heavy cognitive load on the evaluator. Other problems concerned the difficulty of identifying problems and analysing and interpreting the results. In the case of heuristic evaluation understanding and applying the heuristics was difficult for the evaluators. The full results of the study are reported in Dutt et al. However, one final criteria for assessing the utility of the evaluation techniques was to address practitioners' concerns over what exactly to do with the results. More specifically given the results of using the different evaluation methods, what were the design/redesign requirements that could be generated from the problem descriptions to address user concerns and problems?

In the Dutt et al study we provide numerical values for the problems found using the different evaluation methods. However, we also state that the numbers are to be taken lightly due to the analysis and interpretation problems that had to be faced, i.e. in identifying more than one problem arising from a single source, in identifying problems that were specific instances of a general class already counted and those problems which violated more than one heuristic. A number of comparative studies in the evaluation literature report on the utility of the evaluation methods in highlighting numbers of problems but research and pragmatic issues relating to how the problems are counted are seldom raised. The reason for highlighting this problem of numbers, is that similar unhelpful comparisons can be made between the number of redesign user requirements generated by the different evaluation methods.

341

However, looking closely at the lists of requirements, it is fairly transparent that problems are replicated, are instances of general classes, or are otherwise related in some way.

Requirements generated by the different evaluation approaches

The computer system on which the evaluation study was conducted was in the recruitment domain, finding jobs for applicants and vice versa, this involved matching the most appropriate applicant to a job. The system consisted of a number of relational databases holding details of applicants, clients, jobs and so on. Therefore many of the user requirements are necessarily related to recruitment tasks. The procedure for identifying the requirements was for the person who managed the setting up and overseeing of the actual evaluations, to take and analyse the evaluation results and as part of that process make judgements about what requirements would address and eliminate the usability problems. This procedure was supposed to simulate as nearly as possible a designer who would be responsible for the redesign taking the usability evaluation results from human factors people and then generating redesign requirements. The designer who provided the redesign requirements was familiar with the system and tasks that it supported. The user requirements taken from Dutt (1993) are outlined below. The requirements are replicated here just as the designer of the newly redesigned system represented them, however the ordering of the requirements has been changed in order to provide a basis for the discussion that follows.

Requirements generated by both heuristic evaluation and cognitive walk-through

1. There should be faster responses and a more reliable system.
2. All commands available must be shown on-screen.
3. There must be consistency in the placement of commands.
4. All command descriptions must match closely to the task they describe.
5. It must be possible to update parts of the system and exit immediately.
6. Constructive feedback must be given.
7. Feedback to say the search (for applicants or jobs) has been completed must be obvious.
8. It should be made obvious that the index is not the only information given about applicants.
9. It should be made obvious that the index is not the only information given about clients.
10. It should be made obvious that the index is not the only information given about jobs.
11. On-line help must be available at any place in the redesign.

12. There should be an on-screen indication to show how to search through/up or down the applicant index.
13. There should be an on-screen indication to show how to search through/up or down the client index.
14. There should be an on-screen indication to show how to search through/up or down the job index.
15. The screen must not beep or flash.

Requirements generated only by heuristic evaluation

16. All codes must be translated and displayed in English for easy reading (this was noted to be a system requirement but appears also to be an appropriate user requirement).
17. Searching through the applicant index must be more intuitive.
18. Searching through the client index must be more intuitive.
19. Searching through the job index must be more intuitive.

Requirements generated only by cognitive walk-through

20. Must be able to undo a command.
21. The type of commands and system responses must be consistent.
22. The on-screen description of the command to delete must match more closely to the task.
23. There should be only one search facility available.
24. The search facility must be easy to get to.
25. Setting search criteria or parameters should be obvious.
26. The system should show the user where to start entering new information.
27. The problem with the applicant/job action records must be avoided.
28. There should be no screen lags.

Observations about the nature of the user requirements generated

There was considerable overlap between the user requirements generated by the heuristic evaluation and the cognitive walk-through. Of the requirements generated solely by the heuristic evaluation, one is a high level requirement for the use of English and the others give a high level, or non-specific solution, to a problem which exists across tasks, i.e. searching must be more intuitive. There are more requirements generated solely by the cognitive walk-through; they cover high level needs, such as the need for consistency which is pervasive across the system, requirements about specific commands and those that were deemed to be missing, and task-oriented requirements. There was a specific requirement for help and a low level requirement regarding screen lags that is again pervasive across the system.

The requirements differ in a number of ways; in their level of abstraction, how common throughout the system and across tasks and how specific they are as a solution to a problem. Looking at the requirements more closely other differences emerge, in respect of their relatedness, as instances of classes and in the nature of their solution, which could be crudely categorised as 'absence', 'presence' or 'improvement'. Absence is where the solution argues that something is present but should be absent; presence is where the solution argues that something is absent but should be present, and improvement is a kind of catchall category where what is present should be present, but needs improvement in order to alleviate usability problems. Of course, all these categories relate in some way to improvements.

Requirements 1, 2, 3, 6, 16 and 21 are general, system pervasive requirements, 4 and 5 are more specific instances related to the nature of commands. Requirement 7 is a specific instance of the class referred to at 6, i.e. regarding constructive feedback, and 8, 9 and 10 are very closely related, in fact are replications of one problem in different tasks supported by the system. Requirement 11 is concerned with the problem of help whilst 12, 13 and 14 are instances where help is needed and again are replications of the same problem in different tasks. Requirements 17, 18 and 19 are all specific to searching and are closely related and are replications of one problem. Requirement 15 and 28 are solutions which indicate that a system does something it should not do and are examples of the 'absent' category. It is mainly early versions of prototypes or poorly designed systems which have a predominance of usability problems in the absent and present categories. The assumption is that later in the development, after initial evaluations many of these problems will have been eradicated and then the evaluations become a way of assessing how features and behaviour which ought to be there can be improved.

Discussion

First of all, it is important to note that the generation of requirements from evaluations is a complicated process which includes at least the following interdependent stages;

(i)   identification that a problem has occurred, e.g. by disruption to task performance or user error;

(ii) identification of the nature of the problem, often down to the evaluators expert judgement;

(iii) identification of the cause(s) of the problem, again down to the evaluator's judgement;

(iv) problem solution, a judgement of how to eliminate the cause of the problem, output might be redesign requirements... the solution becomes the problem space that the design space has to resolve;

(v)   design solution - how the requirements are to be satisfied, from a number of possible alternative design solutions, with appropriate design rationales.

Given the above process of identifying requirements from evaluation, it is perhaps not too surprising that of the 37 (heuristic) and 32 (cognitive walk-through) usability problems found, only 19 and 24 redesign requirements were identified from the results of the individual evaluation studies. Breakdowns of the process could occur at any of these stages. It is important to reiterate that attaching numerical values to both the identification of problems and design requirements is a vacuous activity given the problems with replications and general classes and their instances. However, other reasons for the discrepancy might exist. For instance, one requirement might be a solution in the following cases: (i) where a number of problems have the same source; (ii) where there are replications of problems, or lower-level instances of a general class of problems, or (iii) where the redesign requirement is at a high enough level of abstraction to solve a number of problems.

A final reason for the discrepancy is that it might be hard to generate solutions to some specific problems. Difficulty could relate to the usability problem identified, for instance, it is easier to generate user requirements for something that is absent (provide it) and something that is present and should be absent (discard it) than it is to provide a solution to a problem where something does and should exist but needs to be better designed. Another answer lies in the difficulty of coming up with solutions to problems in the absence of knowledge about how the user executes tasks. If this is the case then conducting a task analysis on the task(s) to be supported should provide more information about users' task knowledge and execution that then gives rise to more user requirements. This is what we found. The task analysis which took about the same time as the cognitive walk-through yielded 40 redesign requirements (see Dutt, 1993). However, the requirements were quite different, as expected mainly task- and functionality-oriented, with little overlap with the heuristic and cognitive walk-through results. Further work is presently being conducted on the validity of these findings and the implications for the stages in design at which task analysis and evaluation are best conducted and the resources needed to conduct task analyses and evaluation for the gains to be had.

Further questions about the utility of evaluations in generating requirements as solutions to usability problems relate to the improvements that are expected to result. For instance, how do we know that the user requirements led to a better system? This can be partially answered by the fact that further evaluations on the redesigned system led to slightly fewer usability problems and eradication of the usability problems judged as the most severe by independent judges, (Dutt, 1993).

Finally, it is necessary to know if the results obtained are in any way valid and consistent between designers in generating requirements from evaluation studies such that support for the process could be provided. A further series of studies have been conducted where designers not involved in this study have attempted to match the usability problems identified with the requirements generated in order to provide some view on validity. In addition, in a further study designers have taken the evaluation results and generated redesign requirements. The results will give some indication about the nature of the designer's task and whether it is possible to support the process of constructing more usable systems.

References

Dutt, A. (1993) *Evaluating evaluation methods*. Unpublished Advanced MSc thesis, Queen Mary and Westfield College, University of London.

Dutt, A. Johnson, H. & P. Johnson (1994) 'Evaluating evaluation methods'. In, G. Cockton, S.W. Draper & G.R.S. Weir (eds.) *People and Computers IX*, pp. 109-121.

Falzon, P. (1990) Personal communication.

Hamilton, F. (1996) 'Predictive evaluation using task knowledge structures', *Proceedings CHI '96*, Vancouver, April: ACM Press.

Lewis, C., P. Polson., C. Wharton & J. Rieman (1992) 'Testing a walk-through methodology for theory-based design of walk up and use interfaces'. *In proceedings of CHI90*, pp. 235-241.

Long, J.B & Dowell, J. (1989) 'Conceptions of the discipline of HCI: Craft, applied science and engineering'. *Proceedings of HCI89*.

Nielsen, J. & R. Molich (1990) 'Heuristic evaluation of user interfaces'. In *proceedings of CHI90*, pp. 373-380.

Norman, D. (1986) 'Cognitive engineering'. In, D.A Norman & S. Draper (eds.) *User-centred system design: New perspectives on human-computer interaction*, LEA: Hillsdale, NJ.

Payne, S. (1996) 'Cognitive psychology and cognitive technology'. *The Psychologist*, July 1996, pp. 309-312.

44 'Satisficing' in engineering design: psychological determinants and implications for design support

Linden J. Ball, Thomas C. Ormerod* and
Louise Maskill
University of Derby, UK
*Lancaster University, UK

Abstract

We report an investigation aimed at assessing the extent to which expert engineering designers generate and evaluate multiple solution alternatives in accordance with the prescriptive dictates of normative design methodologies. The study focussed upon six professional electronic engineers tackling an integrated circuit design problem. Verbal protocol data revealed a general failure to search for alternative solution concepts and a marked inclination to stick with early 'satisficing' solutions, even when these were showing deficiencies. We argue that whilst minimal solution search in design may sometimes be caused by motivational factors and working-memory limitations, its major determinant relates to inhibitory memory processes that arise subsequent to the recognition based emergence of familiar design solutions. We conclude by exploring the implications of minimal solution search for design support, with particular reference to an agent based indexing system which we are developing in order to facilitate the pursuit of design alternatives in engineering contexts.

Introduction

The way in which engineers develop solutions to design problems has important theoretical implications for psychological models of problem solving expertise in general and design expertise in particular (cf. Goel & Pirolli, 1992). At an applied level, understanding solution development in engineering design can greatly facilitate the formulation of techniques and tools for computer based design support (see Ball, Evans & Dennis, 1994). A useful approach to investigating the design process - and one which we adopt in the present paper - is to compare normative theories of good design practice as espoused in the prescriptive literature (e.g. Pahl & Beitz, 1984) with what designers actually do (cf. Ball & Ormerod, 1995).

The tenet of normative design theory which forms the focus of the present research is the notion that designers should generate and evaluate *multiple solution alternatives* when tackling a problem or subproblem (e.g. Cross, 1994). Adherence to this principle is claimed to maximize the designer's chance of attaining good - and potentially optimal - design solutions whilst minimising the possibility of early commitment to solutions that turn out to be inadequate. The prescriptive literature rarely claims that designers should search for a truly optimal solution, since it is recognized that the space of possible solutions is typically too large for this to be achieved. The emphasis is on deriving the best concept from a *range* of possibilities.

Solution search in design has been considered from a psychological perspective in the seminal work of Simon (1969). Similar to the prescriptive literature, Simon proposes that the search for alternatives is an important aspect of design activity. He also concurs with the view that this search will not be an optimising one because of the limited resources of the human information processing system. Indeed, Simon argues that the impossibility of attaining optimal solutions means that designers apply a 'satisficing' principle by means of which they search for acceptable design solutions and adhere to these after only moderate exploration of the full search space.

What, though, has empirical research revealed about the nature of solution search strategies in engineering design? Studies of software engineers (e.g. Kant, 1985; Adelson & Soloway, 1986) have indicated that both expert and novice designers rapidly develop a kernel idea which is subsequently refined. Ullman, Stauffer & Dietterich (1987) report a study in which graduate mechanical engineers became fixated upon initial solution ideas and failed to consider alternatives. This behaviour was seen both at the level of the overall design problem and at the level of each individual subproblem. Ball et al. (1994), in a study of pre-expert electronic engineers, observed that individual designers rarely generated and modelled alternative solution concepts but focussed upon initial (and often sub satisfactory) ideas which were iteratively improved until they reached a state of adequacy.

The empirical evidence seems, then, to support a view of solution search in design which is at odds with the prescriptive requirement to explore multiple solution options. However, no previous research on this theme has focussed on *expert* electronic engineers. A key aim of the present study was, therefore, to focus on experienced electronic designers in order further to generalize findings concerning the relationship between prescriptive views of solution search and actual design practice.

Methodological aspects of the study

Six electronic engineers (subsequently referred to by their initials) were recruited to the study. Five were professional designers from a large company. They had a minimum of three years' work experience in professional design situations. The sixth participant was an academic with considerable experience of developing commercial designs. All participants had worked on complex multi-levelled design tasks.

The problem used in the study had been written by a professional engineer and required the participants to design an integrated circuit in an image processing application. Some of this circuit's functional requirements were already detailed as mathematical algorithms whilst others necessitated the generation of appropriate hardware-implementable algorithms.

All participants undertook the problem individually and were requested to spend between one and three hours on the task. Participants were asked to think aloud throughout the session and a video camera was used to record all note making, sketching and verbalisation.

The protocol data were coded in a way which focussed on participants' solution generation behaviour. Whenever a solution idea was generated it was coded as being either an *initial* solution concept for a problem or an *alternative* solution concept for a problem. The latter category was further subdivided into: (i) alternatives having moderately to substantially different properties to any previous solution that had been generated for that problem; and (ii) alternatives having minimally different properties to a previous solution. In order to gain some insight into the nature of solution generation at different *levels* of design detail the protocol coding scheme also categorized solutions in terms of whether they were produced at a mathematical level, an abstract hardware level, or a detailed hardware level.

Results

The six participants stated that they had found the design problem novel, non-routine and difficult. JC was the only designer who struggled to make any real headway with the task and he halted his work without attempting many aspects of the specification. He was the least experienced of the designers studied, with just three years of company work behind him. The overall quality of the design solutions was evaluated by the individual who had written the specification. JC's solution was classified as sub-satisfactory in all respects. The other five solutions were classified as: satisfactory or nearly satisfactory as design concepts; requiring a large amount of detailed design work before implementation; capable of operating in real time; and having a fair amount of potential for success. These solutions all involved mathematical algorithms based around iterative constructs which could be implemented as hardware components, such as accumulators and arithmetic logic units. It should be noted that whilst the designers generated many concepts at mathematical and abstract hardware levels, few concepts were produced at the detailed hardware level. It was decided, therefore, to combine the hardware levels into a single category when quantifying the number of solution ideas that were generated.

Table 1
Number of initial and alternative solution concepts generated at the mathematical design level

Category of solution concept	DS	JO	IH	JF	JM	JC
Initial concepts (in relation design subproblems)	5	8	11	5	10	7
Alternative concepts (moderately or substantially different)	1	0	0	0	1	0
Alternative concepts (minimally different)	3	3	2	0	1	2

Table 2
Number of initial and alternative solution concepts generated at the hardware design level

Category of solution concept	DS	JO	IH	JF	JM	JC
Initial concepts (in relation to design subproblems)	32	45	23	26	23	7
Alternative concepts (moderately or substantially different)	2	1	0	1	2	0
Alternative concepts (minimally different)	2	1	1	0	0	0

   Solution generation data for each designer are presented in table 1 in relation to the mathematical level and in table 2 in relation to the hardware level. In line with the protocol coding, each table depicts the number of *initial* solution concepts generated and the number of *alternative* solution concepts generated. The later category is split into those alternatives possessing 'minimally' different properties to an initial concept and those possessing 'moderately or substantially' different properties.

These data reveal some striking aspects of commonality across the designers. In particular, they indicate that the engineers were generally failing to search for moderately or substantially alternative - and potentially better - solution concepts at both the mathematical level and the hardware level. The designers instead showed a marked inclination to stick with initial solution ideas even when these concepts were revealing definite signs of inadequacy. Indeed the present designers tended to iteratively 'patch up' solution ideas in order to make them adequate (as evidenced by the generation of minimally different variants of a solution) rather than devoting effort to the search for genuinely different lines of concept development.

These results clearly support previous findings which indicate that engineering designers often fail to pursue alternative solution ideas in accordance with the recommendations of prescriptive design theories. The present study, in generalising such observations to *expert* electronics design, lends credence to the possibility of developing a generic, domain independent account of design cognition (see Goel & Pirolli, 1992). Whilst the results indicate a failure of designers to generate multiple solution alternatives we also feel that they support a general notion of satisficing as espoused by Simon (1969) since the designers *were* concerned to make their chosen solutions adequate - even if this was through iterative improvements and the 'patching' of inadequacies (cf. Ullman et al., 1987).

Theoretical explanations of minimal solution search in design

One interpretation of minimal solution search in design is that it reflects a lack of *motivation* to seek better solutions when congenial ones are found. An argument against this account is that the present designers expressed a keen desire to achieve *good* solutions and exhibited frustration when ideas were not showing promise - yet still fixated upon these failing solutions. A second explanation of why designers fail to explore alternatives relates to the issue of 'bounded rationality' in cognition. As noted earlier, Simon (1969) suggests that since the search for optimal design solutions is computationally intractable, designers will only generate a small number of alternatives and choose the most promising of these. Even within this view, however, the emphasis is still on exploring a range of competing options. Ullman, Dietterich and Stauffer (1988, p. 45) take the bounded rationality argument a step further and suggest that 'multiple solution proposals (especially detailed proposals) are too complex to be handled well by human designers'. Their argument is that the difficulty is not so much the computational resources needed to search for alternatives, as the resources needed to deal with alternatives once they have been generated.

We propose another bounded rationality account of minimal solution search in design which is related to the properties of the human memory system. To understand

351

this explanation it is necessary to consider how solution ideas come to mind in the first place. What has emerged (see Smith & Browne, 1993) is support for the role of memory as the primary source of solution concepts. Theorists argue that skilled designers possess knowledge structures (i.e., schemas, plans or prototypes) reflecting previously used solutions. Such knowledge drives solution generation through so called case-based reasoning (Kolodner, 1993) which denotes a process of solution retrieval based on information available in the problem.

Given that designers' solution ideas stem primarily from their own memories via recognition-based retrieval, it is valuable to reflect upon the nature of human memory mechanisms since these may be contributing to the observation of minimal solution generation in design. Recognition is often viewed as revolving around processes of 'spreading activation' within memory (e.g. Rumelhart & McClelland, 1986). The essential idea is that incoming cues (concerning, say, key design requirements and constraints) serve to access associated information in the designer's long term memory (including the most salient solution concept in relation to those cues). In addition, the mere recognition of a salient solution idea (which may actually be sub-optimal in a current situation) sets up inhibitory activation so as to block the recognition of alternative solution ideas. Such mechanisms are typically beneficial since they enable rapid determination of the 'best' interpretation of a current situation. In design contexts, however, where the current situation may actually be highly multi faceted (e.g. in terms of the range of requirements and constraints that need to be considered) this mechanism may prove detrimental since it can lead to the rapid fixation upon an initial solution idea and the inability to generate substantially different (but possibly better) alternatives.

Implications of minimal solution search for design support

In light of possible explanations of minimal solution search in design the suggestion is that designers are not deviating from prescriptive design dictates out of choice, but rather because of the inherent nature of their cognitive systems. Indeed we are sympathetic to Ullman et al.'s (1987, p. 16) suggestion that 'it is conceivable that design is such a complex task that there are very few people who do it well. In this case, the methodologists may be correct, and our subjects may need to be retrained or provided with better design tools'. In our view it is unlikely that the retraining option is viable since it would seem necessary to have more than the motivation to pursue alternative designs if one is to overcome cognitive limitations. Instead the option of providing tools to assist designers in developing alternatives seems attractive and is a direction we are taking in our research.

Clearly, the mere provision of an enormous database of information about what solutions already exist for a particular design domain would not, in itself, facilitate multiple solution generation. One difficulty that needs to be overcome for such a database to be useful is that of how to facilitate access to the information that is *relevant* to a current problem. A related issue is how to encode information into the database in the first place so as maximize its effective retrieval in subsequent design situations. A third problem is that such a system must embody mechanisms that can actively promote consideration of alternative designs.

The approach that we are adopting in response to these difficulties is to introduce a degree of system initiated information retrieval, so that the tool can make some decisions on the user's behalf as to when, and from where, to retrieve information. The technology we are utilising in developing such a system is that of 'interface agents' (Laurel, 1993). These are discrete programs which monitor system and user activities. When a specific set of conditions arises the agent activates autonomously to carry out tasks. Interface agents not only offer a solution to the need for system initiated information retrieval, but their autonomous nature also means that they can encode information in a way that is minimally invasive. Agents are also able to undertake multiple information searches, and so facilitate presentation of solution alternatives to the designer who is using the system.

It is finally worth pointing out that our ideas about solution generation in design are not merely focussed on *solution reuse* - as appears to be the current convention, but also on the reuse of the actual process that led to a solution. In this way, our approach has much in common with proponents of 'design rationale' (e.g. Moran & Carroll, 1995) which attempts to improve design productivity by encouraging reflective examination by designers of the design process itself (including information concerning the problem specification, solution options and design critiques).

References

Adelson, B. & Soloway, E. (1986). A model of software design. *International Journal of Intelligent Systems,* Vol. 1, pp. 195-213.

Ball, L.J., Evans, JSt.B.T. & Dennis, I. (1994). 'Cognitive processes in engineering design: A longitudinal study'. *Ergonomics,* Vol. 37, pp. 1753-1786.

Ball, L.J. & Ormerod, T.C. (1995). 'Structured and opportunistic processing in design: A critical discussion'. *International Journal of Human-Computer Studies,* Vol. 43, pp. 131-151.

Cross, N. (1994). *Engineering Design Methods: Strategies for Product Design* (Second Edition). Wiley: Chichester.

Goel, V. & Pirolli, P. (1992). 'The structure of design problem spaces'. *Cognitive Science,* Vol. 16, pp. 395-429.

Kant, E. (1985). Understanding and automating algorithm design. *Proceedings of the International Joint Conference on Artificial Intelligence.* Morgan Kaufmann: Los Altos, CA.

Kolodner, J.L. (1993). *Case-Based Reasoning.* Morgan Kaufmann: San Mateo, CA.

Laurel, B. (1993). 'Interface agents', in B. Laurel (ed.), *The Art of HCI Design.* Addison-Wesley: Reading, Mass.

Moran, T.P. & Carroll, J.M. (1995). *Design Rationale: Concepts, Techniques and Use.* Lawrence Erlbaum Associates, Inc: Hillsdale, NJ.

Pahl, G. & Beitz, W. (1984). *Engineering Design.* Design Council: London.

Rumelhart, D.E. & McClelland, J.L. (eds.). (1986). *Parallel Distributed Processing: Explorations in the Microstructure of Cognition (Volume 1: Foundations).* MIT Press: Cambridge, Mass.

Simon, H.A. (1969). *The Sciences of the Artificial (First Edition).* MIT Press: Cambridge, Mass.

Smith, G.F. & Browne, G.J. (1993). Conceptual foundations of design problem solving. *IEEE Transactions on Systems, Man, and Cybernetics,* Vol. 23, pp. 1209-1219.

Ullman, D.G., Dietterich, T.G. & Stauffer, L.A. (1988). A model of the mechanical design process based on empirical data. *Artificial Intelligence for Engineering Design, Analysis and Manufacturing,* Vol. 2, pp. 33-52.

Ullman, D.G., Stauffer, L.A. & Dietterich, T.G. (1987). *Preliminary Results of an Experimental Study on the Mechanical Design Process.* Technical report 86-30-9, Oregon State University, Corvallis, Oregon.

Acknowledgements

This research was partly supported by an award made under the ESRC's 'Cognitive Engineering' Programme (Grant Reference: L127251027). We would like to acknowledge the assistance of Jonathan Evans, Ian Dennis, Phil Culverhouse and Kenn Lamb during the running of this study.

45 Modelling design processes of groups in industry: an empirical investigation of cooperative design work

Petra Badke-Schaub and Eckart Frankenberger*
Bamberg University, Germany
*Technical University of Darmstadt, Germany

Abstract

In the research project 'Teamwork in Engineering Design Practice' engineers and psychologists are investigating engineering design processes of teams in industry in order to get a more detailed understanding of the interdependencies in design practice. In four projects group design processes were observed and protocol analyses were performed. Additional data concerning the individual prerequisites, the group prerequisites and the environment were also gathered. By identifying phases of routine work on the one hand and 'critical situations' on the other hand the detailed design process was reduced to the crucial phases. Across the four projects 262 critical situations were identified. A further analysis identified the influencing factors of the different types of critical situations and their inter-relations.

Introduction

Successful companies have to meet the general demand for the development of products of higher quality at lower costs in even less time. This requires a parallel cycle of work in product development, as opposed to the traditional mainly sequential cycle. Consequently, engineering designers are collaborating more and more in teams across both departmental and even company borders (Haberfellner, Nagel, Becker, Büchel & von Massow, 1992).

In this situation, engineering designers are struggling not primarily with technical problems but rather with difficulties related to their social environment (Birkhofer, 1991; Ehrlenspiel, 1993).

Obviously, cooperative work in groups is more than merely an exchange of information. It is an inherent component of each type of work in design practice and imposes new demands on communication and cooperation. These demands raise important questions, such as how to organize teamwork in complex working conditions effectively, or how to lead a group and to communicate within a team, or which individual characteristics are important to be a good member of a team?

General aims of the research project

Besides the technical problems, the effectiveness of design processes in industry is determined by several non-technical factors. Thus, we based our investigation on a general starting model of four central influences on the design process in practice: 'individual prerequisites', 'prerequisites of the group', 'external conditions', and the 'characteristics of the task' (cf. figure 1 with examples).

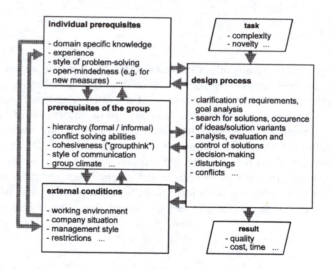

Figure 1   Factors influencing the design process and the result

The overall aim is to identify the factors influencing the design process, stemming from the fields of the individual prerequisites, the prerequisites of the group, the external conditions and the task, and then to build a model of cooperative design work in practice based on these findings. This model describes the interaction of the different factors on the design process and as a result allows conclusions concerning supportive and inhibiting mechanism in a design team to be drawn.

Approach and procedure

The detailed and exact surveillance of design practice has to focus on a very detailed observation of 'single cases' over an extended period of time. In two companies four different projects were observed and evaluated. The first investigation took place in a company producing agricultural machinery. Over the course of four weeks, the design process of a group of four designers redesigning a fruit press was observed and documented. The second investigation was carried out in a company in the capital goods industry. In this company a design team was developing and redesigning several components of a particle board production plant was observed for eight weeks.

Compiling data on the external conditions and on the design process

The external conditions of the design process, such as 'culture', the 'flow of information' and the 'communication' within the organization, and last but not least the 'direct working surroundings' within certain restrictions, are usually stable during the investigation and can therefore be assessed on just a single occasion by interviews and questionnaires. Contrary to this, the dynamic course of the design process requires a differentiated description of short time spans as determined by the duration of the relevant events. Therefore, both direct and indirect methods were used to compile data on the design process.

The primary *direct* method was the continuous non-participating observation of the design work. Sitting in the same room, a mechanical engineer observed the technical activities of the designers (e.g. working steps, subfunctions/ components, ideas and solution variants), and a psychologist concentrated his observations on the social aspects of the design process (e.g. ways of decision-making and group interactions). Furthermore, the video recordings of all phases of team-work and relevant phases of individual design work enabled us to review the description of the design process in specific interesting phases.

In order to fully account for the design process, it was also necessary to evaluate the non observed work of the engineers involved. Therefore, we used *indirect* methods such as a diary-sheet where the designers could note the subproblem(s) they worked on, how they solved problems or when they contacted their colleagues. Moreover, we analysed the documents and asked the designers about their work and their personal opinions on the elaboration of solutions. These 'indirect' data within the design process enriched and complemented the online protocols of the design process.

Compiling data on the individual and on the group prerequisites

The aim of this investigation was to comprehend rules and determining factors of cooperative engineering design work. From studies concerning individual and group-action-regulation behaviour in complex situations (cf. Badke-Schaub, 1993; Dörner, 1996; Rasmussen, Brehmer & Leplat, 1991) we identified suitable investigation methods which would yield statements on relevant aspects of group processes. Regarding these prerequisites, we chose the methods for compiling the variables as listed up in table 1.

Table 1
Methods for compiling prerequisites

Field of data	Variables	Methods
Biographical data	- age, qualification and experience - professional education, career	- semi structured interview - questionnaire
Work environment	- motivation; job satisfaction - evaluation of the organization - evaluation of the actual project	- semi structured interview - questionnaire
Ability for dealing with complex problems	- analysis, information gathering - action planning - dealing with time pressure - dealing with stress - conflict management, etc.	computer simulated microworlds: - fire (individual) - machine (individual) - Manutex (group)
Special competences	- heuristic competence - social competence - group organization	- questionnaire - observing and analysing interactions of the group
Abilities concerning the design process	- clarification of the task - search for conceptual solutions - selection and control - group organization	- diary sheets - marks-on-paper - online protocols (video recordings and tapes)

The biographical data and personal evaluations of the working conditions were compiled mainly by means of semi structured interviews, whereas the ability of dealing with complex problems was obtained by making the person solve three different computer simulated problems. These scenarios were used to study the ability of subjects to tackle novel problems in a complex, dynamic and intransparent system (cf. Dörner & Wearing, 1995). Contrary to design tasks, these computer simulated problems can be solved without any specified knowledge. In addition to the analysis of specific abilities in the computer simulated situations, the specific competences of the designers were assessed during the design work. Group interaction processes and structuring aspects in the design processes as well as in the computer scenarios were described in terms of individual and group behaviour patterns, such as role-taking behaviour and leader functions on the basis of specific event protocols.

Evaluation and modelling

Distinguishing between critical situations and routine work

The preparation and evaluation of the extensive data called for a new approach which connected the data from the different fields (design process, external conditions, the individual and the group) and allowed for both the description of the relations and the generalization of the findings. The basic aim of our method was the reduction of the documented design process to phases of routine work on the one hand and critical situations[1] on the other hand, where the design process took a new direction on a conceptual or embodiment design level. Critical situations were identified according to defined rules fitting the requirements of general problem solving processes (cf. Dörner, 1996; Ehrlenspiel, 1995) and can be classified, for example, into situations of goal or solution analysis, or disturbance or conflict management.

Establishing the model

In order to explain the 'mechanism' of a critical situation, we built a submodel of interrelations between the influencing factors and the process characteristics for each critical situation separately.

In the first investigation,[2] in all 262 critical situations were identified and explained by models of interrelations. Figure 2 illustrates the combination of the submodels of each critical situation to the entire model of interrelations.

Influencing factors and relations

The model of an entire design process represents each relation only once. The importance of the influencing factors can be evaluated by their frequency of

---

[1] This method of 'critical situations' sounds familiar by reference to the 'critical incidents' by Flanagan (1954) or the 'critical moves' by Goldschmidt (1996), but it follows another concept, as the identification of the critical situations takes place according to the requirements of the design process.

[2] In the second invesigation we identified and analysed 200 critical situations in the observed processes.

Petra Badke-Schaub and Eckart Frankenberger

occurrence in all critical situations or furthermore in the different types of critical situations. For example, we can analyse the factors which are mainly responsible for successful goal analysis. Figure 3 shows how factors are interacting in critical situations of the type of 'false analysis'. The thickness of the **arrows** depicts the frequency (in percent) of the relations occurring in this type of critical situation. The thickness of the *frames* depicts the frequency (in percent) of the factors identified in all critical situations of 'false analysis'. These flowcharts show the main mechanisms responsible for the more or less successful course of design work in critical situations. They allow questions such as 'which are the main factors responsible for a good goal analysis?' or 'which are the mechanisms leading to high costs?'

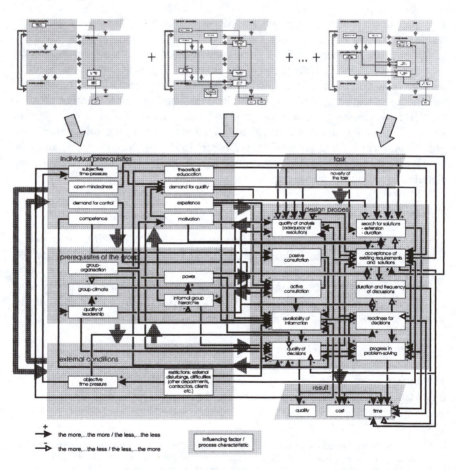

Figure 2   Model of relations of the first entire design process

360

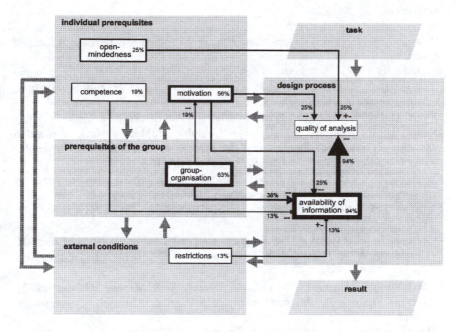

Figure 3   Factors and relations responsible for deficient analysis of solutions
(--: 'the less...the less'+-: 'the more...the less')

Figure 3 illustrates that in the design process of the first investigation non-availability of information was a crucial factor responsible for deficient analysis of solutions. The main reasons for lacking availability of information were limitations in group organization. Insufficient group organization resulted in negative motivation of the individuals because they often felt disturbed in their work.

Discussion

What is the benefit of such a model? Influencing factors from the fields of the individual, the group and the external conditions can be diagnosed in different phases of design work. The outcome of the model for the improvement of psychological theories is located mainly in the field of 'connecting different groups of influencing factors' in a natural surrounding. The description of the interactions of the various influencing factors provides insights into the conditions and consequences of factors in the design process which makes the model useful for design education and practice. Knowledge about important mechanisms of design work helps to develop suitable precautions in a company and allows an efficient and qualified design education at the university.

Petra Badke-Schaub and Eckart Frankenberger

References

Badke-Schaub, P. (1993) *Gruppen und komplexe Probleme.* Peter Lang: Frankfurt a.M.

Birkhofer, H. (1991), 'Methodik in der Konstruktionspraxis - Erfolge, Genzen und Perspektiven', in V. Hubka (ed.), *Proceedings of ICED 91.* Edition Heurista, Schriftenreihe WDK: Zürich.

Dörner, D. (1996) *The Logic of Failure.* Metropolitan Books: New York.

Dörner, D. & Wearing, A.J. (1995), 'Complex problem solving: Toward a (computer simulated) theory', in P.A. Frensch & J. Funke (eds.), *Complex Problem Solving: The European Perspective.* LEA: Hamburg.

Ehrlenspiel, K. (1995) *Integrierte Produktentwicklung. Methoden für Pro zeßorganisation, Produkterstellung und Konstruktion.* Hanser: München.

Flanagan, J. C. (1954), 'The critical incident technique'. *Psychological Bulletin,* Vol. 51, pp. 327-358.

Goldschmidt, G. (1996), 'The designer as a team of one', in N. Cross, H. Christiaans & K. Dorst (eds.), *Analysing Design Activity.* John Wiley: New York.

Haberfellner, R., Nagel, P., Becker, M., Büchel, A. & Massow, H. von (1992), *Systems Engineering: Methodik und Praxis.* Verlag Industrielle Organisation: Zürich.

Pahl, G. & Beitz, W. (1993) *Konstruktionslehre (3rd Edition).* Springer: Berlin, Heidelberg, New York, London, Paris, Tokyo.

Rasmussen, J., Brehmer, B. & Leplat, J. (eds.) (1991) *Distributed Decision Making.* John Wiley: Chichester.

46 Styles of problem solving and their importance in mechanical engineering design

Renate Eisentraut
University of Bamberg, Germany

Abstract

The focus of this paper is on individual styles of problem solving and their influences on the design process. In an empirical study, engineering design students worked on two computer simulated problems, which were used to investigate the subjects' problem solving behaviour in a non design context, and an adaptive design problem. The results demonstrate that individual styles of problem solving determine the way in which designers organize their design processes. Linking the subjects' proceeding to their performance, it furthermore turned out that – depending on the demand characteristics of the situation – each style of problem solving may be adequate in some situations and inadequate in other ones. Results suggest that diagnosing and training individual problem solving behaviour may be an essential contribution to optimize individual design processes and therefore should be a part of design education as well as of further vocational training.

Introduction

It is a widely accepted notion that the design of products is a process of complex problem solving (Wingert, 1985; Goldschmidt, 1996) in which human action regulation plays an important role. Among other things (e.g. the external conditions or the design task itself), the designer's individual prerequisites are one of the major sources of variance in the course of design processes and design results.

The investigation of those individual influences is the general goal of a joint research project in which psychologists from the University of Bamberg and mechanical engineers from the Technical University of Munich are looking at the design processes of engineers in controlled experiments (Dörner, Ehrlenspiel, Eisentraut & Günther, 1995; Eisentraut & Günther, 1996).

Among other individual prerequisites, one focus of our work is on individual styles of problem solving and their influences on the design process. Styles of problems solving are defined as describing an individual's preferred way of action regulation in dealing with complex problems. An essential feature of them is their stability, i.e. individual styles of problem solving manifest in different problem situations.

Methods

Participants of an empirical study were 15 engineering design students. Due to their different stages of study (varying from two to 14 semesters), the subjects also differed in their knowledge of design methodology.

The subjects worked on three problems. Two of them were computer simulated complex problems ('Machine' and 'Fire'), and the third one was an adaptive design problem ('Writing table').

Computer simulated problems

As opposed to the design problem, the computer simulated complex problems do not require specialized knowledge. Nevertheless, they are characterized by the same crucial features as complex problems in real life situations, e.g. opaqueness, interdependencies between variables, dynamic developmental trends or the existence of multiple goals (Badke-Schaub & Tisdale, 1995; Dörner, Kreuzig & Stäudel, 1983). Therefore, the requirements of the computer simulations with regard to planning and organizing the problem solving process are similar to those of any other complex problem. For our purpose, the computer simulated problems offer the possibility to investigate individual problem solving behaviour in a non design context.

In the computer simulated problem 'Machine' (Schaub, 1990), the subjects are asked to operate a process engineering plant that is composed of four production cycles. The main characteristics of the simulation are the various interconnections within and between the cycles, causing any intervention to have long term and side effects on the entire plant. In order to complete their job successfully, the subjects must be able to take those interdependencies as well as the developmental trends of the system into account while they are operating it.

In the computer simulated problem 'Fire' (Dörner & Pfeifer, 1991), the subjects are acting as Chiefs of a group of fire fighters in a large Swedish forests. Their task is to fight the fires which may break out at any time and at any place in the forest area. In order to complete this task, they are in command of several fire fighting engines and helicopters. The main characteristics of the simulation are the high time pressure and the need for acting immediately in the case of fire.

Design problem 'writing table'

In our investigation we used an adaptive design problem. The subjects are asked to modify the height and inclination adjustment of a writing table (Eisentraut & Günther, 1996). It is possible to roughly adjust the inclination of the present table, but not its height. One of the essential requirements is therefore to initiate a motion in another direction and to consider the coupling of the inclination adjustment with the additional height adjustment.

The experiment is carried out in a controlled laboratory situation. The subjects are working in a conventional design workspace with sketch paper and a drawing board. The time is limited to five hours. Before they begin, the subjects are asked to think aloud, i.e. to express all their thoughts verbally while designing. The entire process is recorded by means of a video camera.

Analysis

We have chosen a single case approach for data analysis. The focus of our analysis is on the subjects' proceeding in the design experiments and in the computer simulated problems. As we intend to compare the proceeding in the different problem situations to one another, we use the same system of categories for the three situations. The five categories are goal elaboration, information gathering, prognosing, planning and acting, and effect monitoring. They reflect the basic requirements of complex problem solving (Dörner, 1996) and can therefore be used as a scheme for the analysis of any problem solving process.

Results

Summary of the results

Summarizing the results of our study, there are two points to be mentioned. The first one concerns the stability of problem solving behaviour, and the second one concerns the adequacy of a given problem solving behaviour in a given situation.

First, comparing the subjects' proceeding in the three problem situations, it turned out that the ways in which an individual works on the different problems are quite similar. For example, similarities refer to the amount of information gathering or to the speed of action. We therefore conclude that a person's proceeding in complex problem situations significantly depends on his or her style of problem solving – regardless of whether the problem situation is a design problem, a computer simulated fire fight or the operation of a computer simulated plant. This result concurs with the observations of other authors on the stability of problem solving styles (e.g. Andresen & Schmid, 1993).

Second, we observed that an individual who works on the three situations in the same way (e.g. collects information very thoroughly) may be very successful in one situation, but less successful in another one (e.g. develops a good design solution, but has nearly all the forest area burnt down in 'Fire'). Therefore, our conclusion is that success in problem solving does not only depend on an individual's style of problem solving. Rather, it depends on whether a style of problem solving meets the demands of the situation. In some problem situations (e.g. 'Machine') it may be adequate to collect information thoroughly and to build up a model of the situation before acting. In other problem situations, however, the same way of proceeding may be rather inadequate because they require immediate action without any deeper analysis (e.g. 'Fire').

The subsequent description of two single cases may serve to illustrate those general findings. The subjects A and C were chosen for presentation because they showed very different ways of problem solving.

Two single case studies

Subject A While he is dealing with the computer simulation 'Machine', Subject A demands less information than most other subjects. At the same time, he intervenes much more to the system than any other subject. One reason for this may be that he runs the plant without any automation of processes (e.g., it is possible to have containers refilled automatically). He limits his interventions to an extent where he is still able to keep control of the system. Therefore, he even shuts down one of the production cycles. However, this action also indicates that he did not build up an adequate mental model which depicts the interdependencies within the machine. Nevertheless, he is quite successful, and he ends up with a good result.

In the microworld 'Fire', he does not prepare his engines well before fighting the fires (e.g., he does not take enough care of the villages which are situated in the forest area; although the subjects are told that preventing the villages from being burnt down is a matter of priority). He demands information only in situations where there is enough time to do so. However, he analyses neither the system nor the effects of his interventions in detail, resulting e.g. in the pointless repetition of commands. Once he is acquainted with the system, he reacts very quickly in the case of fire. Because of this, he once again intervenes a lot to the system. However, he is not as successful as in operating the 'Machine', and he ends up with an average result.

In the design experiment, subject A starts with a very short phase of task clarification. He tackles the whole problem swiftly with a very result oriented approach. Thus, he finishes after 2:49 hours instead of five hours available. He starts early to sketch a complete representation of the product, but on a rather abstract level. Several times when new problems arise in the layout he goes back to solve them on a more abstract and incomplete level. That is, he analyses parts of the problem only if this is necessary for his further proceeding. But he does not analyse the entire problem in detail. In the evaluation of the design, his work scored relatively high because it fulfils the requirements of the task and is also convenient to use.

Table 1
The ways of proceeding of subject A in the different problem situations

Machine	Fire	Design problem
	Bad preparation	Short task clarification
Few information requests	Information requests only if there is enough time	Analyses only if necessary (based on abstract, incomplete representations)
	Lack of analysis of the total system	
Lack of a model of the total system	Lack of effect analysis	Lack of analysis of the total system
Many interventions	Many interventions	Swift, result oriented
Lack of automation	Swift reactions to fire	way of proceeding
Shutting down one		(2:49 h)
production cycle		Complete represen- tation early in the process
Good result	Average result	Good result

Comparing the three problem situations (cf. table 1), subject A's style of problem solving can best be characterized as demanding little information, but acting rather swiftly and resolutely.

Subject C While he is operating the 'Machine', subject C is especially interested in information about the background and the functioning of the system. As he analyses the entire system in detail, he identifies the central problem of the machine and succeeds in solving it. His total number of interventions to the system is low, but his interventions are quite effective. In sum, he ends up with a good result.

In the microworld 'Fire', he starts with a good preparation for the fire fight (e.g. by spreading the engines all over the forest area). He demands a lot of information, even in dramatic situations. And he makes quite few interventions to the system. Once again, he succeeds in building up an adequate model of the system, and he makes use of this model in decision making and acting (e.g. by taking the direction

367

of the wind and the fire development into account when directing an engine towards a fire). As in the 'Machine', he is quite successful.

Table 2
The ways of proceeding of subject C in the different problem situations

Machine	Fire	Design problem
	Good preparation	Intensive task clarification
Background information requests	Many information requests	Intensive information requests and documentation
Model of the total system	Model of the total system	Model of the total system
Few, nevertheless effective interventions	Few interventions	Concrete subsolutions early in the process
Focus on the central problem	Developmental trends are taken into account	Lack of changes from layout to more abstract grades
Good result	Good result	Average result

In the design experiment, subject C uses the entire five hours available. In the beginning, he spends a lot of time on clarifying the task. Once again, he thoroughly collects information. He makes a lot of quantitative analyses and calculations, and he is documenting the whole process intensively. Opposed to subject A, he analyses his solutions in concrete but incomplete drawings and then later combines the good ones in a layout. Because of his intensive 'pre-analyses' it is not necessary for him to change from the layout grade back to more abstract grades. However, his solution was judged average, because it does not fulfil some central requirements. Subject C elaborated a desk of high weight which is difficult to handle and not safe for the user.

In sum (cf. table 2), he analyses complex problems thoroughly, collects detailed information and builds up a model of the problem situation before acting. Because of his analysis, he is able to solve problems by few, but effective interventions. His actions are well planned, and he is proceeding step by step, without any major jumps back to earlier stages of problem solving.

Conclusions

The results of our investigation demonstrate that individual styles of problem solving are influencing the course of design processes and that success in problem solving depends on whether a given style of problem solving meets the demands of the situation. But what are the conclusions for design education and design practice which can be derived from those results?

With respect to the influence of problem solving styles on design proceeding, the results suggest that diagnosing and training individual problem solving behaviour may be an essential contribution to optimize design processes and should therefore be included in design education as well as in further vocational training.

As the adequacy of a given style of problem solving depends on the demand characteristics of the situation, a good designer should be able to flexibly use different problem solving strategies and to actually chose the one which best meets the requirements of the situation. Therefore, designers should be trained in the ability to classify problem situations depending on their requirements and in the ability to flexibly adapt their problem solving strategies to the demands of the situation.

References

Andresen, N. & Schmid, U. (1993), 'Zur Invarianz von Problemlösestilen über verschiedene Bereiche'. *Zeitschrift für experimentelle und angewandte Psychologie, Band XI*, pp. 1-17.

Badke-Schaub, P. & Tisdale, T. (1995), 'Die Erforschung des menschlichen Handelns in komplexen Situationen' in B. Strauß & M. Kleinmann (eds.), *Computersimulierte Szenarien in der Personalarbeit* (pp. 43–56). Verlag für Angewandte Psychologie: Göttingen.

Dörner, D. (1996) *The Logic of Failure*. Metropolitan Books: New York.

Dörner, D., Ehrlenspiel, K., Eisentraut, R. & Günther, J. (1995), 'Empirical investigation of representations in conceptual and embodiment design' in V. Hubka (ed.), *Proceedings of ICED 95. Schriftenreihe WDK 23* (pp. 631–637). Edition Heurista: Zürich.

Dörner, D., Kreuzig, H.W. & Stäudel, T. (1983) *Lohhausen: Vom Umgang mit Unbestimmtheit und Komplexität*. Huber: Bern.

Eisentraut, R. & Günther, J. (1996), 'Individual Styles of Problem Solving and their Relation to Representations in the Design Process' in Ö. Akin & G. Saglamer (eds.), *Proceedings of the First International Symposium on Descriptive Models of Design*. Istanbul Technical University, Faculty of Architecture: Istanbul.

Goldschmidt, G. (1996), 'Capturing indeterminism: representation in the design problem space' in Ö. Akin & G. Saglamer (eds.), *Proceedings of the First International Symposium on Descriptive Models of Design*. Istanbul Technical University, Faculty of Architecture: Istanbul.

Renate Eisentraut

Wingert, B. (1985), 'Ist Konstruieren ein psychologischer Handlungstyp?' in V. Hubka (ed.), *Proceedings of ICED 85. Schriftenreihe WDK 12* (pp. 884-892). Edition Heurista: Zürich.

Acknowledgements

The research is sponsored by the Deutsche Forschungsgemeinschaft (Do 200/11-1 and Eh 46/21-3 'Denkabläufe beim Konstruieren').

47 Psychology of pointing: factors affecting the use of mice and trackballs on graphical user interfaces

Chris Baber
Industrial Ergonomics Group,
University of Birmingham, UK

Abstract

Graphical-user interfaces require the use of pointing devices. While there is some research into the relative performance of these devices, there has been little consideration given to the relationship between interaction devices and task activity. In this paper it is proposed that, counter to intuitions, differences in performance with different devices are more likely to arise from the planning required to perform a task than from the operation of the device itself. It is proposed that the nature of dialogue design requires consideration of how devices support planning of activity.

Introduction

In order to directly manipulate objects on the computer screen, the user requires a precise and rapid means of cursor positioning and control. In general, this activity is performed using a pointing device, which is now shipped as a standard with personal computers. In this paper, the psychology of using pointing devices will be considered. Use of pointing devices will be discussed in terms of a simple, hierarchical model of psychomotor skills.

Using mice and trackballs

Clearly, it is important for the user of a pointing device, such as a mouse or trackball, to be able to appreciate the relationship between the movement of the device and the movement of the cursor. It is equally important that the user can assimilate the

Chris Baber

device-cursor relationship in order to develop smooth action sequences; if one needed to operate a pointing device by continually moving a short distance and checking the movement, performance would be both time-consuming and frustrating. Many researchers feel that the mouse is easy to use and trouble free. However, there is some evidence to suggest that not all users are able to master the mouse with such ease; problems for new mouse users can stem from an inability to define appropriate actions or from inability to accurately relate mouse movement to cursor movement (Barker et al., 1990). This suggests that there is more to the use of a mouse than may be at first apparent. Despite these problems, the fact that so many people can use mice with little or no conscious effort suggests that they are able to assimilate this relationship. One of the questions to be addressed in this paper is whether this assimilation is a function of the cursor moving activity or whether it is influenced by the characteristics of a particular device. If it is simply a matter of learning cursor positioning, then there need not be any significant differences in performance between using different devices, say a trackball or a mouse. If, on the other hand, it is a matter of learning to pair device characteristics with task demands, then one might anticipate some relationship between device and performance.

Hierarchy of psychomotor skill in pointing device use

The literature on psychomotor skills is rich and diverse. One avenue of research of relevance to this paper concerns the study of cognitive-motor skills, e.g., typing, writing and drawing. In broad terms, models developed to explain these specific skills tend to employ a hierarchy of levels. For instance, the top level would be concerned with the semantic content of the context in which the skill was to be performed, e.g., labeling an image with different terms can lead people to produce different drawings; the differences arise not only from the end product but also from the sequences of actions performed. In order to progress from the top level to the level of action, further processing is required. The next level concerns the appropriate rules for combining actions and the appropriate actions to use. This requires some definition of syntax, together with recall from long-term memory. Having specified action and sequence, the next level involves specifying a routine for performing the action sequence. Some writers have termed this a motor program, although the term is not without controversy. The final level involves the performance of the action and the evaluation of the performance. Given these levels, it should be apparent that feedback and feed-forward loops will be employed in order to link levels and allow interpretation of lower level activity on the basis of higher level functioning.

Semantic level

I have been collecting reports of 'errors' made by people using pointing devices. For example, one user complained to a leading manufacturer that the foot pedal supplied

372

with the computer did not work; the foot pedal was, of course, the mouse. Another user pushed the mouse over the face of the computer screen, trying to move the cursor. What these examples share is the notion that the errors lay in the interpretation of the object, primarily in terms of defining its operation. As with other aspects of computer technology, people appear to define the devices in terms of properties which the devices share with other objects familiar to the users, or in terms of activities with which the users are more familiar.

Syntactic level

Activity will involve sequences of subactions. Typically, the subactions will vary in terms of duration and requirement for monitoring. For example, pointing will involve large ballistic movements followed by shorter movements of similar duration which involve checking position etc. (see figure 1). Furthermore, when performing sequences of actions there is a tendency to exhibit longer interkey times during third or fifth items than other items (Baber, in press). This is taken to indicate that planning of movement will involve chunks of actions, with updating of plans between chunks.

Taken together these hypotheses point to the need to consider the appropriate ratio of these subactions, e.g., movement in an unfamiliar space with a number of similar objects might have shorter ballistic phases (due to requirements for checking) than movement in a more familiar space or towards unique objects.

Action specification

While the appearance of the device can influence the interpretation and notion of appropriate actions, the layout of the interface can have a bearing on actions are planned. Baber (in press) found that encouraging users to plan actions spatially rather than sequentially led to improvements in performance. However, this effect was more significant for mouse than trackball. Furthermore, later work found no difference in performance between mouse and trackball for pointing to letter sequences forming words or non-words (although there was a significant performance advantage for words over non-words). This supports the notion that performance differences might not simply be device dependent, but relate to some interaction between device and task. One explanation of the 'spatial planning' result relates to the notion of compatibility, i.e., movement of the mouse had a greater mapping onto cursor movement than did movement of the trackball. The notion of compatibility for pointing devices has received scant attention in the human factors literature (Baber, 1996).

Performance/monitoring

Research into use of pointing devices has tended to focus on the performance aspect, in particular using Fitts' law as a paradigm (see over). Results suggest that direct pointing devices yield faster performance than indirect devices; that for pointing, mice and trackballs are similar (although mice seem to be faster), and that for dragging mice are superior to trackballs.

Fitts' law in HCI

Fitts' law predicts that movement time will increase logarithmically with an increase in the ratio of distance from start point to target to target width. The assumption underlying this law was that highly skilled, i.e., well learned, fast and accurate, performance would be limited by the capacity of the human motor system to process information. In order for Fitts' law to be viable as an explanation of human movement it is necessary to make to make the following assumptions (Walker et al., 1993):

(i) positioning movements can be decomposed into one or more discrete submovements;

(ii) each submovement travels a constant proportion of the remaining distance to the target;

(iii) each sub-movement has a constant duration;

(iv) sensory feedback is used to guide sub-movements;

(v) sub-movement sequences terminate as soon as the positioning movement reaches the target

The most commonly referenced expression of Fitts' law is from Fitts and Peterson (1964):

$$MT = a + b \log 2 \, (2A/W)$$

where: MT = movement time, a = a constant, b = a constant, A = amplitude of movement, i.e., distance from start point to target, W = target width.

Table 1 gives values for a and b, and the index of performance, IP, for a selection of interaction devices drawn from a number of studies. The Index of Performance is derived by dividing the tasks index of difficulty, ID, for the total movement time, MT. Index of Difficulty equals 2A/W. Also included is a column for the percentage of errors recorded during performance. It should be possible to derive figures for IP to allow interaction devices to be ranked; those exhibiting the highest IP ought to yield superior performance to devices with lower IPs.

There are several plausible explanations for the differences in values of IP obtained. MacKenzie (1992) provides a detailed account of possible deficiencies in experimental design and analysis across the studies, noting in particular the alarmingly high proportion of negative intercept values. He points to factors such as differences in the manner in which errors are handled; the differences between devices; differences between the characteristics of the tasks used in the study. For example, both MacKenzie et al. (1991) and Gillan et al. (1990) have found differences in performance for pointing and dragging tasks.

Table 1
Summary data of studies using Fitts' law in HCI

Device	IP	a	b	source
Joystick (isometric)	4.5	990	220	Card et al. (1978)
Joystick (isometric)	1.2	-587	861	Epps (1986)
Mouse	10.4	1030	96	Card et al. (1978)
Mouse	2.6	108	392	Epps (1986)
Mouse	60	-107	223	MacKenzie et al. (1991)
Trackball	2.9	282	347	Epps (1986)
Trackball	101	75	300	MacKenzie et al. (1991)

Phases of cursor movement

Any psychomotor skill can be decomposed into a number of phases (Rosenbaum, 1991). While researchers accept that total movement time can be decomposed into sub-movements, there is evidence to suggest that sub-movements are highly variable, both in terms of duration and amplitude (see figure 1). Positioning movements do not end precisely when a target is reached, but incorporate some 'on target' phase, possibly involving verification of performance (see figure 1). In cursor positioning tasks, once a target has been selected, the user will define a path to the object; in effect, aiming the cursor and then, using the device at hand, moving it towards the object. One can expand this simple description by noting that movement needs to be planned and verified. If we concentrate on moving a cursor, using a mouse, we find that movement time can be divided into an initiation period, followed by a sub-movement, often followed by a pause, then another sub-movement and pause, and a verification time (Barker et al., 1990; Walker et al., 1994).

Chunking

Baber (in press) shows that cursor positioning sequences involve chunks of three to four items, with boundaries (marked by longer than mean times) occurring at around three items. It is interesting to note that there were more planning boundaries in the trackball condition than in the mouse condition. It should be noted that these boundaries need not necessarily be solely points for planning, but will also represent points for confirming previous action or for checking device grip. One implication of this is that cursor positioning sequences should be designed to consist of three moves. In general, this guideline appears to be followed on many packages, for

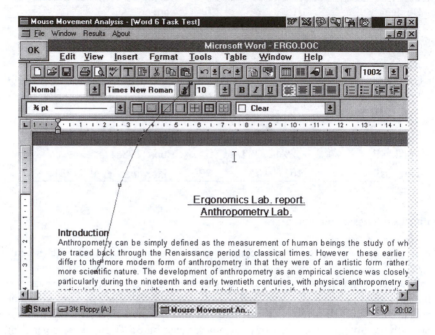

Figure 1   Phases of cursor positioning time

example, to change a word from plain text to bold using ClarisWorks, I select the word, select the style menu and select the bold menu item (i.e., three cursor movements). To change a word in Word for Windows, I select the word then select the B icon. Figure 1 illustrates phases of cursor positioning. Cursor positions were sampled at 50 ms intervals (using software written for this project in C++). Notice that the distance between initial points are larger than later points. This is typical of movement activity, with ballistic phases followed by corrective phases. Notice also the points on the word and on the icon, showing pauses at the start and on-target.

Spatial or sequential use of GUI

Superior performance for spatial over sequential task performance was noted above. However, it is proposed that dialogues are often designed sequentially rather than spatially (even in the age of GUI). For example, in order to enter a command, users still need to proceed through a sequence of stages, e.g., grasp mouse, find cursor, move cursor to File menu heading, press mouse button, drag cursor down menu to Save, release button. Hesse and Hahn (1994) show that interface layout has a bearing on the execution of actions, and the subsequent stages of monitoring the effects of the action. Thus, different layouts of interfaces, and different ways in which a user can interact with them, may require different forms of action planning and execution. This implies that the planning of activity can be influenced by the users interpretation of objects in the display.

Conclusions

In this paper, recent research by the author has been considered in terms of a simple, hierarchical model of pointing in HCI. It is proposed that dialogues tend to rely on sequences of task activity, but that performance could be improved when tasks are planned spatially. However, this performance effect also illustrates the interaction between device and task. It is proposed that one reason why there is some ambiguity in the literature as to differences in device rating arises simply from differences in the nature of tasks employed in the studies. More importantly, it is suggested that dialogue design for interfaces involving pointing devices can be improved by considering the potential of spatial planning. This work raises a number of questions concerning the manner in which people use pointing devices.

References

Allard, F. & Starkes, J.L. (1988), 'Motor-skill experts in sports, dance and other domains', in K.A. Ericsson & J. Smith (eds.), *Toward a General Theory of Expertise*. Cambridge University Press: Cambridge.

Baber, C. (1996), *Beyond the Desktop: designing and using interaction devices*. Academic Press: London.

Baber, C. (in press), 'Cursor positioning with mice and trackballs'. *International Journal of Cognitive Ergonomics*.

Barker, D., Carey, M.S. & Taylor, R.G. (1990), 'Factors underlying mouse pointing performance', In E.J. Lovesey (ed.), *Contemporary Ergonomics 1990*. Taylor and Francis: London, pp. 359-364.

Card, S. K., English, W.& Burr, B. (1978), 'Evaluation of a mouse, rate-controlled isometric joystick, step keys and text keys for text selection on a CRT'. *Ergonomics,* Vol. 21, pp. 601-613.

Epps, B.W. (1986), 'Comparison of 6 cursor control devices based on Fitts' law models' in, *Proceedings of the 30th Annual Meeting of the Human Factors Society*. Human Factors Society: Santa Monica, CA, pp. 327-331.

Fitts, P.M. & Peterson, J.R. (1963), 'Information capacity of discrete motor responses'. *Journal of Experimental Psychology,* Vol. 47, pp. 381-391.

Chris Baber

Gillan, D.J., Holden, K., Adams, S., Rudisill, M.& Magee, L. (1990), 'How does Fitts' law fit pointing and dragging?', *CHI'90*. ACM: New York, pp. 227-234.

Hesse, F.W. & Hahn, C. (1994) 'The impact of interface-induced handling requirements on action generation in technical system control', *Behaviour and Information Technology,* Vol. 13, pp. 228-238.

MacKenzie, I.S. (1992) 'Fitts' law as a research and design tool in human-computer interaction'. *Human-Computer Interaction,* Vol. 7, pp. 91-139.

MacKenzie, I.S., Sellen, A. & Buxton, W. (1991), 'A comparison of input devices in elemental pointing and dragging tasks', *CHI'91*. ACM: New York, pp. 161-166.

Rosenbaum, D.A. (1991). *Human Motor Control.* Academic Press: San Diego.

Walker, N., Meyer, D.E. & Smelcer, J.B. (1993), 'Spatial and temporal characteristics of rapid cursor-positioning movements with electromechanical mice'. *Human Factors,* Vol. 35, pp. 431-458.

48 Communicating human-computer interaction design intent: requirements for recycling throwaway prototypes

Carl Myhill and Peter Brooks*
SFK Technology Ltd, UK
*Northwold Systems and Services Ltd, UK

Abstract

Two long-term participant observation case studies are summarized which investigated a commercial software production process following the introduction of a specialist human-computer interaction role in the development team. Results are presented as a conceptual model of 'categories of influence' in which the majority of categories are issues which effect mutual understanding within the team. Some of these categories are considered 'facts', whilst others are more dynamic and thereby more realistic targets for improvement. The use of visual prototyping is confirmed as a powerful method of sharing mutual understanding of the software under production and is suggested as a way of making improvements to several of the dynamic categories. However, flaws in this mode of use of visual prototypes are apparent from the data but ways in which a new approach to visual prototyping could have considerable potential are identified.

Introduction: human-computer interaction within multidisciplinary design teams

Probably because of its relative recency, the role of the human-computer interaction (HCI) practitioner is not well researched or prescribed. However, with more software companies subscribing to the concept of user-centred design, more companies are aiming to make it more explicit and integrated within the development process of their organization (Karat, 1996). Karat has emphasized, however, that development requires coordinated action of a number of people and that we must move beyond just focusing attention on user involvement to also consider '...the difficult necessity of multidisciplinary communication in design' (p. 20). Even before the advent of multidisciplinary teams, communication difficulties within software teams were recognized (e.g. Brooks, 1995). Erickson (1996) has described software design as a distributed social process in which communication plays a vital role and has suggested that design tools are needed to deal with an indeterminacy which exists because design practitioners are not presented with well-formed problems. Indeed, it is suggested that because human-computer interaction design involves many people from widely varying backgrounds there is a social dimension which '.. considerably expands the scope of messy, indeterminate situations' (p. 35).

There is an identified need, therefore, to examine software team requirements for user-centred design support. Proposals for tools and methods for user-centred design have so far predominantly been in isolation of the social, multidisciplinary team context. Indeed, tools such as integrated project support environments (IPSEs) have been criticized for imposing a structure which burdens the way software is developed (LeQuesne, 1988). This is perhaps not surprising when one considers, as emphasized by Carey, McKerlie, Bubie & Wilson (1991), that the design process is inherently opportunistic and any attempt to rigidly structure it will be either detrimental or ignored.

However, some tools can be identified as having value for assisting a common understanding of the design across the development team. In particular, the use of visual prototypes is recognized as a means to get requirements right before production code is produced (Preece, Rogers, Sharp, Benyon, Holland & Carey, 1995). Although there are many different types of prototypes that can be used within software development (Myhill, Cocker & Brooks, 1994), visual prototypes are typically animated software prototypes which present a facade of the proposed software system in order to allow intended users to understand, and contribute to, what the software would do and what it would look like. When requirements are established it is traditional to view the prototype as throwaway, with programming code used in the prototype being discarded and production code written from scratch (Overmyer, 1991).

The main aim of the study described below was to examine opportunities for increasing user-centred work practice during bespoke software development within a mature software engineering environment. A secondary aim was to examine the potential of visual prototyping techniques which were already adopted within that organization for achieving successful projects A new and dedicated HCI role within a development team was created and offered the opportunity to research the effects on and within that team. Consistent with the research aims, a deliberately exploratory and revelatory case study approach was adopted (Yin, 1994) in which the HCI practitioner (introduced into the team for commercial aims) was also the participant observer (for research purposes).

Overview of procedure and software projects

Case studies were carried out sequentially on two software projects. In this way potential bias due to 'knee jerk' reactions to a new team member and a new role and unfamiliarity within the team and inexperience on the part of the HCI designer in the first software project was eliminated by observing a second project with essentially the same team. In addition, by examining two quite different software developments the scope and relevance of the case studies were broadened and enabled fundamental issues which were identified to be emphasized if confirmed.

In study one a chronological description of software development issues relating to the introduction of HCI considerations was recorded. This chronology and other documentation was content analysed and used as a basis for a workshop involving the participant observer with two other HCI practitioners with research experience. The results of the content analysis provided a structure and focus for study two.

Both software projects were of similar scale and duration (approximately one year). For study one the responsibility for the software user interface was explicitly given to an HCI designer for the first time within this organization instead of being tacitly distributed among programmers. The software developed aimed to utilize knowledge based systems technology to assist mechanical engineers in selecting and specifying flow control valves within process plant design. The software project for study two developed a bespoke water resource scheduling system.

Results and discussion: categories of influence within the HCI role

Many issues relating to the introduction of HCI into mainstream software development arose and influenced the production of the software. Detailed analysis synthesized these into dominant 'categories of influence' represented in a symbolic Venn diagram conceptual model shown in figure 1. The model is symbolic in as much as many of the 'categories of influence' represent concepts which strictly cannot be thought of as exclusive to one category. The model shows three intersecting 'groups' of issues found to affect the integration of HCI: 'people issues', 'representation issues' and 'life cycle issues'. The 'categories of influence' are seen as strongly associated with one, two or all of these groups. Full explanation of this conceptual model is beyond the scope of this paper but there are several features of the model which are considered key and central to the role of visual prototyping.

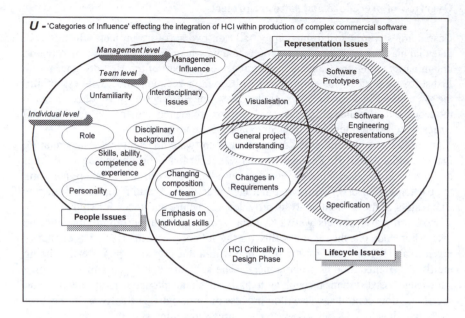

Figure 1   **Venn diagram model of 'categories of influence' affecting the integration of human-computer interaction design practice**

The majority of 'categories of influence' were related to various aspects of comprehension and shared understanding within the software team. Some categories identified relate to aspects which aim to assist comprehension and mutual understanding within the team, e.g. software engineering representations. Whilst others seek to explain why comprehension difficulties may exist, e.g. changing composition of the team.

Many 'categories of influence' provide a context for the comprehension difficulties that existed in the development of the software. These can be considered 'facts of commercial life' (table 1) which would require major reorganization at development process, culture and management levels to be effectively addressed.

After discounting the majority of 'categories of influence' which are 'facts' the remaining categories (shaded in figure 1) are predominantly those which aim to facilitate understanding of the software under production and could be realistically targeted to improve comprehension within the development team (see table 2).

Table 1
'Categories of influence' considered as 'facts' of commercial software development affecting comprehension (reference to other literature in the table identifies results which confirm findings of other authors)

'Categories of influence' considered as 'facts'	The reason for them being considered 'facts'
Characteristics of Individuals in the development team are diverse, i.e. personality, disciplinary background and skills, competence and experience	Hand picked teams are a rarity in software development. People are usually assigned to projects according to their availability rather than personal characteristics
Individual differences are apparent in people's ability to conceptualize the software being produced (Curtis, Krasner, Shen & Iscoe, 1987)	Team members are rarely selected to work on a project because of their ability to conceptualize
Familiarity between team members appears to be an important influence in maintaining a mutual understanding of the software	Team members are rarely selected for a project on the basis of their familiarity
Interdisciplinary teams experience problems understanding each other (Kim, 1990)	Interdisciplinary teams are now a requirement in complex software development
The discontinuity of development teams makes it hard for a team to maintain a shared understanding of exactly what they are aiming to produce	The composition of a development team often needs to change mid project to optimize the allocation of resources and make effective use of specialists
Changes in requirements need to be understood by team members but introduce further scope for misunderstanding	Changes in requirements are endemic to the software process (Curtis, et al., 1987; Harker, 1991; Brooks, 1995)
Emphasis placed on the skills of specialists within a software team (e.g. mathematical modellers) provides further barriers to mutual team comprehension of the development	In reality skills of individual specialists within the software team have become essential
Specification documents written to explain and describe software requirements and the software under development are aimed at such a diverse readership with equally diverse requirements that they become a poor compromise	Limited time and resources restrict the amount of time developers can spend writing specifications, yet these documents still have to serve many purposes as diverse as contracts with the client to technical working documents for the development team

383

Carl Myhill and Peter Brooks

Table 2
'Categories of influence' considered realistic targets for improvements to comprehension in the software team

'Categories of influence' considered realistic targets for improvement in comprehension	Scope for improvement in comprehension
Software engineering representations require training to interpret and do not address 'facts' such as the existence of interdisciplinary teams and individual differences (including ability to visualize)	The development of more accessible representations which would suit the diversity of individuals present
The diversity of uses and readers of written specifications almost dictates that it cannot serve all uses and readers well	Improvement to the quality of the authoring of specifications could generate improvements in their utility (however, such skills are rarely available)
General project understanding, such as knowledge of the domain or project objectives, is often not accessible to all team members	Improvements to team members' general project understanding can only help them make better 'day to day' decisions
Methods used to help team members visualize and maintain a consistent mutual understanding are scarce.	Visual prototypes are the most obvious way to improve team members' visualization and maintenance of a mutual team understanding.
Visual prototypes provide a common representational currency for all team members (as well as users and clients) but are not without problems.	Making more effective use of visual prototypes can improve team members' visualization of the software under production.

Visual prototypes were used in both projects and particularly extensively in the second in order to facilitate communication with the client and users. As more people were brought on to the projects to begin work on the production code, the visual prototypes were an invaluable vehicle for explaining design intent. The visual prototype enabled team members to visualize and share a vision of what the software they were producing should eventually be like. The visual prototype also became a common currency for team members from different disciplines to communicate and understand each other without the need to learn a technical notation.

Utilizing visual prototypes therefore addressed many of the 'facts' that the commercial development context had to deal with as potential pitfalls. They provided a view on the specification that all could understand. They were observed

384

to allow for individual differences in the development team (e.g. mixed abilities and skills) as well as the interdisciplinary nature of software development and did not impose additional structure or administrative burdens.

However, the use of visual prototypes was not without problems. In particular, they were ambiguous and as a result open to different interpretations from different team members. They were sometimes inaccessible to team members because they were (unintentionally) designed to be operated by the person who constructed them. Furthermore, design intent illustrated in the visual prototype often needed to be explained by the HCI designer and design rationale for the HCI design reflected in the visual prototype was not captured or communicated by the prototype itself. Finally, without an understanding of the design rationale there was no real basis for negotiation between the HCI designer and members of the technical core of the team.

Conclusion: the potential of recycling throwaway prototypes

There are many complexities involved in the successful incorporation of human-computer interaction design practice within software development. There is a need to understand and optimize the increasingly multidisciplinary nature of good software design. Communication and collaboration are believed to be central to successful design but they have many barriers to success. Much more research is required and the complexity of the conceptual model developed indicates the wide range of issues which need to be addressed.

Within the current focus on visual prototyping it would appear unnecessary as well as inappropriate to throwaway a visual prototype if this prototype can be 'recycled' into something used to facilitate comprehension of design intent within the development team. Future research should therefore explore the possibilities for placing the visual prototype at the centre of an explanation medium which aims to utilize their positive benefits whilst addressing the flaws in the approach identified. In order to achieve this, four key features of a recyclable visual prototype are identified. It must *reduce ambiguity*; for example, allowing HCI designers to explain every aspect of the visual prototype, including making clear which aspects are well thought out and which require further work. It must provide *accessibility*; for example, through providing 'animated walkthroughs' and 'explanations' which allow any design team member to examine the visual prototype unaided. Related to this, it should *reduce the need for the HCI designer to be involved* in what can be extremely time consuming and often repetitive explanations of 'functionality' to other members of the software team. Finally, it should capture design rationale in order to provide a basis for negotiation between programmer and HCI designer. Such negotiation could lead to the discovery of alternative implementation approaches which the HCI designer was unaware of or could lead to the HCI designer making compromises which could save the development team weeks of work.

References

Brooks, F.P. Jr. (1995) *The Mythical Man Month (20th Anniversary Edition)*. Addison-Wesley: Reading, MA.

Carey, T., McKerlie, D., Bubie, W. and Wilson, J. (1991) Communicating human factors expertise through design rationales and scenarios. In D. Diaper and N. Hammond (eds.), *People and Computers VI*. Cambridge University Press: Cambridge.

Curtis, B. , Krasner, H., Shen, V. & Iscoe, N. (1987) 'On building software process models under the lamppost'. In, *Proceedings of the Ninth International Conference on Software Engineering*, pp. 96-103.

Erickson, T. (1996) 'Design as storytelling'. *Interactions*, Vol. 3, pp. 30-35.

Harker, S. (1991) 'Requirements specification and the role of prototyping in current practice', in J.Karat (ed.), *Taking Software Design Seriously*. Academic Press: London.

Karat, J. (1996) 'User centred design: quality or quackery?'. *Interactions*, Vol. 3, pp. 18-20.

Kim, S. (1990) 'Interdisciplinary cooperation', in B. Laurel (ed.), *The Art of Human Computer Interface Design*. Addison-Wesley: Reading, MA.

LeQuesne, P.N. (1988). 'Individual and Organisational factors and the design of IPSEs' In *The Computer Journal*, Vol. 31, No. 5.

Myhill, C., Cocker, S. & Brooks, P. (1994) 'A practical prototyping process for human-centred software development: when, why and how to prototype'. In D. England (ed.), *HCI'94 - People and Computers IX Ancillary Proceedings*.

Overmyer, S.P. (1991) 'Revolutionary vs. Evolutionary rapid prototyping: balancing software productivity and HCI design concerns', in H.-J. Bullinger (ed.), *Human Aspects in Computing: Design and Use of Interactive Systems and Work with Terminals*. Elsevier Science Publishers: B.V.

Preece, J., Rogers, Y., Sharp, H., Benyon, D., Holland, S. and Carey, T. (1994) *Human-Computer Interaction*. Addison-Wesley: Reading, MA.

Yin, R. (1994) *Case Study Research - Design and Methods (2nd Edition)*. Sage: Thousand Oaks, CA.

Acknowledgements

The work described was conducted while Carl Myhill was a research student within the Department of Applied Psychology at Cranfield University and in which Peter Brooks was an academic staff member. The work was funded by a Postgraduate Training Partnership Award from EPSRC and the DTI. Thanks are due to all PTP scheme collaborators; in particular, management and colleagues of SFK and BHR. Special thanks go to Stephen Cocker for his help with study one.

49 Metaphors in software engineering

Briony J. Oates and Helen Gavin
University of Teesside, UK

Abstract

The nature of software engineering and its methods is discussed, and some limitations of the conventional methods are reviewed, particularly the implicit use of a machine metaphor and a philosophy based upon technical rationality, mechanism and positivism. A method based upon the explicit use of a range of metaphors is proposed, utilising cognitive psychology theory on analogical and metaphorical thinking. A research method for analysing and developing such an artefact is outlined. The use and acceptance of such a method would require a move away from positivism towards interpretivism. It is hoped that the work will lead to improved software engineering practices and computer-based systems.

The nature of software engineering

The discipline of software engineering is concerned with the specification, development, management and evolution of software systems. These systems are abstract, in that they do not have any physical form, so that, unlike other engineering disciplines, software engineering is not constrained by physical laws or by manufacturing processes (Sommerville, 1996). Software systems are usually complex, invisible, and subject to the need for frequent change. Unlike other engineering disciplines, software engineers cannot exhaustively test their end product. There is, therefore, a need to focus on models and the *method* of production, in the hope that a 'good' method will produce a 'good' product.

Avison & Fitzgerald (1995) suggest that methods are needed in order to achieve a better end product, a better development process and a standardised process. Jayaratna (1994) describes a systemic relationship between the three inter-dependent components of the problem-solver (method user), the problem situation (method context) and the problem-solving process (method). Oates (1995) suggests that although there is a single problem-solving role, it is often occupied by more than one person - a method therefore needs to help the individuals communicate and also provide support for the delegation and co-ordination of work in the problem-solving team. Jayaratna (1994) also distinguishes between the created method as documented, the adopted/adapted method as used by the problem-solver, since s/he interprets the created method and adapts it to suit (either consciously or sub-consciously), and the method-in-use, since the method may need to be changed dynamically to suit changing perceptions and circumstances. Bell & Oates (1994) suggest that a method itself could be conceived of as consisting of seven elements: an initial input and final output, a model set, a language set for the representation of the models, a sequence of steps, guidance, and an underlying philosophy.

Different methods have different underlying philosophies. A distinction is often drawn between 'hard' methods, which conceive of information systems as primarily technical artefacts with social implications, and 'soft' methods, which conceive of information systems as social systems which may be implemented technically. Hirschheim & Klein (1989) use two intersecting axes (subjective-objective, and order-conflict) to characterise the different philosophies of systems development methods. The dominant approaches in software engineering are 'hard' methods, in the 'functionalist' paradigm, represented by the objective-order quadrant. This uses rational thinking, which is associated with mechanistic thinking (Dahlbom & Mathiassen, 1993), a world view or philosophy containing ideas of representation, formalization, order, control, and thinking as computation, with the underlying assumption that the world, a body, or society, can be seen as a machine (that is, a machine metaphor is being used to understand and explain something). 'Soft' methods are more interpretive in nature, recognising that individuals may each see reality differently, and providing support for communicating and negotiating different interpretations.

Software engineering is therefore a process involving the interaction between people in an organization, a development team, a method and a product. The product itself has two parts: a technical system as perceived by the software engineers, and its interface, with which the end users interact. The nature of each of these entities, and the relationships between them, is subject to change.

The problems of current methods

Software engineering can be seen as 'technical rationality' (Schon, 1983), that is, deciding upon the appropriate means to achieve a given end. However, like many other professions, software engineering is faced with situations of complexity, uncertainty, instability and uniqueness. Many software systems are designed for organisations, which are complex, dynamic entities. The software engineering process involves working with people within these organisations, who are each unique and unpredictable. Where a team of software engineers is at work, it too is an organisation. The 'means' (software) to achieve the desired end is a relatively new commodity, without a wealth of accumulated experience about the strengths, weaknesses, costs, benefits etc. of particular software 'solutions', so there is uncertainty about the means themselves. The discipline itself is immature, with new models, methods, tools and paradigms regularly being proposed, and often seen as 'silver bullets' (Brooks, 1987).

'Hard' methods are criticised because they do not adequately recognise the social aspects of software systems and their development. 'Soft' methods are criticised because they concentrate on 'problem setting' without addressing the technical aspects of actually constructing a system. Various attempts have been made to link 'hard' and 'soft' methods together, but the necessary 'philosophical shift' between phenomenology and positivism is generally problematic (Jayaratna, 1992). Fitzgerald (1995) summarises the problems in the application of methods as:

(i)   poverty of the rational, technical paradigm (that there is only one interpretation, and the 'true' requirements can be specified);

(ii) goal displacement (focussing on following the method rather than developing a system);

(iii) assumption that methods are universally applicable (rather than recognising the uniqueness of each situation);

(iv) an inadequate recognition of developer-embodied factors (that development is an artistic activity taking place in a complex social context).

It has been suggested that the education of software engineers needs to be broadened, to include the social aspects of systems development and computerization (Kling, 1994). However, the syllabus for software engineers is already full. An alternative might be to introduce the conscious use of metaphors into software engineering methods allowing engineers to transfer knowledge acquired in one domain to a new domain. In the field of organizational analysis, Morgan (1986) shows how a range of metaphors can be used in order to understand and change organizations. Morgan (1986, 1993) suggests that the use of metaphors pervades how we understand the world. By using a range of metaphors we can produce a diagnostic reading of the situation under investigation, a critical evaluation of the significance of the different interpretations produced, and finally the metaphors give us systematic ways of thinking about how we can or should act in a given situation. Morgan (1986) points to a growing literature which demonstrates the 'impact of metaphor on the way we think, on our language, and on systems of scientific and everyday knowledge' (pp. 345-6). This research aims to examine whether the conscious use of a range of metaphors would be a useful technique in a software engineering method.

Metaphors are already used in human-computer interaction for designing the user interface e.g. the familiar desktop metaphor. Metaphors might also be useful in understanding the development team, the development context (e.g. the host organisation) and the end product. Some authors (Coyne, 1995; Avison & Wood-

Harper, 1995) have suggested that method itself should be considered as a metaphor. It should be noted that the use of metaphors would involve a move away from positivism, which is dominant in software engineering, towards interpretivism.

Contribution of cognitive psychology

Payne (1996) argues that the design of technologies can benefit from cognitive psychology and points to three promising research areas in the theory based evaluation of human-machine systems, supporting the design process and the study of cognitive artefacts. This research is aimed at supporting the design process, drawing upon cognitive theories of thinking via metaphors (see for example, Holyoak and Thagard, 1995; MacCormac, 1985), and also offering pragmatic support by, for example, devising suitable documentation techniques to record the metaphors used in problem solving and their influence on decision making. Furthermore, a software engineering method is in fact a kind of cognitive artefact.

Holyoak and Thagard (1995) argue that metaphor and analogy are similar: both are understood by finding a mapping between the target domain (the topic of the metaphor or analogy) and the source domain. For example, using an organism metaphor to understand an organization encourages us to consider how organizations are born, grow, develop, decline and die, and how they adapt to changing environments (Morgan, 1986). Holyoak and Thagard (1995) suggest that the degree to which an analogy is viewed as metaphorical will tend to increase the more remote the target and source domains are from each other. They propose a theory of analogical (and metaphorical) thinking, based on the simultaneous satisfaction of the constraints of similarity, structure and purpose. An analogy is used to build a model in the mind that can be used to understand something about the world. A source analogue is selected (either by active retrieval from memory or by having someone point it out), and mapping is used to guide the construction of similarities between the source and the target. This leads to the generation of possible inferences about the target, which must be evaluated, adapted to the unique requirements of the target, and possibly abandoned. When used carefully, analogy can be a powerful mental tool. Uses of analogy include: to explain or develop a new hypothesis about the target, to solve problems, to plan, to persuade others and to evoke an emotional response. This research will examine how analogical or metaphorical thinking might be used in the software design process, where the 'target' might be any of the entities discussed previously, or relationships between some of the entities.

Research methods

The limited resources available mean that the initial application area must be systems development work carried out by students. At the University of Teesside there is an emphasis on teaching software engineering via group work and projects. Some of the student projects are 'live projects' i.e. they have real clients in an organisation. Students are generally novice software engineers, and sometimes have different objectives from industrial practitioners. Nevertheless, their systems development work can be a useful testbed for a method, allowing early versions to be developed and refined before it is tried out by industrial practitioners. It may transpire that the method is not scaleable to industrial projects, but this should not mean that the method is of no use - students need methods too, and their use of a successful metaphor-based method should enhance their subsequent professional activities with the recognition that sometimes it is useful, or necessary, to see 'reality' in more than one way.

Since one of the outcomes of the research will be an artefact (i.e. a software engineering method), the research method can be described using the basic design method of engineering: analysis, design, implementation and evaluation. (This is a descriptive rather than a prescriptive framework for the engineering of an artefact, since the various stages are not easily separated in practice).

Analysis Literature surveys have indicated some of the problems of software engineering methods and the dominance of a mechanistic philosophy. Empirical data will be gathered by a forthcoming survey of student group work, observing progress, the difficulties encountered and how they are handled. This examination of current practice will allow the researchers to increase their understanding of the process within a specific cultural and contextual setting, and identify where metaphors are already used, or could be used. Supervision of live projects and study of the students' reports on this work will also provide further empirical data to suggest how metaphors might be useful.

Design A method making explicit use of metaphors will be designed. This will draw upon the theories of metaphors described in the literature, and its focus will be guided by the empirical data gathered in the analysis stage. The research method will therefore be interpretive in nature.

Implementation and evaluation Design, implementation and evaluation will be performed iteratively. The designed method will be put into practice via a case-study approach, initially using student projects, but later in industry. It is currently anticipated that the evaluation of the method will be based on interpretive methods, from user-feedback and observation of the method-in-use.

Summary and conclusions

This paper has briefly described the nature of software engineering and its methods. Some limitations of those methods were discussed, namely the implicit use of a machine metaphor and a philosophy based upon mechanism and positivism. The notion of a method based upon the explicit use of a range of metaphors was introduced, and a research method for analysing and developing such an artefact was outlined. It is hoped that the work will lead to improved software engineering practices and computer-based systems. The use and acceptance of such a method would require a move away from positivism towards interpretivism, that is, moving from saying reality 'is' to temporarily seeing reality 'as' (Schon, 1983). Such a movement has begun in the information systems field (Walsham, 1995), but the process of such a shift in software engineering has barely begun. It is hoped that the publication of this paper, and the research it describes, will play a small part in that process.

References

Avison, D. E. & Fitzgerald, G. (1995) *Information Systems Development: Methodologies, Techniques and Tools (2nd edition)*. McGraw-Hill: Maidenhead.

Avison, D.E & Wood-Harper, T. (1995), 'Experience of using Multiview: Some reflections', in F.A. Stowell (ed.), *Information Systems Provision. The Contribution of Soft Systems Methodology*. McGraw-Hill: Maidenhead.

Bell, F. & Oates, B. J. (1994), 'A framework for method integration', in C.Lissoni, T.Richardson, R.Miles, T. Wood-Harper, N. Jayaratna (eds.), *Information Systems Methodologies 1994*. British Computer Society: Swindon.

Brooks, F. P. (1987), 'No silver bullet: Essence and accidents of software engineering'. *IEEE Computer*, Vol. 20, pp.10-19.

Checkland, P.B. (1981) *Systems thinking. Systems practice*. John Wiley: Chichester.

Coyne, R. (1995) *Designing Information Technology in the Postmodern Age. From Method to Metaphor*. MIT Press: Cambridge, Mass.

Dahlbom, B. & Mathiassen, L. (1993) *Computers in Context. The Philosophy and Practice of Systems Design*. NCC Blackwell: Oxford.

Fitzgerald, B. (1995), 'A descriptive framework for investigating problems in the application of system development methodologies', in N. Jayaratna, R. Miles, Y. Merali, S. Probert (eds.), *Information Systems Methodologies 1995*. British Computer Society: Swindon.

Hirschheim, R.A. & Klein, H.K. (1989), 'Four paradigms of information systems development'. *Communications of the ACM*, Vol. 32, pp. 1199-216.

Holyoak, K. J. and Thagard, P. (1995), *Mental Leaps. Analogy in Creative Thought*. MIT Press: Cambridge, Massachusetts.

Jayaratna, N. (1994), *Understanding and evaluating methodologies. NIMSAD: A systemic framework*. McGraw-Hill: Maidenhead.

Jayaratna, N. (1992), 'Should we link SSM with information systems!'. *Systemist*, Vol. 4, pp. 108-109.

Kling, R. (1987), 'Defining the boundaries of computing across complex organizations' in R.J.Boland & R.A. Hirschheim (eds.), *Critical Issues in Information Systems Research*. John Wiley: Chichester.

Kling, R. (1994), 'Organizational analysis in Computer Science' in C.Huff & T. Finholt, (eds.), *Social Issues in Computing. Putting Computing in its Place.* McGraw-Hill: Maidenhead.

Kronlof, K. et al (1993) Method Integration. Concepts and Case Studies. John Wiley: Chichester.

MacCormack, E.R. (1985) *A Cognitive Theory of Metaphor.* Bradford, MIT Press: Cambridge, Mass.

Miles, R. K. (1988), 'Combining 'hard' and 'soft' systems practice: grafting or embedding?'. *Journal of Applied Systems Analysis*, Vol. 15, pp. 55-60.

Morgan, G. (1986) *Images of Organisation.* Sage Publications: London.

Morgan, G. (1993) *Imaginization.* Sage Publications: London.

Oates , B. J. (1995), 'Evaluation of the NIMSAD conceptual framework', in N. Jayaratna, R. Miles, Y. Merali, S. Probert (eds.), *Information Systems Methodologies 1995*. British Computer Society: Swindon.

Payne, S.J. (1996), 'Cognitive psychology and cognitive technologies'. *Psychologist*, July, pp. 309-312.

Schon, D.A. (1983) *The reflective practitioner. How professionals think in action.* Basic Books: New York.

Sommerville, I. (1996) *Software Engineering (5th edition).* Addison-Wesley: Wokingham.

Walsham, G. (1995), 'The emergence of interpretivism in IS research'. *Information Systems Research*, Vol. 6, pp. 376-394.

50 Hypertext, navigation and cognitive maps: the effects of a map and a contents list on navigation performance as a function of prior knowledge

Sharon McDonald and Rosemary J. Stevenson
Human Communication Research Centre
University of Durham, UK

Abstract

This study examined the effectiveness of a map and a contents list on the navigation performance of subjects with and without prior knowledge of the text topic. After reading the text, subjects used the document to answer ten questions. Subjects then completed a cognitive map task. The results showed that performance in the map condition was superior to that of the contents list condition, which in turn was better than that in the hypertext condition (no aid). In addition, knowledgeable subjects performed better than non-knowledgeable subjects, except in the map condition where their performance was equivalent. These results are discussed in relation to the ways in which navigational aids interact with the prior knowledge of the user to enhance or impede performance.

Introduction

In an effort to minimise some of the navigational problems often encountered by hypertext users, a number of navigational aids have been developed. However, the effectiveness of such aids in relieving user disorientation is debatable. The aim of this study is to evaluate the usefulness of two navigational aids, a map and a contents list on the navigation performance of subjects who differed in their prior knowledge of the topic of the text.

The problem of disorientation has many facets, but generally speaking, the disorientated user may encounter problems in deciding where they want to go in the hypertext, and indeed, how to get there. Research has also shown that disorientation is heightened in the case of non-knowledgeable subjects who lack sufficient prior knowledge of the text topic to help guide their movements through the text (Shin, Schallert and Savenye, 1994).

A number of tools have been developed to help users navigate through hypertext. Two of the most popular are the spatial map and the contents list. However, the empirical evidence on the usefulness of these tools, in helping lost or disorientated users is less than clear cut. Dee-Lucas and Larkin (1995), and Wenger and Payne (1994), have shown that the provision of a map increases the amount of material reviewed during browsing. Moreover, Monk, Walsh and Dix, (1988) and Simpson and McKnight (1990) found that a map also improves navigation performance. By contrast, Wenger and Payne (1994) and Stanton, Taylor and Tweedie (1992) found that the provision of a spatial map disrupted cognitive map development. Research into the effectiveness of contents list has shown that they can improve both navigation and memory for text topics (Dee-Lucas and Larkin, 1995).

These findings suggest that a map may alleviate disorientation. However, when we look at learning a different picture emerges. Wenger and Payne (1994) found that a map had no effect on recall, or comprehension. Similarly, Stanton, et al., (1992), found that the provision of a map resulted in poor performance of a sentence completion task, less use of the system, and lower perceived control over the system. Taken together these findings imply that navigational tools such as spatial maps and textual contents lists are suitable for some tasks but by no means all. However, what they fail to examine is how navigational tools interact with the prior knowledge of the user. The aim of this study therefore is to examine the effects of two navigational aids, a textual contents list and a spatial map, on the navigation performance of knowledgeable and non-knowledgeable subjects, and on their ability to represent the document's structure as a cognitive map.

Method

Subjects

Thirty six student volunteers from Durham University served as subjects. Half of the subjects were knowledgeable about the topic of the text (postgraduate students), the other half non-knowledgeable (first year undergraduates). All subjects had equivalent computer experience. Subjects were tested individually.

Materials

The text was taken from Stevenson and Palmer (1994). The text consisted of 45 nodes, and was approximately 4500 words in length. Three hypertext documents were used (map, contents list and basic hypertext). In the map condition subjects were provided with localised spatial maps of the document. In the contents list condition subjects were provided with a scrollable contents list of all the nodes in the hypertext. In the basic hypertext condition, no navigational aid was provided. The navigational tools were non-interactive.

Design

A between subjects design was used. The independent variables were navigational aid (map, contents list, basic hypertext), and prior knowledge (knowledgeable and non knowledgeable). The dependent variables were: the number of nodes opened during reading, the number of questions correctly answered, the mean number of additional nodes accessed per question, (the shortest route to each answer was determined. This figure was subtracted from the actual number of nodes opened by subjects to give an additional node score), and the cognitive map score.

Procedure

Subjects were instructed to read through the hypertext until they thought they had seen the whole document. They then used the hypertext to answer ten questions, using the navigational aids as necessary. Subjects were then given a map of the hypertext with a numbered alphabetical list of all the nodes in the document, and were instructed to mark the numbers corresponding to the list in the correct places on the map.

Results

Reading

Table 1 presents the mean number of nodes opened during reading. A between subjects ANOVA revealed significant effects of: aid ($F_{(2,30)} = 60.0$, $p < 0.01$), and prior knowledge, ($F_{(1,30)} = 11.2$, $p < 0.01$). Tukey HSD tests indicated significant differences between all three groups. (hypertext vs. contents list: $Q_{(2,30)} = 7.6$, $p < 0.01$; hypertext vs. map: $Q_{(2,30)} = 15.5$, $p < 0.01$; contents list vs. map: $Q_{(2,30)} = 7.9$, $p < 0.01$). Map subjects opened more nodes than contents list subjects, who in turn, opened more nodes than hypertext subjects. Knowledgeable subjects opened more nodes (mean = 31.5) than non-knowledgeable subjects (mean = 26.1).

Table 1
Mean number of nodes opened during reading, as a function of prior knowledge and navigational aid (K = knowledgeable; NK = non-knowledgeable)

	Hypertext		Contents List		Map	
	K	NK	K	NK	K	NK
Nodes Opened	21.3	15.3	32.7	24.8	40.5	38.5

Correct answers

The top row of table 2 presents the mean number of correct answers. A between subjects ANOVA revealed significant effects of: aid ($F_{(2,30)}$ = 19.7, p < 0.01), and prior knowledge ($F_{(1,30)}$ = 35.3, p < 0.01). There were fewer correct answers in the hypertext condition than in the other two conditions. Knowledgeable subjects answered more questions correctly (mean = 9.9) than non-knowledgeable subjects (mean = 8.3).

Table 2
Mean number of correct answers, and additional nodes opened as a function of prior knowledge and navigational aid (K = knowledgeable; NK = non-knowledgeable)

	Hypertext		Contents List		Map	
	K	NK	K	NK	K	NK
Correct Answers	9.7	6.2	10.0	8.8	10.0	9.8
Additional Nodes	7.6	11.2	5.4	8.3	3.3	3.7

There was also a significant interaction ($F_{(2,30)}$ = 13.3, p <0.01). Tests of simple effects revealed that knowledgeable subjects performed better than non-knowledgeable subjects in the hypertext and contents list conditions, but not in the map condition (hypertext: $F_{(1,30)}$ = 55.6, p < 0.01; contents list: $F_{(1,30)}$ = 6.2, p < 0.02; map: $F_{(1,30)}$ = < 1). There was also a significant effect of navigational aid for non-knowledgeable subjects ($F_{(2,30)}$ = 32.6, p < 0.01), but not for knowledgeable subjects ($F_{(2,30)}$ = < 1). Non-knowledgeable subjects performed better in the map and contents list condition than in the hypertext condition (hypertext vs. map: $Q_{(2,30)}$ = 11.04, p < 0.01; hypertext vs. contents list: $Q_{(2,30)}$ = 8.03, p < 0.01). However, there was no difference between non-knowledgeable subjects in the map and contents list condition (contents list vs. map: $Q_{(2,30)} = 3.01$, ns).

Additional nodes

The bottom row of table 2 presents the mean number of additional nodes opened. A between subjects ANOVA revealed significant effects of: aid ($F_{(2,30)} = 50.3$, p < 0.01), and prior knowledge ($F_{(1,30)} = 23.3$, p < 0.01). Subjects in the map condition opened fewer additional nodes than subjects in the contents list condition, who in turn, opened fewer additional nodes than subjects in the hypertext condition. Knowledgeable subjects (mean = 5.4) opened fewer additional nodes than non-knowledgeable (mean = 7.7).

There was also a significant interaction ($F_{(2,30)} = 4.2$, p <0.02). Tests of simple effects revealed that knowledgeable subjects performed better than non-knowledgeable subjects in the hypertext and contents list condition but not in the map condition (hypertext: $F_{(1,30)} = 19.4$, p < 0.01; contents list: $F_{(1,30)} = 12.1$, p < 0.01; map: $F_{(1,30)} = p < 1$).

Cognitive map

Table 3 presents the mean number of correctly placed node titles. A between subjects ANOVA revealed significant effects of: aid ($F_{(2,30)} = 50.9$, p < 0.01), and prior knowledge ($F_{(1,30)} = 17.9$, p < 0.01). Subjects in the map condition placed more correct node titles than subjects in the hypertext condition, who in turn, placed more correct node titles than subjects in the contents list condition. Knowledgeable subjects placed more correct node titles (mean = 17.5) than non-knowledgeable subjects, (mean = 12.7).

There was also a significant interaction ($F_{(2,30)} = 4.0$, p <0.03). Tests of simple effects revealed that knowledgeable subjects performed better than non-knowledgeable subjects in the hypertext and contents list conditions but not in the map condition (hypertext: $F_{(1,30)} = 10.3$, p < 0.01; contents list: $F_{(1,30)} = 15.8$, p < 0.01; map: $F_{(1,30)} = p < 1$).

Table 3
Mean number of correctly placed node titles as a function of prior knowledge and navigational aid (K = knowledgeable; NK = non-knowledgeable)

	Hypertext		Contents List		Map	
	K	NK	K	NK	K	NK
Correct Placements	16.5	10.2	13.0	5.2	23.0	22.7

Discussion

Overall, the performance of subjects in the map condition was superior to that of subjects in the hypertext condition, while the performance of subjects in the contents list condition fell between these two extremes. These results indicate that the provision of a map leads to more efficient browsing behaviour, a finding previously observed by Wenger and Payne (1994), and Dee-Lucas and Larkin (1995), and to superior navigation performance, consistent with the findings of Monk et al., (1988), and Simpson and McKnight (1990), who also found that a map led to more efficient navigation.

Subjects in the map condition also produced more accurate cognitive maps than subjects in the hypertext condition, who in turn produced more accurate maps than subjects in the contents list condition. These findings contrast with those of Wenger and Payne (1994) and Stanton et al., (1992) who found that the provision of a map had no reliable effect on subject's structural knowledge of hypertext. The discrepancy in these findings may be accounted for by task differences. Wenger and Payne used a much simpler task. Subjects were given pairs of node titles and were asked to decide if the nodes were linked in the text. In addition, the text used was very small. Stanton et al's, subjects were instructed to draw their maps free-hand. By contrast, our subjects had to label on outline map of the hypertext. This method was chosen because research has shown (Blaut and Stea, 1974) that sketch maps may not adequately represent a person's knowledge because of limitations in their drawing ability.

The difference in performance between subjects in the hypertext condition and those in the map and contents list condition is not surprising, since basic hypertext does not make it easy for the user to know what information is available. Perhaps what is more interesting is the difference in performance of subjects in the map and contents list condition. The performance of subjects in the map condition was superior to that of subjects in the contents list condition, on all measures taken. One reason for this difference in performance might be the way in which the two navigational aids tackle the problem of disorientation. The textual contents list simply provides the user with an indication of what material is in the document, it does not offer guidance on the particular route the user should follow in order to arrive at their destination. The map however, allows users to gain an overview of the hypertext nodes and links and the routes that connect them.

We also found a relationship between navigation performance and prior knowledge. Overall, navigation performance was superior with knowledgeable subjects. Thus prior knowledge in the subject matter can facilitate navigation through hypertext. This result is consistent with those of Shin et al., (1994), who found that novices are impaired in their reading and understanding of hypertext documents. Undoubtedly, the superior navigational abilities of our knowledgeable subjects will have arisen because they have an understanding of the conceptual organisation of the subject matter, that can allay some of the disorientation problems that users may encounter in hypertext. However, our results also showed that the provision of a spatial map, can eliminate the disorientation problems of non-knowledgeable subjects, and bring their performance up to the level of knowledgeable subjects. This result suggests that an appropriate navigational aid might compensate for the user's lack of conceptual knowledge of the text topic.

In conclusion, it appears that the navigation performance of hypertext users improves when they are given access to navigational tools. More specifically, the provision of a localised spatial map seems to eliminate some of the problems typically associated with disorientation, and is especially effective in the case of non-knowledgeable subjects.

References

Blaut, J.M. & Stea, D. (1974). 'Mapping at the age of three'. *Journal of Geography,* Vol. 73, pp. 5-9.

Dee-Lucas, D. & Larkin, J.H. (1995). 'Learning from electronic texts: effects of interactive overviews for information access'. *Cognition and Instruction,* Vol. 13, pp. 431-468.

Monk, A.F., Walsh, P. & Dix, A.J. (1988). 'A comparison of hypertext, scrolling and folding as mechanisms for program browsing'. In, D. M. Jones & R. Winder (eds.), *People and Computers IV.* Cambridge: Cambridge University Press.

Shin, C.E., Schallert, D.L. & Savenye, W.C. (1994). 'Effects of learner control, advisement, and prior knowledge on young students' learning in a hypertext environment'. *Educational Technology Research and Development,* Vol. 42, pp. 33-46.

Simpson, A. & McKnight, C. (1990). 'Navigation in hypertext: structural cues and mental maps', in R. McAleese & C. Green (eds.), *Hypertext: State of the Art.* Oxford: Intellect.

Stanton, N.A., Taylor, R.G. & Tweedie, L.A. (1992). 'Maps as navigational aids in hypertext environments: an empirical evaluation'. *Journal of Educational Multimedia and Hypermedia,* Vol.1, pp. 431-444.

Stevenson, R.J. & Palmer, J.A. (1994). *Learning: Principles, Processes, and Practices.* Cassell.

Wenger, M.J. & Payne, D.G. (1994). Effects of a graphical browser on readers' efficiency in reading hypertext. *Technical Communication,* Vol. 41, pp. 224-233.

Acknowledgements

This work was supported by an EPSRC studentship held by the first author. The Human Communication Research Centre is supported by the ESRC.

51 Personal identification code composed of pictures or numbers?

Karl W. Sandberg and Yan Pan
Luleå University of Technology, Sweden

Abstract

Technical service, as a key to enter social service systems, has gradually replaced the traditional personal service. However, in order to gain access, the user is required to remember items, which they admit to be a difficult task. The study is aimed to compare 'how well' people remember two types of codes (picture code and number code) respectively.

The problems with personal identification numbers (PIN-code)

The end of twentieth century is marked by a technology society which is distinguished by means of technical service. Technical service, as a key to access systems, has gradually replaced the traditional personal service. For instance, with the facility of bank cards, people would rather use automatic teller machines (ATMs) than go to bank during business hours. Needless to say, this technical tool gives the possibility of dealing with a quickly increasing population and updating information. Meanwhile, it is relatively efficient and economic.

However, the cost for this innovation is that the technical items have to be protected with security procedures that are less sophisticated than their data processing counterparts. The reasons are twofold. First, the systems mostly are guarded only by numeric codes, for example, the current popular four digits personal identification number (PIN). It has been proved a difficult task when users have to remember several codes simultaneously. The second reason is those coding activities are relying heavily on memory. Because fastest performance comes only when people have memorised the codes, unfortunately it is also the source of errors.

When users express dissatisfaction with codes, probably for the reason of lack of logic (little relationship between code and its orientated-information).

Meaningfulness refers to those attributes of a code that lead the user to readily associate the code with the item object, instruction, or action that the code represents (Bailey, 1989). By now it has been broadly agreed that users tend to perceive codes more accurately and quickly if they are meaningful.

This argument could obtain the support from Sir Frederick Bartlett. In his book *Remembering,* published in 1932, Bartlett attacked the Ebbinghaus tradition approach to memory, which had dominated psychology for 50 years. He argued that the study of nonsense syllable learning had excluded the most central and characteristic feature of human memory by excluding meaning.

The study of the ability to remember pictures was ignored for a long period in memory research history. Interest in long-term visual memory was revived by some demonstrations in the 1960s that realised the limitless capacity to remember pictures. Standing (1973) found the performance was even remarkably high following single presentation of each of 10,000 different pictures. Initially, pictures of faces always led to high levels of recognition memory. This can prove the influence of 'meaningfulness'on the storage of visual patterns.

We believe the meaningfulness of codes (memorablility) is very necessary with the growing emphasis on user friendliness. Based on this consideration, the present study proposes a new idea 'personal identification picture code' (PIP-code) which refers to the codes which are composed of pictorial images, because PIP-codes provide much more information compared with PIN-codes. In addition, pictures are characterised by their colours, construction, background, and so forth. The 'pictorial superiority effect' (e.g. Nickerson, 1965; Shepard, 1967) is the inspirational root for the framework of the pictorial codes.

Cognitive theories of memory

The saying that 'one picture is worth a thousand words' is usually applied to the effectiveness of a picture in communicating an idea that would take many words to express; it may also apply to the effectiveness of a picture in remembering what was communicated. An advanced explanation would require some memory theories at the level of cognition.

The process of remembering is generally viewed as consisting of three stages: (i) *encoding* or *acquisition* is learning the material in the first place, (ii) *storage* is keeping the material until it is needed; and (iii) *retrieval* is getting the material back out when it is needed. We are all very aware that memory is limited more in getting things out than in getting them in. This has caused complaints that forgetting is easier than remembering. The phenomenon can be explained by the three stages of memory process. Because a failure of any of these three stages will result in forgetting, but the success of all these three stages only results in remembering. It is as if there is only one chance to remember and three chances to forget. However, forgetting does not necessarily mean the memory is lost; it may be merely inaccessible because of the inappropriate retrieval strategies. Then enhancing the retrieval will improve the memory.

Common approaches that enhance the retrieval

Meaningfulness   One determinant of how easy something is to learn is how meaningful it is to the learner. The more meaningful it is, the easier it will be to learn. Words are easier to remember than nonsense syllables. Sentences are easier to remember than words in an ungrammatical order. The reason that meaningful items can be remembered better is because meaningfulness deepens the encoding level so that it makes the retrieval easier.

Association   Association is the process of forming mental connections between what you want to remember and what you already know. This can be done with analogies, metaphors, and examples, and by comparing, contrasting, or re-wording. Although many associations are made automatically, the conscious creation of associations is an excellent strategy for encoding new information (Janet et al., 1994). One way in which association helps memory is to give us, cross-references in our memories.

Interest   Interest helps memory in two ways: it assist us to pay attention and it motivates us to remember. Another way it assist in remembering is that people spend more time thinking about matter that interest them than they do think about matter that do not interest them. One method to develop an interest is seek out items that relate to particular motives.

Visual imagery   Visual imagery is a powerful memory aid in long-term memory. This prominence can be inferred from two pieces of evidence: first, there is a strong relationship between the imageability of a word and the ease with which they can memorise it; and second, imaging plays an important role in mnemonic strategies. The fact that people remember words plus images better than words alone is similar to the effect of leaving two notes is better than leaving only one. This is because pictures are inherently more memorable than words, and pictures are coded both visually and verbally. Therefore, we can take the advantage of this fact by visualising material we want to remember.

The story method   This is the process of making up a simple, yet colourful, tale connecting items that seem to have no connection. Normally both general knowledge about the world (semantic memory) and the personal experience (episodic memory) are an appropriate source for the make up of a story. Eventually, semantic and episodic memory resemble each other in respect of the flexibility or access to the stored information.

Karl W. Sandberg and Yan Pan

A model of personal identification picture code (PIP-code)

Memory researchers have revealed pictorial material is easier to remember compared to either digit or verbal material. Our question here is how to transfer this theoretical evidence to practical application, for instance, using pictures instead of digits, to compose personal identification code. The case could begin with the assumption we were asked to remember one hundred pictures given in random way together. All these pictures were different to each other. The possibility of each picture appeared in front of us is like a picture taken from a new calendar that we had never seen before.

We would not attempt to remember these pictures in the random way they were, presnted, if we were ready to do the task. To solve this problem by the knowledge we have received, we would first classify the pictures into several categories, like human being, animals, vehicles, or buildings or landscapes and others; then find the differences among the same category of pictures; finally we would organise pictures into a certain order that made them meaningful and easier to remember. Objects that we organised in a meaningful, coherent picture would be remembered better than objects in a jumbled picture (Biederman,1972).

Conceptual elements of the PIP-code

The PIP-code model introduces the story-grammar method that defines the story pattern composed of three basic conceptual components: *subject, object* or *place/ time (SOP/T)*. With these elements, we can make up a simplest one-sentence story. For example, Susan (*S*) reads a book (*O*) in the library *(P)*. Subsequently every PIP-code is determined by including at least three different pictures. First one should represent a picture of human being as a *subject*. Second one should represent *an object* by a picture of various articles. Third, one should represent a *place* by a picture of a building or landmark, or *time* by a particular picture that can show a certain time environment, for example, an umbrella symbolising a rainy day. We have given one example in figure 1.

$$S \quad + \quad O \quad + \quad P$$

Figure 1   An example of the three basic conceptual elements of a story

406

The next question is how to make up a story with three elements, meanwhile taking into consideration individual preferences. A simple solution is a no restriction solution. No restriction means encouraging people to freely associate pictures into a story. This 'free-association' also reflects much memory research opinion, because whether a picture represents a person, a thing, or a building is decided by personal semantic knowledge. People's semantic knowledge is similar to each other's because it is built on the general knowledge about the world. However, the behaviour of associating pictures is to an extent a product of the episodic knowledge that a particular an event has with respect to personal experience. The events everybody has experienced are different and people always remember what they had enjoyed best. As to the example figure 1, the story does not matter whether it is 'Einstein was playing violin at Princeton' or 'Einstein was listening to a violin concerto at home'. The ultimate point is using the story to help remember the picture codes, whereas how to associate the story is only of minor interest. In generally, the PIP-code model encourages people to use their imagery to make the story fantasy and use their interests by the method of 'free-association' using three conceptual elements.

Experimental design

The empirical part of the study consisted of three experiments. Each experiment reflected one circumstance about how codes are employed. The first experiment, cued recall of assigned code, attended to when users sometimes have to remember a code for a system (e.g. ATM) in order to get access to its service. The second one, cued recall of self-generated codes, was concerned with when users could sometimes freely determine a code of an object (e.g. suitcase or computer) for the purpose of guarunteieng personal-oriented access. The last, recognition of assigned codes and a backward recall of the cue, which attempted to demonstrate that recognition is easier than recall in future application.

Each experiment was further designed to have code type (PIP-code vs. PIN-code) as the between subjects factor, and code length (three-item codes vs. four-item codes) and the test (the immediate test vs. the delayed test) as within subjects factors. Each condition was completed in two sessions, an immediate and a delayed test. A total of 138 subjects (67 male, 71 female) from Luleå University of Technology and Boden College of Health and Caring Sciences participated in the experiments. Their average age was 28.8 years.

Results and discussion

If we compare the results from all six conditions, experimental (3) × test (2), we find that the PIP-codes attained higher performance than the PIN-codes on five

407

occasions (figure 2), especially in every delayed test. The only exception was in the immediate test of the second experiment. This exception was partly due to the instructional failure in the PIN-codes test. However, the results from the delayed test are more convincing if we attempt to apply PIP-codes. Based on these results, the PIP-codes can be concluded as a relatively memorable type of code compared to PIN-codes.

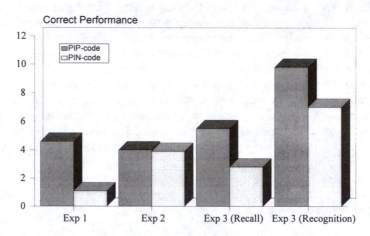

Figure 2 A comparison with the correct performance of the PIP-code and PIN-code in three experiments

The results further provide a confirmation of the story-grammar method for PIP-codes. When the PIP-codes are found easier to remember, this is always when they were composed by the story-grammar method, and vice verse. Supporting evidence is that the subjects remember the PIP-codes better than the PIN-codes in the first and third experiment, but not in the second one. Because in the second experiment the PIP-codes were generated by subjects themselves and they had no consistent learning strategy for memorising the codes like in the other two experiments. The reasons that the method efficiently improves the recall lie in three aspects. First, it uses the pictorial material, the most appropriate material, to compose codes. Second, the method improves the recall by utilising the subjects' semantic and episodic knowledge simultaneously. Third, the method is possible to reduce the transportation errors by way of standardising encoding in sequence of *SOP/T*. The finding of the sequence of the PIP-code is very plainly supported by memory theory 'organisation'. Baddeley (1982) reported material with 'built in' was found much easier to remember in comparison to relatively unstructured material, although it was in fact quite possible to organise the second collection of items in the same way as the first.

However, the method also has its weakness. It lays the emphasis on the internal connection of pictures for every code, but ignores the external connection between the code and their name. Thus, more location errors were obtained in the first experiment than the second one. The former used the assigned codes as stimuli. In the latter the subjects had freely generated the codes. When subjects had opportunities to generate the codes themselves, they tended to select the pictures which fitted more closely with their own viewpoint. The coherence effects assist memory in encoding and storing the information. In short, what we remember is driven to some extent by our emotional commitment and response to the event. With the above analysis, we could say the story-grammar method builds up the theoretical basis for the PIP-codes though the development of the method is still in its early stages.

Some limitations of the study

In considering the practical implications of these findings, it is important to remember the limitations of the study. One is that the study was confined to a group test with the learning material displayed on the screen by an overhead projector. This laboratory testing context is some distance from the ordinary context. Consequently it is impossible to avoid a bias in the results. The other is the student subjects are a very special population. They are characterised by youth and a high level of education which enhances performance. Because of these limitations, we must be cautious in generalising the results from the present study to the PIP-code in more natural contexts.

Conclusion

Experience suggests that many code users are violating the strictures on the traditional PIN-codes methods. Moreover, there is no reason to believe that the multitude of novices will accommodate to those strictures which focus attention mostly on the access granted than the demanded 'user-friendliness'. Relating this phenomenon to the present study, a user-generated PIP-code rooted on a story-grammar method should be recommended as a robust alternative to access systems because it enables trade-offs between security and memorability within an appropriate context and with respect to the cognitive style of users.

References

Baddley, A., (1993) *Your Memory*. Prion: London.
Bailey, R. W. (1989) *Human Performance Engineering*. Prentice Hall: Englewood Cliffs, New Jersey.

Karl W. Sandberg and Yan Pan

Bartlett, J. C., Leslie, J. E., Tubbs, A., and Fulton, A., (1989), 'Ageing and memory for pictures of faces'. *Psychology and Ageing*, Vol. 4, pp. 276-283.

Biederman, I. (1972) Perceiving real-world scenes, *Science*, 177, pp. 77-80.

Janet, F. (1994), *Human Computer Interaction*. Addision-Wesley Publishing Company.

Nickerson, R. S. (1965) 'Short term memory for complex meaningful configurations: A demonstration of captive'. *Canadian Journal of Psychology*, Vol. 19, pp. 155-160.

Standing, L. (1973), 'Learning 10,000 pictures' *Quarterly Journal of Experimental Psychology*, Vol. 25, pp. 207-222.

Shepard, R. N. (1967), 'Recognition memory for words, sentences and pictures', *Journal of Verbal Learning and Verbal Behaviour*. Vol. 6, pp. 156-163.

52 Implementing user interface design standards for 'mission critical' IT systems in telecommunications

Robert Pedlow
Customer Care Program,
Telstra Research Laboratories, Australia

Abstract

The usability of the interfaces to IT systems used by customer facing staff (CSRs) has been identified by Telstra as a key factor in providing high quality customer service. One component of Telstra's usability strategy is to provide a consistent look and feel for CSRs through the use of corporate user interface (UI) design standards based on human factors principles. A number of the systems used by CSRs are 'mission critical' and consequently face intense pressure on their development process. Current approaches used by corporate usability specialists in Telstra to facilitate the implementation of UI design standards are discussed in the context of a case study of implementing UI design standards for one such system. The challenges to implementing UI design standards for this type of system are identified and an alternative strategy based on modifying the UI development tools is presented and evaluated.

Introduction

The implementation of user interface design standards for IT systems has been acknowledged as offering significant advantages for achieving usable systems (Gould, 1988). While standards cannot guarantee usability, they represent an important element of usable interface design (Hix and Hartson, 1993). Consistent user interface design is particularly relevant for software used by customer facing staff in telecommunications. This is an area which has a high level of staff turnover and a need to be able to move staff to other business units quickly with minimal

411

retraining. The implementation of corporate user interface design standards based on human factors knowledge can thus support these business requirements.

Recognising these advantages, in 1993, the Human Factors Research Group at Telstra Research Laboratories produced a set of standards for the design of Telstra corporate graphical user interface (GUI) applications along with a set of guidelines for the inclusion of usability in the software development life-cycle (SDLC). The full set of volumes were circulated widely in Telstra as the Human Factors Kit (HFK), (Telstra, 1993). At about the same time, the Hiser Consulting Group was commissioned to prepare a set of standards and guidelines for Usability specifically for GUI applications used by CSRs. These standards and guidelines addressed issues relating specifically to customer service delivery in telephony that were not included in the HFK. Having developed these standards it was recognised that methods were required to assist software development projects in implementing the standards.

The Customer Support Usability Team (CSPU) was created in the Information Technology division of Telstra to facilitate the implementation of Usability Standards for GUI customer support applications (Miller, 1996). The first method developed by the CSPU team to facilitate standards implementation was to identify a number of development projects of key strategic importance to Telstra and provide these projects with intensive long term consulting by placing a usability specialist with the project team. Whilst this approach has achieved significant success with projects that were in early stages of the software development lifecycle that is 'greenfields' projects, its effectiveness is limited by the number of projects that can be reached. Other methods that have been used include training workshops for project team management and staff and recently, a Usability Representatives Network to promote and support interest in usability in project team personnel (Meighan, 1995).

The telecommunications industry, in common with a number of other customer service industries, has seen the emergence of so called 'mission critical' applications in the customer support area. These are single applications which serve a substantial segment of an organisation's total market and whose success is critical to the overall business success of the organisation. As a consequence of their position in organisations, these applications face a set of intense pressure on their development, which in turn create severe challenges to the incorporation of usability into the development process. Equally however, the potential benefits of improving the usability of the user interfaces to these systems and the potential problems associated with usability defects in the user interfaces to these systems are magnified by the size of the user base and the critical role of these applications for the organisation. The current study presents a case study of the challenges involved in implementing interface design standards for one such system and outlines a potential solution to these challenges.

The case study - system W

Introduction

System W is a Windows GUI client server application intended to provide a single front-end system for staff providing service to one sector of Telstra's telephony market. The system was developed to provide a unified front-end to a range of different character based mainframe or 'legacy systems' (Telstra, 1994).

As part of an initiative to enhance the usability of Telstra's customer support systems, the author undertook a twelve month internal usability consultancy with the project group to advise them on the implementation of interface design standards. The usability intervention with system W met with partial success. It was possible to enhance some aspects of the system's UI including things such as user error messages. However, in the course of the consultancy it became apparent that implementing UI standards for projects such as system W presented new challenges for the existing approaches that have been developed for this task in Telstra. The objective of this case study is to identify some of the features of the situation facing this project team that presented particular challenges to the implementation of user interface design standards.

Method

The case study presented here is based on the analysis of a number of key project documents. The following principles have been adhered to in presenting the analysis of these project documents.

(i)   Information that is commercially sensitive to Telstra has been excluded.
(ii) Information that might tend to identify the project or particular individuals has been altered or omitted.

Within these constraints, the issues have been to the degree possible, discussed from an objective point of view. While some of the discussion examines areas where challenges remain to be met, Telstra has a strong commitment to quality and to continuous improvement in products and systems. Promoting the discussion and analysis of these issues in the human factors community represents one means for Telstra to facilitate this process of improvement.

Findings

The major challenges identified for implementing user interface design standards for system W were:

(i)   Pressure on the project to continually and rapidly incorporate new functionality.
(ii) Time pressure to deliver new releases.
(iii) Project change management.
(iv) Specification of UI design standards.

413

Pressure to incorporate new functionality   Because system W is positioned as the front-end for one customer group, all the products for this group ultimately impact on the system W user interface. This meant that system W project team faced constant pressure to accommodate new functionality to support changing business requirements. This is not an unusual situation for IT development projects however the problem is magnified for mission critical systems. Further, this creates a particular problem for usability since the perception tends to be that support for new products offers a more direct return to the business than enhancing the usability of the UI.

Time pressure to deliver new releases   In a situation common to many major IT projects, system W had critical relationships to other IT systems being rolled out on parallel schedules (Telstra, 1995b). As a consequence of this the project team had to work under great pressure to deliver new releases of system W on schedule.

Project change management   The factors described above i.e. the pressure to include new functionality and time pressure to deliver releases had the consequence of making it very difficult in practise for the project team to deal with any changes including those already accepted (Telstra, 1995a; Telstra, 1996). In effect the project team's processes for management of change tended to be swamped by the sheer volume of changes to be handled. This was essentially a consequence of the status of system W as a mission critical application serving one complete customer group and the rapid development of new telecommunications products and services. This serves to emphasise the practical difficulty of employing existing methods for UI design standards implementation i.e. paper based standards supported by reviewing the UI to ensure standards conformance.

Specification of user interface design standards   Burger (1995) reported that development teams found that because paper based standards are expressed at a relatively abstract level they tend to be difficult for the development team to understand and apply. The system W project group had defined project level UI design standards for system W in the form of paper based documentation. This document essentially codified certain aspects of how the UI should look and provided detailed guidance for programmers on implementation. However while these standards were usable by the developers they were incomplete in the degree to which they specified the look and feel of the system W UI. Thus many aspects of UI look and feel were not documented in the standards and were only specified in visual prototypes of the application. The result of this was that in practise these aspects tended to be inconsistent within the application. For example system W had a large number of forms screens and used accelerator keys to provide quick access to fields as well as providing accelerator key access to menus. However the key press sequence to access menus by accelerator keys involved sequential key presses on some screens while the sequence to access fields involved ALT +key at the same time. Investigation showed that accelerator keys were not defined in the existing standards document. Another example involved the use of different colours for the same field type e.g. mandatory fields, current focus, within the application. This was in addition to other issues because the UI standards system W had adopted did not comply with corporate standards.

Summary

The case study suggests that paper based UI design standards are likely to be problematic for mission critical systems because ensuring adherence to them requires a process of review and correction which presents extreme difficulties for development projects like system W already operating under critical time pressure.

The preferred solution for major projects and indeed for all development projects is for usability to be incorporated into the development life cycle from the beginning. This was a major issue with system W which had been in development for some time before the usability intervention was undertaken. However what became clear during the year and what the case study analysis supports is that many of the challenges presented by system W were due to aspects of the broader situation which are commonly faced in mission critical IT systems development.

Further, strategies for informing development teams about UI design standards e.g. training workshops, while potentially valuable do not provide a solution to the basic implementation problems faced in this situation.

The case study suggests a number of key requirements for UI design standards implementation for mission critical systems.

(i)   There is a need to fully and precisely specify UI design standards before development starts. This is consistent with a recommendation by (Brown, 1996).

(ii)   There is a need to provide UI design standards in a form that developers can pick up and use directly.

(iii) Given the time pressures mission critical systems development operates under there is a need for methods of UI design standards implementation that ensure the correct result the first time.

(iv)   Methods of implementing UI design standards need to have a minimal impact on ongoing development process times.

Telstra like other major telecommunications companies has a multimillion dollar investment in applications used by customer facing staff in their interactions with customers. Major applications of this type are increasingly 'mission critical' in that their function is crucial to Telstra's ability to respond to business priorities and they must be functional for the business to survive. For usability to be relevant to business requirements for these IT systems human factors experts need to recognise the pressures faced by business and develop usability solutions that respond to these needs.

415

An alternative strategy for implementing UI design standards

The proposed alternative to the existing methods i.e. paper based standards, is to embed standards into the tools used by programmers for user interface development. In practise the tools used for user interface development are 'add on tools' for development environments such as C++ . These tools are typically very complex and tend to be understood only by the members of development teams who work with them. There has been a longstanding tendency for these tools to be designed to provide software developers with a maximum degree of flexibility in specifying the look and feel of applications (Robbins, 1995). This tendency while supporting the requirements of developers for powerful flexible tools runs directly counter to the need for corporate software development to support the implementation of UI design standards.

Table 1
Examples of user interface features to be standardised

Feature	Standard
Function keys	Consistent labelling and consistent behaviour
Accelerator keys	Consistent operation
Colours	Consistent colours within and between applications
Fonts	Consistent fonts
Window titles	All windows required to have a title
Menu structure	Standard menu structure

The proposed approach is to customise the software development tools in such a way as to support the implementation and enforcement of corporate user interface design standards at the code level. Thus for standards such as those shown in table 1 the modified interface development tool would directly enforce these standards every time new screens were created.

Potential advantages of this approach

The proposed approach offers two key advantages over existing methods for implementation of interface design standards. First, to a far greater extent than other strategies it 'embeds' UI standards in the development process. Second, this approach is a 'get it right the first time' method. Inconsistent user interface design has a real cost to organisations but the cost is deferred and appears in terms of training and difficulty for end-users once the system is deployed. By comparison, incorporating interface changes to support new products is seen to have an immediate and visible impact on the business. Thus to be acceptable for business for mission critical applications, consistent interface design needs to be implemented with little or no time cost to the development process.

Further, this method of UI standards implementation can be anticipated to represent a direct saving of time for development projects. At the simplest level, it removes the requirement for meetings to decide on UI standards and work to create paper based standards documentation as well as associated reviewing work.

Surveys have shown that, on average, development of the user interface takes up to (29%) of software development costs (Rosenberg, 1989). By enforcing conformance to a standard look and feel, there is potential to significantly reduce this. The approach has been discussed in the context of mission critical systems where it offers particular opportunities. However, once implemented, this strategy can clearly be applied across other systems with significant benefit.

Potential limitations of this approach

This paper has outlined a potential approach for implementing one aspect of usability for 'mission critical' systems, namely, consistent user interface design. However, standards by themselves can not guarantee usability. To design usable applications, we need to understand users and the tasks they will be performing with the applications. A potential advantage of the proposed strategy is that it will free usability specialists time to concentrate on these issues. Rather than acting as 'standards police' usability specialists time can be spent identifying user characteristics and developing and understanding of task and workflow issues. However there is some risk that the type of strategy proposed here could be perceived by non-specialists as a 'magic bullet' to solve all usability problems. Thus if this approach is developed it will be important to inform development groups and business managers that implementing UI design standards does not solve all the usability issues for designing a new system

Also this approach will impact directly on the work of the specialist programmers who currently work with the user interface tools to be modified. There is expected to be a need for specific training and education for these developers who may otherwise resent the reduction in their 'creative freedom' as programmers. Another potential issue is the need for standards enforcement to be combined with flexibility, that is there needs to be some capacity to depart from standards in some cases.

Discussion

The successful implementation of corporate user interface design standards presents a number of major technical and organisational challenges. These challenges are

Robert Pedlow

magnified for the case of mission critical applications development. Equally though the potential benefits to business from implementing user interface design standards are magnified for mission critical applications.

By automating the implementation of usability standards the proposed strategy is expected to free the time of in-house usability experts to concentrate on areas such as task analysis and user profiling. These tasks are more critically dependent on the high level knowledge of human behaviour possessed by usability specialists.

Another issues which became clear when this work was carried out concerned the value of effective collaboration with software engineers. The concept described in this paper was developed as a result of a working collaboration between usability specialists and members of the software development project group. A key issue here is the need for effective communication between usability specialists and software developers. This has been identified by other authors as representing a continuing difficulty for the effective implementation of usability in software design (Mantei and Teorey, 1988). This is not meant to advocate that usability specialists should be programmers or vice-versa. However the present analysis illustrates the importance of both sides understanding enough of the issues influencing the other to be able to communicate effectively.

In conclusion the successful implementation of usability in the telecommunications industry context poses the challenge of developing solutions which responds to the particular needs and pressures of the corporate environment. Through a process of continuing analysis of these issues and feeding back the results into ongoing work Telstra aims to achieve continuous improvement in the usability of its products and systems.

References

Brown, N. (1996) 'Industrial-strength management strategies'. *IEEE Software*, July, pp. 94-103.

Burger, K. (1995) 'Applying usability standards and guidelines within a multi-disciplinary team'. *IHFT 95 Conference Proceedings*, pp. 99-106.

Gould, J.D. (1988) 'How to design usable systems' in, M. Helander, 'Handbook of Human-Computer Interaction'.

Hix, D. and Hartson, H.R. (1993) *Developing user interfaces - Ensuring usability through product and process*. John Wiley and Sons: New York.

Mantei, M and Teorey, T.J (1988). 'Cost/ Benefit analysis for incorporating human factors in the software development lifecycle'. *Communications of the ACM*. Vol. 31, pp. 428-439.

Meighan, F. (1995). 'The usability analyst model: using minimum resources to gain maximum effect'. *OZCHI 95 Conference proceedings*, pp. 301-309.

Miller, A. (1986). 'Integrating Human Factors in Customer Support Systems development using a multi-level organisational approach'. *CHI 96 Conference proceedings*, pp. 368-375.

Robbins, Royice. (1995). Senior Business Consultant AT&T. Personal communication.

Rosenberg, D. (1989). 'A cost benefit analysis for corporate user interface standards: What price to pay for a consistent "look and feel"?' In, Jakob Nielsen (ed.) *Coordinating user interfaces for consistency*. Academic Press inc: Boston MA..

Telstra, (1993). *Human Factors Kit*, Telstra Corporation Limited.

Telstra, (1994). *System W Business Case.*

Telstra, (1995a). *System W, Software Quality Assurance Plan.*

Telstra, (1995b). *Internal project presentation on system W pilot deployment.*

Telstra, (1996). *Strategic information systems plan: Review of system W.*

Acknowledgements

The permission of the Director of Telstra Research Laboratories to publish this paper is gratefully acknowledged. Acknowledgments are due to Royice Robbins (senior Business Consultant AT&T), Joan Scott (Manager: Customer Support Platform Usability Team, Telstra) and the other members of the CSPU Team for their assistance in the development of these ideas. Acknowledgments are also due to Dr Bruce Chisholm (Manager: Telstra Research Laboratories: Customer Care Program) and Dr David Bednall (Section leader: Telstra Research Laboratories Products, Services and Systems Quality) for their continuing support in the development of this work.

53 Script-based spatial user interface: an approach to supporting operators of process control systems

Ivan Burmistrov
Moscow State University, Russia

Abstract

In this paper we propose a novel approach to the interface design for process control industries aimed at support of operators' problem-solving activities. The interface is based on a script approach to human problem solving and uses spatial representation of the experts' procedural knowledge. We describe a prototype intelligent user interface for real-time control systems, the Flexible Script Interface (FSI), which is designed to recommend the correct sequence of actions appropriate in relation to the actual task. FSI is implemented with an interactive script graph which represents a task structure and canalizes user's problem-solving behaviour. The prototype system combines 3D computer graphics visualization technology with decision support and cognitive engineering to produce an intelligent graphic interface for operators of real-time supervisory control systems, such as those used in power production and industrial process control.

Introduction

The design of industrial control centres is advancing toward totally computer-based man-machine interfaces. Computer based interfaces offer many potential advantages over traditional hardwired control panel interfaces including greater flexibility regarding the type of data displayed and its presentation. However, achieving this potential requires development of new interface concepts that change the way operators interact with the plant.

Current theories and guidelines of human-computer interface design give little attention to users' dynamic problem solving process and strategy. This may not present a big problem for users in small tasks, but when a task is sophisticated and requires the support of many and various information and system functions at different stages of problem solving, the compatibility between the interface design and users' problem solving strategy becomes crucial (Ye and Salvendy, 1993).

This paper proposes an interaction style, the Flexible Script Interface (FSI), which is designed to recommend the correct sequence of actions appropriate in relation to the actual task. FSI is an intelligent interaction style that is based on the script approach to problem solving and is implemented with an interactive script graph which represents a task structure and canalizes user's problem-solving behaviour. The main ideas implemented in the FSI are the following:

(i)   Representation of a script in the form of graph directly on-screen.

(ii) Making it possible to interact with the system via such a graph.

(iii) Dynamic visualization of script graph transformations as immediate feed-back to user's actions and data processing outcomes.

(iv) Giving a user on-line assistance with the task by the problem guide.

In this paper, we will discuss theoretical basis for FSI and try to predict those benefits that this interface could provide for its user, as well as present a mock-up of 3D version of FSI aimed at supporting collaborative problem solving in the virtual reality environments.

Domain

Historically, the operator was able to directly observe and manipulate the tool. Today, the operator often interacts with a 'model' of the process, his commands being transferred by computer systems, sensors and effectors. The lack of system transparency thus becomes an obstacle for the process-skilled operator and the operator's knowledge and overall appreciation of the state of the system could be impaired. The manufacturing process therefore again should be made 'visible' to the operator, using computer technology (Stahre, 1993). The problem is how to present information on computer screens in an intelligible and useful form, when the system is hidden from view.

As technology driven systems become more sophisticated the operator's role in system control also becomes increasingly important, even though they become less active in the control process – in highly automated systems human operators are frequently left to cope with the unexpected. Unexpected situations explicitly require a form of mental processing that is deliberate and, therefore, effortful. Thus it would seem axiomatic that information displayed to operators should facilitate 'automatic' tasks and support effortful mental processes. However, the display design philosophies of many current industrial processes do not appear to reflect the needs of the operators for tasks of detection and diagnosis of system failures.

Background

Problem solving scripts

Generally, for the cognitive approach, human-computer interaction is seen as presenting problems which have to be solved. Human problem solving is guided by a person's understanding of the domain of information which the problem under resolution represents. Such understanding, which can be conceptualized as a mental model or schema, organizes and directs a person's selection and usage of information in generating a solution.

One of the concepts of mental model is script, or event schema. Abelson (1981) defines a script as a hypothesized cognitive structure that when activated organizes comprehension of event-based situations. A script represents stereotyped knowledge structure that describes appropriate sequences of goal-directed actions in a particular context. Scripts consist from a number of scenes, which in turn are constituted by sequences of definite atomic operations. Each sequence of operations in scenes has a property of causal chain – every preceding action provides conditions for performing consequent actions.

In their script-based information processing model, Hershey et al. (1990) posit that scripts provide a framework that organizes the set of operations leading to the solution of a problem. They hypothesize that experts, through experience, develop problem-solving scripts, which are streamlined over time so that unimportant variables are dropped from the set of operations. The expert's first step then, is to select the proper script for a particular problem statement. Once this has been accomplished, proceeding to a solution is simply a matter of applying the algorithms called for by the script.

In our opinion, system developers can efficiently improve user interfaces, if they would provide a non-expert user with expert's problem-solving scripts at early stages of user's communication with the system. Such scripts could help a user to form true signposts within the task world and facilitate the building of the good user model of the task.

Spatial reasoning

As cognitive studies have repetitively proven, the representation of our knowledge is key to the effectiveness of our problem solving abilities. Many recent research indicate having the ability to make use of manipulation of spatial information, especially dynamic spatial displays, and, in particular, when users are provided with a display of the functional and procedural structure of a task, may make human-computer interaction tasks easier to perform. Computer graphics displays make it possible to display both the topological structure of a system and information about its current state using colour-coding and animation. Such displays should be especially valuable as user interfaces for decision support systems and systems for managing complex processes.

Virtual reality

Recently, virtual reality (VR) has been applied to a wide range of problems associated with industrial maintenance and manufacturing. Most applications can be placed in one or more of six main categories: visualization of complex data, controlling industrial robots, remote operation of equipment, enhancing communications, operations training, and virtual prototyping and design. These applications are but an initial step in identifying opportunities for using VR in manufacturing organizations. The three-dimensional nature of VR, and the mechanisms for interacting with objects in VR environments, makes the enormous amount of data available much more accessible to decision makers; travelling through, and manipulating objects within, the virtual facility offers a much more causal, natural and direct interaction than working indirectly through programs providing only two-dimensional representations of the problem. We believe that one of the most significant aspects of the technology is its ability to improve decision-making processes from both qualitative and quantitative perspectives.

Overview of the flexible script interface

Script graph

In addition to conventional pure textual descriptions of conditions and sequences of actions, we developed a new form of script representation which is a network representation in form of the event graph. Each node of such a graph corresponds to a definite scene (procedural sequence of actions) and may have several entry and exit points. Arcs connecting nodes correspond to transitions from one scene to another.

The syntax of FSI graphs can be briefly and informally described as follows. There are three types of nodes and three types of arcs in FSI. A node may be:

(i)   an atomic one; these nodes correspond to terminal level of nodes' hierarchy, which provides links to the application part of a program;

(ii) a composite node, or sub-script, which can be decomposed into atomic ones; these nodes represent medium level of aggregation in nodes' hierarchy, which is used to make interface representation more structural and better perceivable by the user;

(iii) a modifier node, a terminal node which initiates propagation of control information through the script graph; selection of such a node can re-configure the graph by creating or destroying nodes or by blocking and releasing links between them.

Arcs, or links, which connect nodes and allow to move from one node to another may be: (i) permitted, (ii) prohibited (temporarily blocked), or (iii) recommended. Prohibited links can change their status to permitted dependent on performing of defined prerequisite actions or as a response to activation of modifiers. User is free to choose transition through any permitted links, but usually only one of them would be marked as recommended.

Guidance

Gritzman, Kluge and Lovett (1995) define the concept of guidance as that the user interface should at any given time be directed towards giving the user maximum help in choosing among a limited set of relevant possibilities to fulfil the task. User guidance is especially relevant to the operator's support in the continuous process industries. A multitude of possibilities offered by traditional human-computer interfaces is not what a user needs when confronted with a task in a complex use setting with many other phenomena requiring attention.

An intelligent agent of FSI, the problem guide, uses procedural expertise about standard scripts and their permissible transformations to direct user's focus, to determine current subgoals, and to correct possible user's misconceptions. It controls dynamics of the script graph and uses mechanism of path blocking and releasing to inform user about consequences of his actions and choices and to direct his goal seeking behaviour. It also provides a user with on-line assistance by suggesting him the shortest way to the final goal through pointing out current subgoals.

Current state of the work

Flexible Script Interface has been implemented for the PersoPlan (Personal Planning), a decision support system based on psychological analysis of individual's motivation in decision making. The last version of the PersoPlan's user interface was restricted to a 2D interface with pop-up script windows. This implementation of FSI has been described in detail in our previous paper (Burmistrov, 1992).

Our current work focuses on the development of the 3D version of FSI which is mainly directed at supporting operators' decision support in process control industries. This section presents a mock-up of 3D interface which in particular is aimed at supporting collaborative problem solving in the VR environments.

Figures 1–5 show our vision of future decision support interface in process control. These pictures were rendered with presentation quality to provide the basis for discussion with and evaluation by the experts in the domain, software engineers and operators.

425

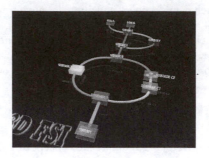

Figure 1   Bird's eye view

Figure 1 presents a bird eye view of the 3D graph with ENTRY node nearest to the viewer, two goal nodes – GOAL A and GOAL B – on the horizon, and a number of intermediate nodes and links between them. The graph represents the hierarchical structure of actions which are performed within the problem-solving activity and the sequence in which they are performed. Sequence generally flows forward throughout the graph from initial node (ENTRY node) to end nodes (GOAL A and GOAL B nodes). One of the main characteristic features of the FSI graph is that it does not present simultaneously the complete collection of actions and transitions, which are permissible in the system. FSI is based on the principles of task context and cognitive economy in its representation of a task structure. In FSI a user is faced with a predefined 'standard' script graph of the top level of task structure hierarchy. This provides a user with a 'general view' of a task structure.

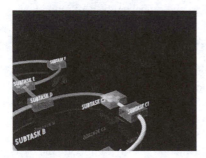   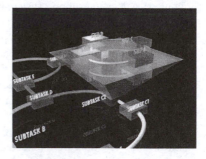

Figure 2   Decomposition of node C2   **Figure 3   Lower level procedural**
**   actions**

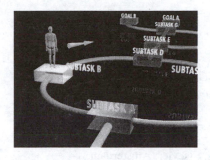

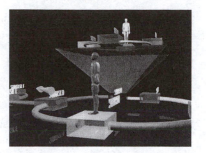

Figure 4   System guide

Figure 5   Avatars used to help co-ordinate progress in joint task performance

Graph nodes can be further decomposed into smaller procedural sequences of actions. Decomposition results in presenting new 'floors' in the representation of the task world. Figure 2 and figure 3 show the decomposition of the node SUBTASK C2 into lower level sub-script of procedural actions, named here STEP A, STEP B, STEP C, and STEP D.

Figure 4 presents the concept of the system guide whose recommendation is represented here as a flying arrow in front of the body icon.

3D FSI may naturally provide support for collaborative problem solving, allowing different team members to perform different actions in parallel in a shared simulated world. Team-mates are represented in the scene by body icons (avatars) of different colour, allowing each team member to get an overview of what is going on in other parts of the task world, to co-ordinate individual efforts, and to keep track of the progress in joint task performance (see figure 5).

Practical implementations of FSI could span the range from true virtual reality with stereoscopic immersion display helmets and gloves to a more modest evolution of 2D graphic user interfaces into 3D versions. It is important to note that VR systems can co-exist and communicate with more conventional systems.

References

Abelson, R. P. (1981), 'Psychological status of the script concept'. *American Psychologist*, Vol. 36, pp. 715-729.

Burmistrov, I. (1992), 'Flexible Script Interface: an intelligent spatial interaction style', in G. C. van der Veer et al. (eds.), *Human-Computer Interaction: Tasks and Organization. Proceedings of ECCE6*. CUD: Rome.

Gritzman, M., Kluge, A. & Lovett, H. (1995), 'Task orientation in user interface design', in K. Nordby et al. (eds.), *Human-Computer Interaction: Interact'95*. Chapman and Hall: London.

Hershey, D. A., Walsh, D. A., Read, S. J. & Chulef, A. S. (1990), 'The effects of expertise on financial problem solving: evidence for goal-directed, problem-solving scripts'. *Organizational Behavior and Human Decision Processes*, Vol. 46, pp. 77-101.

Stahre, J. (1993), 'Humanufacturing– operator decision support in a CIM environment', in M. J. Smith & G. Salvendy (eds.), *Human-Computer Interaction: Applications and Case Studies*. Elsevier: Amsterdam.

Ye, N. & Salvendy, G. (1993), 'Introducing problem solving strategies of users into the interface design', in G. Salvendy & M. J. Smith (eds.), *Human-Computer Interaction: Software and Hardware Interfaces*. Elsevier: Amsterdam.

54 Theories and interface design: designing interfaces with ecological and cognitive task analysis

Marcia Crosland and Eric Sparre*
Georgia Institute of Technology, USA
*Asea Brown Boveri, Sweden

Abstract

In this paper, we report a case study that demonstrates how ecological and cognitive task analytic methods, emanating from divergent theoretical viewpoints, lead to different interface designs of the same information. While both methods seek to enhance performance, they identify different constraints on task performance. We compare the analytic steps of each method and conclude that an integration of the methods into a 'constraint analysis' would be a useful tool for interface designers.

Introduction

The purpose of the current article is to describe how the theoretical assumptions underlying ecological and cognitive task analytic methods influence the design of an industrial process interface. A primary goal of task analytic methods is to identify what constrains people as they perform a task. Despite the importance of constraint analysis, many designers perform such an analysis in an intuitive, informal manner (Shepard, 1995). Two methods are available to guide constraint analysis, ecological and cognitive task analysis. These two approaches differ fundamentally as to how the important constraints on task performance are conceptualized. From a theoretical perspective, the ecological viewpoint (Brunswik, 1952; Gibson, 1966; Kirlik,1995) espouses the notion that task performance is primarily constrained by the availability of data to specify the constraints on goal related actions. However, the theoretical rationale of a cognitive task analytic approach is that task performance is primarily constrained by the information processing demands of the task (Miller, 1973; Fleishman & Quaintance, 1984; Card & Newell, 1989).

Because the design goal is to enhance the efficiency and effectiveness of human-machine interaction, performance assumptions are essential in identifying task performance constraints. According to Rasmussen (1994), the power of analytic techniques lie in their ability to show a system designer 'the big picture' by identifying the crucial aspects of human-work interaction. The particular analytic technique, however, can alter the 'picture' the designer sees changing which aspects of human-work interaction are considered to be crucial.

In industrial systems, there are many constraints on human performance produced by the task of controlling a complex process. Human control of complex industrial systems is constrained by operator perception, comprehension of goal related actions, system state changes and associated cognitive processing demands. The mitre for the quality of human performance in these systems is the selection of a context appropriate action which is critically linked to safety and productivity. Action selection is critical across a diverse range of industrial tasks as follows: (i) process regulation, (ii) optimization, (iii) quick economic changeovers, and (iv) breakdown avoidance and management. In addition, supervising these tasks in industrial systems such as power plants, paper mills, or power networks, is characterized by the complexity of the systems, and their real-time non-linear dynamic behaviour. Such systems place great cognitive demands on human operators and are known to be difficult to control and supervise (Brehmer, 1992). Thus, human perception, action, and cognition are crucial aspects in system control and thus relevant to design.

The purpose of our discussion is to show how task analytic methods can be associated with different views of human performance and how this influences the interface design. We report a case study that demonstrates the impact of theory on the analytic process and how this can lead to different interface designs of the same information. The study describes the design rationale, objectives, and resulting interface designs associated with ecological and cognitive task analytic methods of a simulated industrial process.

Methods

The evaporator The materials for this case study include a simulation representing a forced circulation evaporator commonly used in industries such as paper manufacture, sugar mills, and aluminum production. The process, as described by Carling (1993), concentrates dilute liquors by evaporating solvents from the feed stream. The feed is mixed with recirculating liquor at a high flow-rate and then is pumped into a vertical heat exchanger. The exchanger is steam heated and produces condensate on the outside of the tube walls. The liquor which passes along the inside of the tube boils, and then passes to a separation vessel, where liquor and vapour are separated. The liquor is recirculated with some of it drawn off as a product. The vapour is usually condensed by cooling, in which water often is used as coolant. A goal of the system is to maintain the steady state by manipulating the product flow-rate, steam pressure, and cooling water flow-rate.

Traditional interface   For this case study, we used three simulation interface designs. Two interface designs were constructed using task analytic methods, while a third interface design was used as a reference. The reference design is a graphical display of a simulator constructed by Newell and Lee (1989) which represents the current practice in design. It depicts the structural relationships of the elements within the evaporator and is commonly referred to as a 'P&I' interface indicating pipes and instrumentation. It was built according to the P&I diagram that already existed for the process. Dynamic digital readouts for variables that could be measured in a corresponding real evaporator were added. This includes pressures, flows, levels, temperatures, and concentrations. The separator level is also indicated through a bar graph. This is a common way to indicate levels and volumes. Each of the three controlled valves include automatic control loops. This allows the human operator to request a certain flow or pressure set point which then will be automatically kept by the controller, rather than having to adjust valve openings manually.

Design rationale

Ecological task analysis (ETA)   A design rationale provides the fundamental reasons, principles, and logical basis for design decisions. The design rationale for ecological task analysis (Kirlik, 1995) is that skilled performance is directly related to the efficient selection of appropriate control actions. For each possible action (or class of actions) that can be taken, a set of constraints exists that determine the productivity of the action. As a basis for selection of the appropriate actions during task performance, the action constraints within an operational system should be depicted perceptually on the human-machine interface. The design goal is to minimize the need for complex reasoning about correct control actions. Cognitive processing is necessary only when the perceptual characteristics of an environment fail to direct action.

Cognitive task analysis (CTA)   This approach is theoretically grounded in the assumption that human task performance is directly constrained by the information processing demands placed on the operator. Information processing demands are determined by the general perceptual and cognitive processing demands, as well as, the declarative, procedural, and strategic knowledge requirements of task performance. For each task within a given operational system, there are processing demands posed by the dynamic quality of the system and specific cognitive activities required of the operator. Thus, the cognitive task analysis objective is to identify the information processing requirements of task performance. The goal is to identify possible constraints and organize the interface data to overcome processing barriers

431

(e.g. Wickens, 1995). According to this design rationale, human performance can be enhanced if information processing demands are reduced. Further, the design goal is to reduce information processing by data presentation and feedback tailored to the specific information processing needs.

Design objective   In this phase of design, the methods define the design space, what it contains, and focus attention on certain features and relationships. The evaporative system is analysed as follows:

Ecological task analysis   The objective is to identify context appropriate control actions and constraints. In **step 1**, we identify the three possible control actions as follows: (i) adjust the steam pressure; (ii) adjust the cooling water flow, and (iii) adjust the output flow.

In **step 2**, the overall system goals are listed:
(i) produce as much product as possible within concentration range using the least among of steam and cooling and (ii) prevent damage to the separator from liquid imbalances, and to the heat exchanger.

In **step 3**, list the critical system relationships:
>   PRESSURE ---> Vapour rate + operating pressure ->separator level
>   COOLING--> Condensation rate --> operating pressure
>   FLOW-->Input(flow rate X concentration) = Output(flow rate X concentration)
>   Input flow rate = output flow rate + vapour rate

step 4: identify and list the productive actions and constraints that achieve a system goal.
  (i)   **Action**: Adjust output flow rate - **Goal**: Maintain product concentration.
        Constraints: Input flow rate, input & output concentration.
  (ii) **Action**: Adjust output flow rate & steam pressure - **Goal**: Maintain liquid balance.
        Constraints: Input flow rate, vapour rate, separator level.
  (iii) **Action**: Adjust steam pressure & cooling water - **Goal**: Minimize steam & cooling.
        Constraints: Separator level & operating pressure.

Cognitive task analysis   The objective is to identify the information processing demands associated with the tasks of controlling the operating system. In **step 1**, list the control tasks: (i) pressure, (ii) cooling, and (iii) flow.

Step 2 and **step 3** in CTA are identical to step 2 and 3 in ETA.

In **step 4** of CTA, list the general cognitive activities as follow: (i) detection of deviation, (ii) comprehension of system state, (iii) decisions about actions, and (iv) prediction of future state. The objective of **step 5** is to classify and list the specific perceptual/cognitive activities associated with each control task (see table 1).

Table 1
Perceptual/cognitive activities associated with each control task

Task	Perceptual/Cognitive Activity
Flow	Observe & compare input flow rate to output flow & vapour rate
Pressure	Observe & detect separator level change, Compare to operating pressure & cooling rate
Cooling	Observe & detect change in operating pressure, Compare vapour to condensate fluctuations, Compare to rate of steam change

CTA: Design product The CTA interface is a graphical display (Sparre & Crosland, 1995) which displays the dynamic trend of each element within the evaporator. This display is designed as a graphical representation of the operational environment consistent with the specific information processing activities and activities of the operator. Based on the designers analysis and operators self assessments, a primary activity of the operator is the detection and extensive comparison of the pattern of change between each system element. The trend interface shows the rate of change and goal state for each system element, as well as, providing feedback on the effect of operator actions. The interface design is intended to support the general cognitive tasks of detection of deviation from system goals, prediction of system state, decisions about action selection, and feedback about the effect of operator actions consistent with the design suggestions of Woods, 1995. In addition, it was noted that optimum control of cooling and, thus, operating pressure required comparison between the rate of change of two system elements, condensate and vapour. Therefore, these two elements were displayed together in a trend consistent with the proximity compatibility principle (Carswell and Wickens, 1987; Wickens and Carswell, 1995).

ETA: Design product The ETA interface design was constructed by Erik Sparre at Asea Brown Boveri (ABB). It contains two X-Y diagrams depicting the functional constraints among the elements involved in the maintenance of product concentration and liquid balance.

In the product concentration diagram (mass balance), the relationship between the input and output flow and concentrations is displayed. The flows are shown on one axis and concentrations on the other. Plotting the points for the input flow rate and concentration and output flow rate and concentration will generate two rectangles that will have the same area in a steady state. A line can be plotted from the input flow rate and concentration showing where the output flow rate and concentration will settle. The diagram allows the operator to read each individual variable, determine if steady state is achieved and if necessary take corrective action to achieve a certain concentration value.

The liquid balance diagram depicts the constraining relationship between the input flow rate, output flow rate, vapour, and separator level based on functional equations. It shows that the input flow rate equals the total outflow (output flow rate and vapour rate). If the input flow is different from the total outflow, the separator volume will

433

Marcia Crosland and Eric Sparre

change at the rate of the flow difference. The effect on separator level is easily calculated from this. A large bar graph indicates the current separator value, as well as, the input, output, and vapour flow rate. They are placed next to each other and a balance beam is placed on top, so that it will tilt according to the rate of separator change. The balance beam and flow bars are connected to the vertical movement of the separator bar graph, and the tilting of the beam is scaled so that its tip points at the expected separator value one minute into the future.

Conclusion

The purpose of our discussion has been to show how the choice between ecological and cognitive task analysis influences design through divergent theoretical foundations. While the goal in both task analytic methods is to enhance performance by minimizing the need for complex cognitive activity, the approaches are different. Ecological task analysis identifies constraints on control action selection, while cognitive task analysis identifies information processing constraints.

Enhancing human performance through interface design is accomplished by identifying the information critical to task performance. The type of information required by an operator within any system changes with skill level and system conditions (Rasmussen, 1986). In this line of thinking, skilled operators can accomplish tasks through direct perception when information is available to specify actions but during skill acquisition or fault conditions must depend on cognitively mediated information processing.

Evidence from training research shows that an interface design resulting from cognitive task analysis facilitates the development of efficient control strategies when compared to an ecological interface (Crosland, Walker, Corso & Sparre, 1996). A cognitive design strategy optimizes training and leads to increased operator efficiency. Further research will be needed to show if a cognitive design strategy facilitates fault detection and remediation.

Our findings suggest that an integration of ecological and cognitive task analysis into a 'constraint analysis' would benefit an interface designer. Identifying task constraints is important to facilitating all levels of human performance across task conditions. Future research will be needed to address other pertinent aspects of task analytic methods, interface design and human performance.

References

Berlinger, C., Angell, D., & Shearer, J. W. (1964). 'Behaviors, measures, and instruments for performance evaluation in simulated environment'. *Proceedings, Symposium, and Workshop on the Quantification of Human Performance.* Albuquerque, N. M.

Brehmer, B. (1992). 'Dynamic decision making: Human control of complex systems'. *Acta Psychologica*, Vol. 81, pp. 211-241.

Brunswik, E. (1952). 'The conceptual framework of psychology'. *International Encyclopedia of Unified Science*, Vol. 1(10), University of Chicago Press: Chicago, IL.

Carling, E. (1993). 'Performance, mental models and background knowledge in mastering a simulated dynamic system' in, M. J. Smith and G. Salvendy (eds.), *Human-Computer Interaction: application and case studies*. Elsevier: New York.

Card, S. K., & Newell, A. (1989). 'Cognitive architectures' in, Jerome I. Elkind, Stuart K. Card, Julian Hochberg, and Beverly Messick Huey (eds.), *Human performance models for computer-aided engineering*. National Academy Press: Washington, DC.

Carswell, C. M. & Wickens, C. D. (1987). 'Information integration and the object display: An interaction of task demands and display superiority'. *Ergonomics*, Vol. 30, pp. 511-527.

Crosland, M., Walker, N., Corso, G., & Sparre, E. (1996). 'Training interface design and task analytic methods'. *Proceedings of the 40th Annual Meeting of the Human Factors and Ergonomics Society*, Human Factors Society: Philadelphia, PA.

Flach, J. M. (1990). 'The ecology of human-machine systems I: Introduction'. *Ecological Psychology*, Vol. 2, pp. 191-205.

Fleishman, E. A., & Quaintance, M. K. (1984). 'The description of human tasks'. *Taxonomies of Human Performance*, Academic Press: San Diego, CA.

Gibson, J. J. (1979). *The ecological approach to visual perception*. Houghton-Mifflin: Boston, MA.

Kirlik, A. (1995). 'Requirements for psychological models to support design; Toward ecological task analysis'. In J. M. Flach, P. A. Hancock, J. K. Caird, & Vicente, K. J. (eds.), *Global perspectives on the ecology of human machine systems*. Erlbaum: Hillsdale, NJ.

Miller, R. B. (1973). 'Development of a taxonomy of human performance. Design of a systems task vocabulary'. *JSAS Catalog of Selected Documents in Psychology*, Vol. 3, pp. 29-30.

Newell, R. B. & Lee, P. L., (1989). *Applied process control. A case study*. Prentice Hall: Sydney.

Shepard, A. (1995). 'Task analysis as a framework for examining HCI tasks'. In A. F. Monk & N. Gilbert (eds.), *Perspectives on HCI: diverse approaches*. Harcourt Brace: New York.

Sparre, E. & Crosland, M. (1995). *Trend interface design to enhance operator control [Computer interface design]*. Lund, Sweden: ABB, Corporate Research.

Wickens, C. D. & Carswell, C. M. (1995). 'The proximity compatibility principle: Its psychological foundation and relevance to display design'. *Human Factors*, Vol. 37, pp. 473-494.

Woods, D. (1995). 'Making intelligent and automated systems team players'. *Industrial Summer School on Human-Centered Automation*. Held in Saint-Lary, France, August 21-25, Organized by EURISCO.

Acknowledgements

The authors wish to thank Neff Walker and Gregory M. Corso for their helpful comments during the preparation of this manuscript. This work was supported through the participation of ABB Corporate Research in the Research Affiliates Program of the Graphics, Visualization, and Usability Center of Georgia Institute of Technology.

55 A cognitive psychological framework for the description and evaluation of interfaces

Torsten Heinbokel, Eric Leimann, Heinz Willumeit
and Rainer H. Kluwe
University of the Federal Armed Forces,
Hamburg, Germany

Abstract

In this paper we elaborate a framework of human-machine interaction referring to action theory and cognitive theories of human information processing. This framework provides a scheme for the description of task and interface attributes that can be applied to derive hypotheses concerning the design of interfaces.

Introduction

The design of the user interface is crucial in developing useful and effective tools for the users of human-machine systems. There are two questions of particular importance at different points in the development process. The first question concerns the specification and implementation of interfaces: how can one support efficient control performance by means of an appropriate interface? The second question refers to the evaluation of interfaces: which interface attributes have an impact on the control performance of operators? However, the knowledge about the design of efficient and usable interfaces for complex human-machine systems, for instance power plants, is incomplete. We believe that it is a reasonable research strategy first to identify interfaces and interface attributes that effectively support task performance and enhance efficiency of use, then to develop improved interfaces on this basis and to evaluate them empirically (cf. Andriole & Adelman, 1995). As a first step in this programme it is our goal to develop a coherent framework of human-machine interaction which allows a description of interface attributes. This is intended to provide an integrative approach to the design and evaluation of interfaces that can be applied to derive hypotheses regarding the design of interfaces for process control environments.

A cognitive psychological framework of human-machine interaction

In our view there are good reasons to set up a theoretical framework of human-machine interaction based on a theory of human action and the underlying cognitive mechanisms. In the following we will briefly summarize the action theories formulated by Hacker (1986) and Rasmussen (1986). These theories are intended to clarify the role of cognition in the control of actions.

Actions are defined as the smallest unit of behaviour related to a conscious goal. The goal involves a representation of future results serving as a point of comparison for the action. The goal also provides the motivational basis for the action. An action can be described as a sequence of steps directed towards the attainment of a goal. Action preparation comprises goal formation, orientation towards relevant conditions in the environment, specification of an action programme involving the development of variants. This preparatory phase ends with the selection of an action programme to be executed. The execution of an action programme itself has to be monitored implying that the action programme has to be, at least partly, stored in working memory. However, an action programme is not necessarily worked out completely beforehand. Feedback processing comprises the perception and interpretation of environmental stimuli and the evaluation against the set goal. Feedback loops as described by the TOTE unit (Miller, Gallanter & Pribram, 1960) are the basic units of an action. Feedback loops can be nested in various ways implying that there is a hierarchy of goals where subgoals are instrumental for the attainment of higher order goals.

This distinction refers to the hierarchical aspects of action control. It is assumed that there exist different modes of processing that can be characterized by specific properties of information processing. Empirical evidence suggests to distinguish between automatic and controlled processing (Schneider & Shiffrin, 1977). Automatic processing is described as fast, effortless and performed in parallel. Thus, automatic responses are difficult to ignore, suppress or modify. Controlled processing on the other side is assumed to be conscious information processing. It is slow, labourious and capacity limited. Unlike automatic processing it is perceived as sequential and resource limited. Recent empirical and analytical findings reveal that it makes sense to think of the modes of processing not as a dichotomy but as a continuum (Logan, 1985). Hence, we distinguish similarly to Hacker (1986) and Rasmussen (1986) three modes of processing. The mode in-between automatic and controlled processing is designated skilled processing. It is supposed that in skilled processing action patterns are activated and executed. This mode is related to diffuse awareness (Reason, 1985).

Table 1
A cognitive psychological framework of human action

Steps in the action process	Modes of processing		
	Automatic processing	Skilled processing	Controlled processing
Goal formation		Activation of goals and subgoals: triggered by cues from the environment.	Development of a goal hierarchy: components and dependency analysis.
Orientation	Sensory reception and processing of environmental stimuli: pattern formation.	Signal detection, observation and classification: categorization, recognition, chunking, simple judgements.	Interpretation, diagnosis and prognosis: complex judgements, analogical reasoning and use of metaphors.
Action specification	Activation of movement oriented schemata and cognitive routines: feature match.	Selection of an action schema associated with a cue: 'recognize act cycle'.	Action planning and selection: reasoning, use of heuristics (e.g. means-end analysis), decision-making.
Execution and monitoring	Execution of stored motor programmes (physical execution) and cognitive routines (mental execution).	Execution and monitoring of action schemata.	Execution and monitoring of plans and strategies: encoding and retrieval from memory, elaboration of plan.
Feedback processing	Processing of proprioceptive (e.g. kinaesthetic) and exteroceptive (e.g. visual) feedback on performance.	Detection, observation and classification of external environmental feedback (signals).	Interpretation of feedback involving analysis and synthesis of information, evaluation against the set goals.

439

The steps in the action process and the modes of processing provide the theoretical foundation for a framework model of human action as shown in table 1. The vertical dimension is built by the steps in the action process. The horizontal dimension refers to the different modes of processing. The cognitive processes that belong in the cells of the framework are briefly characterized within the table. It is postulated that there is no goal formation in automatic processing because these processes are under the control of higher order goals and subgoals. Hence this cell is blank.

Different layers of the framework

Different layers of the framework can be elaborated to extend the framework model to a description of tasks, behaviour and interface attributes. The task layer comprises a description of task demands which can be derived from cognitive task analysis. Those operations and cognitive processes that take place in actual control of behaviour are described on the behaviour layer. Arnold and Roe (1987) as well as Zapf, Brodbeck, Frese, Peters and Prümper (1992) proposed error classification schemes based on the same theoretical foundation as applied here. In the following the framework is applied to the description of interface attributes regarding their impact on cognitive performance. For reasons of space we concentrate on an exemplary description of interface attributes concerning goal formation and orientation.

The framework as a scheme for the description of interface attributes

Interaction between the operator and the technical system takes place on the interface. This means that information about the technical system is presented on a display and that the operator controls the technical system with input controls as keyboards or touch screens. In human-machine interaction the user has to translate from psychologically expressed goals and intentions to the physical variables of the system and vice versa (Norman, 1986). Increased capabilities of the technical systems, use of automatic controllers and decision support systems brought about changes of operators' tasks in process control environments. Nowadays, the operators often act as a kind of supervisor, 'setting initial conditions for, intermittently adjusting, and receiving information from a computer that itself closes a control loop (i.e. interconnects) through external sensors, effectors, and the task environment' (Sheridan, 1987, p. 1244).

Interface attributes supporting goal formation   Goal formation refers to controlled processing which is assumed to be conscious information processing.

Functionality of a system is a critical issue in order to support goal development and action planning in controlled processing. That is, an interface should provide relevant functions and procedures to accomplish a task. Goals and subgoals can refer to different levels of abstraction (cf. Goodstein, 1981; Rasmussen, 1986). For example, a goal can be related to the functional purpose of the system, e.g. safe power production, while another goal refers to the physical function of a subcomponent, e.g. repairing a valve. The interface should support means-end analyses regarding different level goals. It should be made obvious to the operator which action alternatives are possible means to achieve the goal. There should be identity cues between actions and user goals (Polson & Lewis, 1990). Hence, the most important interface attributes that have an impact on cognitive performance in goal formation refer to functionality and representation of the system rather than its presentation on the interface.

Interface attributes supporting orientation In automatic processing sensory reception and pattern formation differ dependent on the physical properties of the environmental input. Each sensory modality can be described by specific properties as the capacity of the short term sensory store. Hence, the medium selected for presentation as well as physical properties of the sign code have to be taken into account.

In skilled processing information is perceived as a signal (Hacker, 1986). Performance in signal detection is strongly affected by the amount of information on the display, and the modality and magnitude of the signal (cf. Wickens, 1992). Signals are action relevant stimuli integrated into some knowledge system on the task. Hence, semantic coding referring to the meaning of a sign is crucial in skilled processing. Observed information is classified as a particular instance of an object, event or state of the system. Pattern recognition is facilitated by information integration, for example by grouping of variables in object displays (cf. Woods, 1987). Other important aspects regarding the information coding are: provision of context information like tolerance levels for a particular variable, information reduction by preprocessing of data in order not to overload the operator and the use of clear and familiar presentation formats. Icons specifically match the latter aspect. The larger use of display technology has brought the aspect of sequential versus parallel data presentation to the forefront. Woods (1987) suggest a variety of measures as perceptual landmarks and spatial representations to support information integration if task relevant information is spread over multiple screens.

Orientation and prognosis in controlled processing usually refer to higher levels of abstraction. In controlled processing information is perceived as a symbol (Rasmussen, 1986). That is, perceived information is interpreted for example as abstract entity or indicating relations between abstract entities. Symbolic encoding of information, hierarchical organization of displays and provision of multiple views can support interpretation. Use of analogies and metaphors can be measures to code information symbolically.

Application of the framework

The present section poses the question, can the framework outlined in the previous sections be used to develop hypotheses concerning the advantages of particular interfaces. Since we are doing research in the field of process control interfaces, the following examples and conclusions will be concerned with this range of applications.

Interfaces for process control

Traditional P&I diagrams can be regarded as a standard for industrial process control interfaces. They provide users with an elemental physical representation of a system, for example, a power plant using a set of special symbols for the display of pumps, pipes, valves and other functional units. Usually those interfaces work on a very low level of abstraction, so that Goodstein calls them single-sensor-single-indicator (SSSI) displays (Goodstein, 1981). Over the last few years several alternatives to the widely used P&I diagrams have been proposed. Regarding these alternative interfaces, we will break down those proposals into three different subfields: full scale interfaces, assistant devices and navigation tools.

Full scale interfaces Full scale interfaces display the full range of information that is needed to control the process. Examples are Multilevel Flow Model (MFM, Lind, 1981) or Ecological Interface Design (EID, Vicente, 1992). The MFM is based on the abstraction hierarchy that enables the operator to analyse a given situation on various levels. Lind names five levels that range from the very basic description of the appearance and spatial location of the components (physical form) to the highest level describing the functional purpose of the whole system (functional purpose). MFM provides the operator with a multilevel representation format to give him a better chance to cope with unfamiliar and unanticipated problems. The methodology uses a grammar of abstract icons to describe a power plant in terms of mass and energy flow functions. The EID approach refers to the MFM theoretically as far as the concept of various levels of information is concerned. EID interfaces also intend to show both, low level physical information and higher order functional information. A major difference to the MFM is that EID does not use the abstract and unfamiliar grammar of MFM, but tries to find iconic metaphors and representations that illustrate functional relations within the system in a more intuitive way. Different design philosophies, questions like 'what information should be offered' or 'which symbols or what grammar should be used', are underlying the conception of full scale interfaces.

Assistant devices and navigational tools Assistant devices are tools that support special functions within the whole process of controlling the system. Those tools can be seen in context with single cognitive processes in the control of action. Acoustic signals for example are generally used to draw the attention of the operator to a fault. Object displays (cf. Woods, 1987) are specifically used to enhance the process of integrating given information. Predictive displays are useful in the development of prognoses, 'What-If-Displays' in action planning and decision-making. Safety displays (cf. Woods 1987), as a last example, give feedback on higher levels of the abstraction hierarchy. Finally we regard navigation tools as a unit that should be examined separately from the conceptions for full scale interfaces or assistant devices named above. Navigation tools can also support specific units of the action cycle. Today most process control interfaces still use serial data presentation. But other forms of navigation like different menu structures or the idea of a rolling map have specific advantages that should not be neglected.

Discussion

This paper presents a framework of human-machine interaction. It provides a scheme for the description of various aspects relevant for the design of user interfaces: task demands, behaviour and interface attributes. The different layers of the framework have yet to be fully elaborated. The specification of interface attributes with reference to human action and its underlying cognitive mechanisms is intended to provide a basis for the design and evaluation of interfaces. First, for the specification and selection of an appropriate interface for a given task. Second, for the evaluation of interfaces considering relevant attributes of the task and user behaviour.

References

Andriole, S. & Adelman, L. (1995). *Cognitive systems engineering for user-computer interface design, prototyping, and evaluation.* Lawrence Erlbaum: Hillsdale, New Jersey.

Arnold, B. & Roe, R.A. (1987). 'User errors in human-computer interaction', in M. Frese, E. Ulich & W. Dzida (eds.). *Psychological Issues of human computer interaction in the work place.* North-Holland: Amsterdam.

Goodstein, (1981) 'Discriminative displays support for process operations', in J. Rasmussen & W.B. Rouse (eds.) *Human detection and diagnosis of system failures.* Plenum: New York.

Hacker, W. (1986). *Arbeitspsychologie* [work psychology]. Bern: Huber.

Lind, M. (1981). 'The use of flow models for automated plant diagnosis', in J. Rasmussen & W.B. Rouse (eds.) *Human detection and diagnosis of system failures*. Plenum: New York.

Logan, G.D. (1985). 'Skill and automaticity: relations, implications, and future directions'. *Canadian Journal of Psychology*, Vol. 39, pp. 367-386.

Miller, G.A., Galanter, E. & Pribram, K.H. (1960). *Plans and the structure of behaviour.* Holt, Rinehart and Winston: New York.

Polson, P.G. & Lewis, C.H. (1990). Theory-based design for easily learned interfaces. *Human-Computer Interaction*, Vol. 5, pp. 191-220.

Rasmussen, J. (1986). *Information processing and human-machine interaction.* North-Holland: New York.

Reason, J.T. (1985). 'Absent-mindedness and cognitive control', in J.E. Harris & P.E. Morris (eds.). *Everyday memory, actions and absent-mindedness.* Academic Press: London.

Schneider, W. & Shiffrin, R.M. (1977). 'Controlled and automatic human information processing: I. Detection, search, and attention'. *Psychological Review,* Vol. 84, pp. 1-66.

Sheridan, T.B. (1987). 'Supervisory control', in G. Salvendy (ed.). *Handbook of Human Factors.* John Wiley: New York.

Vicente, K. (1992). 'Multilevel interfaces for power control rooms I: an integrative review'. *Nuclear Safety*, Vol. 33, pp. 381-397.

Woods, D.D. (1987). 'Human factors challenges in process control', in G. Salvendy (ed.). Handbook of Human Factors. John Wiley: New York.

Zapf, D., Brodbeck, F.C., Frese, M., Peters, H. & Prümper, J. (1992). 'Errors in working with computers. A first validation of a taxonomy for observed errors in a field setting'. *International Journal of Human-Computer Interaction*, Vol. 4, pp. 311-339.

Acknowledgement

Preparation of this paper was supported by a grant from the Volkswagen Foundation awarded to the last author.

56 The effectiveness of using combined mimic/emergent features and mimic/multilevel flow modelling displays in a pilot process control environment

Mark Gill and Enda F. Fallon
University College Galway, Ireland

Abstract

Operator performance in monitoring complex automated control systems requires assistance. One method of providing this is through the use of display based performance aids. Emergent features and multilevel flow modelling (MFM) are two methods of display design which have been proposed for this purpose. In attempting to successfully use these methods, difficulties have been encountered due to the manner in which the required data is presented. One possible approach to tackling these difficulties would be to develop a display which combines either emergent features or MFM with a mimic of the process being monitored.

This paper documents the development of two such displays for a small pilot plant process. The results of usability tests carried out to determine whether there was a benefit to be gained in using the respective displays for fault detection and isolation tasks are reported. The combined mimic/emergent features displays did not provide a benefit to operator performance when monitoring the process. The number of continuous variables was insufficient in this case for the effective use of emergent feature displays. The results of the usability testing also indicate that while the mimic/MFM aid was useful, it did not necessarily provide a positive contribution to performance in fault detection and isolation. In order to effectively utilise this type of aid the issue of training needs to be addressed.

Introduction

Industrial progress has led to an increasingly more automated working environment in which computer controlled systems ensure that the desired product of a process is obtained with little intervention from operators. In such systems the main role of operators is one of monitoring and supervision in which they are required to assimilate information from various sources and to assess whether the status of the process being monitored is as desired. Fault detection and isolation are an integral part of this activity. Detection requires the operator to recognise that a fault is present, while isolation requires the identification of the cause or causes of such a fault. Greater plant complexity has led to an increase in the number of familiar and novel faults that can occur in a process resulting in difficulties in their detection and isolation. One way of assuring operator performance in such a scenario is to provide job aids. Several approaches to aiding operator performance in fault detection and isolation have proved successful to varying degrees, e.g. intelligent interfaces (Yoon and Hammer, 1988), and fault tree aids (Hwang and Cheng, 1992). Positive effects have also been noted from the use of representative aiding approaches to interface display design. Two such approaches are the use of emergent features and multilevel flow modelling (MFM).

The concept of emergent features involves the design of a display which combines simple, visual elements resulting in the emergence of new features. Those elements which make up the display (low-level data) are normally scaled in relation to dynamic variables and a characteristic (size, shape, etc.) of the resulting emergent features provides high-level information on the status of the process being monitored. The use of MFM involves the display of a dynamic process as a set of flow structures. The flow structures represent the transfer of energy or mass through the process and show how the process handles this flow under normal and abnormal conditions. The main problem associated with the use of emergent feature displays is that it is difficult to extract both low-level and high-level data from the one display. In the case of MFM displays, problems arise from the fact that while the representation used reflects plant functional structure, it does not always match the user's mental model of the system (Lind, 1991). The use of a mimic, which is responsive to all component changes in the system, in conjunction with these representative aids may alleviate the problems described. In this paper the utility of this approach in a small pilot plant environment is assessed. Two performance aids based on emergent features and MFM were developed. They were used in conjunction with a plant mimic to assist in fault detection and isolation when monitoring a small pilot plant process. A number of 'usability' tests were carried out to assess whether operator performance was enhanced through their use.

Representational displays

Emergent features

Emergent feature displays are used to display dynamic data from a number of sources on one screen in a related manner allowing the operator to perform his task with the help of obvious perceptual clues rather than through labourious inference. The concept can be explained by an example. When simple visual elements are combined, new features sometimes appear that were not present in the original elements. For instance, three straight lines can be joined to form a triangle which produces the features of closure, area and symmetry. These are called emergent features because they arise from the arrangement of the lines without being identifiable with any single line. In a graphic display, each of the lines which make up the triangle can be dynamically scaled so that a regular triangle might represent normal working conditions, while an irregular triangle might represent an abnormality in the system. According to Bennett and Flach (1992), 'this type of display has the potential to improve decision making performance by shifting the burden of responsibility from the cognitive processes that are severely limited (e.g. working memory) to cognitive processes that, with learning, are virtually unlimited, (e.g. object perception and pattern recognition)'.

Multilevel flow modelling (MFM)

Multilevel flow modelling displays describe process plants in terms of flow structures which represent the balanced flow of mass and energy through the plant. MFM displays are normally arranged hierarchically for the purpose of managing complexity. Each of the pages in the hierarchy represents a modular subsystem or flow unit, e.g. functions that can exist separately such as material supply, heating of material, transfer of material, etc. The hierarchical format also shows the relationship between each flow unit, indicating which flow units have to be balanced to allow flow units at a higher level in the hierarchy to balance. A set of standard flow function symbols are normally used. Both Lind (1991) and Duncan, Praetorious & Milne (1989) use six symbols. A brief explanation of each follows:

- **Source**   Represents the source of energy or the flow of energy mass.
- **Sink**   The absorption of mass or energy or a reservoir of mass or energy.
- **Storage**   Represents mass or energy being contained or stored.
- **Balance**   Represents the balance or distribution of mass.
- **Transport**   Movement of mass or energy through the plant.
- **Barrier**   Indicates that mass or energy is prevented from flowing.

447

Pilot plant description

The pilot plant used enables raw materials to be heated, mixed and blended with the aim of obtaining a desired output material. It consists of three sub-processes. Sub-process A is a pre-processing stage where material is heated, recirculated and then transported to the next sub-process at a desired temperature. Sub-process B is a continuous blending process where material from Sub-process A is blended with similar colder material from a different source. The quantities of hot and cold material entering the tank are controlled in response to the temperature and level of the tank contents. Sub-process C is a batch mixing process where specified 'batches' of material from Sub-process B and another source are mixed. The product of the process is extracted from Sub-process C where it's flow and temperature can be monitored.

The process was controlled using an Industrial PLC which had 32 discrete input, 16 discrete output, eight analog input, and four analog output addresses. The PLC was programmed using ladder logic and pilot plant information was displayed using an industrial Supervisory Control And Data Acquisition (SCADA) software package.

Display design

Due to limitations in the technology used, the mimics and the respective representational aids were displayed on the same screen, the former on the left hand side and the latter on the right.

Mimic display

A mimic of the pilot plant containing four pages or formats was designed using the Prism software. The first page contained an overview and the remaining three pages represented sub-processes A, B and C respectively. It was envisaged that operators would use the overview display for monitoring faults and that when a fault occurred they would switch to a more detailed sub-process page to try to isolate it. Consistency was maintained between the spatial relationships of items on the overview and sub-process displays.

For the detailed layout of the displays a style guide was developed based on work by Gilmore et al, (1989), and Ball (1991). The possibilities for presentation were constrained by the SCADA package and consequently in some instances it was only possible to incorporate the SCADA conventions into the style guide.

Each component in the display was responsive to changes in the status of the equivalent components in the pilot plant. Change in status was indicated using colour coding. Green was used to designate that an object was turned on or a valve was open. Yellow was used to designate that an object was off or closed, i.e. standby. Red was used to indicate the occurrence of an error. The tank contents were scaled to increase or decrease in relation to the actual contents of the pilot plant tanks.

Emergent features display and multilevel flow model (MFM) display

Emergent features are based primarily on data that continually changes. In the context of the pilot plant this dynamic data is provided by the continuous variables, level and temperature. However, because of the relatively small number of such variables in the pilot plant, it was only possible to design simple emergent feature displays for Sub-processes B, and C. These consisted of two variables, level and temperature mapped onto a rectangle. The desired or expected temperature and the actual temperature were displayed on opposite sides of the rectangle. Similarly the desired or expected level and the actual level were displayed opposite each other on the other two sides.

The multilevel flow model display was developed using a methodology outlined by Lind (1991) consisting of the following stages; (i) information analysis, (ii) design of means for generation of plant information, and (iii) planning how the information should be presented. The plant was analysed in a hierarchical manner and MFM diagrams were developed for flow structures in each of Sub-processes A, B and C. Each format corresponded to a format in the mimic display. The MFM overview format was a simple flow structure diagram in which the major energy and material flows were labelled. The MFM notation used was that of Duncan et al., (1989), however, due to graphic restrictions imposed by the SCADA system, some slight modifications had to be made to a number of the symbols. The following functions were represented: source, storage, sink, balance, transport, barrier. Failure mode and effects analysis (FMEA) was used to identify the possible faults in each sub-process. Symptoms associated with each fault were subsequently identified and then related to the appropriate flow function.

Assessment

The displays developed above (emergent features in conjunction with a mimic and MFM diagrams in conjunction with a mimic) were assessed to determine whether they were useful in detecting and isolating faults. This was done by introducing faults to the pilot plant process while subjects were monitoring it, and recording their attempts to detect and isolate them. Ten subjects were used for each display. This was consistent with guidelines offered in Bailey (1989) and RACE Project 1065 (1994). The subjects were post-graduate students from engineering based courses. None of the subjects had prior knowledge of the plant or possessed any special skills or training related to it's use. Fault scenarios for testing were selected by first listing all the possible faults, grouping them into fault categories and then identifying basic unrepeated faults. This approach resulted in the selection of 13 faults and ensured

449

that each aspect of the display was tested. Four of these faults were used as part of the process of training subjects in the use of the system. Training consisted of three steps and lasted approximately one hour. The first step was concerned with general knowledge about the pilot plant. The second step was concerned with MFM and emergent feature displays. The final step involved fault scenario simulation. The faults were injected in a preselected order over a period of approximately one hour. Subjects were required to indicate when they had detected a fault and then to isolate it's cause. They were encouraged to speak aloud their thoughts as they performed the task. Task performance was recorded using a video camera and a microphone. A questionnaire was administered after each assessment to determine subject's subjective opinions of the displays.

Data collection and results

The data collected from the usability trials included the time to isolate a fault, and the accuracy of fault detection. The former was measured from the time a fault was first detected. The later was expressed as a percentage of the total faults isolated.

With respect to the Mimic/MFM display, mean fault isolation time was 32 seconds, with a maximum of 53 seconds and a minimum of 20 seconds. Eight of the ten subjects detected ten or more faults while the remaining two detected eight and nine faults respectively. Two of the subjects were observed to have much slower fault isolation times than the other eight. The same subjects had the lowest fault isolation accuracy scores. Subsequent analysis of the questionnaire revealed that both of these subjects rated their understanding of the MFM concept to be poor. The main problem encountered was relating the flow symbols to the cause of a fault.

Overall, analysis of the questionnaire indicated that the MFM display was easy to use, and well layed out. There were misgivings from three of the subjects about the adequacy of the training, while seven of the subjects stated that they would have benefited from further training.

With respect to the Mimic/emergent features display, mean fault isolation time was 16.8 seconds, with a minimum of 11 seconds and a maximum of 19 seconds. All of the 10 subjects detected 10 or more faults. There was no significant variation in performance between the ten subjects. Analysis of the questionnaire results indicated that subjects had few misgivings with respect to the decision aid in terms of general reaction to the system, screen layout and the adequacy of training. However, seven of the subjects stated that they could not see any reason to use emergent features in the context of monitoring the pilot plant.

The Wilcoxon signed ranks test was used to test for significant differences in the time to isolate a fault and accuracy of fault isolation between the MFM/mimic and emergent features/mimic displays. The null hypothesis that there is no difference in the time it takes to isolate a fault was rejected at the $p<.01$ level. However, in the later case, it was not possible to reject the null hypothesis that there is no difference in the number of faults incorrectly detected when using an MFM/mimic and emergent features/mimic displays.

Conclusions

Two main findings emerge from this work. Combined mimic/emergent features displays do not provide a benefit to operator performance when monitoring small processes, particularly where the number of continuous variables is less than three. In the case studied the emergent features aid was viewed as redundant. The use of MFM aids in conjunction with a mimic display to diagnose and isolate faults in a small process plant environment does not improve operator performance when compared with the use of a mimic alone. Further research is required to determine whether this would apply in a more complex process control environment. The issue of training with respect to the use of MFM decision aids should be explored further. Questionnaire data suggests that the level offered in this case was insufficient and that further training could have resulted in improved performance particularly with respect to the mimic/MFM display.

References

Ball, P.W., (1991) *The Guide to Reducing Human Error in Process Operation.* Human Factors Reliability Group.

Bailey, R.W. (1989) *Human Performance Engineering; Using Human Factors / ergonomics to Achieve Computer System Usability.* Prentice Hall International Editions.

Bennett, K.B. & Flach, J.M. (1992), 'Graphical displays: implications for divided attention, focused attention and problem solving', *Human Factors*, Vol. 34, pp 523-533.

Duncan, K.D., Praetorious, N. & Milne, A.B. (1989), 'Flow Displays of Complex Plant Processes for Fault Diagnosis', *Contemporary Ergonomics*, Taylor and Francis: London.

Gilmore, W.E., Gertman, D.I. and Blackman, H.S., (1989), *User-computer Interface in Process Control: A Human Factors Engineering Handbook.* Academic Press: London.

Hwang, S.L. & Cheng, H.W. (1992), 'The effect of information aids on fault diagnosis performance in process control'. *The International Journal of Human Factors in Manufacturing*, Vol. 2, pp 339-353.

Lind, M. (1991), 'Representation and abstraction for interface design using multilevel flow modelling', in G. Weir and J.L. Alty (eds.), *Human Computer Interaction and Complex Systems.* Academic Press: London.

Mark Gill and Enda F. Fallon

Race Project 1065 (1993), *Human Factors Guidelines for Multimedia.*
Yoon, W.C. & Hammer, J.M. (1988), 'Deep-reasoning fault diagnosis: an aid and a model'. *IEEE Transactions on Systems, Man and Cybernetics*, Vol. 18, pp. 659-679.

57 Using conversation to model interaction in the MATHS workstation

Carol Linehan and John McCarthy
Department of Applied Psychology
University College Cork, Ireland

Abstract

The emergence of multi-media computer technologies provides opportunities for creative technical approaches to the design of new equipment for those who are visually impaired. The MATHS project was designed as a response to such opportunities, it aims to develop an interactive workstation to enable visually impaired users to read, write and manipulate algebraic expressions. However it has become increasingly apparent that not only technical but also user issues need to be addressed during the design process. Using analysis of conversation rather than classical task analysis to model the dialogue it is hoped that a more fundamental understanding of users needs could be achieved. Through an understanding of the structural regularities in dialogue in a particular domain tools designed for use in that domain should more closely match user needs and expectations. This paper presents a case study of task analysis followed by dialogue modelling, the aim of which was to identify recurrent structures in conversations and to use these models when designing the interface for the MATHS workstation.

Introduction

This research was carried out in the context of the MATHS (mathematical access to science and technology) project. The aim of MATHS is to develop a multi-media interactive computer workstation which will enable blind and partially sighted users to read, write and manipulate algebraic expressions.

A useful model for designing dialogues in human computer interaction (HCI) is human face to face interaction. Although they are not the same, there are interesting properties of human-human interaction which could be incorporated in HCI design. The comparison between human-human interaction and HCI is not a new one. Nickerson (1987) reviewed the ways in which some characteristics of human conversation are realised in existing applications. Clark & Brennan (1991) examined communication strategies in human-human interaction and the degree to which these strategies carried over into human-computer communication. More recently Clark (1996) argued that an understanding of the techniques that people employ to co-ordinate joint activities is needed before we can adapt these techniques successfully for machines.

While engaged in conversation people seek and provide evidence of their understanding though a process Clark & Brennan term grounding. Many forms of evidence may be drawn upon to monitor understanding, for example linguistic, visual or tactile feedback. This is particularly salient in the context of the MATHS design, because our users are visually impaired and therefore do not have access to all the resources assumed by Clark & Brennan.

We engaged in a process of task analysis, using the Wizard of Oz technique, followed by dialogue modelling, the aim of which was to identify recurrent structures in conversations and to use these to model dialogue when designing an interface for a workstation. In order to investigate such structures we used Winograd and Flores metaphor for complex interaction - the conversation. A conversation is a 'co-ordinated sequence of acts that can be interpreted as having linguistic meaning' (Winograd, 1987). We can plot the basic course of interaction in a simple diagram. The representation is based on changes in states of interaction brought about by speech acts. Speech act theory is 'the analysis of language as meaningful acts by speakers in situations of shared activity' (Winograd and Flores, 1986, p.54). The acts referred to by Winograd are speech acts and a small set of speech act types are possible at each point in the conversation.

The objective of the analysis was to provide designers with user centred recommendations for the input and manipulation languages of the MATHS workstation. This article presents an example of a dialogue model based on requests for information.

Method

The Wizard of Oz technique attempts to simulate a workstation in the absence of a functional prototype. This is achieved by the experimenter behaving as if she were a computer by giving (reading out) and storing (writing down) information only in response to users' requests. The goal in using this methodology was to determine the information requirements, cognitive strategies and labels used by people when doing mathematics.

The technique is structured in such a way that participants have to continually elicit information from the experimenter in order to complete seven mathematical problems, for example:

- $5y^2+3(10+2(6y-4)-5)$. Solve when y=2.
- Factorise $x^2+19x+48$

Eight visually impaired participants took part in this study. Their education ranged from early second level to third level (from 15 to 22 years of age). The face to face interaction was audio recorded. Transcriptions were then produced from the tapes.

Analysis

Systematic analysis of the transcripts was carried out in order to identify relevant sequences of interaction. Through a careful reading of the transcripts categories were developed for each type of interactional event and the transcripts were then coded using this category set, for full details see (Linehan & McCarthy, 1995).

A comprehensive quantitative analysis of all transcripts was also undertaken, during which the type and frequency of each information request, action and error was recorded (Linehan & McCarthy, 1996). Following coding, a number of interactions were chosen for further analysis based on their relevance to our design questions. Models of the dialogue were produced which highlight interesting regularities in requests for information, points of breakdown and the flow of control in the interactions. What follows is an example of one such model, that of conversations for information, and the design implications that emerged from the model.

In this diagram each circle represents a possible state of the interaction and the lines represent speech acts. Each speech act in turn leads to a different state, with its own space of possibilities. There are a few states of completion from which no further action can be taken (these are the heavy circles in the diagram).

Looking at figure 1 we see the interaction beginning with E (the experimenter) presenting information, more specifically a mathematical expression. In response to this presentation S (the subject) requests information, at this juncture there are two alternative paths in the interaction stemming from point three:

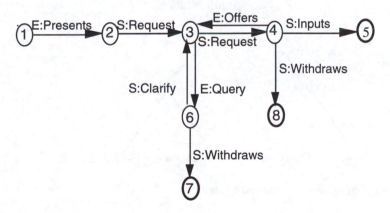

Figure 1   Model of conversations for information

- Points 3-5:

Following a request from S a loop commonly occurred in which subsequent offers of information from E precipitated further requests from S. This loop could continue until;
  (i) S inputs some information (point five), or
  (ii) S becomes overloaded by the task demands of remembering the expression, remembering manipulations done and arriving at a solution and thus withdraws from the interaction (point eight).

- Points 3-6-7:

Alternatively if the request S makes appears ambiguous to E she may seek clarification from S as to the exact nature of the request, at which point S may respond. If E accepts the clarification she can then offer information, however if there is still confusion regarding the request then a loop of queries from E and clarifications from S may develop. There is a danger that if participants are unable to develop a common understanding during this loop that S will eventually withdraw from the interaction and breakdown will occur (point seven).

Even a cursory glance at figure 1 shows that conversations for information are more complex than a simple request-offer-input loop. There are a number of points in the model which could usefully be expanded, particularly those dealing with the issues of subjects requests, points of breakdown, and offers of information.

Requests for information

The label 'request' in the conversation for information conceals the range of different types of requests observed.

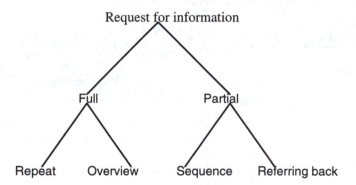

Figure 2   Breakdown of request types

Full information request Frequent requests for repeats following the initial presentation of the expression seems to suggest that in the absence of a visual modality subjects could not easily build a model of the overall structure of an expression.

Overview requests stem from the subject attempting to access the present state of the whole expression during manipulation or inputting activities for example;
S 'minus 15\7\ and so what does the sum read again?'

Partial information Subjects appeared to use two strategies for accessing smaller units of information, in terms of a sequence or to refer back. An example of each strategy is given below:

Sequence		*Referring back*	
S	'30.. the next number?'	S	'the middle bracket?'
E	'12y'	E	'6y minus 4'
S	'36y.. next number?'	S	'what's the very first one..y squared?'

By requesting smaller units of information it could be inferred that subjects were trying to reduce the burden on working memory by breaking up the problem into more manageable units, for example terms, in order to form a mental representation of the expression. However by breaking up or dealing with expressions term by term or in chunks it is likely that blind students may miss out on the type of information conveyed by scanning the whole expression and encounter problems such as parsing errors, forgetting or missing out part of the expression or manipulations done. Perhaps, ideally, blind students as with their sighted counterparts could gain an overview of the expression followed by a more detailed analysis of various sub expressions.

Offers of information

The label 'offers information' is used to cover a range of possibilities. In practice E did not simply offer information to S, there are a number of conditions and consequences attendant on an 'offer of information'. If we examine first the simplest transaction (points two to three), S requests information and E offers it, however implicit in the offer are both E's assumption of understanding S's request and E's selection of the information to be presented. At points three to four there are more explicit attempts made by both S and E to arrive at a mutual understanding, should these attempts prove too effortful or fail then breakdown is likely to occur as S withdraws in frustration. Therefore an important condition for an offer of information is an implicit/explicit acceptance of common understanding between participants in the interaction.

Similarly there are a number of consequences following an offer. These are illustrated in figure 3, overleaf.

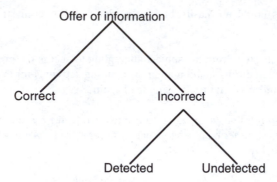

Figure 3   Consequences of an offer of information

If the information offered is correct, that is it satisfies S's request, the interaction may progress to further requests and/or an input.   However E may have misinterpreted S's request in which case incorrect information will be given.   The effect of this 'misinformation' depends on whether S detects it or not.   If S detects that the information given is wrong, that is it does not satisfy the request made, then she may reject the information and re-issue her request.   If the error goes undetected, for example in cases where the information is not that requested but yet sounds plausible to S, then the result is likely to be confusion and perhaps overload for S.

Conclusion

This paper detailed a process of modelling users conversations for information with a human 'wizard' when engaged in mathematics.   The findings show that dialogue directed at gaining information is more complex than a simple request-offer loop. Users requests for information could be subdivided into those for full information, repeats and overviews, and those for partial information, sequences and referring back. Satisfactory offers of information were dependent upon a sufficient degree of common understanding between the user and the experimenter.   In the absence of such understanding the interaction became much more effortful and on occasion broke down.   This finding is interesting with respect to the various resources, linguistic, visual, tactile etc, that Clark & Brennan proposed as contributing to the process of grounding in interaction.   The absence of a visual resource to monitor the interaction process appeared to cause difficulty in two related areas: firstly an over-reliance on users internal memory, and secondly for grounding the activity.   In response to these difficulties a number of user centred design recommendations were formulated.

The system needs to act as an efficient external memory source to relieve the burden on users working memory and to make their problem solving more economical both in terms of length of manipulations and time taken.

It is vital that the user has control over the flow of the interaction to avoid problems of overload. More specifically the system needs to support subjects developing a model of the initial expression in an efficient manner and also to allow the user to control which part of an expression is presented at any one time.

Support should be given for the variety of input and manipulation actions that subjects engaged in. The patterns of interaction observed, for example frequent overview requests during manipulation and input, underline the importance of being able to combine input, manipulation and output activities in a seamless manner.

In conclusion, the approach taken here of modelling the dialogue of people engaged in the joint activity of solving mathematics proved useful from a design perspective for developing an understanding of how such activity might best be supported in the context of a human computer interaction.

References

Clark, H.H. and Brennan, S.E. (1991), 'Grounding in communication'. In, Levine, J., Resnick, L.B., and Behrend (eds.), *Shared cognition: thinking as social practice*. APA Books; Washington DC.

Clark, H.H. (1996), 'Arranging to do things with others'. *Proceedings of CHI '96*, pp. 165-167.

Linehan, C. & McCarthy, J. (1995) *A task analysis of students doing mathematics: contributing to the design of the input and manipulation languages*. EC TIDE Project 1033:MATHS Internal Report no.15.3.

Linehan, C. & McCarthy, J. (1996), Deriving information requirement in the design of a mathematics workstation for visually impaired students. I, Sasse, M.A., Cunningham, R.J. and Winder, R.L. (eds.) *People and computers xi:* Proceedings of HCI'96. Springer:London.

Nickerson, R.S. (1987), 'On conversational interaction with computers' In, Baecker, R.M., and Buxton, W.A.S. (eds). *Readings in human-computer interaction: a multidisciplinary approach*, pp. 681-693.

Winograd, T. (1987), A language action perspective on the design of cooperative work. *Human-Computer Interaction*, Vol. 3, pp 3-30.

Winograd, T. & Flores, F. (1986) *Understanding computers and cognition: a new foundation for design*. Addison-Wesley: Norwood, N.J.

Acknowledgements

The MATHS project is being carried out as part of the Commission of European Communities TIDE (Technology Initiative for Disabled and Elderly People) programme. The MATHS project consortium consists of researchers from University College Cork (Ireland), Katholieke Universiteit Leuven (Belgium), University of York (UK), University of Bradford (UK), F.H. Papenmeier (Germany), and GRIF, S.A. (France).

58 Proposal for the development of an IT-infrastructure for the disabled person

Karl W. Sandberg
Luleå University of Technology, Sweden

Abstract

The aim of this paper is to discuss how we will undertake a common project to develop IT systems in support of service providers working with disabled persons in Europe. Effective communication is an important factor in providing socio-political services. This is especially important in regions with low population densities where the physical distance between service providers and users is great. There is an important, but currently understated, need for development of IT to support the elder and disabled persons in our society. However, these people have special needs which can be addressed through the use of IT. There is an increasing need for access to timely and current information concerning the law, national and regional policy and is a praxis of concern to the less able members of society. Access to a wide range of information via computer and networks is increasingly common at local, regional, national and international levels. This can, at one level, be the use of 'fax databases' where information can be obtained via fax by ringing the appropriate database whilst at the other extreme, 'multimedia' or by connection to Internet and the World Wide Web.

Introduction

Most disabilities are correlated with age, i.e. the number of and degree of impairment increases with age. This is an aggravating factor, as cognitive skills in general decrease with age and thus also learning capacity. This is a challenge for engineers and human factors people, who must ensure that telematics equipment has a good human-machine interface and is self-explanatory in its operation. Individuals with severe disabilities are able to operate computers using available IT. However, access to IT is still limited for many persons with disabilities; a number of obstacles to complete access remain.

More than 50 million people in Europe have various kind of disabilities - 100 million are over 65 years of age. There is an important, but currently understated, need for the development of information technology (IT) to support the disabled person in our society.

Use of information technology

The development of devices to provide unrestricted access to information technology for the disabled person should be viewed as a priority by researchers, practitioners, and consumers. Information technology (IT) has been integrated into education, employment, and everyday functions such as banking. Without devices to access this technology, disabled people will be further excluded from the mainstream of society. Access to standard hardware and software is needed to enable disabled people to be fully participating members of our technologically oriented society and to prevent IT from becoming obstacles to this participation.

In addition to the broader societal implications, access to IT is important on a more personal, affective level. Being able to independently use the same equipment in educational and employment settings has a positive impact on self-image.

Information technology for disabled people

Table 1, shows a number of applications of relevance to disabled people.

Text telephony system is a substitute for ordinary telephones for those who are postlingually deaf, hard of hearing or speech impaired. Deaf people who use sign language, some people with speech impairments and some with mental disabilities need *video telephony* for their remote communication. Remote document reading can help overcome visually impaired people's problems through the use of graphics and pictures in information. Telefax can be used by blind people to transmit copy including graphics to a reading centre, where the text is read and the pictures described via the telephone. Blind people also have access to daily newspapers. With the current speed of technical development, it is an illusion to believe that basic as well as dedicated research and development in the field of remote communication will automatically be undertaken on behalf of people with disabilities. A good example is the utilisation of video communication facilities for providing *sign language telephones* for deaf people. Emergency alarm systems are common among elderly people and people with disabilities. These devices are provided by the municipality and connected to a service centre. Studies need to be undertaken on the future of terminal based service facilities, like dispensing money, paying at point of sells and carrying out bank transactions.

Table 1
Applications of relevance to disabled people

Interpersonal communication	Relay, conversation alternative media	Remote activities	Care services
Voice	Text telephone relay	Information access	Social services
Text	Video telephone relay	Teleshopping	Telemedicine
Video	Text interpretation	Transactions	Navigation support
Special media	Electronic books and newspapers	Telework	
	TV (closed) test captions	Distance learning	
	TV audio description	Entertainment and leisure	

How to develop IT for disabled people

The need to include disabled people in the process of developing information technology can not be stressed enough. We ought to treated disabled people as problem-solvers, not problems to be solved Their perspectives, values, and feelings need to be considered in judging the usefulness of information technology and in determining the need for additional research and development. The research and development should be based on the life experiences of disabled persons and the interests of researchers.

Aims of EuroConnect

Regional developments within county of Norrbotten in the North of Sweden will be made. Specifically:
- To quantify the need for IT support for this section of society in the county of Norrbotten.
- To develop complementary IT systems for the service providers working with the disabled people together with the Organisation for the disabled in county of Norrbotten.

- To develop complementary IT systems for users from this section of society. For example enabling physically challenged to carry out meaningful work from home.
- To train users in the use of the above IT systems.
- To systematically evaluate the above IT infrastructure from the user's perspective.

Project phases

Year one - Preparatory work

With the expressed aim of providing IT support for the physically challenged citizens of Norrbotten, a proposal for an initial system configuration will be developed.

Year two - Implementation phase

The IT services and staff necessary to support the initial system will be put in place and users will be trained to use the system. Ongoing support and development will be provided to ensure that the system is used in an effective way.

Year three - Evaluation phase

The initial system configuration will be evaluated from the user's viewpoint in parallel with continued support and development.

It is necessary to have a formal systematic approach for comparing a user's abilities and goals with available IT technology in order to develop a human service system. Applying systems theory and human factors engineering research to develop a model for analysing disabled people's requirements needs to be applied in situations where the use of IT technology is being considered.

A key feature will be the emphasis on maximising the use of standard IT technologies to achieve cost-effective solutions. The project needs to be a series of cross-sectional projects, and in particular concentrate on those which undertake the validation of applications from a number of different sectors. Such proposals will receive favourable attention at the evaluation stage.

It will focus on how emerging technologies, many of which are multimedia-based, could be configured and adapted through projects into useful, user-friendly and cost-effective applications. Such applications would offer realistic solutions to basic problems and requirements experienced by companies, institutions and the citizen. In addition, emphasis will also be placed on best practices and proven methods, techniques and tools to achieve these goals.

This approach means that in all projects, the full involvement of users at all phases of a project is necessary. An approach based on co-operation between users and suppliers for mutual benefit will underpin the selection of projects. The project will have number of phases.

(i)   Identification of user needs.
(ii) Translation of user needs into functional specifications.
(iii) Building a demonstrator.
(iv) Validation with users in a real-life situation.

References

Behrmann, M. M., and Lahm, E. A.(1984) 'But it will be obsolete tomorrow: evaluating ultimate needs of users vs. the capabilities of devices'. In, J. E. Roehl (ed.), *Proceedings of Discovery '83: Computers for the Disabled.* Menomonie, Wis.: Materials Development Center, Stout Vocational Rehab. Inst., Univ. of Wisconsin.

Steyaert, J., Colombi, D & Rafferty, J. (1996) *Human services on information technology: an international perspective.* Arena: Aldershot.

Vanderheiden, G. C. (1984) 'Curbcuts and computers providing access to computers and information systems for disabled individuals'. In, J. E. Roehl (ed.), *Discovery '83. Computers for the Disabled.* Menomonie, Wis.: Materials Development Center, Stout Vocational Rehab. Inst., Univ. of Wisconsin.

Wright, B. A. (1983) *Physical Disability - A Psychosocial Approach,* (2nd edition). Harper & Row: New York.

59 Application of human performance theory to virtual environment development

Richard Eastgate, Sarah Nichols and Mirabelle D'Cruz
Virtual Reality Applications Research Team (VIRART),
University of Nottingham, UK

Abstract

Virtual reality is an exciting new technology with increasing application in industrial and educational settings. However, as the technology is still in its evolutionary stage, virtual environment (VE) developers are faced with many technical limitations when designing VR applications. These result in the VE including less detail or fewer features than the real world which it represents. Therefore the developer is required to decide what level of detail and which features to include. Previously these decisions have tended to be made on the basis of size of objects, ease of programming, individual programmer's preferences, or arbitrarily. In psychological and ergonomic research, theories that explain the ways in which humans behave in certain situations already exist. This paper discusses utilising an existing theory to consider the VR user's role in participation within a VE, with a view to aiding the VE development process.

Introduction

Virtual reality (VR) is an exciting new computer technology which has experienced increased prevalence and technical power over the past few years. The major research interest has been in technological improvement, however, more recently, the focus has gradually moved towards the development of VR applications (Wilson, D'Cruz, Cobb & Eastgate, 1996).

VR applications are often developed with a number of goals in mind, such as enabling more effective visualisation, testing a new design, or teaching a new concept. An effective VE will successfully achieve these goals. However, as VR

467

technology is still developing, many applications are restricted by the limits of the current technology and the time and resources available for VE development. Therefore, whilst these applications are usable, the VE may not be as detailed or as complex as would be ideal. In order for VR to be used in the most productive way, and to maximise the achievement of the goals, VE development time needs to be optimised and technical limitations need to be dealt with in a way that will cause minimal loss to the virtual experience.

Overcoming limiting factors in the VE development process

There are a number of factors that have an influence on the way a VE is developed and consequently, how it eventually performs. Some of these factors have a stronger influence than others, but all are interlinked in some way. These factors include the following:
- Purpose of application.
- Target user population.
- Developer's ability and experience.
- VR system (hardware/software).
- Time available for development.
- Money available for development.

The two factors which have the biggest influence on the complexity of the final VE design are the time available for development and the ceiling of processing power permitted by the VR system (Eastgate and Wilson, 1994). The combination of VE complexity and finite system processing power limits the rendering speed of VE presentation. It is important that rendering speeds are sufficient to avoid causing usability and/or utility problems. When faced with the restrictions outlined above there are various solutions available to the developer. More than one of these techniques would normally be used in combination; the facilities offered by the VR system software and the developers' ability and preferences are most likely to influence the choice.

Texturing large amount of three dimensional detail can be replaced by a bitmap texture pasted onto a single facet in a VE. Depending on the subject matter these can increase rendering speeds and will generally be quicker to create than three dimensional geometry. Whilst textures are a good way of adding realism to a VE they can only be used in specific circumstances.

Distancing This is a widely used technique whereby if a virtual object is more than a specified distance from the viewpoint of the participant it is replaced by a simpler model or disappears altogether, thus reducing the amount of processing time required to render that object.

Reducing the screen resolution This is an indiscriminate solution which results in a reduction in the amount of detail visible to the participant. This will make some tasks in the VE more difficult (e.g. reading a sign) and will also reduce the realism of the VE making the experience less enjoyable. It is also possible to selectively reduce the screen resolution around the periphery of the screen, whilst maintaining a high resolution in the centre, (Watson, Walker & Hodges, 1995).

Selectively including objects Reducing the number of objects in an environment will increase rendering speed and decrease development time. The decisions as to which objects to include tend to be made on the basis of size of objects, ease of programming, individual programmers' habits, or arbitrarily, with little understanding of how these decisions will affect the participant. Thus this is an easy technique to implement but a difficult one to implement correctly. The dilemma is in deciding which objects to include and which to omit.

Of the solutions listed above, selectively including objects stands out as a technique which can both decrease development time and increase rendering speeds. It is applicable across all hardware and software platforms and will be compatible with future VR systems. What is required is a set of guidelines to help the developer through the process of deciding which objects to include and which to omit. These rules will have to be developed with reference to the specified purpose of the VE, and user behaviour within a VE. The resulting VE should not be significantly inferior (at achieving its specified purpose) to a hypothetical one in which all objects are modelled. Indeed, it may be found that omitting the right objects may increase the effectiveness of a VE. An analogy could be drawn with descriptive passages in a book. It would be impossible for an author to describe a scene in all its detail and it would not be of any benefit to the reader. By describing specific features of a scene the author can communicate far more effectively with the reader and complete the description within a few sentences.

Application of human performance theory to VE development

Work has already been carried out categorising the requirements of the participant, and the ways in which the VE should be designed to meet those requirements (Eastgate, 1995). What was unknown was how an individual participant would respond to the VE, and whether this response would allow the objectives of the application to be met.

Much research, particularly in the field of psychology and ergonomics, has already identified the factors involved in determining human behaviour in real world environments. Areas in which this has been applied are human error analysis (e.g. Reason, 1990) and task behaviour (e.g. Wilson & Rajan, 1995). These use as a basis, a model of Skill-, Rule- and Knowledge-Based behaviour, which suggests how human behaviour is affected by the information presented within a system (Rasmussen, 1986).

This model can also be applied to VE design with a view to firstly avoiding situations which may result in user error, and consequently to developing VEs which give the user the right amount of information at the right time to afford a meaningful virtual experience. Table 1 shows the basic characteristics of each of these types of performance.

Table 1
Skill-, Rule- and Knowledge-based performance
(derived from Rasmussen, 1986)

	Description	Example
Skills	Sensorimotor performance which takes place as (more or less) automatic behaviour after a statement of intention.	Riding a bicycle
Rules	Goal-oriented performance controlled by a stored rule or procedure. The rule may have been derived from past experience or learned from other people's experience.	Interpreting and acting upon familiar road signs.
Knowledge	Goal-controlled or model-based behaviour used during unfamiliar situations. A plan is developed using knowledge, reasoning and experience to predict the outcome of actions.	Navigating in an unfamiliar environment

At present, it is not possible to implement real world skill-based behaviour in a VE, as the input and output devices are not sophisticated enough to provide the realistic interaction and feedback required for sensorimotor performance. This is best illustrated by considering a relatively simple, automatic action such as opening a door. If it were to be executed in the same way in a VE as in the real world, it would require an input device which monitored a combination of precise physical placement of the hand, multi-directional application of force, balance control, and provided continuous feedback to the operator. This would be a complex process, and if it were modelled, any slight discrepancy between the VE response and the expected real world response could cause the automatic behaviour to become disrupted and inefficient. When designing a VE, where appropriate, skill-based activities will have to be replaced by metaphors such as pointing at a door to open it.

It should be possible both to model real world rules in a VE, and to teach rules in a VE which can then be applied in the real world. For example, if a user is in a VE, and is instructed to open a door, they will already be in possession of several rules which will help them in the execution of this task. For example, they will know:

i) A door is a way to pass from one space to another.

ii) A door will open to let you pass through it.

iii) A door is usually of a specific size, and so will provide some indication of the scale of an environment.

Equally, a VE developer has the opportunity to abuse this principle, and consistently model rules that misrepresent the real world, thus providing the user with an incorrect mind set which may be hard to dislodge.

Knowledge based behaviour is used in problem solving situations. A mental model of the situation is formed, and this model will be used as a basis for a plan of actions. However, if a user is presented with misleading or inadequate information, then they may be unable to form a plan, form an incorrect plan, or may form several plans, and be unable to determine which of these will be successful. A VE developer who is aware of this can ensure that the design and content of the VE encourages the user to develop the correct mental model, and therefore be more likely to adopt a successful strategy in the VE, or in the real world once they have been trained in a VE.

Applying SRK to VE development

In order to illustrate how the consideration of the SRK model can lead to an effective VE the example of an actual VE training application will be presented. This application is intended to teach users how to replace the network card in a computer. Two specific scenarios from this experience can be used to illustrate how the understanding of human behaviour enhanced the design of the environment.

Figure 1 shows the initial scene that the user is faced with on entry to the room containing the task. The actual room in the real world setting is a typical office environment, which is cluttered, and contains many items not relevant to the task. If none of these peripheral objects were included, then the user could have problems relating to a room which lacks items that enhance a sense of direction, scale or atmosphere.

A user will already be aware of some rules which help in the correct interpretation of the VE. When viewing the initial scene, they will be aware of several objects in front of them, and will make inferences about the environment based on the in formation obtained from these objects, and their associated properties. The objects consist of two windows, a radiator, and two desks. The inclusion of these objects has the following effects:

- An outside wall is expected to have a window. A lack of windows would be a contradiction to expectation, and therefore may be a distraction.

- The windows and radiator are simple objects which add to the 'atmosphere' in the virtual room.

• The desks will provide information about the scale and function of the room.

Figure 1   Situation in VE requiring rule-based behaviour

A desk is likely to be of a certain height. As one of the desks is in the far corner of the room, this information can be used to estimate the overall size of the room. As the visual information provided by the VR system is inferior to that provided in the real world (e.g. it will have a lower resolution, smaller field of view etc.), this use of rules transferred from the real world can aid navigation throughout the task. A desk also has a function, implying that the room that they have just entered is an office. Thus, using a minimal number of objects, the user is given a large amount of the information necessary to understand the environment.

Within this training application the user's attention can be directed towards relevant features and information to encourage the user to successfully complete the task. A user who performs the VE task successfully, with the minimum contradiction or confusion, will be more likely to apply the correct mental model when attempting the task in the real world.

Figure 2 shows all the elements necessary to complete the task - a computer, a screwdriver and a new network card. The first part of the task is the removal of the outer casing of the computer. The options available to the user are minimal, and therefore it is likely that the user will come to the correct decision to use the screwdriver to undo the screws in order to achieve their goal. If however, a spanner was also present, the user would have additional unnecessary information, and may form an incorrect model of how to remove the outer casing, and attempt to use the spanner.

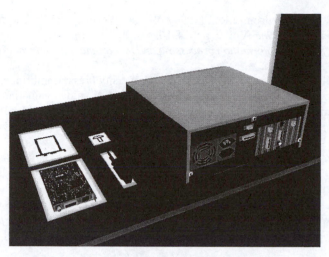

Figure 2   Situation in VE requiring knowledge-based behaviour

Discussion

A technology-based approach to VE development may become obsolete due to the rapid advances in VR hardware and software systems. However, the approach presented in this paper is based on fundamental cognitive processes in human behaviour. Therefore, it can continue to be applied and evaluated in VE development as the technology evolves.

There are some factors which are not considered within this theory, but may still influence the effectiveness of a VR application. One of these is the fact that individual users' abilities, attitudes and requirements of a Virtual Experience will differ. Therefore it may be difficult to develop one environment which is the most effective design for all users. In addition, a developer may be under pressure to design more aesthetically pleasing VEs rather than focussing on the needs of the user.

However, it is hoped that by expanding upon this theoretical approach, and combining it with other VE development research, practical, generic guidelines can be devised to enable the production of usable and effective VEs, with minimal development time and computer resources being used.

References

Eastgate, R.M. (1995) Categorisation of features in a Virtual Environment. *VIRART Report /95/137.*

Eastgate, R.M. & Wilson, J.R. (1994) Virtual Worlds. *EXE: The Software Developers' Magazine*, Vol. 9, pp. 14-16.

Rasmussen, J. (1986) *Information processing and human-machine interaction*. North Holland: Amsterdam.

Reason, J. (1990) *Human Error*. Cambridge University Press: Cambridge.

Watson, B., Walker, N. & Hodges, L.F. (1995) 'A user study evaluating level of detail degradation in the periphery of head-mounted displays'. In M. Slater (ed.) *Proceedings Conference of the FIVE Working Group*. QMW, University of London. December 18-19, 1995.

Wilson, J.R., D'Cruz, M.D., Cobb, S. & Eastgate, R. (1996) *Virtual Reality for Industrial Applications: Opportunities and Limitations*. Nottingham University Press: Nottingham.

Wilson, J.R. & Rajan, J.A. (1995) 'Human-machine interfaces for systems control'. In J.R. Wilson & E.N. Corlett (eds.) *Evaluation of Human Work: A practical ergonomics methodology*. Taylor & Francis: London.